THE FRAGILE PEACE

The Fragile Peace
Paul Anthony

First Published 1996 by Janus Publishing Company, London
Copyright (©) Paul Anthony 1996
Second Edition (Revised) 2012
Published by Paul Anthony Associates
Copyright © Paul Anthony 2012

Cover Design © Margaret Anne Scougal 2012

Published in Great Britain in 2011
by Paul Anthony Associates
http://paulanthonys.blogspot.com/

By the same author

≈

Bushfire

The Legacy of the Ninth

Sunset

The Conchenta Conundrum

Moonlight Shadows

≈

To Margaret – Thank you for never doubting me
To Paul, Barrie and Vikki – You only get one chance at life. Live it
well, live it in peace and live it with love for one another.

To my special friends – Thank you. You are special.

Foreword

≈

This novel was conceived in the autumn of 1994 in the aftermath of the ceasefires announced by both the Provisional Irish Republican Army and the Loyalist paramilitaries in Northern Ireland. This book uses as a backdrop the 'Irish Problem' between 1969 and 1995. It is a work of fiction, weaved with fact.

My private research has taken me through countless newspapers, journals, magazines and television documentaries. In addition, I have spoken with many friends from the island of Ireland, This, in order to piece together a brief history of 'The Troubles' which you will find at the rear of the book detailed in chronological order. This novel was first published in 1996 by Janus Publishing Company of London and has been revised and republished in 2012 following popular demand.

To the journalists, writers, academics and producers who have walked this path before me, I offer my thanks. To my Irish friends, I extend my gratitude, in the hope that one day they will find the peace that they deserve. I do not seek to offend those who mourn their fellow man. If you are offended by the content of this book, then perhaps you are on one side of the fence and will never quite understand the other person's position. Perhaps, you yourself are part of the dilemma. One man's democracy can be another man's prison. No one can deny the Irish problem. The history of Ireland cannot be hidden in a peat bog of denial.

My words tell the story of 'The Troubles' from many perspectives. I concentrate on two particular characters from different backgrounds. Both characters live their lives independently of the other, little knowing that they will one day meet. Indeed, both characters throughout this period enjoy a relationship with an individual who comes to love them both.

You, the reader, may better understand 'The Troubles' when you have read this book. You may choose sides en route. If you do so then you will have unconsciously contributed to the great divide that exists in Northern Ireland.

During the period 1965 - 1994 many hundreds of people died as a result of 'The Troubles'. In the main they died because of what they believed in and what cause they'd dedicated their lives to.

They died in Ireland, the mainland and elsewhere. Those who died were mainly Irish or English, but other nationalities did not escape death. Some died from the bullet and some died from the bomb. Some died as a result of injuries sustained during 'The Troubles'. Some died merely because they were in the wrong place at the wrong time.

Those who died were young and old, male and female, guilty and innocent. They were Catholic and Protestant, Republican and Loyalist.

Some were terrorists, some were police officers and some were members of the armed services. There were those who died because their duties as firemen or ambulance men led them to the front line of the terrorist war. Sometimes the front line was represented by the brave bomb disposal officer who died alone whilst making the street safe for others. A few of those who died were members of the Intelligence Services – the silent few.

The dead are all silent now. This book is for those who died. They will forever rest in someone's memory.

Whether it was on an Irish street, an English shopping precinct or on a lonely Scottish hillside, they all died.

The search for peace must not die.

Indeed, Ulster, according to Article 2 of the Irish Constitution, is an integral part of Eire. This has little practical effect due to the partition which is apparent within the island of Ireland.

The partition is characterized, according to 1979 figures, with the indication that 34,000 Irish citizens usually reside in Ulster, whereas the 1971 Census showed that 36,000 Ulster-men and 84,000 persons born in Great Britain were usually resident in Eire.

As you, the reader, consider the chronological historic notes of 'The Troubles' at the rear of this work, you may wish to acknowledge that the word 'Brief' denies every second, of every week, of every month, of every year, of the 25 years that we have to come know as 'The Troubles'.

Yesterday's memories are tomorrow's heartaches.

All sides involved in 'The Troubles' have strived for their own kind of peace. Now a 'fragile peace' ensues.

Well over 3,000 people lost their lives during 'The Troubles'. This all occurred in the advanced civilised society that we have proudly named the United Kingdom.

Many other lives were saved. Every round of ammunition recovered during 'The Troubles' probably related to the potential saving of someone's life.

Special people in special places know who they are and what they did. They are used to being the unsung and the unnamed. They have chosen their path in life and walk it with a silent pride.

This is my story...

PART ONE
GROWING UP
≈

The dark grey Land Rover crept slowly through the Galliagh estate back towards Madams Bank Road, the River Foyle and the Strand Road police station. On the south side of the Foyle lived the Protestants and on the north side, lived the Catholics. The two seldom met. The sprawling city was divided as much by the river as by religion, politics, culture and the upbringing of its citizens. To the Protestants it was Londonderry and to the Catholics it was Derry.

Here, religion, beliefs and aspirations were determined by examining which side of the street you walked on. Occasionally, you could find a few streets in which the Catholics and the Protestants lived together. You could tell which was which. The Protestants painted their kerbstones red, white and blue, for the monarchy; the Catholics favoured the colours of the tricolour, green, white and orange. They rarely spoke to each other and sought comfort in their own respective communities: North and south, Catholic and Protestant. They were poles apart.

The occupants of the Land Rover wore the dark green uniform of the Royal Ulster Constabulary. They were both in their mid-twenties, married with young children, and Protestants. The driver was Gordon, named after his father, and his passenger was Brian. They were doing an ordinary job in an extraordinary city.

Swinging lazily into the Shantallow estate, the vehicle trundled slowly through the quiet streets of the Republican camp. It was dark, early evening and the air was damp. It was just starting to get a little breezy as the tide turned on the coast, bringing with it a fresh bout of weather.

Hidden, frightened faces behind partially drawn curtains moved back from the windows, lest they be seen by the policemen. Who wanted to solicit a wave or an acknowledgement from the police in this land? After all, it was a Protestant police force, wasn't it? Run by the 'Brits' in London?

The Land Rover drew to a halt and Brian peered cautiously through the bullet-proof windscreen. The armoured bodywork of the vehicle creaked and sighed as its weight was thrown forward when the brakes were applied. The army personnel carrier following the Land Rover also stopped and a patrol swiftly clambered from the rear passenger compartment onto the nearby footpath.

Rifles and submachine guns were brandished at the faceless buildings and the hostile streets. Apprehensive eyes searched the rooftops and high rise windows looking for the unusual, the out-of-the-ordinary, the suspicious.

The troops were young men, drawn mainly from the Home Counties and the south of England. To the Irish they spoke with a strange English accent. To some, the army was a friend. To others, it was the enemy. In some quarters it was preferable not to take sides at all and have as little to do with the army as possible. They had been there since August, 1969. The troops were nervous.

'What's going on? Why have we stopped?' shouted the army sergeant moving his fingers to release the safety catch on his assault rifle as he raised it across his chest in readiness.

Sitting on the crown of the road in the middle of Shantallow were a group of children. Aged about twelve, they wore short trousers, long-sleeved grey pullovers and scuffed, worn-out shoes. They were children at play, positioned across the road, as pearls on a rope.

The Land Rover was prevented from continuing its journey.

One of the children sang a gentle haunting song, 'God made the land and God made the sea. To be sure, I hope He shines down on me.'

Removing his cap, Gordon leaned out of the Land Rover and shouted, 'Clear off! Get off the road, will yer?'

Mumbling something softly to his partner about Catholic kids, Gordon reached into the rear compartment for his weapon. He favoured a habit of never leaving the vehicle without his gun. As he was about to get out of the Land Rover he heard the faint sound of an old Irish melody drifting towards him again.

'God made the land and God made the sea. To be sure, I hope He shines down on me.'

The young child singing bathed in light from a nearby street lamp and remained seated cross-legged on the road, apparently oblivious to the policeman. The other children slowly moved from the roadway to the footpath.

The Land Rover idled about forty yards from them, its headlights illuminating the scene.

The engine continued to tick over. Gordon gently pressed the accelerator with the gear stick in neutral whilst his hands rested firmly on the steering wheel.

From the window of a high rise building overlooking the street, a middle-aged man in a long black coat put down his binoculars and pressed the transmit button of his walkie-talkie radio. The man spoke quietly, 'Now!'

It was all over in a matter of seconds.

On the wasteland, approximately fifty yards from the Land Rover, two young volunteers hoisted a home-made mortar tube out of a battered old blue suitcase and aimed it slightly above the roof of the Land Rover.

The taller of the two laid his walkie-talkie radio to one side and rested the mortar tube on his shoulder, whilst the other youth loaded it. He pulled the trigger.

There was a loud explosion and in less than a second a shell pierced the air and collided with the front offside of the Land Rover. The vehicle erupted into a ball of fire as the impact of the lethal home-made device lifted it off the ground and spun it round so that it turned at a right angle to its original axis.

The two young occupants of the Land Rover were heard screaming in the face of death when they were thrown about like peas in a drum.

A cloud of black smoke climbed the sky, billowing upwards in a horrible spiral.

The man in the long black coat stepped away from the window and pocketed his radio. As he walked quietly out of the room that had been seized only hours before for the 'hit' a motor bike rode off at high speed.

Simultaneously, a door opened nearby and an anxious mother gathered up her twelve-year-old son and took him indoors.

The voice of the twelve-year-old asked, 'Did Ah do alright, Ma? Did Ah do what you wanted, Ma? Did ya like ma song, Ma?'

His mother listened for the sound of approaching footsteps and men running. She heard nothing. She held the child closely, saying, 'Hush, Liam Connelly, will yer now? It's late. Now, go yerself ta bed before yer da' gets home.'

She guided the child up the stairs, whispering, 'Off to sleep with you now. To be sure, your uncle Padraigh will be upon us tomorrow, so he will, and he'll be wanting to hear about yer schooling. Off wid yer now while I make yer father's dinner. Don't you go waking yer sister up at this time of night or yer father'll have something to be saying.'

The smile of satisfaction on his mother's face was enough for Liam. He knew he'd done well. If Ma was pleased, all would be well in the world.

A telephone rang in a remote cottage situated between Dundalk and Dublin in the Republic of Eire. The Irish voice answering it belonged to Seamus Kelty, 'Yes?'

From the comfort of his home on the Creggan estate, in Londonderry, a man wearing a long black coat spoke, 'You have a party of two booked in for the fishing on the river at the weekend now. Unfortunately, they aren't going to be making it, that's for sure. Could you be cancelling the two rods?'

Seamus Kelty smiled and eased himself back into his chair, savouring the moment of triumph. He replied, 'Thank you.'

Kelty often received such calls; he replaced the telephone on the cradle end considered how well things had gone that night.

Damien Devenney also cut the connection. He slid his black overcoat from his shoulders, stoked the fire and sat back in the leather armchair, allowing himself the distinct pleasure of small glass of Jameson Irish whiskey before turning in for the night. Damien only drank Jameson when a good job had been successfully completed or when he toasted the dead. It was a smooth drink. His throat tingled, ever so slightly, as it flowed down his gullet. It was the only slight discomfort he endured that night. He relished the drink.

Liam climbed the stairs to his bed, passing the tricolour and the framed print of the 1914 Proclamation that declared the Easter Uprising and took pride of place in the family hallway. He crept passed his sister Shelagh's room, noting she was sound asleep.

Mother Connelly turned to the lounge curtains and drew them even tighter across the front window, not wanting to look towards the burning Land Rover.

A good job done for the cause tonight, she thought. Our Liam! Only twelve, but he will do alright one day.

Settling down for the night, she pulled the bolt across the front door. Her husband, Declan, would be a while before coming home from his work at the Fruit of the Loom factory.

The door closed on the carnage outside in the street as the air gradually filled with the sound of screaming men, hastily given orders and distant sirens rushing to the scene through the Brandywell and Pennyburn.

Within the hour a crowd of teenagers gathered, inspired by older, unseen men. They threw stones at the police; the fire brigade and the ambulance service, as they tended to the burning Land Rover and the latest casualties to be written in the history of 'The Troubles'.

Baton rounds were fired to disperse the crowd.

Another young woman had been widowed at an early age. Another young boy would grow up in a harsh land with only a crumpled photograph and a hazy memory of a father he never really knew.

In the coming weeks the Royal Ulster Constabulary ceremonially buried one dead colleague, the policeman Gordon, and medically discharged another due to the extensive injuries sustained in the attack.

Another name was added to the Book of Remembrance displayed in the foyer of the RUC police headquarters at Knock, in Belfast.

After a time, a burnt-out stolen Honda motor cycle was found dumped in a field near the road to Letterkenny, over the border. The army carried out a series of early morning raids, searching for arms, explosives and the latest homemade mortar device. Big black army issue boots kicked in soft wooden doors, causing more work for local council repair men. The prime suspects were rounded up, held in the police cells and interrogated at great length. The police followed up with extensive enquiries in the area and learnt nothing of importance.

Nobody saw anything. Nobody knew anything. No one wanted to help anyway. It was a land of frightened people.

The RUC put their trusty informants - 'touts' - to work and in due course were close to discovering who pulled the trigger. But by then it was far too late, since the evidence was long gone and the young offenders more than likely elsewhere.

It was only a short drive to the border and the sanctuary of the Republic until the heat and furore died down and things returned to normal.

Until the next time.

The jewel in the Irish Sea called Ireland had been mercilessly desecrated yet again by another mindless murder, another act of inhuman insanity, and another act of alleged political self-determination.

This is Shantallow, Londonderry, November, 1970: The birthplace of 'The Troubles', the home of the Provisional Irish Republican Army.

≈

It was one of those nights when the damp autumn air carried your breath in a misty cloud that disappeared into the atmosphere as soon as you'd said your piece. The sky was black save for a few stars that were fighting to get through the darkened clouds that you knew were there, although you couldn't quite see them.

The adults dug their hands deeper into their pockets and shuffled their feet to keep the cold out. Neck scarves were pulled in closer in a fervent battle to keep warm. Mothers inspected their offspring's Wellington boots, wondering how to prevent the children from running into the house and depositing mud all over the carpets.

The ladies stepped gingerly over the small pools of water that lay here and there in the local farmer's field whilst men folk walked with an air of resigned authority, carrying their tea flasks and sandwiches underneath their arms. The damp and the mud both had to be endured in the name of family life. It was a family night: The night when magic is made by striking a match and introducing it to the blue touch paper.

They approached the bonfire excitedly looking eagerly into the sky to see yet another rocket, from a rival bonfire far away, explode harmlessly into the heavens.

Clutching the box of fireworks tightly to his side, Billy knew Dad would let them off as soon as the farmer, Mr Lindsay, got the bonfire going and Mum would pretend to be frightened by the noise and the sparks as usual. In the distance, hidden in the dark and mysterious shadow of the fellside, the church clock tower struck seven and farmer Lindsay, with proud ceremony, stepped forward.

'Stand back everybody. Here we go!'

Tilting his flat cap onto the side of his head, Lindsay took a match from his waistcoat pocket and walked towards the bonfire. He took a long taper and lit the huge bonfire that dominated the centre of the field.

Slowly the flames climbed towards the top of the bonfire where Guy Fawkes sat resplendent in cast-off jacket and trousers stuffed with old straw. Lindsay walked round the bonfire, inserting the taper at carefully selected points to make sure that the fire took a firm hold.

This was his field and he had lit the bonfire every year since the end of the Second World War. As a village elder it was a big responsibility to make sure the bonfire was a success. Farmer Lindsay set his cap yet again and motioned with his arms to the assembled villagers that they best hadn't come too close just yet. It was his moment.

The evening rolled on. The night birds sought sanctuary in far-off trees as the cold breeze whispered the embers through the air and the smoke swirled round and round as it spiralled upwards to the stars. Gasps and cries of delight echoed across the field as the rich smell of fireworks began to fill people's nostrils and more and more pyrotechnical wizardry launched into the autumn heavens. The bonfire crackled and roared as it reached a climax. Flames reached out to devour old wood and dead leaves that Lindsay and the village elders were piling on.

Playing with a sparkler, Billy made circles in the air like the conductor of an orchestra. A crackerjack detonated, by kind permission of Lindsay, who was ever-present, organising and jollying the assembly.

Billy jumped as the crackerjack danced a dance of fire. The firework box lay at his feet.

Father leaned forward and collected the box saying, 'Come on, Billy Boyd, our turn now.'

Mrs Boyd smiled quietly as she pondered on how quickly Billy had grown and watched him walk beside his father to the area of the field where the men folk were letting off the fireworks.

The field was swelling now with most of the villagers gathered at the annual pilgrimage. A large trestle table had been erected by Lindsay and a variety of Roman candles and coloured cascades were displayed to the gathering.

A fiery Catherine wheel spun endlessly round from a pole embedded in the soft earth. The sparks lit up the arena as the fire warmed the congregation. A rocket aimed for the moon, only to explode in a fountain of coloured sparks that showered the scene as it plummeted into a neighbouring field.

Mrs Boyd directed Billy to the sky, not wanting him to miss the unfolding spectacle.

A police minivan trundled slowly along the lane which bordered one side of the field. Its driver carefully motioned the steering wheel from left to right as he negotiated the potholes in the rough track.

Billy could see the van approaching and made out the shape of the blue light mounted on the roof of the minivan. He knew one day he too would be a policeman.

The driver parked at the gateway to the field and got out of the van. He waved in acknowledgement at Lindsay and walked towards the bonfire with a big smile on his face. 'You've a good turnout again, Lindsay. It's to be hoped them beasts of yours are all safely in the barn?' he said, easing himself out of his overcoat.

Lindsay replied, 'That they are, Johnny me lad. How goes it with you this night? Making yer rounds on bonfire night is no place for an old codger like you. Will the police not give you a night off?'

The village bobby laughed, removed a box of fireworks from inside his tunic pocket, and handed them to Lindsay. 'You'll be needing these soon when you run out, Lindsay. Best make sure the kids have a good time tonight.'

'Thank you kindly, Johnny me lad. There's tea over there if you've time to keep the cold out.'

Lindsay motioned towards a small card table on which a collection of tea flasks and coffee cups were receiving the avid attention of the villagers.

Nodding to Lindsay, the policeman joined the throng. He placed his helmet on the table, helped himself to a mug of tea, and was immediately buttonholed by the vicar who decided it was a good moment to discuss the recent outbreak of petty vandalism at the church hall.

On the other side of the bonfire, Billy set up his fireworks on the trestle. 'We've been doing about Guy Fawkes at school this week. Dad!'

'Oh! And what do you remember about Guy Fawkes?' enquired his father, as Billy's mother bent forward to listen to the answer.

Billy thought for a while before responding with, 'Well, he planted a big bomb under the Houses of Parliament hundreds of years ago but the coppers caught him. We have bonfires now every November the fifth to celebrate.' Billy lined up his Roman candles, like soldiers waiting to go forward to do their duty.

His father laughed, 'Well, that's not quite the whole story, but it's near enough for this time of night, I expect.' Raising his head to the skies, he saw smoke hanging in the air since the breeze had dropped. It reminded him of his younger days when he had been a sergeant in the Second World War in France. He recalled how the RAF bombed the way ahead for his infantry platoon when they marched on Germany. Now he wore the regimental badge on the breast pocket of his blazer to remind him of those who died.

He sought out his wife's eyes. Ann Boyd was a nurse who had fallen in love with the dashing young sergeant. She had no regrets about the marriage and neither had he.

William Boyd looked into his child's eyes and wondered what future his son would have.

A rocket dropped towards the River Eden.

In the distance Saddleback could be seen rising above the land. The Eden sprang to earth just above Kirkby Stephen and meandered lazily through the county before it dissected Carlisle and spilled into the Solway Firth. Across the Solway and beyond the Isle of Man lay Ireland, not more than a couple of hour's journey from the Cumbrian coast.

The table was engulfed by fire.

The Roman candle sitting right in front of Billy ignited without warning as a rogue rocket from a distant bonfire plunged downwards, landing on Lindsay's trestle and causing instantaneous havoc. It landed in Billy's box and was still warm enough to ignite the contents.

A cacophony of sound and a flash of light followed as fireworks exploded at will. Sparks flew across the table and people shielded their faces with hasty arms. Those nearest turned and ran away from the developing scene.

Lindsay, and the policeman, together tried to push the trestle over onto the soft earth in an attempt to defuse the situation. A rocket launched itself from the table on a horizontal flight path, miraculously cutting through the crowds without claiming a victim.

The vicar dropped his cup of tea in the excitement and took control. 'Calm now! Calm!' he cried, raising his arms as if to prevent the turn of events.

Billy screamed, holding his hands to his face where the firework singed his eyebrows.

'Water. Quickly!' shouted his father.

Mr Boyd's arms enveloped his son, lifting him up cautiously as Mrs Boyd and the vicar rushed in, carefully dabbing his eyebrows.

The vicar became over-excited and dropped the water container.

Mrs Boyd held her son closely and cuddled him into her bosom. She comforted him as she inspected his angelic face to make sure there was no permanent damage. 'No harm done, Billy, just an accident, not to worry. You'll be alright. It's just singed your eyebrows. They'll grow back,' said his mother tenderly.

Within minutes, normality returned. The fuss and the excitement that epitomised Guy Fawkes Night subsided. It was over for another year.

It was November the fifth, 1970, and young Billy Boyd, aged twelve, had experienced his first contact with an explosive substance.

≈

Hugh Devenney sat in the Dun Low public house in downtown Derry, drinking a pint of Smithwicks beer. It was lunch-time and there were a small number of men in their early twenties clustered in groups standing at the bar.

On the table nearest the window Devenney placed his pint next to a small glass of Jameson whiskey, which waited for some attention. Most of the customers, at some time or another, had come across the middle-aged schoolteacher. He was a regular in the Dun Low at lunchtimes. The school, near St Peters, was only a five-minute walk from the city centre pub and many of the regulars had been taught by him. It was said Devenney liked younger women, but it was never discussed in his presence. He never spoke of the 'Troubles' and kept himself to himself. He was a good teacher with many acquaintances but few friends.

A respected man in Derry, it was rumoured that Hugh's brother, Damien, was a leading member of the Derry Brigade of the Provisional Irish Republican Army, the 'Provos!'

Sipping his beer, Hugh waited patiently as a clock behind the bar moved. Idling his time, he watched anxiously out of the window and studied a red leather miniskirt that a girl in her late teens wore as she carried out her lunchtime shopping.

Through the crowd of shoppers in the street outside he caught a glimpse of a long black coat shuffling along the pavement. Within a moment or two the front door of the public house opened and a large brutish-looking man walked into the Dun Low.

It was Eugene Kelly. Aged thirty, with shoulders dominating his upper torso, his arms were muscular and his hands appeared over-sized in comparison with the rest of his body. Sporting close-cropped blond hair, he wore a good quality dark blue suit with a cheap raincoat.

On entering the bar Eugene scoured the customers lined up drinking. Looking to his left and right, he nodded to one or two who acknowledged him and took a seat from where he could simultaneously study the front door, the exit to the toilets, and the rear door.

The licensee was pulling a pint of Smithwicks for him before his backside touched the seat. No money changed hands as one of the bar regulars passed the drink to him.

When satisfied that all was well in the pub, Eugene took out his racing newspaper and studied the form. He needed to get a bet on sometime today. His existence depended on gambling.

Glowering over the afternoon runners, he was immediately followed by an older man wearing a long black overcoat. Kelly was henchman and bodyguard to the figure in the long black coat.

Damien Devenney saw his brother Hugh seated at the usual table.

'Bless all here,' offered Damien, looking towards the bar.

There was a flurry of waved acknowledgements and nodded agreements as Damien moved swiftly towards his brother, removing his black overcoat en route.

He extended his hand and it was seized gustily by Hugh.

The two sat down and Hugh guided the Jameson gently towards his brother saying, 'I guessed you would be needing this, so I did.'

Raising his glass, Damien held it to the light, inspecting the content for quality and blend.

'You've heard then, my little brother. It's no time to drink to victory when we lose a good man now. Still, I'll drink to Declan Connelly, that I will. God rest his soul,' said Damien.

Turning to the bar, Damien lifted his glass high and toasted, 'To the memory of Declan Connelly: A good Catholic and a good Republican, who died last night. May God rest his soul and may his enemies rot in hell.'

The Jameson, having been revered sufficiently, slid neatly down Damien's throat.

Turning quickly to the optics, the barman filled another glass with Jameson which he placed on the bar. Eugene lifted it from its resting place and repositioned it on Damien's table.

Eugene ignored the schoolteacher.

The barflies concurred hastily, raising glasses on high and praising the recently departed. Muttered conversations turned to the subject of Declan Connelly as different cliques praised the latest volunteer who had died for the cause.

Eugene remained unmoved by the ad hoc ceremony being acted out before him. It was his job to watch the doors and windows for the unwanted. Kelly knew everyone in the bar, but remained impassive. He knew those who were in the organisation and those who were just on the periphery. He also knew those who were not members of the Provos as well as those he would have to keep in line if they engaged in loose talk. Today there would be no loose talk. The boss was having his weekly meeting with his brother. Eugene turned his attention to the horses and the prospective starting prices.

''Tis a sorry business, it is, Hugh,' offered Damien.

'What happened to yer man?' enquired Hugh.

20

'He was on active service, sure he was. Up there in Limavady the boys had found a good Loyalist man whose time had come to depart this earth,' replied Damien.

'How was that then, Damien?' asked Hugh.

'Sure, the man walked on the wrong side of the street, sure he did, ma wee brother. He spoke out against us, so the boys decided to help the Protestant on his way. Declan Connelly, God rest his soul, slipped a wee parcel underneath the Loyalist bastard's car. To be sure, Declan tripped the switch as he was putting it down. He went up at the same time as the car. Poor Declan Connelly, blown to the four corners of Limavady and not enough of him left for a proper funeral. The Loyalist bastard was in his house asleep. May the Orangeman rot in hell and all his sons and daughters with him,' said Damien.

The second Jameson slid unceremoniously down the throat. He placed his hand over the top of the empty glass signalling to Kelly that he did not want it refilled.

Kelly moved in to tend his charge.

'No, Eugene. Two's enough. No loose talk. What I've said is common knowledge but no more. Leave us now while I talk to ma brother,' instructed the Provo leader.

Kelly retired without a word, ever obedient, ever faithful.

''Tis a terrible day then, Damien. A terrible day. He'll be buried like a hero, sure enough. A martyr for the cause; a hero who died for his beliefs, a man who died for a free Ireland, a man to tell the children about,' said Hugh.

Hugh Devenney took a long pull on his beer.

'And the bastard Brits will laugh in the safety of their English castles and tell the press that he died from an own goal. That's what they'll call it, Hugh. An own goal!' said Damien.

Hugh responded, 'Sure, I know that, Damien, but yer mustn't worry yerself now. 'Tis a battle lost but a war still to be won. Look to mother Connelly and her kids just now. I'm thinking the poor woman has two young 'uns, Liam and Shelagh is it not? Don't worry on Limavady. The Orangeman will have his day, that's to be sure.'

Damien reached for his long black coat and started to draw it over his shoulders. Leaning down to Hugh's ear he advised, 'Tell the youngsters, Hugh. I want the name of Declan Connelly written in the history of the Republican cause. Do yer hear me now, Hugh? A hero.'

With that, the two brothers shook hands and Damien departed. Eugene was through the front door and onto the street, checking security, before Damien said his goodbyes to the assembly at the bar.

It was little more than twelve months since the Kingsmill massacre when ten Protestants had been shot dead by the Provos at a bogus road block in the village of Kingsmill, South Armagh. Retribution from the Protestants was always anticipated.

By mid-afternoon Sinn Fein counsellors from the Derry office were helping to organise the Connelly funeral whilst 'volunteers' were seeing to mother Connelly's immediate financial needs.

The organisation looked after their own.

Liam and Shelagh Connelly were in their late teens by now and already well aware of the Republican movement. They had been fed on the history of the movement since their early days.

However, in the weeks to come, their friends and neighbours would revere and respect the Connelly name in Shantallow. A Connelly had died for the cause.

Hugh Devenney finished drinking his Smithwicks before placing the glass on the bar. Nodding farewell to the licensee, he made for the street.

The sudden Derry daylight dazzled him during his march back towards the school to take the afternoon session.

Declan Connelly's death would be another story to tell his carefully selected group of teenagers: The teenagers who were being groomed for the Provisional Irish Republican Army.

Hugh had never been on active service for the Provos and probably never would be called upon to participate. He couldn't fire a gun and knew very little about bombs and explosives. He knew everything there was to know about politics and the history of the Republican cause, but he kept a low profile and held his counsel wisely.

Many knew who his brother was, but very few knew that Hugh Devenney was the local leader of Fianna, the young wing of the Provos. The kids of today were the Declan Connellys of tomorrow.

It was Hugh Devenney's job to make sure that the boys knew why they were fighting. This was not a game. It was a war, handed down from generation to generation. The names changed and the deeds altered slightly - but the objective remained the same - to win the war against the Brits and bring about a free Ireland.

≈

August 1976

An orange sash fluttered against his chest as his legs stretched out in front of him, clawing back the distance between himself and his opponent. His heart was pounding and he felt the sweat forming in rivulets on his neck and throat. Already his eyebrows were moist as the perspiration slowly descended onto his face.

His spikes tore into the soft summer earth when his body angled to one side on the bend. His arms pumped wildly and his mouth and cheeks formed into a playful grimace. And August sunshine tanned his skin as the large crowd cheered the athletes on.

There were only eight runners in the last event of the Police Cadets 1976 Athletics Meeting, but Billy Boyd was determined to win the five thousand metres even if it killed him in the process.

They ploughed onwards past the grandstand, where his classmates sat cheering, waving and jumping up and down in their seats.

There were four teams of cadets who wore the coloured sashes of their teams: Orange, green, blue and red. They'd competed all afternoon and at the end of the day the Orange and the Green were equal on points.

Brewster, the youth ahead of him, wore a green sash. First through the tape would win the cup for his team. The other six were so far behind they didn't count.

Painstakingly, Billy entered the last lap. The two athletes, sensing the end of the race, accelerated slightly, each trying to push the other into a physical and mental torture chamber from which there was no return.

The green sash headed the field by a yard and the team trainer, Sergeant Ferguson, felt confident of his man Brewster. The crowd leapt to their feet and pressed forward when the race swung into the back straight. Standing next to Ferguson was Sergeant Miller, all six foot seven of him, worried as to the outcome.

It was only a sports event. A bit of fun to end a three-month course before the cadets went off to the District Police Training Centre at Bruche, Warrington, where they would learn the noble art of policing.

Ferguson and Miller were joined by a superintendent from the west of the county, who had a reputation as a bit of a gambler.

'Well now, gentlemen, who do you recommend? The orange or the green?' queried the super.

Ferguson replied, 'My boy, sir, Brewster, green sash, good swimmer, good runner, balls like an ox. Cleator Moor lad, from your own neck of the woods. Breed 'em tough out there they do, sir. As well you know,' he offered.

The sound of Cleator Moor inspired the superintendent right away. Cleator Moor was on his patch.

'The other one?' he asked.

Miller replied, 'Fortunately, he hasn't got balls like an ox....'

Before Miller could speak further, the superintendent interjected, 'One round of drinks on the bar, six o'clock, on the green. I'll bet on the Cleator Moor boy.'

Ferguson beamed and said, 'Good decision, sir.'

Miller decided Ferguson was a clown. Miller, however, was no fool. He knew when to keep on the right side of senior police officers, even when they were foolish gamblers. Where was the harm in a round of drinks? Apart from that, he might even win if Boyd got a move on.

Miller took the bet. 'Done! The orange will win.'

The superintendent wondered whether or not the chief constable would be in the bar at six o'clock. Probably not. Still, time for a couple before he headed back to base. He'd drawn the short straw to attend the meeting. He might as well take solace in a couple of drinks before he travelled west.

Ferguson and Miller walked out onto the field, their blue tracksuits adding to the colour in the arena. Between them, they stretched the tape across the winning line as the last runner entered the final lap.

At the crown of the last bend, Brewster was ahead of Boyd. The noise was deafening as they entered the straight for the last time, with Boyd catching his fellow cadet by the second. Those teenage years spent running up and down the Cumbrian fells paid off as Boyd pulled out and levelled with the opposition, shoulder to shoulder, man against man.

The tape was in sight as Boyd matched the enemy stride for stride all the way down the final straight.

Ferguson and Miller pulled the tape across the track, ensuring there was no give in the line. They were willing their respective men on.

The small wooden-built grandstand erupted in a spectacle of excitement as the cadets and their families and friends cheered for their favoured runner at the top of their voices. Young people with youth on their side and hope in their hearts.

Brewster held the inside lane nearest to Sergeant Ferguson whilst Billy powered down the outside lane.

Inching ahead, Billy Boyd dragged the last measure of physical endurance out of his body. With no more than a yard or so to go, he dipped. His torso aimed for the tape. His opponent followed suit.

There was only a matter of inches in it.

Ferguson dropped the tape from his fingers when he realised that his man was beaten. The tape fluttered in the breeze.

Sergeant Miller held the other end of the tape tightly in his hand as the two runners dipped together.

When the tape left Ferguson's fingers the tension in the line relaxed and, as it fell to the ground, Brewster brushed the tape first. In a micro-second Brewster glimpsed from the corner of his eye and realised Boyd was fractionally ahead. Boyd crossed the line first but Brewster had chested the falling tape first. Boyd was the winner by inches.

To the distant observer in the grandstand it looked like a draw. The confusion of the dropped tape added to the enigma. Only those at the trackside could discern the truth.

The two runners collapsed in a heap as they finished the race. The cheers of the crowd were replaced by questioning exchanges.

Who had won?

The superintendent took the initiative and declared, 'Draw! A draw, I say. What a splendid result! Well done, lads! It's a draw.'

No one was getting a free drink from the superintendent that night, not if he could help it.

Draw! The word spread like wildfire from the track to the front row of the crowd and up through the grandstand. Draw? Incredible! Mistake?

Slowly the realisation seeped in and puzzlement changed to applause: Loud rapturous applause for a great race from two fit young men.

Ferguson helped Brewster to his feet and offered, 'I thought you got it.'

Brewster penetrated the Sergeant with his eyes. 'Bollocks! I bottled out. I heard him coming and I got too worried about him. He inched me out, you fool. He won. Only just, but he won.'

Brewster threw his arms round Boyd's neck as he pulled the green sash from his chest and said, 'Well done, Billy. Great race! You just got me, you lucky sod.'

'Thanks,' cracked Billy.

'Too close that one. I'm knackered. I just got you on the line. Our cup then, Sarge?' asked Billy Boyd.

Miller looked across at the superintendent before he answered Boyd. He could see the look of consternation in the super's eyes. A reputation at stake.

'No! A draw, Cadet Boyd. Now, off to the showers with you both,' said Miller.

The superintendent smiled and addressed the small group. 'Agreed. That's it settled then. A draw! Good result! Well done, lads! Excuse me. I must speak with the chief before I go. Sergeant Miller, you train your cadets well. Congratulations!'

The superintendent wandered off in search of his quarry.

Considering the declaration, Boyd commented, 'Draw? Draw? I won fair and square.'

Anticipating problems, Miller countered, 'It's only a game, Billy. It's not important who won. It's the taking part that counts. Don't you realise that?'

Miller guided Billy towards the showers in the opposite direction to the superintendent.

'Pure crap, sarge. I'm no loser. I was born to win, not draw. Do you hear me? I was born to win,' countered Billy Boyd shrugging away from Sergeant Miller.

Boyd stormed off.

Miller closed his eyes, shook his head and wished he was back on the beat again. He would never get the hang of dealing with these kids.

The Cadets dined, showed their families around police headquarters and returned home for a two-week holiday before going to the police training centre. A new life was ahead of them.

≈

December 1977

The Commandant and his class instructors looked out eagerly through the conference room window across the parade ground and examined the latest batch of police recruits being put through their paces by the drill sergeant.

The drill sergeant was an officer in the Cheshire Constabulary and a former member of the Welsh Guards Regiment. His big black boots shone so brightly that it was said the sergeant shaved by them in the mornings. His trousers were razor sharp and the creases in the arms of his tunic were accentuated when he marched out. His cap carried a peak that was slashed to the core. It sat on his shaven head and slanted down over his forehead in true Guards fashion. A pace stick glistened in the sun and never left the sergeant's side. A curly black moustache dominated his face and finished off the portrait of the man who ate policemen for breakfast. He was smartness personified, but then he would remind you in no uncertain terms that he was a Cheshire man. His name was Nixon but everyone called him 'Sergeant'.

The Commandant turned to his instructors, 'What do you make of the present bunch then?' Pausing, he allowed the question to be considered before asking, 'What manifestations of man and womankind are we about to unleash on the poor unsuspecting British public? Do they deserve my police officers, I ask, or do they deserve each other?'

He raised his eyebrows to the gathering. They were used to him, those former physical training instructors and teachers of legal academia. They'd joined the police service on a second career ticket in order to carry out their first choice career within the cosy confines of a police training centre. He loved to antagonise them. It prevented him from becoming bored. He was an old-fashioned copper at heart, the Commandant.

His sarcasm was answered by a young Inspector, keen to impress the dinosaur from another age.

The Inspector replied, 'They'll do alright, sir. They've been a pretty good bunch, this lot. We've done as before. It's the usual mixture of brains and brawn with a liberal application of discipline and common sense, mixed together for three months, broken down, reconstituted and put back together again. Good swimmers; fit, all first aiders and all through their police law exams.'

The Commandant considered the remark with some suspicion. 'Yes! But are there any good coppers in amongst that lot?' he said, aiming the question at the gathering of senior officers.

'That remains to be seen, sir. We'll have to wait and see,' replied the Inspector.

Out on the parade ground four uniformed classes, each containing thirty young men and women, lined up in open order for inspection by the Godlike Sergeant Nixon.

Nixon floated over the parade ground towards them with his pace stick flashing in the sun He'd nicknamed his pace stick 'Excalibur' and it was seen by the recruits as a potential weapon to be castigated with. Sergeant Nixon used 'Excalibur' to good effect, matching the pace stick stride for stride as he measured his military march towards the police corps.

The gentle melodic sound of Sergeant Nixon's gleaming black boots whispered on the tarmac as he marched briskly through the ranks. No buttons undone. Boots clean. Uniform pressed. Ties straight. Hair above the collar line. No stubble on the men and no make-up on the women. This was a parade ground for disciplinarians, not a catwalk for the fashion conscious.

His eyes searched every crevice of his charges, seeking out the untidy. Who would dare to disgrace his parade ground? He marched on, immaculate in his every move, robotic.

A gap! He stopped, paused, and confronted the space.

Sergeant Nixon considered the gap for a moment and then retraced his steps, checking those present. Who was missing? A gap where there shouldn't be a gap! He was annoyed. He fumed. He exploded in a fit of controlled anger.

'Boyd! Where are you, Boyd? You disgrace of Cumbrian fell sheep. Where are you? You great northern clodhopper. Out shearing the sheep are we?' screamed the drill sergeant.

The young recruits broke into spontaneous laughter. It would be one of those mornings when a chuckle would keep the spirits up. They were few and far between at times. Life at the district police training centre could be hard. No-one got an easy ride

'Silence in the ranks! You were not granted permission to laugh,' ordered Nixon.

His moustache bristled, perhaps even tingled slightly.

Silence fell over the assembly. No one argued with Nixon. The penalty for upsetting the sergeant was a dawn parade in full uniform and a dog's life for the rest of the week.

The figure of a proportionately built, dark-haired young man could be seen rushing towards the parade ground from the nearby residential blocks. The young man was striding out, swallowing up the ground between himself and the parade. The figure was nearly dressed in a police uniform. The tunic was undone and he was carrying his helmet in a nonchalant manner. Quite what he was supposed to do with the helmet, he hadn't quite figured out.

The young man shouted a jovial reply, 'Coming, sergeant'.

'That man there, stand still!' screamed Sergeant Nixon.

The command pierced the airwaves and drilled sharply through the eardrums.

Rooting himself to the ground at the sound of Nixon's order, Boyd stood like a statue.

'Sergeant! Yes, sergeant!' shuddered Boyd.

Nixon homed in on his quarry, his moustache bristling in anticipation and devilment. The drill sergeant increased his marching tempo and accelerated towards the young Boyd in brisk military fashion. Left! Right! Left! Right!

No messing with his boots gleaming and a backbone as straight as a die. He said, 'The helmet, lad! Are you going to piss in it or wear it?' asked Nixon.

Behind the drill sergeant one hundred and nineteen recruits strained their necks round to watch the admonishment whilst at the same time trying to stifle a laugh.

The sergeant, however, carried eyes in the back of his head, specially implanted there by the noble Welsh Guards two long decades previously.

'Eyes front, you lot! No one gave you permission to watch.'

The uniformed contingent waited anxiously. There was nothing better than watching Nixon in full flow and they had a ringside seat. The theatre continued.

Boyd offered an apology, 'Wear it, serge. Sorry!'

Nixon narrowed his eyes and sharpened his claws. 'Constable Boyd, you will be even sorrier at six o'clock tomorrow morning when you present yourself in number one uniform outside my office. I don't like laziness, laddie. You are late for my parade. I consider that a personal insult Do you understand that?' asked Nixon.

'Right, serge,' replied Boyd.

'It's Sergeant Nixon to you, you Cumbrian clodhopper. Double time around the square - Now!' ordered the drill sergeant.

'Yes, sergeant,' replied Boyd woefully.

Boyd made the parade ground and started to double march round the square to the quiet amusement of his classmates.

'Sergeant!' shouted Boyd.

'Yes, Boyd,' came the reply.

'What's a clodhopper?'

'Move it, Boyd! Before I insert one up your backside.'

A guffaw exploded from the rear ranks but died quickly when Nixon swivelled his neck towards the offending area. The parade continued minus one.

Boyd spent the next hour in double time mode round and round the square.

Other police officers went through their paces, polishing the marching performance that would soon be given at the passing out parade. They all knew it backwards.

Taped military music filled the air as it circulated the centre via strategically placed loudspeakers. It was not surprising. It was a time when its members were drawn largely from those who liked to call themselves 'ex-servicemen'. It was a disciplined organisation, or so it thought.

The sweat trickled down Boyd's blue shirt as his boots became scuffed and his serge trousers became unkempt. There was a good two hours' work at least tonight on his uniform. The perspiration from his body continued to soil his garb. Six o'clock at the sergeant's office meant out of bed at five. Lovely. It wasn't a problem. It reminded him of his home in the far north.

As Boyd continued doing the parade ground circuits he spied the music studio, where a civilian staff member was selecting the next rendition. Would it be 'Hearts of Oak' or some other suitably stirring piece of music to stimulate patriotism and inspire the young? He wondered - and the germ of an idea became a plan.

Rejoining his class, Boyd marched off in troop order to the showers. By lunchtime he was back in the classroom block, hard at his studies. He concentrated deeply, putting his mind to the subject in hand.

Nightfall came.

Lights were out all over the centre. The bar was closed and the gymnasium complex was still, save for the smell of sweat which tended to hang in the air when the caretaker had forgotten to switch on the extractor fans. Water in the swimming pool was crystal clear and lay like a mirror, waiting invitingly for the early morning plunge. Only the soft murmur of a pool filtration system could be heard in the still of the night.

Classrooms were a dark abyss of abandoned learning, clustered with empty chairs and lonely desks. Chalk dust hung in the air where the blackboards slept the night away.

Near the reception area, where all visitors were directed on arrival, there was a small fish pond surrounded by plants. Its occupants hung lazily suspended in the clear water. Sleeping fish and sleeping students.

The guardroom contained two pressed senior students on night security patrol. One read a car magazine whilst the other patrolled the site with a high-powered maglite torch. A two-way radio system occasionally crackled as the outside officer ran through his security checks with his colleague in the guardroom.

This was good practice. The young man would probably spend the best part of his next two years shaking hands with every city centre door knob in his town of posting. It was typical of night duty, potentially the loneliest job in the police service. Checking door handles at the front and rear of city centre shops was a basic part of night duty in many northern towns in those days, making sure all was secure in the still of the night.

It was three o'clock in the morning. The only people awake now were policemen, nurses, other night workers, cats, criminals and Billy Boyd.

The bedroom window closed quietly behind him as his feet touched the earth and he moved silently away from the ground floor room that had been home for three months. He made the hedgerow that bordered the residential block.

Black trainers complemented the dark blue hooded tracksuit that Boyd favoured for his mission. He crouched at the end of the hedgerow waiting for his eyes to become accustomed to the light. The moonlight was sufficient to work by, but it threw subtle shadows across the high rise concrete buildings.

Boyd saw the police patrol pass him by. The torch flashed from side to side as the young bobby guiding it whistled nervously in the night. Allowing him to pass, Boyd watched him walk off towards the far car parking area.

The Cumbrian policeman approached the parade ground and skirted the edge in order to attack the music room with the minimum of exposure. He paused, crouched down as low as he could, listened, and looked. The coast was clear.

Withdrawing a yellow, plastic-handled screwdriver from his trouser belt, Boyd slowly inserted it into the window fastener and worked the tool backwards and forwards until the clasp gave in. He pushed the screwdriver upwards and released the catch. Leaned up, he inserted his left hand, opened the window, climbed in, and pulled the window closed behind him. He crouched down in the room, allowing his eyes to become accustomed to the darkness.

The night security unit continued to patrol the car park at the far end of the site, oblivious to the events developing in the music studio.

Boyd found what he was looking for. He located the cassette tape that bore the legend 'Passing out Parade', pocketed the tape and checked everything was situated in the same position as when he had entered. He climbed out of the music studio window and returned cautiously to the safety of his own room.

In the privacy of his sanctuary he carried out his deed.

The five o'clock alarm sounded. Boyd was fully awake, silenced the clock, and eased himself gently from his bunk. He showered and dressed before stepping into the crisp morning air.

The street lights of Warrington provided an amber halo effect over the sky to the west of the centre. He thought it was a pity there were no Cumbrian fells in the background. He usually went jogging at this time of day when he was at home. Boyd set off for his dawn appointment with Sergeant Nixon. En route he had one last matter that required his personal attention.

It wasn't long before he found the night patrol and alerted the weary officer to the fact that a window in the music studio didn't look as if it had been closed properly. He'd spotted the insecurity on the way to see Nixon.

The night patrol worried. The premises had been checked just after midnight and were secure then. Not to worry. Acting on the advice of Boyd, a visit was made to the music studio.

Boyd accompanied the patrol to back them up. In a blaze of light the night officers scoured the studio and checked to see if anything was missing. All correct. No problems. It was assessed someone had merely forgotten to close the window properly.

In a final misdemeanour during the search of the studio, Boyd replaced the 'Passing out Parade' cassette tape whilst no one was looking. Mission accomplished!

At six o'clock precisely, Boyd rattled on Sergeant Nixon's door.

Nixon relished the moment and was eloquent in his mastery of the English language. As he administered a severe caution for misconduct and professional incompetence on the parade ground, or rather, the inability to make the parade ground on time, Nixon managed every parade ground insult in the book plus one or two others he made up on the way.

Billy Boyd stood impassive throughout the tirade, fully acknowledging he was in the wrong when he dared to turn up late for the sergeant's drill instruction and inspection. Boyd ate humble pie whilst

Nixon made mince meat out of the insulted Cumbrian. When the dawn chorus of castigation finished, Boyd remained silent.

Nixon replenished his throat with a large glass of milk that massaged the sides of his larynx as it slid down into his stomach. He wondered if Boyd would ever learn that military discipline was a fundamental requirement for the modern police service. It was just as well that his fellow class instructors had voted Boyd the best recruit of the current crop. Best, that was, in matters of physical fitness and intelligence.

Nixon would tell you that such points were of no concern to him. If a policeman couldn't behave properly on the parade ground then a character defect must obviously be apparent. Discipline was sacrosanct.

Boyd slammed his bedroom door behind him in the sure and certain knowledge that, despite all Nixon said, he was a policeman, not a product of a quasi-military regime. As far as Boyd was concerned, the police service was for civilians in uniform, not for the would-be soldier. Any attempts to remove his individualism would be bitterly resisted.

Boyd decided that morning that he would never become the stereotype that men like Nixon strove to produce. He would make his way in the world through brains, not bullshit. Boyd was from a new generation. Times were changing. He was a young man in a brave new world.

The final day arrived at last.

Nixon marshalled the big white police horses from Lancashire Constabulary into the holding area to the side of the parade ground. The horses would lead the band onto the square and herald the start of the passing out parade. The contingent of recruits would follow and line up in front of the makeshift grandstand. Here, the Deputy Chief Constable of North Wales would take the salute following the marching display by the recruits.

The grandstand filled with proud families and friends waiting to see their son or daughter enact the final events of the three-month initial training course.

Preening himself in the mirror, carefully removing the last element of dust that had settled on his tunic jacket, Boyd surveyed his boots. They shone up at him! And then he fidgeted with a white lanyard he wore to signal to others he was class leader. The instructors had voted him class leader some weeks earlier. This reflected both his popularity and the abilities apparent in his approach to life on the centre. He was a bright and personable young man, although some felt he liked bucking the system. Time would tell.

He left the room and joined the others mustering for the start of the parade. It was a beautiful day with Excalibur flashing in the sun and Nixon proudly pacing the parade ground on his final inspection.

Nixon marched sternly through the ranks with the Inspecting officer. His moustache bristled and his boots creaked with excess polish. The Inspecting officer nodded satisfactorily as the ritual wore on. Salutes were exchanged and the Deputy Chief Constable addressed the gathering. Prizes to the students were presented for various achievements amidst thunderous applause.

Finally, Sergeant Nixon brought the eager contingent of young recruits to attention and ordered them into close order for the anticipated marching display. The civilian in the nearby music studio fingered through the cassette tapes and eventually found the tape bearing the handwritten legend 'Passing out Parade'.

He carefully inserted the tape into the machine.

Nixon saluted the grandstand, which was awash with uniforms and splendour, about-turned, and saluted the students. It was up to them now.

The sergeant marched off giving the signal for a marching display to commence.

In the music studio, the play button was depressed and the spools whirled round, gathering the thin tape inwards. Strains of 'Hearts of Oak' pierced the loudspeakers and the recruits set off at a brisk march. Left, right, left, right.

Midway through the seventh bar, pandemonium broke loose. Unexpectedly the strains of 'Hearts of Oak' were replaced by the melodic sound of 'Tip toe through the tulips, through the tulips, by the willow tree, come tip toe through the tulips with me'.

The beat totally confused the marchers. Left became right and right became left.

The corps was thrown into a scene of comical chaos as the marching display faltered into a spectacle of one hundred and twenty police officers trying desperately to make sense of inappropriate music.

The scene was worsened when 'Tip toe through the tulips' was replaced by the sound of 'The Dambusters' followed closely by the Beatles favourite 'She Loves You'.

Staff in the music studio looked on horrified.

The Commandant set his eyes on Nixon and decided he was in charge and he, Nixon, would pay dearly for this major foul-up.

The Inspecting officer dropped his neck backwards and looked into the heavens for divine inspiration. None was forthcoming.

Nixon's face reddened and his temperature reached boiling point when he realised he'd been had. But who by? There were quite a few out there he had had cause to speak to over the months. Which one was it?

The families in the grandstand loved it and, thinking it was part of the display, roared with laughter at the sight unfolding before them.

Chaos was eventually replaced by sanity when the tape returned to 'Hearts of Oak' and continued on its scheduled route through a succession of military marching pieces. No matter, the contingent got it together at last and regained their composure.

Nevertheless, the display never quite achieved the effect Nixon desired and the debacle ended with the march past having to split ranks when one of the Lancashire police horses desecrated the parade ground.

Recruits marched off the square and wheeled towards the reception area coming to a halt opposite a fish pond. Three cheers were given and the final tradition occurred when helmets were thrown into the air in a glorious signal that it was over.

Nixon stood by the pond trying to avoid the Commandant.

Boyd gathered his helmet from the ground, kissed goodbye to some of his female colleagues and shook hands with others. Embracing some of his closer male friends, he promised to write to everyone for an eternity.

Squaring his helmet on his head, he straightened his tunic and marched towards Nixon and the Commandant, who by now appeared to be in the middle of a heated debate.

Boyd brought himself to a halt and crisply saluted them both with a flourish from his right arm. 'Sirs, thank you both for a wonderful three months. I have learnt many lessons and will not forget them.'

The Commandant melted. 'Well, thank you, Boyd. Good luck,' he said shaking Boyd's hand.

'Sergeant Nixon!' cracked Boyd.

'Yes, Boyd?' responded the sergeant.

'I looked it up,' offered Boyd.

'What did you look up, Boyd?' enquired Nixon.

'Clodhopper, sergeant. It means peasant and in Cumbria we do not have peasants. Indeed, many would say that to call a Cumbrian a clodhopper is to give personal insult. Not recommended in today's modern police service. Goodbye,' said Boyd.

Nixon didn't take it all in right away, but by the time he had worked it out, it was too late.

Police Constable Billy Boyd turned smartly on his heel and briskly marched off into the police service. He found his old banger of a motor car, loaded it with his battered and weathered suitcases, and drove crazily onto the M6 motorway. The top student was returning to his beloved Clodhopper land and a hopeful career in the police force.

Bruche Training Centre knew they'd had him. Cumbria feared the worst.

≈

1978

The house on the Pennyburn estate in Derry had been carefully selected because of its anonymous facade and easy access. Situated on the corner of a cul-de-sac, the occupant of the upstairs bedroom had a reasonably good position from which to observe the comings and goings in the street.

Hugh Devenney was first to arrive. Using the front door key, he settled into the house, filled the kettle, and switched it on before drawing the curtains and turning on the radio. Then he waited patiently for his students to report. They would arrive cautiously at five-minute intervals: The Fianna, coming to hear the propaganda that was the history of the Republican movement.

Sean Brady turned into the street. He stubbed his cigarette out and walked right round the cul-de-sac on the footpath. In circling the bottommost part of the cul-de-sac, he looked back up towards the direction he had just come from. Sean's eyes were on the mouth of the cul-de-sac. No one appeared. On completing the circle he checked the long road he had walked along then lit another cigarette and waited.

Sean was the leader of the unit and waited for the others to make a safe entry into the house before he joined them.

Minutes ticked by before Dermot Dougan appeared. Ignoring Sean, Dermot turned into the cul-de-sac and walked round the full extremity of the footpath. There was no signal from Sean.

Taking the gate off its catch, Dermot walked down the path to the front door. His light knock was answered by Hugh who welcomed him into the house. Dermot was interested in explosives and occasionally had been known to try and assemble small bombs. He was to be sent to a quarry in Limerick where his skills would be tested further and upgraded by the organisation's experts. He was a quiet young man with a soft voice and a love of animals. His parents did not know where he was that night.

Eamonn Murphy was nineteen years of age. He parked the Ford about a quarter of a mile from the house, having travelled across the Craigavon Bridge and the Foyle Bridge in order to shrug off any would-be followers. He was a good driver with a love of high speed cars and a record of stealing vehicles to order for the organisation's hierarchy.

Eamonn walked quickly, ignored Sean at the sentry point, and jumped over the hedge into the garden. He made the path and was ushered into the house by Hugh, who immediately admonished him for failing to comply with standard counter-surveillance instructions.

The noisy one, Eamonn turned everything into a joke. He looked at Hugh with mischief in his eyes then looked through the window and feigned amazement at sighting Sean mounting observation.

Hugh motioned him to help himself to tea and directed him to a seat.

Outside, Sean lit another cigarette as the minutes passed by.

A crippled old lady approaching him walked slowly down the street with the aid of a walking stick. A headscarf was tied tightly at her chin and a worn, navy, baggy duffel coat covered her body down to her knees. The bottom of her legs carried wrinkled stockings and flat-heeled shoes. She was breathing heavily and appeared to be asthmatic. The woman paused opposite Sean but there was no signal from him.

She walked into the house and was welcomed by Hugh. It was only then that the young woman, Bridget Duffy, removed her scarf to display long flowing blonde hair. Bridget removed the duffel coat to reveal a magnificent figure. With a prominent bosom, good looks and an engaging smile, she was also a master of disguise.

Hugh studied her figure with great interest. His groin ached.

Sean was still thinking about Bridget's latest disguise when Seamus Rafferty rounded the corner on his pedal cycle. Seamus whistled as usual and steered his cycle into the cul-de-sac and dismounted. Removing the cycle clips from the bottom of his trousers , he gently rested the cycle on its side against the hedgerow, and entered the house carrying the latest list of RUC movements on a small piece of paper secreted in his left sock. Seamus had been admitted into the Fianna due to his hatred of the police and his skills in targeting their every movement.

The group of young Republicans, in their late teens and early twenties, was almost complete. Sean waited for a newcomer to arrive.

Liam Connelly had been selected by Hugh. If Liam had been followed he would run the risk of betraying the group. Sean was the firearms expert, a terrific shot, and he had grown up during an era that knew only violence. He was a potential killer. Liam Connelly would be Sean's first victim if the group were betrayed that night.

Liam saw the leader of the pack standing on the corner of the cul-de-sac. He walked straight past Sean but then stopped. In the distance, a police Land Rover entered the far end of the street. Liam regained his composure and merely crossed the road.

Walking past the Land Rover, Liam ignored the occupants.

Meanwhile, Sean Brady stepped into the shadows and observed the goings on. He saw the Land Rover pass Liam and continue its slow patrol of the Derry estate. The Land Rover drove on past the meeting house.

 Sean observed that the occupants did not look at the house. He also heard not a sound from the vehicle radio. The minutes passed by and Liam came back into sight.

Liam circled the cul-de-sac and entered the house. Hugh seated him and five minutes later Sean Brady entered.

Sean nodded to Hugh that all was well. His arrival completed the latest active service unit Hugh had been instructed to put together by his brother, Damien.

There was something about Liam Connelly that Seamus Rafferty took an instant dislike to. Perhaps it was his youthful looks or the edge of his tongue. Perhaps it was because of the sighting of the RUC Land Rover, which Sean had recounted to the assembly. Seamus was suspicious He couldn't put his finger on it yet but Liam just didn't feel right. He quietened down to listen to the schoolteacher.

Hugh continued to chronicle the history of the Republican cause and spoke of how the Welshman, Patrick, landed on the shores of Ireland in AD 432 and brought religion to the population. Patrick toured Ireland meeting the Druids, who played their harps as he spread the word of God.

The harp became the emblem of Ireland. More recently, Hugh spoke of the period of the 'Plantations' when the British ceded the nine most northern counties of Ireland to the English and Scots on the mainland. In 1608, the Colony of Ulster was founded when the British Government ceded lands to the English, who took with them the Protestant religion and a degree of wealth that placed the Irish peasants in a position of subordination.

The schoolteacher portrayed the long and bitter struggle for a free state over the centuries. In the latter days of his obligation, Hugh concentrated on laws now separating six counties from the Republic and the armed struggle that had grown in magnitude since the 1916 Easter Uprising. The movement, argued Hugh, declared an allegiance to the thirty-two county Republic, proclaimed in 1916 and overthrown by force of arms in 1922, and thus suppressed to this day by the existing British imposition of counties and twenty-six partitioned states. Internment ended in the spring of 1975 but was professed as an example of British arrogance and Imperialism. Imprisonment without trial, it was said, was an indication of the contempt the British held for Irish people. Martyrs were recalled when a host of Republican heroes who died at the hand of the British were revered in the name of Republicanism. The doctrine of bringing fear to the Protestant population and the security forces, who maintained the peace, was declared to be that of the bullet and the bomb.

These elements would free the movement from the slavery of British repression. Terror was the enemy of democracy. Terror rules. Yes, 1977 was a time for peace. A time for a ceasefire if you will but if was also a time to plan for the war ahead. Little was said of the political democratic institutions that exist to deal with grievances, other than that they were legitimate targets belonging to a system that had failed the Irish Catholic.

Little was said of the massive criminal organisation that was growing across Northern Ireland in the name of PIRA and was seen to be terrorising people from all religious persuasions.

Nothing was said of the millions of pounds racketeering contributed to PIRA coffers through illegal gambling, protection and armed robberies. Some individuals were sustaining eloquent lifestyles on the back of terrorism. The issue of collecting monies from the sale of soft drugs was side-stepped, since PIRA made it clear they did not condone drug abuse.

The tensions of the 'Troubles' are like an open sore in consideration of the point that, in order to gather funds for a military response to PIRA, the Loyalist paramilitaries regularly resorted to supplying drugs to the people of Ireland. Do two wrongs make a right? What, for that matter, is right and what is wrong?

Hugh Devenney continued into the night until he eventually closed the green book that was his political bible.

The group were becoming restless and needed action. Hugh would have liked some action with Bridget Duffy. He slid the book into a briefcase and addressed the gathering.

'That's all for tonight, to be sure. I think we'll call it a day. Indeed, I think the time has come for yous to go on about yer business. Sean here will look out for you all. Now that's the way it is, people. I'll have no more to do with yous. Do you all understand that? The time has come to carry the fight outside. Sean will see to all your needs and he'll be telling you the when's and where's. My piece is ended. I fight my comer here in the armchair. I'm too old for the streets now.'

Sean accepted the opening Hugh had made for him. 'That's right. Thanks be to Hugh, but I take my lead from Damien now,' he said.

Sean drew long and hard on his cigarette and continued, 'We all know what's to be done. Tonight we go to our homes. You need only wait until I contact you. No loose talk. I'll be in touch when things are to be done. If we all look after each other, there'll be no problems.'

Seamus Rafferty didn't like it. He pointed towards Liam and asked loudly, 'And who's this boy that yer wanting me to look after? Jesus, I don't know the boy from Adam and yer wanting me to work with him.'

Sean closed with Seamus and stared into his face.

Seamus felt Sean's breath on his cheeks.

'Sure, Liam was sent to me directly from Damien. Did yer mind that?' declared Sean.

'So!' cracked Seamus.

'So you must learn the discipline, Seamus. Liam is in because I say so and Liam is in because Damien says so,' ordered Sean.

Sean had encountered a test of his strength and did not intend to weaken in the eyes of the group.

'Excuse me!' intervened the newcomer parting the two. 'My name is Liam Connelly from the Shantallow. My father was Declan, God rest his soul. My uncle is Padraigh O'Toole. No man speaks for me. Damien sent me, sure he did, but he sent me for to fight the Brits, not yous boys.'

Seamus and Sean relaxed slightly before Seamus queried, 'Would that be the Padraigh O'Toole who put them together for Declan?'

Liam knew he was referring to putting together bombs.

Dermot followed the exchanges and announced, 'Sure that would be right now, Seamus. It was a sad day when Padraigh made one that went off prematurely in the hands of Liam's father.'

Hugh took an interest in the debate. 'And where would your uncle Padraigh be now, Liam?' he enquired.

Sean denied an answer. 'Sure, that's not a question to be asking, Hugh. No loose talk here,' replied the self-appointed leader.

Liam ignored the helpline and answered, 'It was too much for my uncle Padraigh. After the funeral he crossed the water. I've never seen him since.'

Considering the point, Bridget added, 'That's a pity, Liam. Could you be finding out where he is now?'

''Why, Bridget?' probed Liam.

'One day we'll cross the water for the cause. Sure, would it not be good to know where we could find such a man?' suggested Bridget.

'I doubt it,' replied Liam closing the subject as he looked at Seamus Rafferty, wondering whether or not the wounds of yesteryear would be reopened.

The joker in the pack stepped forward and introduced himself, 'Eamonn Murphy is ma name and joining losers is ma game. Sure, there's one of us with an uncle who can't make bombs and a father who can't plant them and then there's Seamus who thinks he's God and Sean who acts like God. Sure, Dermot thinks he can make bombs, but he's frightened of the clock ticking and will yer take a look at Bridget, to be sure? Wid a bosom like that now and her blonde hair flowing in the wind, they'll be seeing her on the ferry at Stranraer before we leave Larne. I'm thinking we should all be staying here at home wid the schoolteacher and read the books. Sure, we could throw books at the soldiers and save Damien a fortune in the bullets. What do yer all say to that now?'

Pushing Eamonn playfully in the stomach as the tension dropped, Bridget countered with, 'And you'd be still trying to drive over the water when we're on the ferry, boyo. You are a thick Irish clown, Eamonn, that yer are.'

They broke up and left the house separately, just as they had arrived. It was darker now.

Across the way from the meeting house lay a derelict house. Some months ago the Loyalists from the Ulster Volunteer Force firebombed the house and the occupants fled. The house had been empty ever since.

In the roof space one man crawled on his stomach, trying to find a better camera angle through the half brick that he removed from the gable end of the building. The man used the infra-red camera and photographed all the occupants of the meeting house as they left. The cameraman was a member of the intelligence services. He was aided by one soldier with a radio and one with a submachine gun and hand pistol, who was briefed to protect the trio.

In the silence of the night they returned to their base and developed the photographs. Within a week the photographs were in the possession of the intelligence community. Within the month everyone concerned had been identified and the tout who had told the police of the meeting was paid handsomely for identifying a newly formed active service unit.

Many people in the district of Londonderry would have been surprised to learn that the tout responsible for this intelligence coup was one Eugene Kelly, bodyguard to Damien Devenney. The offer of a large amount of money proved too much for Eugene. He was on the other side now, playing the odds. The longer he played the game, the less chance he had of staying alive. He would never know everything that Damien was involved in, but he knew enough.

Hugh Devenney arrived first and left last. His part was ended. He had done as his dear brother Damien had asked. It was cold. He hurried home to the comfort of his fireplace. Tomorrow they would meet again the Dun Low and talk of old times and parents long departed.

Liam Connelly walked back towards the Shantallow. He hoped to spend time with his sister, Shelagh. He didn't know how long he would have before he got busy but he knew Sean wanted him to finish a job at the 'Caw' estate on the south of the Foyle. The meeting had gone well. The blonde woman, Bridget, had been the problem. When she asked where his uncle, Padraigh O'Toole, was living, he had lied. He knew where to find Padraigh and how to get to Padraigh's home without using the recognised travel routes. It would remain his secret, locked away in his devious mind. The months rolled by.

≈

1979

Seamus Rafferty spent his time following the RUC around, noting when and where they went. He tried desperately to find out where some of the local RUC officers lived but was constantly frustrated by the elaborate counter and anti-surveillance methods they employed to protect themselves during the journeys between home and work.

Damien sent word down to select a Loyalist for a 'hit' and Seamus obliged with a visit to the Caw estate south of the River Foyle in Londonderry.

Eamonn was called upon to choose a suitable vehicle for the getaway and picked out a grey saloon car.

Dermot exercised his long fingers and got to work on a small device. It was the size of a sandwich box and carried a magnet on its lid.

Sean and Liam carried guns. They oiled, cleaned and checked the weapons in order to maximise their effectiveness and prevent malfunction.

Bridget walked the streets checking out the site for any protection issues they needed to address. It was her job to be sure that they were not being watched by others. It was also her job to ascertain what defences the target had in his area. Who looked out for the target? She also had to be sure that the target always turned up at the same time and at the same place every day. Only then could they guarantee a kill.

They were targeting a leading member of the Ulster Defence Association. They would take their time to do it right.

The day of the 'hit' arrived.

At lunchtime the active service unit left their homes in Derry and went about their business. Eventually, they met at predetermined rendezvous points. Seamus reported the target was in residence whilst Bridget declared that the protection in the area had not been changed. Dermot handed the sandwich box to Liam. They got into the car Eamonn Murphy had stolen from the Creggan earlier in the day.

Eamonn drove the car. Sean sat in the front seat with the gun underneath his seat. Liam sat in the rear with the deadly sandwich box beside him and his gun nestling down the belt in the small of his back.

Taking the vehicle through the outskirts of Shantallow, Eamonn found the River Foyle on his nearside. It was approaching tea time. The three men were nervous but Eamonn managed his full repertoire of jokes to quell the tension. The grey saloon with the three terrorists on board crossed the Foyle Bridge and turned into the Caw estate. Threading their way through the streets, they turned into a road where the target lived.

The house was quiet when they saw the silhouette of the target in the front lounge. At the end of the street Eamonn swung the car to the right and turned right again towards a block of council garages at the rear of the target's home. He turned round to point back towards the escape route and then pulled up, turned off the car engine, and sat quietly. No one spoke. The clock ticked on.

The area was deserted save for the passing traffic that could be heard in the distance. The trio looked cautiously out of the car window, checking out rooftops and bedroom windows that might give an enemy position away.

Sean felt perspiration trickle down the back of his neck. Liam thought that his heart was beating so loud that everyone for a mile around would hear it and Eamonn fingered the ignition key.

It would be a quick getaway, controlled but fast, he thought.

Getting out of the vehicle, Sean peered over the car rooftop towards the entrance to the garage area. He signalled to Liam some minutes later by tapping lightly on the car rooftop. Liam swung his legs out of the car and walked towards the garages.

The sandwich box was under his arm.

He found the garage with its 'up and over' type door.

Sean moved to his side and remarked, 'It's as quiet as the grave, Liam.' Standing with his back to the garage wall just to the side of the door, Sean eyed the bedroom windows again.

Liam eased the garage door open and entered.

He removed the dowel pin from the bomb and placed the slender piece of wood into his pocket. Liam knew the bomb was now live and the timer device inside Dermot's box of tricks was working. Dropping onto his knees, he felt the underside of the car and moved the sandwich box into position underneath the driver's side. The magnet found its target and hung tightly to the underside of the car with a dull 'clunk' when the magnet met the metal.

Withdrawing, closing the garage door behind him, Liam's perspiration rolled down his face and matted his hair. His pulse was racing.

Sean checked both ways and scanned the rooftops and offered, 'Let's go.'

The two men retraced their steps to the grey saloon car. Eamonn fired the engine. Liam and Sean climbed in and they drove off, gathering their speed selectively.

The timer ticked on.

The Loyalist commander left the house by the back door and walked to the garage. His bodyguard was ahead of him as usual and as predicted by Bridget. They reached the garage. The bodyguard lifted the 'up and over' door and entered the garage.

Remaining at the entrance to the garage with his back to the door, again as prophesied by Bridget, the Commander surveyed the area.

The bodyguard knelt down and looked underneath the car. He checked out the underside by dropping onto his hands and knees. He saw it. 'Out, John! Quick ...' he yelled.

The timer completed its last action by bringing together two pieces of metal. The fusion sent an electronic spark through a thin wire down into a detonator. The subsequent explosion caused a large fireball that blew the car upwards into the ceiling of the garage. The car roof crumpled on impact.

The bodyguard didn't see the fireball.

The initial blast effect pushed his head against the car bulkhead and he was decapitated. The garage was engulfed in flames and the door blew outwards into the commander. His back broke instantaneously but he was thrown away from the area of the explosion into the dirt, where only an hour earlier a grey saloon car had been parked. The broken masonry, hot metal, and the debris of the explosion fell to earth.

The commander was still alive but died on the operating table later that night.

An old woman with black hair walked nearby. She was said by witnesses to have an unusually prominent chest for one so old. This woman watched the explosion unfold and then left the area on foot, without speaking to anyone, it was said.

At seven o'clock that night a female voice spoke on the telephone to a reporter at BBC Ulster. The caller claimed the attack on behalf of the Provisional Irish Republican Army. A code word was given to indicate authenticity.

The RUC officer banged the desk with his fist. The tout had not been aware of the attack that was to be carried out. The tout had failed.

The bombers were home free. Two more names were added to the death count.

Liam Connelly stood casually by the window of the local Sinn Fein office on the Racecourse Road north of the River Foyle in the City of Londonderry, or Derry, as it was known in the particular locality where it was situated. The well known and well frequented office served part of the Republican community north of the river.

It was no more than a week since the Loyalists lost one of their leaders in the bomb attack on the Caw estate.

Liam laughed and joked with staff whilst he waited for Sean to tend to his private business with a Sinn Fein counsellor in the back office.

Glancing outside, Liam saw the yellow-coloured transit van glide up to the side of the gutter and park near the pavement by the 'phone box. There were three men in the vehicle. Liam didn't recognise any of the occupants.

'Sean!' he called. 'Come here a moment, will you?'

There was no answer, just the sound of a whispered conversation from within the small compact office situated near the rear entrance.

The van doors closed and two of the men stood on the pavement. One carried a dark blue holdall. The sound of the van's engine could still be heard, with the driver remaining in his seat.

I don't like this, thought Liam. The two men approached the Sinn Fein building. Liam saw revenge in their eyes and hatred in their hearts.

'Sean!' screamed Liam.

The taller of the two men produced a sawn-off shotgun from beneath his coat. The smaller, ginger-haired man dropped the holdall he was carrying and pulled out a home-made machine gun. Without a word or a signal to each other, the two Loyalist paramilitaries closed with the building and raised their firearms.

'Get down!' shouted Liam loudly. 'Everybody down! It's a hit! Get down now!'

The occupants of the Sinn Fein office scrambled for cover hitting the floor when the first bullets ripped through the glass windows and exploded into the wall behind them. Suddenly the building was a shooting gallery, with paintings and framed declarations that hung on the wall slithering and sliding as the bullets resonated against the brickwork and caused complete mayhem.

Outside, the two Loyalists pumped round after round into the building from the pavement. When the shotgun was emptied, the assailant merely discharged the dead rounds and refilled the twin chambers. His deadly load erupted once more into the office building. The pellets penetrated the building, seeking to blind and disfigure. The home-made machine gun was no different. Once the magazine was emptied, the gunman knelt down, took another magazine from the holdall and pumped his cargo of hatred into the Republican enclave.

Glass in windows shattered and light bulbs danced in frenzy as the interior of the building became engulfed in a cauldron of lethal ammunition.

Workers buried themselves beneath their desks and hugged the wooden floor for fear of death.

Pushing his back further into the wall, Liam peeked one eye out into the street to see the attackers continue their violent onslaught. Suddenly, it was over. There was no sound. The firing stopped.

The man with the holdall bent down again and removed an object from the bag.

'Petrol bomb! Out the back quickly!' ordered Liam as he watched carefully from his delicate position. 'Move! You've got time if you're quick! Leg it!'

The shotgun disappeared beneath a coat as the first terrorist moved back to the van and jumped into the front of the vehicle. He tapped the driver on the elbow, signalling him to make ready for a quick departure.

The remaining paramilitary removed the top from the bottle, doused the taper and lit it with a match. He drew back his arm and threw the petrol bomb into the building through the space where once glass windows had provided some shelter from the unfriendly elements.

Then he was gone, backing away into the escape vehicle. The yellow van moved off at speed, the driver screeching his tyres as his vehicle lurched forward and out of the area, back towards the Protestant lines.

Crash!

A petrol bomb landed in the centre of the floor. The office was empty save for Liam.

Liam smelled the burning petrol as it burst onto the wooden floor and fanned out haphazardly across the deserted office. Acting quickly, he grabbed the fire extinguisher from its wall mounting, manipulated the mechanism, and moved adroitly round the Sinn Fein building, dousing the fire wherever he could and killing the flames.

A breeze from the rear door greeted him as Sean Brady rushed into the main office, panic written on his face. 'Bastards!' screeched Sean. 'Bastards! I'll kill every one of them, sure I will!'

Flames reacted to Sean opening the door. Fire billowed upwards with flames reaching for Sean's face and his clothing. Feeling the heat from the inferno, Sean covered his eyes, frightened of being burnt, and screamed as the fire enveloped him.

Ignoring the flames, Liam smoothly sprayed foam onto the floor in front of Sean. He smothered the fire, saving Sean from terrible burns. Liam worked the extinguisher round, concentrating on the seat of the fire before moving the device outwards away from the centre.

'Are they out, Sean? Did they get out unscathed?' asked Liam.

'Aye! Sure they did. Just as well you were on the lookout, Liam,' remarked Sean. 'They would have got them all if it hadn't been for you.'

'Sure, it pays to keep an eye out, Sean. You never know what's around the corner, sure you don't know,' acknowledged Liam.

The Sinn Fein office was wrecked, a shadow of its former self. The attack had been over in less than three minutes. Three minutes of hell! Three minutes of hatred and revenge! Three minutes of arson! Three minutes of potential murder!

No windows remained to keep out the cold, just a charred floor and a desecrated empty office. The Loyalists had retaliated. The cauldron of sectarianism continued to boil.

Today an attack on a Sinn Fein office, tomorrow - who knows?

≈

PART TWO
IN POSITION

1982

A police patrol car sped eastwards chasing its quarry. A flashing blue light and a deafening two-tone siren announced to the sleeping occupants of the market town of Wigton, and the driver of a stolen car, that the chase was well and truly on. The huntsman was chasing the fox.

Dawn broke in north Cumbria and sunshine cast its first shadows over the fells. The never-ending cat and mouse game between law keepers and law-breakers was being acted out once again.

As chaser and chased headed at high speed towards the city of Carlisle, neither driver took time to take in the distant views of the rising Caldbeck Fells to the offside or the silent Solway Firth to the nearside. The cattle in the fields shied away from the hedgerows near to the main road as the two cars roared noisily away from Wigton and on towards the distant city some ten miles to the east.

The radio in the police patrol car crackled when a young female voice sounded through the radio speaker and enquired, 'Current location. Tango Zero Five?'

The police driver lifted his radio handset to his mouth and responded calmly, his eyes fixed on the road ahead. 'I'm on the A595 east from Wigton towards Carlisle, speed seventy-five miles per hour and climbing, one male driver and it looks like one passenger.'

There was a pause as the policeman studied the profile of the car in front of him. He made out the number of occupants in the vehicle in front of him and reported further. 'Yes, control. It's one male driver and one male passenger. Both teenagers by the look of them. Just the two up and increasing speed. He's not going to stop, control. Request assistance, please,' he said.

The control room operator looked at the clock above her. It was nearing six in the morning, 26th September 1982. She heard the sound of the siren coming through the police radio and visualised the patrol car weaving in and out of the early morning traffic.

'All patrols. All patrols City area, be advised of Tango Zero Five in pursuit of a red Ford Granada XHH 147T. Vehicle stolen Cockermouth during the night. Two male occupants also suspected of burglary at Workington Gun Shop. Current location A595 Wigton towards city. All patrols acknowledge.'

She signalled the sergeant to her side and filled him in on developments as the mobiles outside responded to the message on their radios. The police drivers softly cursed under their breath. After a long night shift no one liked chases at this time of day. The shift was ready for their beds, not more excitement.

The sergeant said, 'Thanks, Sarah. Get the dog man on the route in case they dump it and make a runner. Tell the Inspector he might like to think about firearms, seeing as how they probably did the gun shop last night. Now then, get pandas one, two and three out of the morning briefing and up to the city boundary. Four and five can remain loose in the city centre until we see how it goes.'

'What about the walkers?' enquired Sarah, looking down the deployment board.

'Good point, my love,' replied the sergeant.

He paused and looked at the map of the city which dominated the wall in the control room. 'Pull the walkers down towards Hardwick Circus. If we haven't got it by then, the traffic on the roundabout will balk it whatever happens. Anyway, it'll probably turn off before then and head back to marrowland,' he said.

Sarah ignored the reference to her native West Cumbria, directed the men as instructed by the sergeant, reached for the radio microphone, and adjusted her headset with the apparent intention of concentrating further on the job in hand. She updated her VDU and pressed the 'talk' button.

'Tango Zero Five? she enquired.

'Tango Zero Five, go ahead. I'm approaching Thursby. Still high speed, now at 100,' came the reply. 'We're all over the road! He's driving like a madman! Advise all patrols. Caution! Caution! Caution!'

Sarah could hear the siren wailing in the background and moved her headset slightly downwards towards the earlobe in order to lessen the noise level coming through to her brain. She, too, was tired and needed to take the device from her head.

Her neck was stiff. 'Tango Zero Five, Roger. All patrols are responding,' she radioed.

Sarah fingered her keyboard and the computer display adjusted the data on current patrol deployment. Updating herself from the display, she reached for the button on the desk that would signal the call for further patrols to be dispatched from the station.

The buzzer in the briefing room sounded and the alarm brought the early morning briefing session to a close. A tannoy on the wall declared the current state of the chase as the morning shift hit the streets to join the game.

Sarah advised 'caution' using the tannoy system, knowing the early birds would be drawing their radios and hurrying to their cars.

On foot patrol. Billy Boyd collected his pocket radio and made for the large roundabout called Hardwick Circus. It would be all over by the time he got there, he decided

The stolen car reached over one hundred miles per hour on the straight when it hurtled towards the city boundary. The young driver gripped the steering wheel of the stolen Granada. His knuckles were white with the tension in his hands and the strength of his grip on the wheel.

Under-steering round a right-hand bend, he felt the nearside tyres kick up gravel from the extremity of the roadside. At the following left-hand bend he over-steered and nearly lost control of the car as the back end twitched. He was driving on the edge of his questionable ability since the car was too big and too fast for him.

His friend in the passenger seat was leaning over into the rear seating compartment and wrestling with a navy blue holdall that slid across the back seat whenever the stolen car lurched round a tight bend.

Eventually the passenger managed to get his hands into the holdall and find one of the guns. It was an air pistol. He removed the weapon from the bag and caressed it. The pistol was the answer to his prayers.

He didn't want to go back to detention centre again. It had been hard enough the first time round. He had no intention of being caught by police and thrown in the slammer again.

'This'll frighten him,' cried the terrified youth.

Winding the window down, he pointed the gun out of the nearside window towards the chasing police car. The speed of the stolen car caused him to rock uneasily as he took aim.

The police driver braked. His car bonnet dipped and the vehicle moved from nearside to offside, with headlamps on full beam, siren sounding and blue light flashing.

'Where do we go?' shouted the driver of the stolen car.

With one eye on the rear view mirror and one eye on the road ahead, he was approaching the advanced stages of panic and had no particular idea of how to escape. He was not thinking of giving himself up. It did not occur to him, and it had not been part of his unfortunate upbringing to even consider the point, that all he needed to do was stop.

Speed limit signs signalled the entrance to Carlisle.

More police cars joined the chase. Some positioned themselves in front of the stolen car. Others could be seen running parallel.

Police cars moved in to try and box the stolen car. The speed of the chase reduced as the passenger inadvertently dropped the air pistol out of the window when the vehicle lurched from side to side looking for an escape route.

'I've dropped the gun. Move it! Don't slow down now,' he said.

The driver worried; panic etched on his taut face, the skin youthful but with a growth of stubble visible on the end of his rounded chin.

'I'm boxed in, for God's sake! You should be driving. It was all your idea!' he argued.

'Get on the pavement and scatter them!'

They neared Hardwick Circus where the stolen car braked hard and the passenger was thrown forward.

A gap occurred in front and the driver steered his motor onto the footpath as he tried desperately to overtake the police car down its nearside and on the pavement.

'Tango Zero Five to control,' shouted the police driver on the radio. 'We're at Hardwick Circus now. The road is blocked. A gun has been dropped out of the nearside window. Suppose they could be further armed. Don't know but. . . Oh no! Standby! He's going to crash it. No! He's up on the footpath. Stand by! Stand by!'

Sarah, the radio controller, could hardly hear the radio due to the sirens in the background but she tried to picture the scene. Knowing where the vehicles were in the city, she visualised the pandemonium.

Boyd saw the circus of cars approaching and moved from the pavement to a low level wall bordering the footpath. He found what he thought was the safest place until, without warning, the Granada mounted the kerb and headed straight for the wall upon which he stood.

Releasing the wooden truncheon from his right-hand pocket, Boyd threw it as hard as he could at the approaching car windscreen.

The windscreen shattered, obscuring the driver.

Boyd's truncheon carried on through the windscreen, glanced from the gear stick, and bounced harmlessly into the rear seat landing close to the navy blue holdall.

The stolen car, now completely out of control, careered into the wall as the front nearside wing crumpled on impact. The rear offside wing of the car followed round in a semicircle and collided with a lamp standard bordering the roadway. The vehicle came to rest on the footpath. Steam escaped into the air from the fractured radiator and the Granada dismally groaned in its final anthem of death.

'Tango Zero Five to control. Crash! Crash! Crash! Two out and running over the road into the park,' radioed the police driver.

The passenger in the Granada ran about five yards before a mixture of physical shock, mental disorientation and three of Carlisle's finest brought him crashing to the ground.

Before he was able to draw breath, one of the officers placed the hand-cuffs on him. He was out of the game. The driver fared somewhat better. Gathering his senses together quickly, he reached onto the back seat, seized the holdall and set off as fast as his legs would carry him.

He vaulted the wall into the neighbouring park. The first handgun fell from the holdall as his feet touched the ground on the opposite side of the wall. Increasing his speed, he penetrated the bushes using his free hand to shield his eyes from the branches. Ahead he saw the statue of Queen Victoria looking down disapprovingly on the developing scenario.

He made thirty yards before police realised what was happening and set off after him.

More guns fell from the thief's over-laden holdall.

Joining in the chase, Boyd sprinted past his colleagues, covering the ground like a gazelle. Within minutes he had caught his target. A rugby tackle that would have graced the hallowed turf of Twickenham brought the young tearaway to the ground.

The thief's face hit the soft grass before he was up again, on his knees, striving to escape. Down he went again, unable to break free from the grip.

Overpowering the youth, Boyd manacled him as his captive continued to kick out desperate to retain his liberty. The two combatants rolled down the embankment towards the river in a grotesque embrace. Guns and ammunition boxes scattered across the river bank before Boyd eventually punched his prisoner in the face and subdued him.

Other uniformed officers arrived and the prisoner was bundled unceremoniously into the rear of a large police van where he joined his partner in crime.

The sergeant arrived at the scene. 'Nice one, boys. Not so sure about the truncheon, though,' he offered, looking directly at Boyd.

Boyd ignored the sergeant's look and spoke out loud, 'I had a stick. He had a car. What's the problem? You can't drive when you can't see!'

The sergeant studied the wreck of the Granada. The shift was directing the early morning traffic around its remains.

'Glad it's not mine,' acknowledged the sergeant, motioning the men towards him with his hands.

'So far, so good. Now for the hard part,' he announced.

His men waited for him to explain.

'All we have to do now is search the route from where the car crashed to the point where Billy arrested the Grand Prix driver. Line up and we'll do it right. Billy! Take the middle of the line and we'll form up on you. Two yards. Spread out. Take your time. I want these guns found before the park fills up,' instructed the sergeant.

Reluctantly the thin blue line retraced their steps and formed up on Boyd. The contingent set off line abreast to search the park. Daylight came. The line of police searched through the shrubbery towards Queen Victoria's statue. Whenever a weapon was found it was made safe by the firearms officer, labelled and placed into an evidence bag. Quite a number of guns had fallen out of the holdall during the attempted escape.

The ammunition rounds proved harder to find, being smaller and likely to lodge between the roots of bushes. It was nearly breakfast time before the line had reached the river bank. The blue personnel carrier drove down the tarmac strip into the park and the driver steered the van onto the rough track that bordered the river bank.

Bringing the vehicle to a halt, the driver jumped out, opened the rear door, and shouted, 'Tea up! Compliments of the boss. He says you'll all be happy to have breakfast here by the river bank. He's right. It's so peaceful here relaxing by the river. The odd bit of fishing, an early morning dip or just a lie down while you contemplate your navels. This, my friends, is our modern police force. You've never had it so good.'

Tuning to the interior of the van, he began unloading the flasks and the sandwiches that had been sent out to the team when a clump of soil landed on the side of the carrier near his head.

A voice from the line cried, 'Get back in the van and warm your fat backside. It's about all you're good for. Nothing more than a chauffeur. I'll take the tea flasks, sir. I'll take the sandwiches, sir. Yes, sir. No, sir. Three bags full, sir. Get back to the nick where you belong and leave us workers to get on with it.'

The banter and scuttlebutt continued until the team broke ranks and settled down for a break.

'The boss says don't leave the park until all the guns are accounted for. There should be twenty-six weapons, according to the CID out at Cockermouth. I must go now. It's too cold for me out here. I'll be back for the flasks later when it's warmer and the sun is shining.'

The crusted remnants of a half-eaten sandwich whistled through the air towards the driver, followed by a cry of 'Hop it!'

The carrier returned to the warmth of a cosy police station. The search resumed once the team had finished their brew.

Carlisle Cricket Club lay on the far side of the river bank. Access to the club was from the main road that led from Hardwick Circus north into the south of Scotland. A cinder track bordered the club premises and petered out into the earth that gave way to the river bank. The going became rough and the grass grew longer, uncared for.

A man walked on the path with his young son. The boy saw police on the opposite bank and the man told him to keep away from the riverside. The river here ran swift and deep, with a notorious history of suicides and accidents.

The police continued their search of the river bank looking for the last of the guns.

There was a splash and a cry for help. The youngster fell into the river and the Eden was dragging him under.

His father ran along the side of the bank, unable to swim and too frightened to jump into the water. He shouted at the policemen to do something, and starting to panic as the youngster disappeared under the surface.

Menacingly, the Eden took the boy chillingly towards its terrible churning confluence with the muddy River Caldew.

The sergeant and Boyd were the nearest to the scene. They saw what had happened and began to run along the river bank.

The man on the opposite bank was running parallel with them, shouting at his son to kick the water with his legs.

The boy couldn't hear. At the age of nine, he was fighting for his life. One moment he was above the surface with his arms high in the air, the next he was under the water. He was struggling to survive.

The sergeant ran up the bank towards the footbridge that crossed the Caldew near the confluence. He could see the lifebelt the city council had strategically placed nearby. However, time was running out.

Trying to read the situation, Boyd wondered, would the youngster drown before the sergeant threw the lifebelt into the water or would the sergeant be in time?

Using the speed he was famous for, Boyd accelerated towards the confluence of the two rivers. Here, the rivers met in a bubbling froth of mighty water that created whirlpools of unequal supremacy. The rivers jostled each other for sovereignty; with white water rising to the surface to pound the rocks before subsiding into a broader, deeper, serene channel.

Boyd ran like the wind, his legs pumping at great speed.

The sergeant was bemused but the father on the other side of the river was angry.

Ignoring the drowning nine year old, Boyd merely ran on until he was some fifty yards past the youth then he stopped, bent down, placed his hands on his knees and took a deep breath. Drawing in a lungful of oxygen, Boyd stood up straight again, took off his shoes, removed his tunic and his trousers, and dived into the icy water.

The sergeant worked it out first. He realised Boyd had successfully forged ahead of the current flow and, instead of trying to catch up the boy by swimming, he needed to position himself in front of him in the water.

The current grew stronger and the sound of a bubbling mass ahead of the two grew louder.

The sergeant ran to where the rivers met hauling the troublesome lifebelt with him.

Striking out strongly for the far side of the bank, Boyd had a vague idea of where the kid was. Swimming freestyle, his head moved to the left to snatch a lungful of air. He felt the muscles in his calves begin to tighten with both the cold and the second untimely exertion of the day.

From the corner of this eye he saw the boy.

The youngster headed towards him, face down in the river.

Changing to breaststroke, Boyd praised the crucial seconds he needed to absorb oxygen as he tread water. When the youngster floated past him, head down, Boyd seized the boy around the shoulders and dragged him towards the bank.

Supporting the child by keeping his hand underneath the boy's chin, out of the water, Boyd back-kicked away from the centre of the river. The river reacted violently, trying to suck Boyd and his charge back towards the confluence and a watery demise. The battle raged on with Boyd and the child on the edge of survival.

A lifebelt suddenly splashed into the water and with his free hand, Boyd caught hold of it. The belt was attached to a line which the sergeant secured around a fallen branch.

Buoyancy from the lifebelt, and Boyd's strength, kept them afloat. Exhausted, Boyd struggled to blow air into the youngster's mouth.

The father scrambled to the side and cautiously waded to the shallowest part of the river. He used his coat to form a rope-like line. The man held one arm of the coat while Boyd held the other. Every few seconds, Boyd blew air into the boy's lungs then rested by balancing himself on the two lifelines that the sergeant and the father had provided. It was a precarious and ungainly situation.

Coughing back into the world, the youngster spewed out a large mouthful of dirty water. Suddenly, the boy was thrashing his hands about as it dawned on him what had happened.

He was coughing up water and becoming more and more agitated. Strong arms pulled the two drowning rats to the riverside. The man seized his child and held him close, using the warmth of his body to comfort the youngster.

Others arrived at the scene and ran towards the small group. Billy Boyd lay on the grass bank totally exhausted, passed out, and dropped into oblivion.

An ambulance arrived with a blare of sirens and flashing lights and conveyed the child and Boyd to the casualty department of the nearby Cumberland Infirmary. The clear-up squad moved in, rescuing Boyd's personal belongings and returning the lifebelt to its home. The sergeant took refuge in the police station, resting in the matron's room, and gathered himself together with a blanket draped round his shoulders. It had been a close thing.

The hours passed.

At the hospital Boyd stirred in the cubicle. Gradually, he opened his eyes and saw the figure of a man he vaguely recognised. It was the boy's father. A deep Irish accent filled Boyd's ears.

'Jesus, you're alive! To be sure, I thought you'd had it now. Well, young'un, I don't know what they call yer but you've just saved me son's life. That ya have! God bless you, lad!'

Boyd was still coming round, but responded. He raised himself onto one elbow and looked hazily at the Irishman. 'Alright? Is the boy alright?' asked Boyd.

The Irish face beamed from ear to ear. 'He is that, thanks to you. The doctor people and them there nursing wimmin say he's going to be fine. Just fine.'

Offering a handshake, Boyd introduced himself. 'I'm Billy Boyd. Who are you?' he enquired.

Padraigh O'Toole, me boy, and I'm pleased to be meeting ya, sure I am.'

'Padraigh! What kind of crazy name is that for a Welshman?'

'Welsh? I'm as Irish as they come, sure I am. Now then, you've a crazy name that ya have. Billy Boy! Billy Boy the Protestant!' suggested Padraigh.

The Englishman replied abruptly. 'It's Boyd, not Boy.'

'Well, from now on you're Billyboy in my book that ya are. Billyboy! Still, no matter. Thanks, Billyboy, for giving me back the son I nearly lost. When you get yerself out of here take yerself up to the Catholic club on the Scotland Road. I'll be potting the black with yer, that I will, just to be saying my thanks. They know me there. Ask for Paddy.'

They shook hands again, warmly this time then Padraigh withdrew.

Boyd lay there drowsing, wondering what was meant by 'Potting the Black.'

Padraigh turned into the corridor that pointed the way to the exit. He was taking his son, Michael O'Toole, home. Lifting him up, he cuddled him before taking him home to Mother O'Toole. Padraigh was happy and sang an old Irish tune.

'God made the land and God made the sea. To be sure, I hope He shines down on me.'

The hospital door closed behind father and son.

That week Padraigh O'Toole introduced Billyboy to the quaint and honoured ritual of 'potting the black'. It was the same week in which the Provisional IRA laid a bomb attack in Rotten Row, London, injuring fifty persons and killing eleven soldiers of the Household Cavalry. The horse 'Sefton' was amongst the injured animals.

≈

1986

It was a summer's day in the occupied counties. Shelagh Connelly tidied the council house on Shantallow estate. Dutifully, she polished the mantelpiece, moving the gilt-edged photograph of her beloved dead father whilst she carefully rearranged the ornaments and bric-a-brac that furnished the lounge. Only her brother, Liam, really knew how hard times had been since the death of their father.

Declan Connelly had died by his own savage hand when placing a bomb underneath a Loyalist's car in Limavady. Her mother fell into ill-health from a cancerous disease and spent most of her life in pain. Shelagh enjoyed being wooed by half the male population of Derry but it was Liam who kept the family home going with regular bursts of short-term employment in the local labouring trade. She, herself, added to the family income from her own job as a waitress in a cafe down on The Diamond. Fortunately for them all, Liam always managed to find spare cash from somewhere when the bills mounted up. She had grown so close to Liam in recent years that the brother and sister bond was exceptionally strong, now virtually unbreakable. Life had not showered the unfortunate Connellys with many riches, but they had managed to survive so far.

Opening the letter from Padraigh O'Toole, Shelagh found a bundle of £10 notes that he'd sent to them to help out. There were ten such notes, making £100 in all. Padraigh's money meant they could have the odd luxury in life now and again.

She secreted the cash in an old china teapot used as an ornament. The teapot rested on the side of the mantelpiece. Counting out the notes, Shelagh realised there was now £500 in the teapot. They had been prudent with Padraigh's money and between them she and Liam had always saved a cash reserve for emergencies.

Dusting complete, Shelagh sat the teapot on the corner of the mantelpiece as the kitchen door opened and Liam Connelly walked in.

'Now then, Shelagh. How goes it with you today?' asked Liam.

He kissed his sister on the forehead, moving back the curls that threatened to cover her eyebrows.

'Fine, Liam. Ma's upstairs asleep, so don't go making too much noise. Are you staying in tonight?' replied Shelagh.

'No, Shelagh. I have business out. I won't be long though. Just an hour or so,' said Liam.

Shelagh frowned at her brother's remark. She was never very happy when Liam spoke in that urgent, aggressive tone. She wondered what manner of activity was being planned that night but thought better than to ask.

'Be careful, Liam. We couldn't make it without you. Sure, if it wasn't for Uncle Padraigh sending the money now and again, we would really struggle,' she offered.

'He's a fine man is Padraigh,' acknowledged Liam.

Liam went upstairs to check on his mother. She was sleeping lightly and lifted herself up to rest on her elbow when she heard him in the room. They talked quietly until she fell back against the pillow and drifted once more into an easy sleep.

When hunger set in, Liam helped his sister in the kitchen preparing the meal. They talked together of their uncle Padraigh, over the water on the mainland, and of how he regularly sent the family money since the death of their father.

Shelagh read out loud the latest letter to Liam and recounted the number of times Padraigh had written to them, imploring them all to abandon Derry and cross the water to join him. Shelagh told Liam of the latest hundred pounds. Liam responded by telling her to spend it wisely. Padraigh wrote of his family in England and how he'd found useful work and a new lifestyle away from the politics and the terror that were the hallmark of Northern Ireland. Padraigh repeatedly told them of the need to renounce the bullet and the bomb whilst persuading others to work for a peaceful settlement. Above all, Padraigh told them how much he loved them and how he dreamt that, one day, they would live without fear in a land of peace and harmony.

A noble cause, but perhaps naive and out of touch, thought Liam.

There were those who thought peace could be achieved through the peaceful process of politics whilst others believed peace would only come about following violence.

Liam still believed violence would bring peace. After the meal the telephone rang. It was Sean Brady for Liam.

'Right, I'll be there,' replied Liam.

Replacing the telephone, Liam pulled on his hooded anorak, bade his sister farewell, and set off to meet Sean. He didn't think he would be out very late tonight but there was much to do.

Watching him go. Shelagh worried after him. She knew he was an active member of the local PIRA brigade. A trusted member, he was no longer the young pretender, no longer a terrorist in waiting. Her brother was a terrorist. It was as simple as that.

Liam walked through the Republican estate towards the meeting point. He heard his friend, Sean, approaching on the motor cycle before he saw him.

The bike pulled up beside him as he walked along the footpath.

'Sure jump on, Liam, and hold tight,' said Sean Brady.

Liam mounted the pillion seat and the two set off for the border. Cutting through the estate, they headed out towards Buncrana. The night was closing in. Twisting the throttle on the narrow country roads, Sean made for a border crossing point where neither police nor army checkpoints were the routine.

Damien Devenney was a worried man. In recent months a number of his best people had been arrested by the RUC. It seemed that as soon as the organisation smuggled in arms and equipment, the security forces recovered them from one of the many hiding places in Derry. Damien had a mole, but he didn't know who. Was it someone in Derry Brigade? Or was it someone in Dublin? Someone, somewhere, was engaged in loose talk with the police.

Driving the Ford through the countryside towards Buncrana, Damien was interested in who else travelled this lonely road tonight.

Meanwhile, Eugene Kelly carefully bided his time. Damien had left the house early, telling him his services that night were no longer required. Eugene responded by promising to attend at the crack of dawn to look after his charge.

As Damien drove away, Eugene strolled casually towards the centre of Derry and deliberately walked quickly past the first two telephone boxes he came to. The street lights of Derry cast shadows over the pavement. He glanced behind him, just in case he was being followed.

At the third kiosk, he entered and dialled a number.

'Yes!' said the receiver.

The voice on the other end of the telephone was non committal. Nothing else needed to be said to the tout on the 'phone.

Eugene spoke quickly, 'To be sure now, he's just left about five minutes ago. It's the black Ford, so it is, and it's a bridge near Buncrana. Somewhere on a country road, don't know the exact place. There's a motor bike involved, with two on it, but that's all I know. I think it's a bomb to put down somewhere tonight. It must be already primed and ready, that's for sure. I can't find it all out. It might just be dets. When do ah get ma money? I want to see the lady. I want ma money,' he said.

The policeman taking the message on the confidential line made his notes and checked the time before replying, 'Thank you. Make the usual meet at the same time as last week. The lady will be there.'

The telephone line went dead.

Eugene still held the telephone in his hand when the call was brought to an abrupt end by the unknown man from the police. He had done his part again but he hadn't heard what he wanted to hear. He was dissatisfied and angry. He was their man now. He ached inside. Eugene Kelly, a tout, swore quietly.

'Bastard RUC!' he swore.

The kiosk door banged noisily behind him when he slammed it against the metal jamb.

The policeman finished his note and lifted the telephone that gave him instant access to his counterpart in the intelligence community.

Within a matter of minutes a well rehearsed sequence of events was put into operation. Army patrols were redeployed, moving closer to the border at the designated time. In addition a Lynx helicopter containing infra-red night vision equipment diverted towards the Buncrana area. The RUC special task force also responded by quietly moving its grey armoured Land Rovers into predetermined positions so that all roads leading back into Derry were covered.

The web was being set and, with luck, the fly would be trapped on its return.

Drawing up short of the border in a lay-by, Damien checked his watch. When the hands had moved on five minutes he turned the Ford directly around and drove back towards Derry.

The two motor cycles stopped on either side of the bridge. The countryside was deserted and it was nearing nine o'clock. One bike remained in the Republic, the other in the province.

Dismounting, the two operatives from the province made their way cautiously underneath the bridge.

Sean kept one eye on the Republic whilst regularly checking the road behind him. He felt the smoothness of the gun's barrel resting in the trouser belt by the small of his back.

At the side of the river bank directly underneath the bridge they found the parcel. It was small and slipped easily into Liam's inside pocket. He considered the texture of the parcel with his fingers.

'Detonators, Sean, by the feel of it. Do you want me to have a look?' enquired Liam.

Sean eyed the road, searching for the unwelcome and the unexpected, before replying, 'No! Pocket it and we'll be on our way. Damien said not to touch, so we don't. Understand?' he offered.

'Sure, no problem,' replied Liam.

They mounted the bike and flashed their lights at the other side. The rider in the Republic waved, turned his trials bike round and manoeuvred it skilfully through a gateway into a field.

In seconds, the bike disappeared over countryside with its rear wheel bouncing on the uneven surface. No lights were visible. The rider knew the area well, and within the hour was nearing his home in Donegal.

Sean and Liam waited for the sound of the motor cycle to leave their ears. They would not return to Derry until they were sure of the road behind them. Sean lit a cigarette and drew deeply on it.

'This is our third such trip, Liam,' remarked Sean.

'So?' enquired Liam.

'Doesn't it bother you that the others keep getting caught?'

'It must bother Damien, but I trust you, Sean. I know you're committed to the cause and I know who isn't talking to the RUC, that's for sure. One day the tout will be caught and he'll go the way of all traitors: Two in the back of the head. You can whack him, Sean. Whack him and leave him in a ditch by the side of the road. We'll booby-trap the body and take some RUC out when they move the corpse. Dermot can make us the booby trap, sure he can,' suggested Liam.

'Who's that you're thinking of, Liam?'

'You and me, Sean, I know it's not you and me,' explained Liam.

'It could be our friend who has just ridden off over the hill. Did you think of that? Perhaps the wee man from Donegal is telling them now that we're here with the parcel. If the police know it, then the army know it and they can shoot us down like dogs. It could be a short life, Liam.'

'I think the tout is in Derry, Sean. Come on, let's get back.'

Sean stubbed his cigarette out, fired the machine, turned round, and headed back towards Derry.

Damien travelled slowly back towards the outskirts of Derry and parked the big black Ford on a grass verge and left the car.

The Provo leader made the top of a nearby hill and looked down on Derry through a night image intensifier that had been relieved from a dead soldier's body many months ago in South Armagh. In the distance above him he could vaguely distinguish the sound of a helicopter. Below him he saw the outline of the RUC Land Rovers. They were strategically parked in at least three locations where Derry could be accessed. He studied the hedgerows looking for the soldiers. He couldn't see them, but he knew they were there.

It was enough. They had been set up. The only people who knew about the delivery in addition to himself were Seamus Kelty from the Headquarters brigade, the quartermaster from Donegal, Liam Connelly, and Sean Brady. This meant there was a tout in the organisation somewhere. But where? Dundalk? Donegal? Or Derry? There was no way the RUC could have got so lucky recently. It had to be a tout, he thought.

Damien returned to the car. He had to stop Liam and Sean. He needed those detonators. The current supplies would see the summer through, but not much more than that.

Spinning the Ford round, Damien headed back towards the Buncrana crossing point.

Damien drove fast, waiting for the motor cycle to approach him.

As he drove, he mulled over the recent months. Six of his men had been taken within hours of collecting guns and ammunition from the various points on the border the organisation used to transfer equipment from the Republic to the province. He added more names to his list. He decided Bridget Duffy knew enough to be a threat to him. Furthermore, a woman might break easier than a man if taken by the police or the army. He drove onwards, watching the mirror to see if he was being followed.

It came to him like a bolt from the blue. Shelagh Connelly! Of course, Liam probably told her everything he did. The Connellys were good Republicans with a father who had died for the cause. It followed that many would place them above suspicion. Shelagh - a woman to break easy! She would tell the RUC all they wanted to know. It explained why the Connellys never went short of money, even when Liam was out of work. She was on the RUC payroll. Liam probably didn't even know she was talking to the police. It was often the way. He recalled how many men had been taken recently whilst they were on active service. He calculated Liam and Sean had been out on at least three cross-border operations, not counting a number of other jobs in Derry. On many occasions people had been arrested, but never when Liam and Sean were out. The reason was credible. Shelagh either would not tell the RUC of her brother's involvement, or, the RUC had made a deal with her never to arrest Liam. The pieces fell into place. It was Shelagh Connelly.

Damien convinced himself and decided to trust only his brother, Hugh, and his bodyguard, Eugene, who was above suspicion. Eugene would lay down his life for Damien, or so the Provo Commander thought. They would carry out the discipline inquiry and if that meant that Hugh got his hands dirty, then so be it. Damien didn't want the cohorts from Seamus Kelty's camp turning over Derry. Derry was his. He sorted his own problems out.

Rounding the bend, Damien saw the motor bike coming towards him. He flashed the lights frantically.

'Jesus son of Mary!' cracked Sean.

Recognising the Ford, Sean closed the throttle as soon as he saw the lights flashing. He grasped the brake with his left hand whilst his right boot pressed the front brake. The front suspension forks dropped down and he pulled the machine into the nearside.

'What's the matter, Sean?' asked Liam.

'It's Damien, Liam. Something's wrong. He shouldn't be out here. Watch yourself now,' advised Sean.

Sean waited for the Ford to turn round and come back to where they had pulled in. The car came to a standstill and Damien joined them.

'We've been set up, boys. The road ahead is crawling with police and army. Listen out. There's a pork chop in the sky and it's looking for you two,' declared Damien.

Sean and Liam automatically looked into the heavens, searching for the helicopter.

'There's no time. Head back into the Republic and lie low for a few days. Watch yourself mind. They may have the Garda out, but I doubt it. Just be careful and keep yer heads down,' ordered Damien.

Liam enquired, 'What about the detonators, Damien?'

'Who told you they were dets, Liam? Come on now. There's too much at stake here. Who told you about the dets?' challenged Damien.

'Sure, it's just a guess, Damien. What else would it be now? It's too small for much else,' smoothed Liam.

Damien responded, 'Keep them safe, Liam, but bring them to me soon. Just don't get caught tonight.'

Liam asked, 'What about Shelagh? She doesn't know I'm here. She's expecting me back.'

Damien answered, 'Don't worry yerself about her. I'll take care of her. On yer way, Sean. Ride like the wind before they close in behind us. I'm clean. I'll take my chances here. It'll be alright. They'll find nothing on me. Now go quickly.'

Lighting up the machine, Sean fired the engine and they sped back towards the Republic.

Damien made his slow way back towards Derry. He had nothing to fear from the security forces. The night intensifier was well hidden in the countryside. He would be checked and searched but nothing would be found either on him or in his vehicle. He would be home soon, still free.

The motor cycle sped towards the border as the trap closed in. The helicopter dropped off its patrol near the border and the troops took command of the roadway. A vehicle checkpoint was set up and the troops lay in the ditch on the approach to the stopping point. Anything pulling up short of the stopping point was a likely target.

The RUC patrol cars blocked the road and the occupants donned bullet-proof vests. Caressing their carbines, they released the safety catches as the secret war heated up.

Speeding onwards, the motor cyclists leaned easily to the nearside and the offside as the vehicle negotiated the winding road. Dark clouds filled the horizon as the last vestige of moonlight dipped over the hillside.

Sean saw it first and yelled above the engine noise, 'Jesus! It's a checkpoint! Five minutes ago it was dead, now it's swarming, Liam. They're all over the place.'

'Don't stop, Sean. Straight through or we've had it,' bellowed Liam.

'Here goes!' hollered Sean increasing speed.

The RUC officers knew they'd struck lucky when the motor bike appeared at high speed. Their carbines pointed towards the machine.

In the ditches bordering the roadside, troops drew a bead on the target as it sped towards the stopping point. They shuffled and eased themselves carefully into shooting positions. Head shots would be favoured by the marksmen and body shots by the lesser able.

Professional soldiers didn't aim to injure. They aimed to kill. This was war. The motor cycle had to stop. It had no place to go. The young troops prepared for the fire-fight.

The policemen radioed in the engagement. The wireless crackled, adrenalin accelerated, and perspiration began to trickle.

'Target acquired.'

The army helicopter turned back towards the scene of the impending engagement. The scanning equipment that revealed the picture of body heat below was activated eagerly by the pilot. The helicopter propeller blades whirred eerily above them. The pilot adjusted his height and trim and increased speed.

'Roger! Target acquired. Grid reference Zulu Charlie 3278.'

The radio operator acknowledged the RUC at the same time as the pilot turned and banked the machine tighter.

Sean twisted the throttle round so tightly that the back wheel fought for grip on the tarmac surface and the front wheel began to lose its traction. He accelerated towards the patrol cars in the middle of the narrow country lane. There was just one chance and they would take it. He focused his eyes.

A ginger-haired corporal stood rigidly between the hedgerow and the police patrol car. There was no more than a two-foot gap, but no one was going past him that night. The corporal dropped onto one knee, raised his rifle and brought the weapon's front sight level with the back sight. He aimed towards the machine, searching for the rider's head. He felt the weapon nestle into his shoulder and embrace his cheek. He took long and careful aim. He was a true marksman at the height of his profession and he made every micro-second count.

He inhaled, taking his time. It seemed like a lifetime.

This was the crucial time. It was often the last seconds of someone's life. They often called it the killing time. This was the corporal's killing time.

The sound of gunfire ripped through the air as the other platoon members opened up on the speeding motor cycle. Red hot, death-laden, pointed, metallic bullets pierced the atmosphere searching for their prey. The killing time arrived.

The motor cycle was too fast. Ricochets bounced from the ground behind and in front of the machine. One bullet smashed the exhaust pipe, another penetrated the fairing, passing right through the fibreglass moulding and missing the rider's knee by no more than an inch.

The two riders hunched low, presenting the smallest possible target to the army.

It was a duck shoot, but the landed gentry expected the ducks to slow down and give in, perhaps even present themselves as an easy target. These two ducks were martyrs to the cause. Death would be quick, but it would be glorious - and death wouldn't happen without a fight. No mercy shown; no quarter given.

Selecting a section of roadway, Sean changed down a gear but noticed a soldier stood directly in his path.

Pulling the revolver from his trouser belt with his left hand, Sean's right hand fought to steer the machine and keep the throttle wide open. The engine noise reached fever pitch in lower gear.

The corporal started to exhale in the last half second of the killing time. His eyes were focused; his mind totally at peace. His bullet was dedicated to the unerring path of death. His target was acquired. The time had come to kill for the regiment; his moment of courage, his moment of valour, his moment for Queen and country. His killing time.

His finger took the pressure on the trigger.

'Squeeze, don't pull...'

It was his last thought.

Sean unmercifully sprayed the ground in front of the motor cycle an instant before the corporal pulled the trigger completely through.

Bullets flew over Sean and Liam's head as the motor bike hurtled through the air.

The first stray, haphazardly aimed, panic-stricken bullet, fired by Sean over the motor cycle fairing, smashed into the corporal's left eye socket, diverted into the brain and exited the top of the corporal's skull in a bloody deluge.

The corporal was dead before he hit the ground, killed before his time: Another young life taken in the savage butchery of terrorism. The remaining bullets killed earth, grass and hedgerow, adding only to the noise that filled the air.

The helicopter zoomed low, lighting up the killing ground for all to see. The infra-red, heat-seeking scanner housed near the co-pilot revealed a mass of sprawling figures pointing towards a thin red blur moving across the screen with such speed that it resembled a hideous computer game being acted out in a children's amusement arcade.

A bullet entered Sean's right leg above the knee and passed through the flesh, exiting on the inside of the thigh and embedding itself in the motor cycle under the rider's seat.

Screaming in agony, Sean felt the red hot metal tear the inside of his limb on its deadly journey as he fought to control the machine.

The corporal fell.

The policeman nearest to the soldier took a step backwards, aimed his pistol at the machine, and fired. His bullet zipped across Liam's right wrist where he felt the hot metal graze his skin.

The corporal's body hit the ground as Sean Brady drove the motor cycle over him. The front wheel of the lethal motor cycle crushed the corporal's vertebrae, fought to regain traction, wobbled and headed off through the checkpoint at high speed.

Bullets pursued the weaving motor cycle in a frantic desire to bring down the killers but Sean had chosen his escape route. The fact that a member of Her Majesty's armed forces was in his way was an irrelevance to the determined and committed man from PIRA. He was resolute.

The radio murmured and the army helicopter light swooped low, magnifying proceedings but casting confusing shadows.

A wild burst of gunfire shot into the heavens by Sean saw the helicopter bank steeply to the left and turn away from the scene.

When patrol cars turned to follow the terrorists, Sean turned the Honda motor cycle into a farm track. Mud splattered as the machine weaved from side to side, coating the hedges with brown dirty water.

Battling to ignore the searing pain in his right leg, Sean slewed the motor bike into the farmyard, searched for the entrance, and found the field gate. It was open.

Within minutes the Honda was into the fields and bouncing towards the Republic and safety.

A disappearing cloud of dust pointed the way for the pursuers. They abandoned the chase and called it in.

'It's a shoot. Suspects have crossed the border and made good their escape. One male, no further description, has been shot in the right leg. Second male, no further description, shot in the right arm. No descriptions of motor bike, but it has a big front fairing on it. One down here wearing khaki. Where are the Garda?'

There was a long pause before a gruff voice responded.

'Roger.'

In Strand Road police station, Londonderry, the senior police officer in charge of the botched operation looked at the map on the wall. A tall red-headed woman stood beside him. He looked across to her.

'Where are the Garda? They said they would be there.'

The red-headed lady continued to study the map. Without turning her eyes from the wall, she countered, 'Still considering their political position, probably.'

The army major smirked and changed his personal radio to another channel. He wanted more information on the 'khaki' casualty. The major knew he'd lost a man to the 'Troubles.'

The police commander snapped his pencil and quibbled, 'My backside. They'll consider it one day when the Loyalists blow up half of Dublin. Bloody politics! Bloody politicians!'

He left the room with his obvious disappointment surrendering to bad temper.

As the policeman closed the door behind him, she quipped, 'PIRA only have to get it right once to win. We have to get it right every time.'

The red-headed lady continued to study the map on the wall and examined the road from Londonderry into County Donegal. She listened to the helicopter pilot reporting that the suspect motor cycle had rejoined the highway on the Burnfoot to Fahan road. The pilot announced on the radio he was returning to base since he was off limits in the Republic's air space.

Fingering the wall map, the red-head traced the green line that was the road from Burnfoot into the Inishowen Peninsula.

Evading the security forces by a mixture of luck, good judgement, ingenuity and a pure determination to remain free, Sean and Liam eventually travelled into Eire. On the outskirts of Burnfoot the motor cycle pulled in and Liam examined Sean's leg.

Luckily for Sean, the bullet had been of small calibre. The rifling from a bigger calibre bullet would probably have ripped half of his leg out. The bullet was from the handgun of one of the policemen.

Had it been from an army rifle, Sean would have lost his leg. He was a very fortunate man. The bullet had passed right through the thigh. The injury was essentially no more than a severe flesh wound.

The back of Liam's hand bore the path of the bullet. He would be scarred for life but he needed no medical attention, other than a cleansing of the wound.

At Burnfoot they turned left and headed towards Buncrana. Short of Buncrana they neared Lough Swilly and turned left again towards Inch Island. It was a narrow road but they crossed the tranquil Lough and journeyed through Inch and Carnaghan towards Mill Bay.

Passing a telephone kiosk, they found the deserted bungalow belonging to Damien Devenney standing on the coast looking out over Lough Swilly. The key was located in the dry stone walling outside.

It was just like Damien had said it would be, many months ago, when he explained procedures to be followed in the event of an escape to the Republic.

Sean hid the motor cycle in the garage and entered the bungalow.

They fell exhausted by the fireplace. Liam made the fire and the meal. Sean slept. When he woke, they drank hot tea. Rifling the medicine chest in the bathroom, Liam tended to Sean's thigh and his own hand. Sean would limp for a long time but the bleeding had stopped and there was no risk of disease at the moment. They were safe.

That night they looked out across the Lough. It was one of the serene beauties of County Donegal. The pair drank a half bottle of Jameson whiskey that Sean found in the drinks cabinet in the front room before they fell into a long and deep sleep. Pain, excitement and fear blurred into an alcoholic cloud.

In the morning Liam checked Sean's wound and applied a clean dressing. Time would be a good healer. A thin scar started to form on the back of Liam's right wrist.

Damien Devenney didn't drink Jameson that night, but he did wonder if his operatives had found their way to Inch Island without mishap. He reckoned that if they had made it, he would have the detonators in good time for the planned autumn campaign. He knew if the two men kept their heads down and stayed put, then they would not be seen in Londonderry for at least a fortnight or more. Ample time for what he planned. And time to deal with the tout - Shelagh Connelly. It would be over by the time Liam returned.

Dawn broke.

Strand Road police station was on tick-over with the police commander safely tucked up in bed. Damien would not rise until after nine in the morning. Shantallow was slumbering. Londonderry slept on.

All except Eugene Kelly, that is. He had a date with a young lady that morning, but it was no love affair to speak of. Eugene rose later than he ought, dressed, snatched a piece of toast, and headed on foot towards the Foyle Bridge. Crossing the river, he stretched northwards towards Strathfoyle. The River Foyle flowed seaward on his left. He continued, passing the hospital, waiting for the red-headed woman to announce herself. She would appear, when she was ready.

He walked on, walked alone, and waited.

The area was deserted but she watched him walking close to the railway line as she drove a van bearing the name of a Belfast florist on its side. But the lady driving the van was no florist. She was an intelligence officer. Closing in, she picked him up.

'You're late, Eugene,' she remarked contemptuously.

'I slept in. I'm sorry. Did you get them?' he enquired.

'No! They got away. Your information was too late and too imprecise. There wasn't enough time to close the border down completely. A soldier was killed. Shot dead. Another half hour and we would have got them. This is no good to me, Eugene. I don't pay for rubbish like this. It's not good enough. You're right next to the man and all I get is a near miss.'

Eugene felt hurt. Risking his life for the information, to say nothing of the money, he snapped back, 'It's not my fault. When I got to know, you got it,' he responded.

'Yes, but not in time. I can't work miracles.'

'What about ma money? I'm owed for the others.'

Tossing her head in that dismissive manner, she allowed a spray of red hair to resettle on her shoulders and stated, 'Correct, but only quarter pay for last night's episode. Get with it, Eugene. You're in this for money. You know it and I know it. If it's there, I pay you. If it's not, I won't,' she declared.

Eugene considered her remark. She was right. He was interested only in the money. One day he would have enough to take off for sunny climes. His belief in the cause was weaker than the others. His job was bodyguard. It paid well, but not as well as the police and the intelligence service. The money helped feed his addiction for gambling and the good life. All he needed was that one big win and he would be gone. With thoughts duly gathered, he countered, 'Last month you took four out because of me. All arrested with arms and blow on them. Come on, you owe me. Don't give me a hard time,' he threatened.

'I'll give you whatever time I want to give you. I call the tune, remember. The "blow" you refer to was a couple of pounds of home-made explosives. I'll be happy when you tell me where I can put my hands on a couple of tons. Do you understand me? If you want to get rich then I'll make you rich, but under my terms. Got it?'

Eugene ached inside. He was addicted to money, couldn't live with it and couldn't live without it. He said, 'But. ..'

'No buts. Anyway, here's something to be going on with. Whatever the parcel was, it didn't get across last night so I managed to get you this,' she said passing over a bundle of cash.

Taking it, counting the cash, Eugene slid the wad into the back pocket of his trousers and asked, 'Thanks. Can I go now?'

'Tell me, what's going on? Who were the two on the motor bike? Who pulled the trigger last night? Where are they now? What is Damien's next step? Understand?'

'I can't help you just now, that's for sure. If I hear anything, I'll ring the number,' he replied.

'Be sure you do, Eugene. Be sure you do. I'll see you on Sunday morning. Make sure you have the answers to the questions - and don't be late,' she ordered.

Leaning across him, the red-head opened the passenger door.

He stepped out into the street to her words, 'Take care, Eugene.'

Eugene held the door open and offered, 'There's bound to be a witch hunt on for the tout. They'll know there's a tout, that's for sure. If I'm suspected, I'm for it. What do I do?'

'Simple, Eugene. Say nothing and be careful. Goodbye!' she said. Heaving the door closed, she drove off without waiting for his reply.

Eugene watched the florist's van disappear towards Limavady. It was incredible, he thought. She had no interest in his safety, no guarantees for him. Just a red-headed bitch from London and he hated her.

He fingered the notes in his back pocket. He'd made good money this morning. Turning towards Derry, Eugene made a start on the long walk back home. He could take the flak from her if the money was that good.

The red-head followed the road for Limavady and then cut across to Maghera, skirted the northern end of Lough Neagh, and dropped the van in Belfast where she caught the next flight to London. She was pleased with Eugene Kelly. Much of the recent successes enjoyed by the RUC and themselves were due to him. Her biggest problem would be to keep him happy with the money. She only hoped the organisation didn't suspect Eugene was the tout. That was a problem she could do without.

It was a short flight. She dozed before they touched down at Heathrow. By nightfall she had filed her reports, dined in a Covent Garden restaurant and enjoyed a long luxurious bath. She washed Londonderry right out of her hair, for the moment.

Sean and Liam rested. The leg was still aching but Sean hid the pain, only stifling an occasional grimace. Liam adjusted the dressing. His thigh was healing nicely.

Damien set up a busy day. His mind was working overtime. He met Eugene as he was leaving the house. Eugene looked tired, and when Damien asked if he had slept well Eugene told him that he had taken an early morning walk to kill a headache. Damien worried over the health of his bodyguard, whilst Eugene wondered whether or not Damien suspected him of being the informer.

They got into the car and drove to the Dun Low public house for opening time. A telephone call en route summoned Seamus Rafferty and Hugh Devenney to the pub. The meeting was called and they gathered in the corner of the bar within ten minutes of opening time.

It struck eleven. Only Damien spoke. The speech was swift; the briefing concise, the objective simple. Find the tout! Prove it was Shelagh Connelly.

One drink was taken and the four left the premises. They got into a car Seamus borrowed from a friend and headed for Shantallow.

Hugh Devenney sat in the back of the car with Damien. Seamus drove. Eugene rode shotgun in the front passenger seat.

Hugh spoke out loud. 'It must be her then, Damien. It figures. All that money explains it, sure it does. But what about Liam?'

Damien looked his brother in the eye, 'Liam is okay, I say. I'm sure his loose talk has been picked up by Shelagh and reported by her to the RUC. Poor Liam will be warned when this is over, but he will understand. Loose talk is not allowed. Liam will understand. It was his sister, sure it was. Hugh, you get your way with Shelagh. I know you'll like it. Seamus, you look to take care of Liam if there's any problems with him in the future. Eugene, you search the house when we get in. I want a bank book or a policeman's name on a piece of paper with a telephone number. Better still, I need hidden money in the house somewhere. Do you all understand?' he instructed.

Eugene turned to Damien and replied, 'Sure I do. I'll find some evidence for you, boss. I'll find it. The bastard wee touting woman that she is.'

Seamus Rafferty concentrated on his driving but glanced into the driver's mirror to engage Damien's eyes, No problem, Damien. It's no surprise to me that it's Liam's sister. I shouldn't wonder if Liam isn't talking too!'

Damien said, 'Drive, Seamus. When I want your opinion I'll ask for it. Liam does well for me. I've seen him at work. I know this man. He's no tout, just his sister. But...'

Looking out across the Foyle, thinking out loud as they sped towards Connelly's home, Damien offered, "But if I'm wrong, then Liam is yours, Seamus.'

Seamus smiled. Seamus didn't quite know why he disliked Liam but he was sure he'd be proved right. The four men drove on. The schoolteacher, Hugh, thought of Shelagh Connelly, reminded himself of her looks, and felt a stirring in his groin at the idea.

Damien settled down fully in control of the situation. The episode today would spread further fear of his name in Derry and, more importantly, raise his profile in Dublin. Seamus Kelty would know that Damien Devenney was in charge in Derry. A tout was being brought to justice - a PIRA version of justice, that is.

Meanwhile, on Inch Island, Liam removed the fairing from the motor cycle to change the appearance of the bike for the return journey to Derry. He briefed Sean as to his intentions. Liam would return to Derry by a circular route and check out if it was safe to return home. He would contact Damien and arrange a doctor for Sean before contacting Shelagh to make sure she was all right, It was decided that every night at six o'clock, Liam would telephone the kiosk they had passed on the road to the bungalow and make sure Sean was well and up to date with affairs. It was important Sean knew when the doctor would arrive and it was equally important Sean knew when it was safe to return to Derry. If Liam failed to make a telephone call, then Sean was to assume Liam had been taken into custody and he was on his own.

The two men shook hands.

Passing over the handgun to Liam, Sean suggested, 'Sure, you'd best be taking this now just in case, Liam.'

'Thanks, Sean. You know I don't like to carry a gun but I think I will this time. I want to be sure there are no other reception committees waiting in Shantallow.'

Handing him the package containing the detonators, Sean asked, 'What about these, Liam?'

Taking the package, Liam slipped it inside his anorak and replying, 'I'll take them, Sean. It's a good bargaining strategy No doctor, no help from Damien... No detonators from me. Okay, to be sure?'

Sean nodded.

'Good luck, Sean. Mind how you limp to that phone box now.'

'Good luck, Liam.'

Liam kick-started the bike and headed back towards the province. On reaching Burnfoot, he turned right and joined the road that led him away from Derry and took him deeper into the Republic towards Letterkenny. At Newtown-Cunningham, Liam turned left and dropped down into St Johnstown. Here he joined the highway taking him back onto the A4 and into Londonderry.

Travelling leisurely, not wishing to attract attention to himself, he reckoned the police and army would still be searching for two men on a motor cycle fitted with a fairing. There were many such motor cycles in Derry. He was gambling he would not get stopped at a checkpoint. If he were stopped, then he would use the versatility and speed of the Honda to escape. Remaining cool was the secret. Loose and cool.

Liam entered Derry without mishap along the Foyle Road. He watched his speed and saw two policemen standing near the Craigavon Bridge look at him He ignored them and made his way slowly along the embankment towards Queen's Quay and the Shantallow estate. In so doing, he drove directly past the Strand Road police station. About one hundred yards after the police station, he turned left and parked the Honda near a row of shops. He had virtually parked right under the noses of the police. Stay loose; keep cool, remain arrogant and cocky, that was how you could be one step ahead of the chasing pack.

Liam Connelly started to walk the remaining distance to the Shantallow. It was mid-afternoon in Londonderry.

Bridget Duffy called on Shelagh Connelly that afternoon. Bridget had no knowledge of the events of the previous night but she liked Shelagh and took the trouble to call upon her occasionally. The two girls were of the same age and had much in common. Bridget was fixing Shelagh's hair. Shelagh was worrying over her brother, Liam

'Why didn't he ring me, Bridget, or is that a silly question?'

Bridget continued back-combing the curly hair and remarked, 'Sure, he wouldn't be using the telephone. Shelagh, if Damien was involved. If you've heard nothing from Damien then don't worry. Sure, some things take their time now.'

'I wish we were out of here, Bridget. I'm tired of it all.'

'Where would you go, woman?'

'Anywhere to find peace, sure I would,' replied Shelagh.

'How's your mother, Shelagh?' enquired Bridget.

Shelagh rolled her head from left to right, loosening the tension in her shoulders and replied, 'Just the same now. Good days and bad. Oh, where's that bloody Liam?'

A car drew up outside.

Damien Devenney, Hugh Devenney, Eugene Kelly and Seamus Rafferty got out of the car. The four men stood proudly on the footpath outside the house, almost defying the entire estate to witness their arrival. Soon, the estate would know it was a tout's house. There was no harm in standing out for all to see. The people on this estate relied on the Provisionals to police the area and prevent Loyalist attacks. No one would dare give evidence against Damien's cohorts. Some lived in fear.

Seamus remained with the car. Eugene took the back door. Hugh and Damien took the front. Hugh knocked on the door.

'Who could that be, Bridget?' asked Shelagh.

As Shelagh went to open the front door, Eugene shouldered the back kitchen door and entered the house.

Hugh pushed the front door open as soon as Shelagh turned the latch and grabbed Shelagh by the throat, gripping her tightly and pushing her back into the lounge.

Closing the door behind him, Damien saw Bridget in the lounge.

'You! Woman! What are you doing here?' enquired Damien

'Nothing, Just visiting. I'll be gone. You have business, Damien I'm sorry. I didn't know you were coming,' said Bridget.

Damien said, 'Sit down, woman. Over there. Sit! I may need to speak to you yet. Be quiet. Don't speak. Understand?'

'Yes, Damien,' shivered Bridget.

Bridget sat in the corner near the television as Hugh pushed Shelagh into the sofa. Eugene pressed her shoulders down. Hugh smacked Shelagh on the cheekbone with the back of his band.

Shelagh started to weep.

'What have I done, for God's sake' she asked.

'We've come for a tout, my love,' smiled Damien savouring the moment.

'Liam's no tout, Damien. Sure, he's no tout!' countered Shelagh.

'No. You've got it wrong, Shelagh. You're the tout, not Liam.'

Open-mouthed, Shelagh stared back at Damien. 'No! No! Not me!' she cried.

'Search it, Eugene,' ordered Damien.

Releasing Shelagh, Eugene turned his attention to a chest of drawers and rummaged through them as Hugh fingered Shelagh's cheekbone with the back of his hand.

Hugh's fingers caressed her cheek and travelled gently downwards towards her chin.

'I'm a fair man, Shelagh. I know you've been touting for the RUC. Tell me and I will spare you pain. I owe that to your father, God rest his soul, and to your brother Liam. From my respect of them, I will promise you no pain if you tell me the truth. Speak now or my promise will not hold and you will die a slow death. These are my words. Listen to them well,' said Damien.

Before she could reply, Hugh whacked Shelagh another blow on the face and then repeated the process of caressing the wound with the back of his hand. His fingers moved across her cheeks, gently touched her chin and sought her bosom. Hugh found her breasts and started to fondle them.

'Not me! Not me!' she screamed and then sobbed pitifully.

'For Jesus sake, Damien, leave the girl alone,' pleaded Bridget.

'Sit. Watch, Bridget. You may be next,' suggested Damien.

Eugene turned to the mantelpiece. He lifted the lid of the teapot and saw the wad of money. By now everyone in the room was watching Hugh fondle Shelagh. Hugh's fingers now held her pubic area.

Shelagh was screaming.

Damien's voice could be heard. 'Tell me, Shelagh. Tell me.'

Eugene removed a piece of paper from his pocket. The slip of paper bore a telephone number and the name of a well-known Detective Sergeant in Strand Road police station. He placed the slip into the teapot and removed Padraigh's letter. Eugene quickly scanned the letter and saw in the first paragraph what he did not wish to read. The money was a gift from an uncle. This was no good to Eugene. Finding the wad of money was his get-out. It was the reason to point the finger at Shelagh. It was the reason to save himself from suspicion.

Crumpling the letter into his fist, he casually threw Padraigh's letter into the fire. Shelagh's defence went up in flames. He turned to Damien with the contents of the teapot.

'Ask her about this, Damien. There's £500 here in used £10 notes and a telephone number.'

Damien smiled and thought, Eugene, faithful Eugene. He'd furnished the evidence that would get him off the hook with Seamus Kelty in Dublin. Eugene, the saviour.

Damien demanded, 'Speak child. My promise is about to die. This is your last chance. Where did the money come from?'

Taking the teapot from Eugene, Damien spilled the contents into his hand. He saw the money, three safety pins, a button and a slip of paper with a telephone number and a name on it. He recognised the name of the RUC man immediately.

'Damien, please, there's a letter from my uncle. The money is a gift. Get this brute off me,' pleaded Shelagh.

Damien had dismissed her before she spoke. He took the black silk hood out of the inside pocket of his long black overcoat and placed it over her head. Tightening the hood with the drawstring, Damien took out a gun, cocked it, and handed it to Hugh before turning to Bridget and saying, 'You are lucky Eugene found the money, Bridget. It could have been you. Watch, Bridget, and never forget what you are about to see. It may happen to you one day if you find yourself in loose talk. Take her, Hugh. She is my gift to you.'

Slapping Shelagh once again, Hugh pushed her back against the sofa, placed the gun to her leg, and fired one shot into the knee.

Shelagh's kneecap disintegrated in an explosion of blood and broken bone. She was barely conscious as he hit her about the head again and again. Hugh ripped her top open to expose her naked breasts.

'Eugene! Carry on the search please, my friend,' ordered Damien.

Eugene responded by clearing everything off the mantelpiece with the back of his hand. He emptied a magazine rack and kicked the television over. A mirror smashed against the floor and a standard lamp fell back against the curtains. He had saved himself. The red-headed bitch from London had been right. Be careful and say as little as possible. It had worked out right for him.

Lifting Shelagh by the hair, turning her round, Hugh pushed her against the sofa. Blood from her knee began to soak into the cushion. He unzipped the throbbing member from his trousers. His mind was a twisted perversion of insanity. There was a rustle in the back kitchen.

The door was ajar.

Liam walked into the Shantallow estate and circled the area of the house repeatedly until he was sure there was no one from the security forces watching out for him. Time had taught him that it paid to be careful. He was still unsure whether or not he and Sean had been recognised the night previously at the Buncrana incident. If he was wanted, it would be a safe bet that there was a surveillance operation on his house. He kept his eyes open.

There was no watch that he could see. He felt safe. Safe, that is, until he saw Seamus Rafferty sitting in the car outside the house. Liam began to feel uneasy.

He knew something was wrong and went down the cutting between the houses, climbed over a trestle fence, and clambered into his own back garden. Feeling for the gun Sean loaned him, Liam saw that the rear kitchen door had been forced, heard the sound of voices from within, and listened intently. He moved nearer.

Liam began to seethe with rage. He crept into the kitchen and stepped round the paraffin heater that was burning on a low setting near the sink unit.

The door into the sitting room was ajar. Cautiously, he peeked through the slender gap and gasped with anger.

Hugh unzipped his stiffening penis and prepared to enter Shelagh.

Shoulder-charging the door open, Liam entered the room, crouched low with weapon drawn, then stood up, pointing the gun all round. His heart was pounding and the adrenalin was thumping through his bloodstream when he aimed the gun at Hugh Devenney and screamed, 'Back off, you bastard!'

Looking up in total surprise, Hugh's sadistic smile vanished when he saw a gun pointing into his face. Slowly, he backed away from the girl.

Moving backwards, displaying his erect penis, Hugh's trousers hung grotesquely round his ankles.

Damien and Eugene both held their empty hands upwards, showing the palms to Liam, fingers spread out, and took a step back.

Bridget moved directly to Shelagh and comforted her. She placed her arms around Shelagh's shoulders and hugged her.

A shot rang out.

Hugh Devenney's penis exploded as the bullet blew the head off his organ and entered his belly. He fell forward, clutching his lower stomach in excruciating pain.

'Jesus! Ma brother! Ma brother!' screamed Damien.

Damien moved towards Hugh but stopped in his tracks when the gun was pointed towards him by Liam.

'You're an evil bastard, Damien,' threatened Liam.

Liam took it all in and saw the scene of turmoil and carnage developing before him. Deciding to finish it, he moved over the slumped body of Hugh Devenney, knelt down, and fired two shots in quick succession into the left temple. Both bullets penetrated the skull and ended the schoolteacher's life instantly.

The carpet was littered with mucus, skin, broken bone and blood.

The back door burst open and Seamus Rafferty rushed into the living room. His last vision was of Hugh Devenney dying.

Liam, caught unawares by the sudden entry, turned immediately and fired twice more into Rafferty's chest. The second bullet pierced Seamus's heart.

Staggering clumsily over the side of the sofa, looking wide-eyed into Damien's face, Seamus finally fell onto the fireplace and died minutes later. No one tended to him.

Liam regained control by turning and panning the gun towards Damien and Eugene. The after smell of the gun's discharge lay on the air.

Upstairs, mother Connelly had heard part of the interrogation, the screaming and the gunshots. Bed-ridden, racked by pain and approaching the end of her miserable life, she lifted the telephone by the bedside and dialled 999. She told the police the house was being attacked, presumably by some Loyalist gunmen. Mother Connelly was unaware of the true drama being acted out downstairs when she fell back into unconsciousness unable to replace the telephone on the handset.

Damien decreed, 'Liam! That's ma brother you've killed. I tell you now; you're a dead man. Forget the past. Get out now. If you're in Derry at midnight tonight, you're a dead man. You've killed one of us. You're out, Liam. You're out! Do you hear me? There is no place safe for you on this island. Leave!'

Damien's anger was fierce, his voice commanding: The voice and deadly promise of a senior brigade commander in the Provisional Irish Republican Army. Damien's declaration was cold, sudden and lethal.

Liam took it for what it meant. He was banished from Ireland.

'Yes, and that was ma sister. She never touted in her life. She never knew enough to tout, you fool,' snarled Liam.

Bending near his sister, Liam stroked her hair with his free hand whilst the other hand pointed his gun towards Eugene and Damien. He moved the weapon towards the shining skull of Eugene Kelly.

'Now you, Eugene, you are different,' threatened Liam.

Eugene felt death about to engulf him. He stepped backwards with terror in his eyes but realised there was no place to hide.

A siren sounded in the distance.

Liam changed his plans. His mind was racing. He collected the £10 notes that lay near Damien's feet, watching the two PIRA men the whole time, not giving them an inch. The gun wavered from Damien to Eugene, preventing both men from moving forward.

Handing the £10 notes to Bridget, Liam withdrew to the doorway.

The sirens were growing louder. Time was running out.

Liam ordered, 'Bridget, take ma mother and ma sister out of the house. Take them to safety. Sean will contact you. The money is for Shelagh. She'll need it. I won't, not where I'm going. Do this for me and I will never trouble you again.'

Bridget replied, 'It's done, Liam. I never wanted any part of this. You must realise that?'

Ignoring the remark, Liam watched as Bridget gathered up his sister, Shelagh, who was unconscious, bleeding from her knee. The siren was still some way off but grew louder as Liam considered his options. Backing into the hallway towards the front door, constantly training the gun towards his newly acquired enemies, his hand found the door catch.

Liam turned and was gone. Out of the house, over the road and into the gardens, he ran as fast as he could.

Running to the doorway, Damien screamed, 'I'll kill you, Liam! You're a dead man running! A dead man running.'

Liam Connelly ignored the threats.

Damien returned inside, anger and hate inscribed on his face, and yelled, 'Burn it, Eugene. Burn it!'

Bridget took the mother and daughter out of the house whilst Eugene emptied the contents of the paraffin heater around the lounge. The fuel soaked the furniture. Damien found another bottle of paraffin in the kitchen cupboard. The two men doused the house downstairs. The gun used to kneecap Shelagh was left near the body of Seamus Rafferty and doused with paraffin.

The siren grew louder and was joined by an orchestra of sirens from a variety of emergency vehicles making for the Shantallow estate.

The bonfire was ready.

Damien lit the paraffin and the house went up in flames.

The first police Land Rover at the scene blocked the entrance to the street. A green army personnel carrier entered from the opposite end and closed the area down. Troops slowly moved into position, using the natural cover of dustbins and hedgerows as they prepared to meet the unknown.

A young RUC constable removed a submachine gun from the rear weapons compartment of his armoured vehicle and jogged towards the house. The weight of his bullet-proof vest slowed him down but did remind him that he might be glad of its protection.

He had no need to look for the house numbers on the doors. The Connelly house was well known and, in any case, a plume of smoke was curling out of the downstairs windows. The young policeman depressed the switch on his personal radio and advised, 'At scene. House on fire. Road closed. Stand by!'

The radio report was acknowledged as he saw two men emerging from the burning house into the road. The young constable took no chances when he levelled his weapon at the two men and challenged, 'Armed police! Freeze!'.

Damien and Eugene became statues.

'Hit the ground,' ordered the policeman.

The two men dropped to their knees in the middle of the Derry roadway. Knowing the drill, they bent forward and lay spread-eagled on the tarmac.

'Spread yer legs. Arms out in front of you. Now! Move!' demanded the policeman.

The two PIRA men hugged the tarmac and did exactly what the policeman said. The RUC man trained his weapon on the two suspects from behind the safety of the car that Seamus Rafferty had used to drive Eugene and Damien to the house.

'Place your hands behind the back of your heads. Spread your fingers out so that I can see them. One false move from either of you and you'll both become statistics. Do it!' instructed the RUC man.

The two men complied.

The policeman radioed in, 'Two detained at scene. I have a view of the house. Now well alight. First mobile to respond to my location, please. Two turkeys netted but not yet trussed.'

The reply came back. 'Roger! Mobiles with you in less than a minute.'

The constable settled down to await the arrival of the cavalry. He didn't intend to rush things in this street. He altered his position behind the car slightly and crouched as low as he could. There was no need to give a sniper a clear shot, he surmised. The nose of the submachine gun pointed at Damien. The policeman heard the sirens growing louder around him. The army were sealing off the estate. He could see the troops moving in closer from the far end of the street. He waved them in. No further action would be taken until the forces were there in strength.

The house could burn down for all he cared. It was the Fire Service who put out fires and they wouldn't attend until the police told them the area was under total control.

The Connelly house burnt on.

Liam stopped running and walked into the roadway some distance from the burning house. He could see the smoke spiralling upwards above the rooftops. An obliging bus was passing and he hopped onto the boarding deck at the rear. This would take him into Derry town and the comfort of his Honda motor bike.

Within minutes, Shantallow was sealed. Two women were taken to hospital, one suffering from an apparent sexual assault and gunshot wounds to the knee, the other suffering from shock and a crippling terminal disease. A woman with them was taken into custody for questioning. The older lady from the house, a Mrs Connelly, died later from natural causes. A heart attack, they said.

Two known members of the local PIRA brigade were held for questioning about the incident on Shantallow. The house was saved from total destruction by the Fire Service but was declared uninhabitable until such time as extensive work had been carried out by the local council.

Later that night the bodies of two men were recovered from the carnage. Both had died from gunshot wounds. The house was boarded up by the council.

Bridget Duffy declined to answer any questions when interrogated by the police during her seven days of incarceration at Castlereagh. She was more frightened of Damien and his friends than the police.

Eugene and Damien co-operated completely with their interrogators. They stated that one Liam Connelly had returned home unexpectedly and found Hugh Devenney having sex with his sister. Liam had lost control of his temper and had shot his sister, together with Devenney and a Seamus Rafferty, who had tried to prevent the shooting. Before leaving, Liam had set fire to the house in order to teach his sister a lesson. It was said that Liam had disliked Hugh for years and was jealous of the relationship between Shelagh and Hugh.

The PIRA men told their interviewers Liam was a dangerous man. He had two guns with him when he came into the house. They did not know where the guns were now.

The PIRA men lied through their teeth.

Police officers who heard the statements were not impressed. The IRA men were not believed. Such men usually never spoke to police during interview. Police investigators were uneasy about the whole matter.

Shelagh Connelly gave a different story when she was well enough, but by now the situation was so muddied with innuendo, suspicion and counter-allegations that any chance of building a strong police case against Eugene and Damien was fast diminishing.

In any event, a certain red-headed lady privately advised senior investigating RUC officers that there was no need to rush into a prosecution against Eugene Kelly, or for that matter Damien Devenney. The tout had done well. He had lived to tell the tale, was still on the hook, was still in their pocket. The Provos thought Shelagh was the tout. They should be encouraged to think that. Events at Shantallow had been no more than a domestic matter: An internal feud involving certain members of the Provisional IRA.

Sure, there had been two murders and an attempted rape, but they could be turned to the advantage of the security forces. It was unfortunate Eugene did not recall the address of Padraigh O'Toole on the letter he read. It was, of course, understandable, seeing as he was trying to protect his own skin at the time. Eugene couldn't be expected to remember everything in the heat of the moment. Eugene, the tout, was safe to infiltrate PIRA further. His work of providing information on arms movements and terrorist activities could resume when he was free. The investigation could not proceed until Liam Connelly was traced.

The RUC agreed up to a point. No case could be built against anyone until Liam had been interviewed. Liam Connelly must be found.

His name was circulated to all police forces in the United Kingdom as wanted for double murder and arson. Liam Connelly was said to be armed and dangerous, only one handgun that was attributable to him having been recovered from the burnt-out house. Liam was on the run, wanted.

The PIRA men walked free, untouched, for the present time.

And the Intelligence lady was content. She was still in control.

Damien would have agreed with his captors. Liam must be found. He threatened to kill Liam Connelly for taking his brother's life.

Liam was a man stalked by death. He looked over his shoulder. He was unique. He was wanted by both a terrorist organisation and the security forces.

Such was the complexity of the intelligence war: A dirty war with no morals and, at times, no apparent sense. The rule in the intelligence game was simple. Win. Win by whatever means possible, but win.

Meanwhile, Liam had made his way south on his trusty Honda, unaware of how the scene was to be played out in the coming weeks. Fortunately for Liam, he was no fool. He was cautious.

On the night of the Shantallow incident, Liam rode the Honda to Pomeroy, in County Tyrone. Here, near the crossroads, he dismounted the machine and at six o'clock precisely telephoned Sean at the Inch Island telephone kiosk. Both men at that time were unaware of how the security forces would react to the murders and arson in Londonderry.

Liam dialled the number.

Sean answered and listened as Liam delivered a briefing of the day's events.

'Sean! Damien was thinking Shelagh was the tout. He's out of order. He's way out of line. It's all gone wrong here.'

Hobbling about in the telephone kiosk, moving his weight onto his stronger leg, Sean complained, 'Slow down, Liam. Take it slow and tell me what happened.'

'Hugh Devenney was raping ma sister when I arrived back at the house. Look, I've killed Hugh and Seamus,' admitted Liam.

'Jesus, what happened?' probed Sean.

'They were torturing Shelagh to make her talk, but she knows nothing for God's sake. Damien and Eugene are after me. They've put me out of the country. I'm banished. I'm making for the mainland, Sean. They fired the house. It went up in flames. Bridget has ma mother and ma sister. Get hold of Bridget and look after them for me. I'm gone now. Take care of yourself, Sean.'

Sean responded, 'Wait, Liam. Slow down, sure you must. How will I know where you are?'

'You won't, but Shelagh will work it out eventually one day. She'll know where to find me,' replied Liam.

Sean remembered an earlier visit to the mainland he had made on behalf of the organisation some years previously and promptly advised, 'Make for Kilburn in London, Liam. The Red Cockerel pub. Take the fight to London, Liam. You'll find friends at the Red Cockerel. People like us. Join them. Strike at the heart of the Brits in London and Dublin will have to let you back. That's the way to get back here, Liam. Believe me. Hit the bastard Brits in their own backyard, I say. Do you hear me now?'

'I hear you, Sean. Tell Damien I'll do the same to him if he ever touches ma family again. Even if it costs me ma life,' threatened Liam.

Sean shuddered at the thought of Liam taking on Damien but felt he had given good advice to his friend. 'I will, to be sure. I'll get Eamonn to collect me from here. What did you do with the dets, Liam?'

'Dumped them,' lied Liam. 'Look, Sean, I'll be a wanted man. I've no time. I need to be away now. I'm on the run. Take care, good friend!'

Replacing the telephone, Liam mounted the motor bike. Checking the packet of detonators in his inside pocket, he decided they would make a good trade for a passage to the mainland. He kick-started the Honda and drove into County Armagh.

By nightfall, Liam was riding down Newry Road in the picturesque port of Kilkeel. The beautiful Mourne Mountains overlooked the tiny port that stood guard at the entrance to Carlingford Lough.

Liam found the terraced house near the harbour and recalled how his father, Declan, once told him many years earlier that if he ever needed to leave the country quickly then he should call at this address and ask for a man called Quincy.

He knew why his father had told him. It was the accepted way of the secret organisation that dominated some parts of Ireland and he had remembered the rule of the terrorist. Always have a bolthole. Somewhere to run to and hide in safety. His father had probably saved his life.

He knocked on the door. 'I'm looking for Quincy,' said Liam.

An old grey-haired man in his seventies, with a weather-beaten face and a stubbly chin, peered out from the darkened doorway and enquired, 'Who wants him?'

Liam stood tall and proud and responded, 'The son of Declan Connelly, late of Shantallow, Londonderry. My father told me Quincy would help.'

The door started to close.

'No one of that name here, boy. Be gone will ya now,' said the man from Kilkeel.

Liam put his foot in the door and offered, 'No! Ma father taught me a song. He told me that God made the land and God made the sea. To be sure, I hope this good night that the God above is shining down on me, Quincy.'

On hearing the words, Quincy smiled broadly and opened the door fully, permitting entry.

'Jesus be! I knew your father well. You've got the look of him, that's for sure. Come yourself in and rest a while. Would you be having a ticket for the ride?' quizzed Quincy.

Liam was welcomed into the house with open arms. Once inside the warmth of the tiny house, Liam revealed his package and proudly said, 'Detonators! Once the property of Damien Devenney, Commander, Londonderry Brigade: A gift to you, the brigade quartermaster in these here parts. For use only against the Brits mind you, Quincy. I'm told yous boys here in the south are running out of equipment for the cause.'

'Nonsense, me boy. Wherever did you get that idea now?' replied Quincy.

Quincy's wife handed Liam a scalding hot bowl of soup.

Cupping it in his hands, Liam felt his fingers tingle as the heat warmed him.

Inspecting the detonators with old eyes, Quincy knew good equipment when they saw it and revealed, 'We've more kit than we know what to do with, Liam. Still, I'll find a use for these. Now then, sit you down and speak well to me of your father and your mother. Jesus! I knew them well in my younger days. Here, drink you the soup, boy, and then we'll drink to bygone days. Lights out at eleven bells. We leave on the morning tide.'

At dawn, Liam boarded Quincy's fishing vessel that plied the Irish Sea. Eight small fishing trawlers left the port of Kilkeel that morning. They were destined for the fishing grounds between the Isle of Man and the mainland. At the height of the season and when the fishing was good, it would not be unusual to find over a hundred such vessels fishing that broad channel between Ireland and the north of England.

Standing at the stern of the vessel, looking back towards the Mountains of Mourne as they disappeared into the morning mist, Liam watched his last view of Ireland fade.

Humming the tune he had been taught by his father, he felt the gun in his inside anorak pocket.

'God made the land and God made the sea. To be sure, I hope He shines down on me.'

The tears welled in Liam's eyes, rolled down his cheeks and fell onto the ship's wooden handrail. The island in which he had been born a boy and had been made a man slowly disappeared from view.

One hour after they had left Kilkeel, Liam threw the gun into the Irish Sea and turned to his duties. They fished the Irish Sea mainly for prawns and shrimps but anything that swam could be sold and eaten. Liam played a deck hand in the six-man crew. He worked his passage, taking to the galley below deck only when an aircraft flew overhead or a naval frigate came into view.

Ten days later they neared St Bees Head, off Cumbria. The hold was full since the catch had been good.

That afternoon they put into Whitehaven port and offloaded their catch, selling it to the local fish merchants. They kept a little back for the occasional local resident who wandered down to the quayside to barter for one or two fish. The two local port officers boarded the Irish fishing trawler, bought fresh fish from the captain as usual, and interviewed the crew members of each vessel under the terms of the Prevention of Terrorism Act. It was the usual routine with Irish shipping in the port.

By then, Liam Connelly had reached Whitehaven town centre and had made a telephone call from a public kiosk to a well-known Catholic club in Cumbria.

That evening, the Irish terrorist, Liam Connelly, wanted by the police for murder and arson, sat in the bus station across the road from Whitehaven docks. Rain pounded the Whitehaven streets and washed the town's grime into the sewage system. Buses came and went and the people who got on and off spoke in that strange West Cumbrian accent that portrayed them as belonging to 'Marraland', West Cumbria. The people were friendly and unsuspecting, nodding at the quiet young man who patiently in the bus station.

Liam Connelly, believed armed and dangerous, wanted by the police and wanted by the IRA, boarded the evening coach bound for the city of Carlisle.

The all-night petrol station in Scotland Road, Carlisle, lay on the outskirts of the city, virtually opposite the Coach and Horses public house. The small family owned filling station lay near the intersection where the M6 motorway ended and became the A74 highway for a further ten miles before bypassing the village of Gretna and penetrating the Scottish lowlands.

The petrol attendant that night was a young, bespectacled, ginger-haired local youth, who was tired and looking forward to a beer at the nearby pub when his relief turned up. The youth knew nothing about the drama being acted out in the dark outside. It was nine at o'clock at night.

Detective Sergeant William Miller Boyd fingered his square chin in a pensive mood as he looked impatiently at his wristwatch. He hunched his broad shoulders forward to ease the tension from his back.

Billy Boyd was the front seat passenger in a plain coloured car used by the local CID. The driver was a fellow detective. Both men were aware that three other cars, each containing two officers, were positioned at various strategic points nearby. Police had in fact quietly surrounded the petrol station and were waiting to see if the informant's tip-off had been correct.

The radio whistled its familiar tune. The first detective, Michael, radioed in. 'Point Alpha. All quiet.'

A colleague, Mark, responded. 'Bravo quiet.'

Michelle was one of two females in the team. She too joined in the radio procedure. 'Charlie! Same at this end.'

Sergeant Billy Boyd picked up his radio handset and said, 'This is Delta. Thanks for that. Keep your eyes open. It won't be long now. Delta out.'

Replacing the handset, Boyd settled down to play the waiting game.

The night dragged on whilst halogen street lights cast mysterious pools of light on the roadway, distorting figures and throwing shadows to the disadvantage of the team watching and waiting.

A dark blue transit van drove slowly down the road passing the garage. The van was fitted with two rear doors which were hand-painted in black. They windows were tinted making it impossible to ascertain how many occupants were in the vehicle.

Two people in the front of the transit took another look at the garage as they passed it for the second time that night.

Opening his till, the garage attendant took cash from an elderly customer and pressed the buttons on his computerised data box to show payment had been received. Radio Cumbria played softly in the background. It would soon be time to cash up and place the money in the night safe. It was a three mile drive to the bank and he began to count money from the till.

First, he separated twenty-five pounds in mixed notes and coin for the float and then took cloth bags from the drawer and placed them on the glass-topped counter. There were three bags marked five, ten and twenty pounds. He separated the day's takings into the relevant bags. He bundled the twenty-pound notes together and then turned to the ten-pound and five-pound notes. It had been a busy day.

The dark blue transit van swept the street once again before it finally pulled up at the petrol pumps. Two men alighted from the front of the van and went to the rear where they opened the double doors. One of the men, Craig, was more nervous than his colleague, Lawrence. Turning, Craig looked down the road into the city searching for something or someone, anything out of the ordinary.

Nodding to each other in silent agreement, they reached into the back of the van where they gathered their silk balaclavas. Rummaging in an old green rucksack inside the van, they pulled out two pick-axe handles. In black leather bomber jackets, jeans, trainers and balaclavas they looked a grim sight but with the aid of the pickaxe handles they looked frightening. The van doors closed.

Making their way across the petrol station forecourt to the garage entrance, their approach was quiet. They could see the lone figure of a young man illuminated by the garage lights. He was cashing up and counting the cash they had come to rob.

The police radio sounded, 'It's the blue transit. Two men! They are at the rear of the van. Stand by.'

Boyd was three hundred yards from the scene but the halogen lights of the garage illuminated the area well enough for him to direct matters. His colleague observed through night binoculars and remarked, 'I think we're in business, Sergeant Boyd. Pick-axe handles! Wait! Yes! Balaclavas! It's time.'

Boyd remained cool, considering his options, weighing up the evidence emerging in front of him. 'Not until they are inside,' he ordered.

Seconds ticked by before Boyd reached for the radio and bellowed into it, 'Listen to me. Hold your positions. Any second now. Wait! Wait!'

The young attendant in the garage filled the third bag with a handful of notes as the front door opened.

'Down! Down on the ground!' Screamed through a balaclava mask with a pick-axe handle held aloft by a dangerous and determined man.

The second robber stood by the door, keeping it open for a quick escape whilst looking outside for those who might seek to interfere.

The petrol attendant reacted by opening his mouth wide and looking nonplussed. He stood still, shell-shocked.

Craig, smashed the pick-axe handle onto the till and then hurled the wooden stave at the glass counter. It shattered into a hundred pieces. Glass splintered everywhere, littering the floor.

Craig roared at the top of his voice, raising the stave above his head in a threatening manner, 'Give me the money!'

Boyd spoke loudly into the radio handset, 'This is Boyd. It's going down. All units strike, strike, strike!'

Engines revved and tyres screeched as four cars covered the short distance to the filling station from their various hiding places. The first car stopped in front of the transit van and the two occupants rushed into the garage. The second vehicle slotted behind the rear of the transit. The other two cars arrived and police ran into the garage shouting 'Police! Police! Standstill!'

Lawrence never knew what hit him when the detective, Mark, shoulder-charged him to the floor and overpowered him.

The pick-axe handle fell to the ground as Mark and his fellow detectives pinned the crook to the floor and placed the handcuffs on him. The other robber, Craig, who was much taller and broadly built, decided to make a fight of it and wielded the pick-axe handle towards Boyd and the CID squad. 'Who wants some of this then? Come on, you pigs. Who wants to be first?'

Craig moved into the centre of the shop, moving the massive piece of wood menacingly from left to right threatening police as he tried to make for the exit and freedom.

The youngest detective present, Michael, was also the quickest thinker present and selected a can of Coke from the shelf nearest him and threw it directly at the robber.

The Coke can struck the robber directly in the nose and blood splattered outward, spraying the shop floor with crimson.

Dropping his pick-axe handle, the robber automatically went to cover his face with the sudden pain. The squad closed him down. A struggle followed with blows exchanged but Michael and his friends overpowered and outnumbered the thief. Both men were handcuffed and dragged out into the waiting police cars.

Withdrawing his black leather wallet, Boyd flashed his warrant card and introduced himself to the filling station attendant, 'Police! Sorry about the mess. Their choice, not ours. I'll need a statement from you tonight. One of my team will take it. Are you okay?'

'Jesus! Where did you lot come from? I was never so pleased to see a copper in all my life. Another minute and they would have had me.' replied the attendant.

Boyd laughed. 'You were never in any real danger. We just didn't have time to tell you what was going on. Sorry about that, but that's life.'

Sitting down on a stool, the attendant fingered the bridge of his nose, pushing his spectacles upwards as he eased the sleep from the corner of his tired eyes.

'I'm glad you can smile. Did you see the size of them? They were like gorillas.'

Chuckling, Boyd, shook his head and cracked, 'Who do you mean? The police or the robbers?'

The young man laughed. 'Is there a difference?'

'Well, we get paid for doing this,' replied Boyd. 'They don't. They'll pay their debt to society in due course, courtesy of the court.'

'What will they get?' enquired the petrol attendant.

Boyd considered the point and pursed his lips. There was a pause before he answered, 'Electrocuted, if I had my way. Now then, my lady officer, Michelle, will look after you and take your statement. We'll tell the owner what's happened and get him down here too.'

Returning to the squad nearby, Boyd offered, 'Okay, boys and girls, it's a wrap! Book them in at the nick. Good work Michael, Mark. Now then Michael - statements please. Steve - can you recover the van to the nick? Peter! Get the forensic team up here to tie the knots and seal up the case. Otherwise, good work! Snooker in one hour at the club for those who can make it.'

The team acknowledged their leader.

'Good tip, Sergeant Boyd. Good tip!' cracked Michael.

Boyd headed for the police station. It was a good result and a good piece of information from one of the many informants that worked for him. He wrote his notes, tidied up the paper work and bedded the case down for the night. Then he jumped into his sports car and headed to the club. It was time to pot the black and the Catholic club was no more than a ten-minute drive from the police station.

Boyd was first at the bar with, 'Five pints of bitter and two lagers to start with, my man, if you please! That will do to be going on with.'

The barman reached for two pint glasses, placing one under the bitter tap and one under the lager. He drew down on the pump handle.

Padraigh O'Toole was at the bar and waved across to Boyd.

'Now then, Billyboy. What brings you here this night? Snooker perhaps?'

The other detectives chuckled. The big bearded Irishman was the only one alive who would have dared to call Boyd Billyboy.

'Not tonight, Pat. There's no competition,' replied Boyd.

It was the gauntlet thrown down. The Irishman picked it up.

'Sure and who do you think taught you the game, you big daft Englishman?'

Boyd responded, 'Okay! One round. Pot the black. You pay!'

'Why me, to be sure?'

'Because you're a thick Irishman. Now line up the white ball.'

Pat nodded to the barman who was following the conversation. The barman turned to the optics; two vodkas were placed on the bar. The two men eyed up the vodkas almost daring the other to touch the glass. Boyd was first to speak, 'It's not white!' suggested Boyd.

Pat quipped, 'No, but it's near enough now.'

The two men sank the vodka then Boyd signalled to the barman. Two Campari appeared on the bar.

Pat studied the thick gooey liquid, noting the deepness of the red as he held the wine glass by its stem in order to study the drink.

'The red is it, then?' asked Padraigh.

Boyd watched his Irish friend carefully and replied, 'Yes, bonny lad. Then you can pot the black. Get the red away first.'

The two men drank Campari. Once they had finished, the barman placed two pints of Murphy's stout on the bar. He loved this crazy game that the two men regularly played. The club made a fortune when the two friends played 'Pot the Black'. The drinking ritual had absolutely nothing to do with the game of snooker or, for that matter, billiards. It had everything to do with the colour of the alcohol. Similar to snooker players, the drinkers started with the white, took a red and then finished on the black. Once the red and white had been taken any colour drink could be selected. Just like snooker, only sillier.

Stroking his beard, studying the black stout as it settled in the glass, Padraigh noticed a head of froth appear on the beer. It was the kind of froth that only the Irish could master to his taste.

'Tell me, Billyboy, what would you be celebrating tonight? An Irish sweepstake win, perhaps?'

Boyd countered, 'No chance. I don't gamble. Cheers, Pat!'

'Cheers, Billyboy.'

The pair sipped at their Murphy's. By now, the bar had filled gradually with a collection of locals as well as Boyd's detectives. The humour was good and the late night club licence added to the atmosphere. Two of Boyd's team challenged two locals to a game of snooker. The challenge was accepted. This time a table, balls and cues were used and a few side bets were laid on who would win the match.

Padraigh and Boyd moved to a seat in the corner of the room, away from the bar. They sat down, placing their glasses on a small table in front of them. The club was well furnished and the armchairs in which they rested were comfortable.

Pat spoke first, 'You get no better, Billyboy, playing the game of pot the black. I remember when you were just a boy. Look at you now!'

'I'm keeping well, Pat. Yourself?' asked Boyd.

'Tired, older, but happy. What was it tonight then?'

'An armed robbery. No guns, just coshes. We got them though. It seems like it never ends, Pat.'

Pat replied, 'That's right now. I know what you mean. There's no such thing as peace, Billyboy.'

Taking another drink of Murphy's, Boyd laughed it off. 'Peace would just make life dull, Pat!'

'That depends where you're living, Billyboy!' suggested Padraigh.

'Any news from home, Pat? Ireland?'

Padraigh O'Toole considered the question. In all the years he had known Boyd, he had never been asked such a question by him.

Lying, he replied, 'I've just a sister over there, a nephew and a niece. Brother- in-law left them years ago. It's all in the past, Billyboy.' He lied again when he said, 'They're travelling people. We've gone our own way and lost contact with each other these last years.'

Boyd offered, 'I'm sorry, Pat. What about your son?'

'Sure, Michael is doing well on them oil rigs up in the north of Scotland. He works from Aberdeen.'

Boyd chuckled, 'I hope he doesn't fall off, Pat.'

'Sure, he can swim now, Billboy. Thanks to you.'

'And your wife, Pat, is she well?' enquired Boyd.

Pat beamed at the mention of his dearly beloved. 'Linda! Sure, she's well. At home with the cat and the TV. A marvellous woman, sure she is.'

Boyd continued, 'Tell her I sent my love. Linda's far too good for the likes of you, Pat.'

The Irishman chuckled and responded, 'Sure, she'll be pleased on that. She'll not forget the day you dragged poor Michael from the Eden. Sure, I owe you, Billyboy. It'll not be forgotten.'

Boyd thought back to the thundering river 'You'd have done the same for me, Pat. Still, if you owe me, get the Murphy's in.'

Boyd drained his glass and handed it to Pat who went to the bar.

The telephone behind the bar rang and the barman answered it.

'Sure, it's two Murphy's, so it is, if you please now,' said Pat.

The barman replied, 'Phone call for you, Pat. Someone from Whitehaven. Take the call. I'll get the beer.'

The barman handed the telephone to Pat who took it. He was puzzled; he didn't know anyone in Whitehaven.

Boyd chatted to the locals nearby for a few minutes until Pat returned. Pat looked as white as a ghost. He was visibly shaken and landed heavily as he sat down by Boyd.

'Here's your drink, Billyboy. Sure, I must go now. I'm tired. Let's pot the black at the weekend,' suggested Padraigh.

Pat sank his Murphy's in three large gulps.

Concerned for his friend, Boyd knew better than to ask. If Pat wanted him to know what was troubling him, he would tell him soon enough.

'Fine, there's one thing you can do for me though!' remarked Boyd.

'What's that, Billyboy?'

'I' moving on,' declared Boyd.

'What do you mean?' questioned Padraigh.

Boyd explained, 'A new job. They've transferred me out of the CID.'

Pat's eyebrows rose. 'Where to?'

Boyd answered, 'A special terrorist squad.'

'Terrorist! Billy!'

'Yes, one night you can give me a history lesson. Tell me what it's all about over there. I've spent all my career chasing thugs, not terrorists. That okay with you, Pat?' asked Boyd.

'Sure, Billyboy. Sure, it is now. Terrorists! Indeed...' Padraigh paused, unable to finish the sentence he had started. 'Billyboy!'

'Yes, Pat?' replied Boyd.

Pat's mind was racing in turmoil but he said, 'Nothing, Billyboy. Nothing. It'll keep.'

'No! Go on. What's on your mind?' probed Boyd.

'I must get home, Billyboy. The good woman will be waiting for me. I wish you good night,' said Padraigh.

Boyd responded in the usual manner. 'May God shine down on you, Pat,' he said.

Padraigh O'Toole drained his glass, buttoned his coat and bade farewell with, 'Sure hope so, Billyboy. I sure hope so.'

Walking from the bar, Pat covered the short distance to his home on foot in less than fifteen minutes. His mind was uneasy, uncertain and worried.

Just after midnight that night, Liam slipped quietly into the house and slept in on the living room sofa. The following day Liam told his uncle, Padraigh O'Toole, all there was to tell about Derry PIRA, Damien Devenney, Eugene Kelly and the incident at the house in Shantallow. The story was to remain a family secret. The events were not spoken of again in the house. There would be no loose talk in Pat's house.

Liam would be safe in Carlisle as long as Pat could see to it. By the end of the month, Pat arranged permanent accommodation for Liam, as well as a part-time job in a twenty-four hour wagon park on the edge of the city. Liam was on the mainland to stay and Pat took him under his wing.

Detective Sergeant William Miller Boyd packed his bags and caught the early morning train to London. Boyd had joined a specialist crime unit and his job was to catch terrorists. The journey south from Cumbria to London took him further and further away from one of the most wanted terrorists in the United Kingdom, Liam Connelly.

Stepping from the packed London train at Euston railway station, Billy Boyd walked briskly up the slight ramp towards the platform exit. He declined the waiting porters and carried his battered suitcase across the attractive marble concourse. The place was vibrant with people, rushing from one place to another, going about their daily business

Taking the steps down to the taxi rank, Boyd took a cab towards Marble Arch. The journey was reasonably peaceful as the vehicle carefully threaded its way through the London traffic into the West End.

His four star hotel was near Oxford Street. He tipped the cockney taxi driver, walked into the plush hotel vestibule, registered, took the lift to his room, and unpacked. He showered, watched the lunchtime news on television and dressed in a double-breasted dark suit, light blue shirt and complementary silk tie. Finally, he added a tie pin.

Boyd walked casually to the Piccadilly area, where he found the Intelligence Service building. Boyd produced his police warrant card at the glass-fronted reception desk.

He sat in the visitors area until the necessary security checks were completed. Eventually, he was allowed access to the building and escorted to the lecture room.

It was his first introduction to the Intelligence Service. It would not be his last. He knew why he was there. The service wanted his expertise as a detective to help fight the secret war against terrorism. And he was looking forward to the challenge.

He sat down with the others, introduced himself to those around him and waited for the lecture to begin.

The lights dimmed and the spotlight focused on the speaker. The gentleman giving the lecture was a smart young man of about thirty years of age, dressed in a plain grey suit, white shirt, light blue tie and dark shoes. He welcomed the gathering and spoke at some length on the history of the Intelligence Service revealing how the service had remained disaffiliated from any political party throughout its entire being. Indeed, the speaker argued part of the strength of the Intelligence Service was evidenced in its lack of accountability to a political master. The 'master' to whom the service was accountable was evidenced in the need to defend the United Kingdom from its enemies both within and without its sovereign territories. Yes, there were politicians of different political persuasion, who for relatively short periods of time held political power, but no one was beyond the reach of a service dedicated to the long-term preservation of the United Kingdom. There were critics of the service, but in the main the critics were those who sought to undermine society for their own good.

The Intelligence Service sought to preserve peace in Britain and maintain a capability that would deny its enemies the ability to subvert and terrorise British society. The points raised were not unfamiliar to the policeman Boyd.

The young man droned on and ended at tea time. It was the right time since the group were becoming restless and Boyd's long journey was starting to have an effect on him. He was nodding off.

Tea was taken and small talk between the participants was the order of the day. After a fifteen-minute break, the lectures recommenced and the audience sat down again. The previous male speaker introduced a young female member of the Intelligence Service. After the usual introduction, the speaker informed the audience the young lady was to speak on 'Northern Ireland and associated problems'.

She was Boyd's cup of tea.

Introducing herself as Antonia Harston-Browne, the audience observed a tall, good-looking girl, with long red hair flowing down her back and covering her shoulder blades. Of slim build, with an hour-glass figure to match, Antonia wore a dark blue, two-piece, executive-style suit, set off with a silver brooch worn on the lapel. The neatly tailored skirt stopped short, well above the knee, giving the potential to reveal a well shaped pair of legs.

The audience comprised mainly of males with only a handful of females present. The males in the audience were immediately attentive.

Antonia Harston-Browne had a commanding way with her that was supported by very good looks.

Waking up, as did many others in the room, Boyd eyed her legs.

Ignoring him, Antonia addressed the gathering on various views relative to Irish history arguing that the Republicans from the Catholic community had been deprived of the six counties of the north by a British state that had invaded Ireland centuries ago and left the Protestant religion dominant in Ulster. This was soon to become the seed of war and the origin of the Irish Republican Army and its various competing derivatives, such as, for example, the Irish National Liberation Army.

Harston-Browne continued to lecture like a staunch Republican, dissecting the 'Troubles' and their relevance to the 'Anglo-Irish' society. She would have been passed for a leading terrorist had it not been for the surroundings, the decor and her clean-cut upper class cultured image.

Changing tack, Antonia pointed out that Loyalists from the Protestant community grew up in Ulster. It was their country and their home. They were entitled to the protection of the British government. Continuing in this style, she played Republican and Loyalist, revealing the feelings that underlie the great religious divide in the six counties variously referred to by the different Irish communities as Northern Ireland, Ulster, the Province or the occupied counties.

Policemen and policewomen, who had spent their lives chasing muggers, pickpockets, burglars, fraudsters and armed robbers, listened intently. Understanding the views of the opposing sides was fundamental in the battle to be waged.

Antonia, however, argued a common theme. Whether or not the terrorist was a Republican or a Loyalist, it was evident their organisations were underpinned by ruthless, dangerous criminals. For every would-be terrorist who could spout the political and historical argument at length, there was a plethora of so-called volunteers and activists who dedicated themselves to the spread of terror throughout their community, often for their own personal ends.

Indeed, the history and politics of Ireland were often thought to be so long-drawn-out and complex that you could not simply package the problem into two distinct, easily understood, arguments.

Moreover, the committed terrorist, whether Loyalist or Republican by nature, was driven by greed, violence, self-determination and self-indulgence. These were the people who would never support a true and lasting peace in Ireland: people who desecrated Ireland with their protection rackets, murders, shootings, kneecappings, and robberies; people who feasted on beatings, intimidation, illegal gambling dens, illegal drinking houses and drug dealing, people who had terrorised a whole country for as long as many a soul could remember, for a half forgotten, often misunderstood and ill argued cause. Some folk couldn't even remember what had started it all. Some didn't care what started it all.

The result was the lethal, ever-downward decline of a country polarised by bigotry, hate and fear: A country torn apart by the Loyalist bullet and the Republican bomb: a country defiled by a relatively small group of people who killed at the drop of a hat without thinking through the consequences of their actions. People who had no respect for others; no respect for life, no respect for the countless thousands of women and children who walked in fear of death.

These were the very people who made their way in life by stealing from the poor. They collected the 'dues' from door to door on the housing estates and in the pubs, clubs and cafes, so that money could be sent to the families of those imprisoned for the 'cause'. What cause? Whose cause? Did it matter what cause?

Two large men standing over a frightened woman demanding money for the 'cause' are unlikely to be challenged by the weak and elderly. The collector took his share of the 'dues', of course. These were the people who made money by selling drugs to young kids in the street. Money for the drug dealer and a little money for the 'cause': money for the terrorist to buy guns, to buy ammunition, to buy explosives to support the families of those in jail.

These were the bigots who killed because you were of a different religion. You could be killed because you got in the way, didn't agree, lived in the wrong area, worked in the wrong place, or wore a uniform. They could shoot you, bomb you or just beat you to death. The Republican terrorists called themselves Irish. The Loyalist terrorists called themselves British. Such people deserve no nationality. They are inhuman. Never mind your politics! Never mind your religion! How many lives were lost because someone gave to the cause? These people; these volunteers, these activists, these terrorists, they are an insult to the thousands of Irish people who seek peace and humanity. They were beasts of death. Vile, heartless creatures who did not deserve to breathe the air of life. They were, are, and always will be, the enemy of mankind.

Antonia Harston-Browne drove home her lecture fiercely and then rounded off her speech, shuffled her papers into a buff folder, smiled, and stepped away from the lectern The afternoon session was over.

The schoolchildren could go out to play that night but had to be back in class for nine o'clock the next morning, she joked. 'Drinks at the local,' were announced.

Boyd followed the red-head out of the classroom to the cloakroom. He studied her legs, closed in and pounced.

'Good evening, I enjoyed the lecture. Can you recommend a good pub nearby?' asked Boyd.

Keen to assist, the red-head liked his cheek, wondered how deep his blue eyes were, and replied, 'If you were listening, then follow me. I'm sure half the class will turn up at the pub across the road. We all tend to stick together on these things you know. Anyway, who are you?'

'Bond! James Bond!' cracked Boyd.

No hint of amusement; indeed the lady was not at all amused.

'Ha-ha! Read the book, saw the film. Been there, done that. Not funny anymore,' replied Antonia deliberately swishing a bundle of red hair across her shoulders in an act of rebuttal and contempt.

Responding, Boyd, cajoled, 'Yes. I know, but I just couldn't resist it I've been waiting to say that since they told me I was coming here. I'm Boyd, William Miller Boyd, actually. I didn't quite catch your name?'

She bristled again. The blue eyes were losing their appeal.

'Antonia Harston-Browne! You must learn to remember things if you're going to be any good to us.'

Considering the name carefully, Boyd commented, 'I don't work for you. I work for the police. Anyway, that's far too much of a mouthful: Antonia Harston-Browne. Hyphens are most inconvenient, don't you think? They should be done away with. I'll call you Toni! Toni Brown!'

Antonia Harston-Browne had never been called anything other than Antonia Harston-Browne in her entire life. She was shocked, but recovered quickly and reacted sharply, 'Then I'll call you Billy, if that's the way it's going to be! Billy! Where's your short pants?'

Boyd countered, 'Good! Everyone calls me Billy. I only wear short pants when I'm running. Actually, I have a very good memory, so I really hope that your service can come up to scratch. I don't suffer fools gladly.'

The lady was lost for words.

Boyd continued at high speed, 'Look, perhaps we should have a partnership right from the start. You do your part of the job and I'll do mine. I promise not to get in your way, so please don't get in my way. Come on; let's get to the pub first. I don't like to queue at the bar. Tell me, does this pub do Murphy's or is it the usual River Thames water filtered into a beer keg and sold at a ridiculously high price? Have you ever tasted northern beer? They make it with hops in a place called a brewery. Its a fairly new idea I believe, certainly hasn't reached London yet. You can taste the beer, you know. That reminds me, have you ever played Pot the Black? We must try it one night. Have you ever been north of Watford gap? Do you see the United Kingdom ever extending beyond the M25 motorway ...?'

Boyd continued to prattle on as if he had been inoculated with a very sharp gramophone needle. Easing the overcoat onto her shoulders, he pushed the door open and walked into the street with her, still talking ten to the dozen.

Antonia Harston-Browne giggled to herself. She had never been chatted up in such a cheeky manner before.

They walked and talked their way past four bars before they found a suitable establishment that Boyd duly pronounced fit for human inhabitation.

Entering the bar, they ordered Murphy's and were closely followed by those classmates who managed to keep up. By then the entire party knew she was really called Toni Brown, and had recently recovered from a sex change operation. Boyd was, of course, the senior hospital surgeon who had performed the miracle transformation and had been obliged to rush down to London to ensure all was well with his patient.

The conversation got no better once the ebullient Boyd had decided to teach the southerners how to play Pot the Black. Boyd, in his usual cheeky manner, then barred half of the class immediately, dictating that those suffering from colour blindness would be unable to understand the complicated northern rules.

Vodka flowed. Campari flowed. Murphy's flowed. The black was potted. The ice was broken. Boyd's life in the Specialist Crime Unit began.

1988

A little black kitten picked out its spot and sprang from the carpet onto Dermot Dougan's knees causing the Derry man to flinch slightly as the cat's claws dug sharply into his trouser leg.

'Ouch! Get down, my pretty one. Sure, I'll no get this done if yer in ma way. Sure, be off wid yer now and lie by my feet.'

Dermot stroked the cat's throat and massaged her tummy with his fingers. Lifting her gently to the ground, he stroked her delicately behind the ears before turning his attention to the bomb he was making. The cat purred happily, stretched its tiny paws, and cuddled into his feet where Dermot felt the kitten nibbling the ends of his slippers.

Closing her eyes, the cat eventually drifted into sleep.

'Sure, cat, you don't want to be near this one when it goes off. You'll lose your tail, pretty one,' muttered Dermot.

Moving the timer into position, Dermot carefully secured it with a thin piece of dowelling. The timer would not be activated until the small piece of dowelling wood had been removed. At that point the timer would start its deadly countdown and the device would explode a micro-second after the two metallic contacts triggered each other sending an electronic spark into the detonator to explode three pounds of semtex.

Dermot checked wiring and connections and confirmed they were in order. Reaching across to the other side of the table, he found the video cassette case and eased the device fastidiously into it. The case was tailor-made so that the dowelling pin could protrude from the end of the case. It was in the right position to be extracted without causing the device to be tampered with. The easy activation of such a dangerous device had to be well and truly above suspicion. The excellent job had been completed by a true master craftsman.

Sean Brady watched intently from the other side of the room and then tried to peer over Dermot's shoulder.

'How many is that now. Dermot?' enquired Sean.

The bomb maker looked up at Sean and then scanned the table counting the objects before declaring, 'Sure, that's five so far, Sean. Just like you said. If yer wanting more then you'll need to go back to the hide tonight and bring some more 'blow' back.'

'No! That's enough, Dermot. Good job done. If yer finished, then tidy it up. Clean as a Catholic father's chalice. Nice and clean. No traces!'

Eamonn Murphy was standing by the net curtains looking out of the second floor window into the busy Maida Vale Street. The flat was situated just off the Kilburn High Road, about two miles from Marble Arch, at the junction of the Edgware Road and Oxford Street, London.

'I hope they are alright, Dermot, or I'll be back to haunt you, that I will. If I don't make it because you got yer fingers where yer thumb should have been, then I'll haunt ya from ma grave. I promise you,' cajoled Eamonn.

'Quiet will yer now, Eamonn? Can you no see the kitten's asleep, so it is,' replied Dermot.

Dermot stroked the dozing lazy cat. It was the young offspring of a neighbour's cat and he had befriended it when they had first arrived. The cat had latched on to him ever since and was now accepted by the others as part of the furniture. Apart from that, no one really wanted to upset Dermot. He was too important to the cause not to have him on your side. Dermot made bombs. The cat stayed.

Eamonn shook his head, saying, 'Jesus yer are worried about a bloody cat when you've blown up half of London this year. Sure, and half the police in yonder Scotland Yard are after us. To be sure, Dermot, yer a troubled man that ya are. Cats indeed!'

'Quiet the pair of you, now. I can't be doing with all this. Yer giving me a bad head,' snapped Bridget Duffy. She joined Eamonn at the window and continued, 'Just get them finished, Dermot, and we can get back home away from this Godforsaken place. I don't like it here.'

'Don't you like London, Bridget?' queried Sean.

Bridget's blonde hair twirled across her shoulders when she turned lightly and answered, 'It's safer back in Shantallow, Sean. I know the streets there. It's different here. When you go out it's as if everyone was watching you.'

Nodding in agreement, Sean replied, 'They might be, Bridget. They've got spies everywhere. We've to be keeping on our toes. Away from the window now, the pair of yous.'

Dermot placed the final bomb into a large shopping bag and announced, 'That's us ready then, Sean. Five to put down in the West End. Oxford Street is it?'

Taking control, Sean addressed his team, 'Eamonn, bring the van round to the back lane. Bridget, get the shopping bags together. We'll put them in the car once Eamonn is back. Now then, Dermot, we'll leave you to clean up. Don't miss anything. We'll see you at the rendezvous point, like last time. So, come on! Into the city. Hit! Run! Hide! Now let's do it.'

The four members of the PIRA active service unit went about their allocated tasks. Today, the target was Central London.

Oxford Street: Full of hustle and bustle at lunchtime; full of Londoners selling a mixture of goods to a mixture of people. But Oxford Street was more than that. It represented modern London where Londoners from many different ethnic backgrounds sold their wares to tourists at sites which varied from that of the corner barrow boy to the international department store.

It was in the popular Green Man public house just off Oxford Street that Detective Sergeant Billy Boyd stood waiting for his colleague. He was sipping half a pint of beer and minding his own business. She was late as usual. Boyd checked the time on his wristwatch.

The lunchtime karaoke session was in full swing since office staff from the many businesses in the area used the pub regularly. Londoners never needed much of an excuse to party. There was always someone leaving or joining an office in the area.

The karaoke played on. Noise permeated the atmosphere into the street outside. London was in a party mood.

Antonia arrived at last with her red hair tied in a bun at the back of her head. She wore a black trouser suit high at the collar and trimmed with brocade. Her shoulder bag bulged with an assortment of alleged female necessities.

Pecking Boyd on his cheek in a sisterly fashion, Antonia eased herself onto a stool and sighed in a fashion betraying a long hard day.

Boyd summoned the barmaid.

'Hello, Billy. Any news? Perrier, please!' said Antonia.

Boyd ordered the drink and answered, 'I had a meet with one of my Irish friends this morning. Kilburn area. That's all he's got. I don't think he'll get much more than that personally, but you never know, do you? I phoned it in to control about ten minutes ago. What about your mob, Toni?'

'Looks like the same team as last year.'

'Is that so?' commented the interested Boyd.

'So I'm told, Billy.'

Collecting their drinks from the bar, they moved to an empty table by the door. The music was loud, comical, raucous and not at all conducive to a quiet lunchtime meet..

Puzzled, Boyd asked, 'How do you know that?'

Antonia replied, 'I'm told that the bombs that went off last week were all semtex-based, between two and four pounds usually. When the lab boys examined the remnants swept up from the road, the bits and pieces of the timer and the way it had been assembled suggested it's the same bomb maker. That probably means the same ASU as last year's attacks. But you never really know, of course. Just my assessment of it all.'

Taking a sip of the Perrier water, Antonia pulled the slice of lemon out onto the edge of the glass and continued, 'They're all small bombs. Just the kind to keep everyone on their toes without causing any major damage. Big bombs, little bombs. What's the difference? The bomb damage is covered by television every night. It's like a nightly PIRA advert for God's sake. Any bright ideas from you or the team at the Yard then?'

Boyd took a gulp of beer and offered, 'No bright ideas at all, I'm afraid, Toni. I have men on the street now, just looking, keeping their eyes open. Although, to be fair to them, it's like searching for a needle in a haystack. Are there any suggestions at all from across the water?'

Nodding firmly, Antonia responded, 'The RUC reckons it's Derry or Belfast faces. Probably between four and six in number, maybe one or two women. Short stay, do the business and out quick. Fact is, they could be new to us. Just be patient. We'll find them, trust me.'

Looking at his watch again, Boyd knocked back his drink. 'Come on. Let's take a walk. We can still make the afternoon meeting without any problem. I'm sure our bosses will have some answers later today. Let's take the tube at Bond Street. It's just round the corner.'

Draining their glasses, they returned them to the bar and stepped into the street turning away from the general direction of Mayfair and made towards Oxford Circus.

About two miles from their location and only minutes earlier, a phone call had been made from a telephone kiosk near Regent's Park to a national newspaper. The call purported to come from a member of the Irish Republican Army. An authentic codeword was used. The message was passed by the newspaper to the police in New Scotland Yard and indicated bombs had been placed in Oxford Street and would detonate in about half an hour. Nothing else was said.

Boyd's personal radio crackled causing him to adjust the earpiece. The reception was bad so they moved into a shop doorway where he used his mobile 'phone to make contact. He pressed the illuminated digits on the mobile and spoke to the duty dispatcher in the radio room.

Boyd took the message at the same time as the two police cars moved into position at Marble Arch and Centrepoint. The Metropolitan police had been alerted. They were in the process of sealing off the mile-long street.

Within minutes the department stores and boutiques would have a choice to make. Close down, lose business and search for a bomb, or ignore it and carry on regardless. It was the same old PIRA tactic: Imprecise information. No definite locality where the bomb had been put down. No specific timescale as to when it would detonate and no consideration for the massive police response that was obviously required to deal with the threat made.

Relaying the problem to Toni, he took out his note book, reminded himself of who was where, and started contacting his own men on the radio net. He had six detectives in the area, all in plain clothes, on the look-out for the suspicious. Given the length of Oxford Street and the mass of shoppers around, it was an almost impossible task.

A police motor cycle roared past with its siren blaring.

Toni advised, 'The tube station, quickly. We might just get a look at some faces in the crowd, you never know. Keep that radio plugged in.'

She strode off at high speed, beckoning him to keep up.

Another police car roared into the street escorting a police personnel carrier which contained about a dozen officers from the local station. An armed response vehicle, liveried in fire service red and adorned with police signs on all four sides, swung into Park Lane and crept towards the top end of Oxford Street.

Its nervous occupants checked their weapons and loaded the ammunition, just in case they were needed.

Meanwhile, at the rear of Oxford Street, in nearby Wigmore Street, Eamonn Murphy tapped the steering wheel impatiently.

Sean joined him in the van and snapped impatiently, 'Where is she for God's sake? We should be away by now. Dermot's called it in and half the police in London are descending on us. Where the hell is Bridget?'

'Should we go, Sean?' suggested Eamonn.

'Wait two more minutes,' ordered Sean.

Bridget had been delayed. She'd placed one bomb in a department store near the escalator. The shopping bag rested beneath a display of dresses with its timer moving slowly towards detonation. She then walked towards Bond Street underground station but thought she was being followed by a man in plain clothes.

The man was in his mid-twenties and he was dressed in trainers, jeans, tee shirt and a blue fleece jacket.

Bridget didn't panic. She was disguised as an elderly lady wearing a headscarf, raincoat and Wellington boots and merely walked round the block until she felt safe. She stopped at the corner of the tube station near a barrow upon which a selection of leatherwear was for sale and placed the second shopping bag down beside a leather bag.

Then Bridget walked away making for Wigmore Street, still looking over her shoulder for a man wearing a blue fleece, and fifteen minutes later than planned.

The timer was on countdown.

One of Boyd's men was not happy. It was the detective they called Mickey. He spoke to Boyd near the tube station.

'It was an old woman. Well, no it wasn't. There was just something wrong about her,' said Mickey, thinking it through, trying to make it right. Then Mickey pulled the collar of the blue fleece jacket into his cheeks.

'What do you mean?' questioned Boyd.

'What did the woman do?' probed Antonia.

Mickey pondered, 'I know this sounds crazy but her bosom didn't fit her. She wore a raincoat. From the front she looked young but from the rear she was different. The bosom was way out; I mean she had a big pair of...'

'Yes, I know what you mean,' acknowledged Antonia. 'Go on.'

'They were too big and firm for her age,' suggested Mickey.

The timer moved another fraction of an inch round its circular path. The metal contact neared its counterpart.

Eamonn Murphy stopped the van in Primrose Hill.

Dermot Dougan joined the escaping group. All smiles, they bundled together for the ride north.

'Yes, that's it! I've got it! When I saw her first she had a shopping bag. The second time I saw her she didn't have the bag,' explained Mickey.

Boyd shouted, 'Where? Where did you see her exactly?'

A thin piece of metal, filed and honed to perfection by Dermot Dougan, gently kissed its opposite pole and activated a small carefully selected detonator. The electronic pulse sent a shiver down a thin blue wire into two pounds of semtex explosive mixed with a home-made fertiliser compound.

And then the bomb exploded.

A plastic video casing was torn apart and a shopping bag disintegrated.

If you were near enough to the bomb and could slow the world down to a snapshot in time, you would be able to hear the bomb first, see it second, and feel it third.

Those near enough that day included Billy Boyd, Antonia Browne, a handful of detectives, two railway workers, a husband looking to buy a leather shopping bag for his wife and an Asian street vendor trying to sell a bag to the husband. Those who survived first experienced an almighty bang, followed by a searing light and a shock wave that lifted everyone off their feet and threw them like autumn leaves against the street furniture.

The sound wave from the bomb hit thin glass windows causing the glass to splinter and shatter before falling downwards onto the unsuspecting public below. On many occasions the broken glass landed harmlessly on the pavement. On other occasions, the glass fell onto the human body and caused horrific cuts to the head, face and trunk.

Thrown off his feet by the shock wave and into a shop wall, Boyd lay motionless whilst Antonia Harston-Browne smashed into a litter bin, tumbled over it, and lost consciousness when she landed unceremoniously on the ground.

People further way from the immediate scene ran in panic not really knowing where to hide. In a frenzy of uncertainty, innocent members of the public crashed into each other when they sought refuge offered by the shops and offices in the area. Cars mounted pavements to get out of Oxford Street when a taxi ran into the rear of a London bus.

The Asian barrow boy selling leatherwear died instantly. He was standing directly above the bomb when it detonated and exploded outwards disembowelling him. His stomach and lower torso detached themselves from the rest of his body.

The gentleman buying the leather shopping bag for his wife was much luckier. He managed to fight for and keep his life in the coming weeks. However, he lost both legs and would probably have died had it not been for the skill and dedication of the doctors and nurses who cared for him at the nearby hospital.

Two detectives, three uniformed police constables, one member of the Intelligence Service and eleven members of the public were taken to hospital suffering from a variety of cuts and bruises inflicted as a result of what came to be recorded as the Bond Street Tube Station bomb attack.

A small bomb, but lethal when so many people were nearby. During the next fifteen minutes, four other explosions occurred in the Oxford Street area. They all contained between two and four pounds of explosive materials. They were all small bombs. All caused similar injury.

By the end of the day three people had been killed and forty-six injured. The reality of Belfast days arrived in London yet again.

The number of dead and injured was determined as much by luck as by the placing of the bombs. If a bomb was detonated when no one was around, then there was a good chance that only damage would occur, with slight injury to distant passers-by. If you were too near when the bomb exploded then you either died or were maimed.

Small bombs hurt as much as big bombs.

Eamonn Murphy was telling jokes. The van headed north on the A1 through Hertfordshire as adrenalin flowed freely. It had been a successful day: a good day for the cause.

Eamonn joked, 'Here's one! Here's one now. Are you ready?'

The van occupants listened carefully for the next rendition.

'Go on, Eamonn,' enthused Bridget.

'Here are the football results. Tottenham Hotspur two. Arsenal nil.'

'What's funny about that?' challenged Bridget.

'Nothing, but how do you feel about Derry Brigade five, London nil?' quipped Eamonn bursting into an uncontrollable fit of laughter.

The others joined in, seeing the hilarious side of his remarks. There was no remorse for the day's proceedings either intended or offered. The day had been one of pure business.

Studying the map thoughtfully, Sean turned the pages of the atlas plotting the course north and decided, 'Right, up here to Scotch Corner, Eamonn, then over the back roads. We'll be in Newcastle by nightfall. I'll ring Damien then. With luck we'll be home for a while unless there's more business to be doing.'

Dermot stroked the cat. She licked his fingers. She had found her master, purred lovingly, and snuggled into the Irishman.

Eamonn enquired, 'What will Damien be saying now, Sean?'

Looking out of the window into the English countryside, Sean thought of Liam who he knew was living somewhere out there. He thought of Liam's sister, Shelagh, with whom he had gradually fallen in love since the killing of Hugh Devenney at Shantallow. He wondered what Liam would make of his love affair with Shelagh now.

Sean shook off his daydream and answered Eamonn with, 'Damien will be saying that five bombs means five more steps towards peace. Five more reasons why the Brits should do what we say. Five more reasons for continuing the armed struggle. Bloody heroes, that's what we'll be. Five bombs in one day. Bloody heroes for the cause, make no mistake. We'll bomb the Brits to our way of thinking, that we will.'

Back in London, Billy Boyd checked on his men in hospital. Boyd was fine. So too was Antonia Harston-Browne. They were both shaken but no bones broken. They had talked about bombs for a long time. Now they had experienced them first hand. It was an experience they would not forget.

In Oxford Street, what remained of the dead had been put into body bags for the trip to the mortuary.

There were no jokes in the West End that night.

1990

Hustle and bustle adequately described the large general office in New Scotland Yard. It was a hive of activity with telephones ringing incessantly. Definitely not the place to be if you wanted peace and quiet. It was the headquarters of the specialist crime unit.

The recently promoted Detective Inspector sat looking out over the London rooftops searching for inspiration. He tapped the ballpoint pen on his knee and felt quite frustrated at recent events.

Present in his office were Antonia Harston-Browne and a selection of well-informed special crime unit detectives. They numbered twelve drawn together because of their detailed knowledge of one particular terrorist attack. They had other credentials though. Each distinct experts, specialists on various facets of Irish terrorism, and every individual knew how the so-called 'intelligence system' worked. There was one inspector, two sergeants and nine constables. But the team was tired having suffered too many long hours and too few successes. The secret meeting was about to start.

Boyd's office door closed and proceedings commenced.

The door bore the legend now familiar to many in that building: 'Detective Inspector W. M. Boyd, Special Crime Unit'. The corridor outside quietened and the occupants of the office settled down.

Swivelling his leather armchair round to face the group, Boyd rubbed his eyes with his hands, rolled his neck from shoulder to shoulder in order to relax his muscles, and put his pen down on the blotter. He looked around, acknowledging his special friends, and spoke to his team.

'Thanks for coming in, everyone. Help yourself to coffee. The pot is full. This seems a good time to catch up on things and look toward jobs in the pipeline. Toni is our contact for this team as you know. Thanks to you people we have been putting the current picture together and since Toni is with us, she can outline the position so far. Toni! Over to you!'

Swinging her red hair across her shoulders, Toni smoothed out her skirt and glanced down at her papers. Nodding towards Boyd, Toni looked up and spoke to the assembly, 'Thanks, Inspector, here it is then. 1988 saw the three PIRA operatives killed out in Gibraltar when they were putting together an attack on the colony. Following on from then, Michael Stone killed three of the mourners at one of the funerals of the Gibraltar three in Belfast. It gets much worse. Two army corporals are killed when they get mixed up with a Republican funeral in Belfast. Do you remember the television pictures? They were horrific. Last year the MP, Ian Gow, was blown up in his car here on the mainland in Sussex. Then we had the bomb at the Deal barracks, school of music. We lost eleven bandsmen there. Put simply, we are being blitzed. The list is only the main jobs. I haven't bored you with the little ones. No sooner is a player removed from the picture than another takes his place. Or her place for that matter. Now, I want you to look at the wall chart over here.'

Walking purposefully to the rear of the room, Toni casually examined a chart on the wall and used a wooden pointer to guide her captive audience through the complex information displayed before her.

'These are particular attacks on the mainland between 1986 and 1990. They all have one thing in common. Anyone cares to hazard a guess?' she ventured.

A number of voices replied in virtual unison, 'Small bombs!'

Toni responded, 'Correct. Somewhere out there we have a small, dedicated, active service unit. Their only function appears to be to put down small devices whenever and wherever they can. Now, on its own, and in comparison with the matters I have just referred to, this doesn't appear to be too much of a problem...'

A female detective sergeant called Anthea intervened, to the amusement of the group, saying, 'Unless you are the one that's underneath one of those bombs, that doesn't really seem to be a problem.'

Acknowledging the remark, Toni offered, 'Yes, you are absolutely right. Tell me about it. I've still got the marks from the Bond Street bomb. What I'm really trying to get at, of course, is the tactic. Hit, run, hide and return when we least expect it. Keep the propaganda in the news. Keep people frightened. Keep us on our toes. They try to stay one step ahead whilst we always seem to be one step behind. We need to try and change that situation - sooner rather than later, I suggest.'

Boyd joined in, 'The way to win is to be ahead of the game either by knowing what they are going to do or anticipating what they may do.'

Toni responded, 'As far as this team of ours is concerned, I want to thank you all for the work put in on this ASU. I think we are starting to see the light at last.'

'How's that then?' enquired one of the detectives.

'In 1988,' replied Toni, 'When the Oxford Street bombs went off, we picked up the investigation and this team has been more or less on the case ever since. Probably because some of you were in the immediate area of Bond Street station when that one went off. Anyway, since then Boyd and I reckon that we've looked at every photograph taken in London on that day. This, of course, is thanks to your endeavours. I think every one of us here would like to catch the people who put bombs down without any thought for others.'

There was a general chorus of 'Hear! Hear!'

The telephone on Boyd's desk rang and he answered it and quickly dealt with a query from an external office.

Ignoring the interruption, Toni turned her attention to the wall by her side and continued, 'On the wall chart here,' she gestured with the pointer, 'We have a chronicle of PIRA attacks which we are attributing to our target ASU. We shall be studying these more carefully during the remainder of the week. Indeed, I know Inspector Boyd already has one of you putting together a comprehensive forensic package on this. Proving links between the attacks, etc, etc. Your police world, not mine. Now, can I turn your attention to the video?'

Moving to the television in the corner of the room, Toni found the display panel, switched the set on, and pressed the 'play' button. The colour television quickly hummed to life and the first sequences of the videotape began to feed through onto the screen. The medium size screen settled to show the shadowy picture of a man. It was a very old black and white still photograph.

Antonia announced, 'This is a photograph of a man called Sean

Brady. It was taken in 1977 in Londonderry. Brady, we believe, at that time was about 20 years of age.'

By activating the remote button, the video sequence ran on. She didn't really need her notes but Antonia glanced down to refresh her memory and pressed on. The sound of telephones ringing in the outer office could be heard in the background.

Toni revealed, 'This is a photograph of Eamonn Murphy, also a Derry man. He is noted for his driving abilities. He's a little older and has been questioned a few times by the RUC but released every time. The third photograph is of Dermot Dougan. We know he is a bomb maker.'

'How come you are so sure of that then, my love?' asked one of the officers. It was a Lancashire accent.

She replied, 'From the usual intelligence sources. He has never been arrested, never been imprisoned and, as far as we can tell, this is the only photograph of him we have.'

'Pretty usual for a bomb maker,' offered Boyd.

Toni agreed, 'About right there, Inspector.'

The group of investigators watched closely as the next frame came into focus on the screen when Toni ran the video on.

'Number four is Bridget Duffy,' advised Toni. 'She has been held on a number of occasions by the RUC at Castlereagh. Indeed, she has been arrested four times under the Prevention of Terrorism Act but never convicted. My friends in Derry tell me she is scared stiff of the PIRA hierarchy. More scared of them than us. No, I can see you all about to ask. She has never worked for us, although obviously we have tried to get her onto our side in the past.'

'Yet they, PIRA, still use her?' A question came from the floor to the approval of the team.

'Indeed! Strange, isn't it!' observed Toni. 'Perhaps she has some kind of death wish. I don't know.'

There was a short pause before Toni went on, 'The next photograph is of Hugh Devenney. A schoolteacher from Londonderry. Brother of Damien Devenney who is one of the main men in Derry PIRA. The next is Seamus Rafferty. Both Rafferty and Hugh Devenney were killed by the last one, number seven, Liam Connelly, son of Declan Connelly. Declan Connelly scored an own goal in Limavady, circa 1976. Declan was a bloody good terrorist. One of their best in the province.'

The detective sergeant, Anthea, followed the silent video show with interest and enquired, 'Where does all this take us then? Anywhere?'

'Absolutely,' replied Toni. 'Let me explain. Between 1976 and 1979 this man, Hugh Devenney, recruited on behalf of his brother, Damien, a bunch of terrorists whom we reckon have been together ever since. The team has a bomb maker in Dermot Dougan. A driver in Eamonn

Murphy. A bomb planter and targetter in Bridget Duffy and a leader and killer in Sean Brady. We know Bridget Duffy is reckoned to be a master of disguise and Brady is an out and out killer. He was close friends with Liam Connelly. There was a bust- up of some kind. Liam Connelly killed Rafferty and the schoolteacher and he's never been seen since.'

'What was the bust-up about?' asked a male detective.

'That depends on who you talk to,' replied Toni. 'However, at the end of the day Liam Connelly is wanted by the RUC for a double murder on his own people. PIRA also want him for killing their own men.'

Boyd growled, 'We should give him a medal when we find him. Two less to worry about, thanks to him.'

'Yes, that may be so,' suggested Toni, 'But there is the possibility that Liam is serving his penance by hitting back here in London in order that he can return to the PIRA fold. We just don't know.'

Boyd offered, 'I don't like it. I can't live with that one. It doesn't ring true. What really happened in the bust-up, I wonder? Any ideas, Toni?'

Deliberately ignoring the remark, Toni went on, 'I believe Connelly, Dougan, Murphy, Duffy and Brady are the ASU we are searching for. Let me explain to you all why I believe that to be the case.'

Helping himself to a beaker of coffee, Boyd added two sachets of sugar and settled down into his chair.

Toni continued, 'The 1977 photographs I have shown you were taken by an army patrol in Londonderry. Now, I know the people in the photographs have changed slightly with the passage of time, but please note the following photographs taken in the Oxford Street area at the time of the Bond Street attack.'

Humming into life again, the video ran through into the next sequence as Toni used the wooden pointer to direct their attention to the television screen.

Toni announced, 'I will suggest to you that the photographs here are of Sean Brady, Eamonn Murphy and Bridget Duffy. The three are in a van parked in Wigmore Street. This street, as you all know, runs parallel to Oxford Street. A security guard from a nearby department store took the photographs because he thought they were about to carry out some kind of robbery nearby. Apparently the two men were looking suspicious. They were then joined by a woman and they drove off at quite high speed. There is a witness statement from the security guard in Anthea's filing system. Unfortunately, on the day in question the guard did not ring the police. One of your guys, Inspector, collected these on the follow-up house to house enquiries in the area.'

Boyd nodded in agreement.

One of the younger detectives enquired, 'I hope that isn't the whole case. I presume we have more than that?'

Boyd intervened, 'No, we still have to make the case. Stay with us for a moment while we run it by you. Go on, Toni. Take us through the sequence.'

Continuing, Toni stated, On its own, that isn't much. Now look at the security video film taken from Bond Street station provided by the British Transport police.'

The video ran on. The picture of a woman was captured in the frame and was seen to be identical to the female in the photograph taken in Wigmore Street.

'And again, a further photograph from a Japanese holiday-maker; the photograph is of his wife, but note the woman in the background,' counselled Toni.

The group leaned forward to take in a better view.

'I reckon that is Bridget Duffy getting into a van driven by Eamonn Murphy. See? There's Sean Brady in the passenger seat,' suggested Toni.

The group studied the picture, nodding agreement. The video ran on, flickering in the corner.

'And there is my proof to you,' added Toni.

The video displayed an enlarged photograph of the previous picture.

'Quite clearly, it is the three that I have referred to,' Toni declared emphatically.

Boyd walked into the middle of the office, smiled at Toni and continued the saga, 'It's pretty damn close. That's what I say. However, that is not the end of it all. About two weeks later, my man Mark is turning over every piece of paper that the Metropolitan Police ever produced when he finds a crime report for a stolen cat, I ask you. Anyway, it transpires that three Irishmen and an Irish woman, a good looker by all accounts, rented a flat up near Kilburn High Road. They paid the rent, kept their heads down and gave no trouble to the landlord. Problem is when they went, it was the day of the bombings, and they took with them the neighbour's cat. Apparently this tame kitten attached itself to one of the Irish blokes and the owner hardly ever saw it. When they went so did the cat presumably with the Irish. Mark's team went up and got some artists impressions. This is the result,' offered Boyd handing out sketches. They were A4 size, in pencil.

'Now, I know you've seen the sketches before, but now compare the sketches with the photographs you've just seen. I say this because I reckon the fourth member of the team, who kept the cat, is one Dermot Dougan, not present in Wigmore Street. But why? Anyone?' probed Boyd.

A number of voices piped up. 'Tidying up? Clean up the flat? Hide any loose gear? Phoned in the bomb warnings? Drove a back-up car to the West End? Come on, guv. Which one?'

Boyd chuckled and offered, 'I don't know, but you get the idea, don't you? If he's the bomb maker, he wouldn't be putting it down in Oxford Street. He's much too valuable to risk, just two other points. The RUC tells us that at the relevant times there is no trace of any of these people in the Derry area. It doesn't actually mean a lot on its own but then it does raise the possibility that they were in London. Point two: The van that the Kilburn team left the flat in is the same colour and the same style as the one in our Japanese friend's photograph, etc, etc. Now, I add to that a list of vehicles checked by a BM patrol on a motorway service station in Yorkshire later that night, the night of the bombings. Please note that, according to our research on the vehicle sightings, one blue van remains unaccounted for The alleged owner does not exist and neither does his address. It's all false. When all this started to come together, our friends in the anti-terrorist squad searched the Kilburn flat. Nothing of use was found. Our Irish friends did a good job and swept the place clean. It was as clean as a whistle,' suggested Boyd.

There was a murmur of conjecture around the squad room.

Boyd went on, 'That brings us more or less up to date. It's my belief we have latched on to the team. This is only one of hundreds of pieces of jigsaw that we have been chasing. This is the one I like. It doesn't entirely fit, but it doesn't entirely fall down either. The photograph, artist's impressions, and the circumstantial evidence tell me we are on the right track. I also remember getting the information about an ASU moving into Kilburn from one of our Irish friends. Now, all we have to do is find them. Any problems so far?'

Anthea challenged, 'Not enough for court?'

Boyd agreed, 'No way. Find them, hunt them and catch them at it.'

Anthea enquired, 'How?'

Boyd took a deep breath and paced round the office. He looked first at Toni and then back towards Anthea. Grimacing initially, he addressed the team, 'You might as well know that neither my bosses here nor Toni's bosses really believe we are on the right track. Basically, we have a gut feeling about this which is supported by some interesting circumstances and some pretty little pictures from a holidaymaker. We have nothing else, so we are going to run with this line of enquiry until we run them all down. That way we will prove whether or not it's them or someone else. Put simply, we are going to put all our eggs in one basket for the time being. You know yourself the top landing never likes to spend time and money on gut feelings.'

Boyd let the message sink in. No one liked to be on a loser in this game but they all knew Boyd's reputation for tenacity. They also knew that Antonia Harston-Browne was supporting Boyd. The doubters weighed it up and fell in line.

Anthea was the spokesperson who chimed in first when she declared, 'Okay, so the powers-that-be don't think we are right. Well, some of them wouldn't believe you if Sean Brady walked into New Scotland Yard, rammed a bomb up the Commander's backside, lit the blue touch paper and retired. They would still want to know if we are sure. Most of them don't know where Ireland is, couldn't care less about Ireland and think the biggest problem in their tiny little world is where to park the cars at Hackney dog track. So what we do is get off our backsides and get out there and find them.'

Boyd smiled and responded, 'Thank you, I couldn't have put it better myself.'

'Just one thing, guv!' quipped Anthea.

'Go on, Anthea,' replied Boyd.

'You've nothing on Liam Connelly in the video show that makes me want to put my money on him.'

'You're right, I don't think he's in the game, but Toni disagrees.'

Toni's shoulders hunched up and the palms of her hands opened up in a gesture of resignation when she joined in with, 'I think Liam Connelly is a murderer and well capable of running this team. He could easily be a courier between PIRA and wherever they are laid up. Someone must be feeding them with money to sustain their lifestyle over here. I doubt if any of them are in full-time employment. Connelly could easily prove to be the moneyman. What I do know is this. Find Liam Connelly and we'll find Sean Brady.'

'And this is how we will do it,' revealed Boyd. 'Back to basics. The long walk. Pubs, clubs, cafes, car parks, shops, newsagents, bus stations, railway stations and anywhere we can find people. Between us we have contacts all over the country. The Irish always lead us to the Irish. Talk to the Irish to find the Irish. Gather round. This is the battle plan. The starting point is the last sighting. Yorkshire. It's on the wrong side of the Pennines for a lad like me, but no matter. That's where we start. Up north. Fill up the coffee mugs; it's going to be a long day. Toni, bottom right hand drawer of my desk, one bottle of Bushmills Irish for dispensation, if you please.'

Boyd took control and moved to centre stage.

Toni found the Irish whiskey, secured some glasses and poured the drinks. Anthea helped distribute the glasses whilst Toni settled down to listen to Boyd's battle plan. Boyd wasn't the kind of man who let life slip by. Toni liked him because he was a winner, that was becoming obvious. He liked to win and Antonia Harston-Browne backed winners. She, too, didn't like to be second in this game.

The office door remained closed into the late hours. The battle plan was drawn up. It was a good one. Toni liked it.

≈

1991
Six Months Later

His shaven head bobbed above the rest of the crowd in the busy Derry Street whilst Eugene's broad shoulders and heavy woollen overcoat gave him the appearance of a wrestler making for a Saturday afternoon bout. His sheer size dominated the walkways as he carefully picked his way through the mass of people going about their business.

Strolling into the betting shop, Eugene walked up to the kiosk where he laid his bets for the afternoon races. He waited patiently for the betting slip to be checked and stamped before nodding to the attendant and turning to leave. He pocketed the betting slip, looked up at the charts on the wall to check the going for tomorrow's races, and then stepped out of the bookmaker's into the street.

Just ten minutes to spare before he met the redhead from London, Eugene hopped onto a passing bus and made across town through the Bogside as quickly as he could.

Toni saw him coming. He was late again. If he would only grow his hair! The shaven head was a giveaway. Toni watched him bob along through the quiet park. The red-head had been on his tail for thirty minutes, or thereabouts. She was happy he wasn't being followed by anyone else.

Antonia Harston-Browne felt safe when she cut across his path and took a seat in the park where he couldn't miss seeing her.

She checked the contents of her black leather shoulder bag. Inside she removed the racing magazine and placed it on the park bench beside her. Rummaging, she found the small handgun, moved the safety catch to the 'off' position, and carefully replaced the weapon near the top part of her shoulder bag, covered only by a discarded headscarf.

The sun had come out through the grey clouds and was shining, brightly. It was far too warm for Eugene's thick woollen overcoat. The temperature was rising.

He was puffing at the long walk. Eugene was growing older, probably a stone or two overweight, and glad to see her on the park bench. Mopping his head with a handkerchief, he sat down beside her. Brooke Park, Londonderry, was reasonably quiet at this time of day. In any case this would be over in a matter of minutes.

Eugene glimpsed the racing magazine lying on the park bench between them and wondered how much money was folded inside the pages this time.

Toni saw him looking down at the magazine, could read his mind, knew she had him where she wanted him. She took the initiative and spoke first, 'You're late again. I could have made this meet ten minutes earlier and I'm supposed to be one of the so-called weaker sex. Eugene, you're grossly overweight and badly out of breath. Cut out the booze and lose the cigarettes. Get some exercise. Listen to me, you fat idle Irishman,' she snapped, 'You're no good to me dead.'

He felt like hitting her with the hammer that he called his fist. Better still, he could have shot her dead with the handgun hidden in the leather holster underneath his armpit.

Eugene bristled indignantly, 'How about a simple hello, or is that too much to ask?'

'You're right. It's too much to ask. You have five minutes to talk. I got your call. I came as soon as I could. This had better be good. I don't like these meets during the daylight hours. Give me it, now,' she ordered.

The sunshine intensified, the clouds parted and the temperature rose. Neither trusted the other fully, but the game was being acted out between them. Eugene was playing the odds, risking it all on a daytime meeting in the middle of a park in the Republican enclave of northern Derry. He was walking on the edge. All it needed was for someone from PIRA to walk by and see the two of them talking together. Questions asked of Eugene, with no apparent answers, could jeopardise him.

'As far as I can find out there is a price on Liam Connelly's head. Yer man Liam? Well, he killed Hugh Devenney and Seamus Rafferty. You know all that. I told you when it happened. Liam is over the water in England somewhere. He's probably up north. I can't see him making for London. Word would get back to Derry very quickly if he showed up in Kilburn or Luton. You'll not find him where the Irish live. He will hide, will that one. So no one knows where he is. No one really cares either, as long as he doesn't come back.'

'What about the others?' asked Toni.

'Well, I never really knew them. Damien always kept things close to his chest. He's no fool. For instance, you could work for him, for all I know,' ventured Eugene.

'Do me a favour,' she replied.

'Put it this way, Damien tells me only what he wants me to know. He's always been like that. That's why he's still walking round free. To be sure, it soon came out that Liam and Sean Brady had been doing the business for Damien all those years back. But listen to me, woman. Eamonn Murphy! Dermot Dougan! They meant nothing to me then and they mean nothing to me now. Kids on the block. That's all they ever were. Kids on the block. I do what I'm told by Damien. I'm his enforcer.

I keep him alive and I see to it that no one gets too close to him. I keep the Protestants from the UDA and the UVF out of his hair. I'm not his confidant, I'm his bodyguard,' revealed Eugene.

She deliberately looked him right in the eye and said sarcastically, 'Big word for you, Eugene. Confidant. What about the Bridget Duffy woman?'

'I didn't think she had the balls for it still. But there you go, to be sure, Yer man, Sean Brady, could be seeing to her. Bridget is a bonny woman, that's fer sure,' he replied.

'Why didn't you know this years ago?' Toni asked.

'Because Damien didn't tell me years ago, you silly bitch. How many times must I tell you? I killed and maimed for him but I didn't organise his bombing campaign,' said Eugene.

'Okay, where are they now? What's the current word on them? Come on, out with it, Eugene.'

Eugene knew she wanted them for the events in London and elsewhere on the mainland. Cocky and arrogant, he spoke up, 'Sure, that information doesn't come cheap, lady,' suggested Eugene looking away from her and across the park, deliberately ignoring her. 'It can be pretty expensive, that's fer sure now.'

Her eyebrows rose slightly but she challenged, 'What price is it?'

Eugene's confidence grew. He allowed time to digest the moment, swallowed hard and countered, 'Let's say fifty thousand pounds.'

'No, Eugene, let's say two bullets in the back of the head delivered by South Armagh brigade. You! Why you'd be dumped in a ditch with a booby-trapped bomb round you. Don't push me on this one. You'll be rewarded when it's over and when I decide. Now speak up and tell me, lest I drop your name to the next Republican prisoners that we take into Castlereagh. I wonder if they would like to know that you were talking to an officer from Intelligence? A few photographs of you and me together taken by my friends might just raise one or two questions.'

Eugene Kelly's head started to sweat again, partly from the sunshine, partly from the encounter with the woman.

'You wouldn't do that to me after all the years I've worked for yous? You'd be nowhere without me.'

'Watch me, Eugene. Watch me. I'll do it. There's no such thing as an indispensable man. I'm a woman. I should know. No one messes me about. I am winner, not a loser. I don't like being second. You know that.'

Rising from the park bench, she lifted the racing magazine and made to leave. She was back in command again and she knew it.

'Wait! Wait! Okay! I'll tell you.'

Antonia froze and took the opportunity to check out the surroundings. Seconds ticked by before she looked into his eyes as if considering the offer. She would make him squirm a little more.

Finally Antonia exhaled loudly. Her mind made up, she sat back down beside him and said, 'Eugene! Are you listening to me?'

'Yes,' he replied anxiously.

'Don't ever push your luck again. You have thirty seconds. Talk!'

Her voice had been cold and flat with hardly a trace of emotion.

Eugene thought she would take great delight in tipping off someone from South Armagh about him. He reckoned she must make a harsh lover for a man. God! She scared the life out of him at times. He rattled off all he knew as quickly as he could.

'Yer man, Liam Connelly, went to the north of England. That's all I know. No one really knows where. Sean Brady is in Tramore in the Republic staying near the sea in a guest house or a holiday flat, something like that. He's with a woman. I reckon that will be Bridget Duffy. Eamonn Murphy is living somewhere near Leeds in Yorkshire. Dermot Dougan is near to him. Perhaps only five or ten miles away from Eamonn. I'm told now that they share a woman, to pass the time of day, you understand. They are lying low waiting for the word,' revealed Eugene.

'Where is Tramore?' Antonia asked.

'On the coast, just south of Waterford,' replied Eugene. 'It's in the Republic, woman.'

'What word do our friends all wait for, Eugene? What's going on?'

'The word that will come to Damien Devenney from Seamus Kelty that it is time for the team to hit London again,' replied Eugene.

'Who will bring the word?'

'Damien's decision! I don't know. What I do know is that I heard Damien on the telephone the other night talking to Kelty down in Dundalk. They were talking in that funny way about fishing rights being renewed and such like. I know what that means. Seamus Kelty had been to see Brady down in Tramore. You'd best be getting back before another one goes off in London, girl.' advised Eugene.

'How do you know it's that team?'

'Do people like that go on holiday in Leeds and stay indoors most of the time? Believe me, woman. I heard the telephone conversation. Damien drove to a public telephone kiosk the other side of Letterkenny in order to make it. I ran shotgun for him and watched his back. He made the call and he was told to keep things quiet until the New Year. Something about peace talks and Dublin. I know how these units work. That's the team. Kelty and his friends in the south think they are heroes. Try the little villages outside Leeds. I heard Wetherby mentioned. Is there such a place? Boston, near Wetherby?' suggested Eugene.

'And Liam leads them?' Antonia asked.

Eugene greeted the chance to get even when he twisted the truth

114

and prevaricated, 'Yes! Send him home in a body bag. If you find them by Christmas, they will be getting ready to continue the struggle in the New Year. They will strike at the Houses of Parliament, Downing Street, Whitehall, places like that. They will strike in the centre of London and rip out the heart of government. I've heard them talking. The war in Northern Ireland will be won on the streets of London. That's what they say. Sean Brady is the most committed member of the team. He will die for the cause. You will not take him alive.'

Pausing to take breath, Eugene drawled on, 'One more thing. Dermot Dougan has a cat. It's a joke amongst the hierarchy in the provisional army council. They're calling Brady and the ASU the pussy cats. Can you believe it? That's it. I've no more to tell you.'

Eugene, head down, looked directly into the ground. He dared not look into her eyes. He disliked informing on his own countrymen..

Toni recognised the look in his eyes: Greyness, fatigue and despair, from a man who lived on the brink; a man who walked the fine edge that all touts knew. The fine edge that existed when a man lived a lie every day of his life. One slip could end his life. For a brief moment she felt sorry for him. He was just a tout trapped in the system. And the system could only end if she freed him or if PIRA killed him for touting.

'Thank you,' she replied and then pushed the magazine towards him along the bench.

There was a picture of a horse jumping the sticks at Chepstow on the front cover of the glossy magazine.

Toni stood up and walked away, resetting the sunglasses on her nose. She would write up her notes and make for a secure telephone.

Before she had reached the park gates, Eugene picked up the magazine, scanned the pages and pocketed the few hundred pounds she had left for him. Why did she feed him money like this, he thought? To make him come back for more? She'd penetrated his mind, knew his weakness, knew his greed. He hated her and loved her at the same time.

Eugene continued leafing through the magazine. Between the pages was a note giving a figure. The figure indicated how much money had been put in a London bank account for him towards his retirement. He could not get to it, but he knew how much was there.

Perking up, Eugene studied the form for the next day's racing. and ran his fingers down the list of runners and riders. He was playing the odds again.

Antonia was happy. Boyd had been right. The two Irishmen his team had traced to the Wetherby area would prove to be Dermot Dougan and Eamonn Murphy. Boyd had banked on Leeds, calling it the centre of Yorkshire. From Leeds, he had worked outwards, following every piece of tittle-tattle until he had arrived at Boston Spa and Wetherby. The two locations were only four or five miles apart and situated just off the AI road, not all that far from Leeds. The man with the cat in Boston Spa was obviously Dermot Dougan. The man down the road in Wetherby would prove to be Eamonn Murphy. She still could not figure out where Bridget Duffy was though. Eugene had mentioned two women. One with Sean Brady and one with Eamonn and Dermot. No matter! The trap was closing. All would become clear soon. A holiday in the beautiful town of Waterford was called for, and the search would need to move into the north of England. Once Sean Brady had been located in Tramore there would only be Liam Connelly to find. Eugene had proved more than useful, she thought.

Toni resolved to keep the matter secret. The fewer people who knew about Eugene, the better. Loose talk could result in a leak of information. A leak of information into the wrong ear could result in the demise of a tout. Eugene needed to be protected. There was no need to tell the likes of Boyd, not until she was forced to.

≈

The small guest house looking out over Tramore Bay, towards Brownstown Head on the southernmost coast of Eire, was named the 'Saratoga Shack'. It was situated about eight miles from Waterford and was owned by the infamous Muriel St Clair.

Muriel St Clair was said to be the mastermind behind the local black-market in 'poteen': an illegal alcoholic drink, made from potatoes and famous for a kick like a mule. It was no surprise to find the area awash with intrigue. The Tramore region has a long and mysterious history of smuggling, as do many other parts of the rugged, but beautiful, southern Irish coastline. The area is not dissimilar to that in Cornwall and the south-west peninsula of England.

The Atlantic Ocean hammered mercilessly against the daunting cliffs, showering the rocks with a million droplets of spray.

The summer sunshine pierced the windows of the hostelry and casting beams of light on the dishevelled bedclothes where the young couple made love earnestly.

He took her fiercely, with little consideration for her own desires. When it was eventually over, he turned onto his back and reached for the cigarettes.

Sean offered her one and, when she declined, lit his own and reclined against the pillows. She nuzzled into his chest and blew the hairs on his torso as he smoked has cigarette

It was the first time Sean had been able to relax for about three years. Once Seamus Kelty had summoned him, he had returned to

116

Northern Ireland and collected Shelagh Connelly. He and Shelagh had travelled south to Dundalk where he had met Kelty who had then briefed him on the mainland campaign ahead and what needed to be done. Once Brady had been given his brief he had taken Shelagh south and holidayed in Tramore with the good wishes of Seamus Kelty and the good moneys of the Provisional Irish Republican Army.

The two were happy. Shelagh Connelly had fallen in love with Sean Brady. Love had grown from the days on Inch Island when Bridget Duffy had taken her there and looked after her following the terrible events in the Shantallow house. Sean had been the only man in her life for many months. Gradually she had fallen for him. Now she loved him deeply. She loved him not like a sister loves a brother but as a woman loves a man.

It was morning and the setting was one of tranquillity. Sean was thinking ahead, wondering how best to carry out the brief given to him by Seamus Kelty. The leading PIRA man had given Sean a menu of terrorist activity to choose from.

Propping himself up on one elbow, Sean roused Shelagh and asked, 'Shelagh! Where's that brother of yours gone to?'

'Sure, I told you I would never tell you that now, Sean. I promised Liam I would never tell.'

'But once you said, did you not, that he would go and join Padraigh O'Toole?' suggested Sean.

'Aye, that I did,' she answered.

'And did he, Shelagh? Did he join the man, Padraigh?' asked Sean.

Shelagh was mystified. She wasn't used to being questioned at this time in the morning and wondered what all this was leading to. She looked into his steel grey eyes as she gently smoothed his jet black hair with her hands and said, 'I told you, Sean. Sure, the rule in the house was never to speak of where Padraigh lived.'

'Yes, but that was before I had decided to make an honest woman of you and get you and me married.'

'Married? Married!' She shouted joyfully. 'Are you serious, Sean?'

Shelagh jumped up from the crumpled bedclothes, exposing her firm naked breasts.

'That I am, woman. Why do you think I ask now? I'll be needing to ask Liam and yer uncle Padraigh to the wedding, that I will.'

'But it's all so quick, Sean,' replied Shelagh swinging her legs over the side of the bed as if to dress.

Sean pulled her back into bed by the waist and held her tightly.

'Quick is it? How long have I known you, woman? Since you were a wee girl, that it is. Now, marry me and have done with it!' said Sean.

'Yes!' she said, 'Yes! That I will.'

They wrestled as lovers do. She pulled him over on top of her and he responded immediately. This time he was gentle and loving, taking his time to satisfy her. By the time they had finished, he had the address in Carlisle where Liam could be found.

They made love most of the day.

At nightfall they slept, and by the following morning the way ahead had been decided in Sean Brady's mind. He needed two return tickets to Amsterdam, a couple of shovels, a little bit of equipment and Liam.

≈

SOME MONTHS LATER

Dermot Dougan was feeding the cat. They had called her 'Scrappy'. The kitten had grown faster than any of them had imagined. He placed the food down beside the paraffin heater, stroked the cat's back and settled by the window.

Eamonn Murphy was due with Bridget in the van any minute. The weather in the village of Boston Spa was horrible. It was snowing heavily and the January wind howled round the detached house Sean had rented before he left for Ireland and his meeting with Seamus Kelty. It was one of a number of houses in the north of England that had been rented for long-term holiday use by tourists.

Scrappy heard the noise first. She postured at the door and purred angrily as Eamonn and Bridget walked up the path. She was Dermot's cat and she did not take too kindly to intruders.

Hearing the crunch of the snow on the footpath, Dermot realised his friends had returned from their Christmas visit to Amsterdam. He went to the door, nudged Scrappy from his feet and welcomed his friends.

'Come you in now. Sure, the snow is a terrible thing, is it not? Have you had a good trip now?' enquired Dermot, ushering them in towards the fire and helping them from their wet clothes.

Bridget kissed him on the cheek to acknowledge his welcome and replied, 'Aye! Sure, it was a good break, Dermot, even if it was only a few weeks. How goes it with you?'

Dermot answered, 'Too damn cold, to be sure. How about you, Eamonn? Are yer well, my boy?'

He clasped Eamonn by the hand and shook it firmly.

Eamonn responded, 'That I am, Dermot. Sure is good to see you. How's that damn cat?' Eamonn bent down to stroke Scrappy.

Dermot poked the coal fire, saying, 'The cat's well, Eamonn. Come, eat, hot drinks, settle by the fire and tell me of Amsterdam. How is that beautiful place? It's so long since I've been there.'

Pulling a chair closer to the fire, Eamonn knocked the residue snow from his boots into the fireplace, looked through the window, and motioned with his head towards the fields beyond whilst saying, 'And what of our friends?'

'Still there,' nodded Dermot. 'They have been watching us all winter. When you went there was a flurry of comings and goings for a day or two, but I think it was because they thought I might have gone with you. Be careful what you say, my friends. No loose talk.'

Dermot moved to the window and closed the curtains tight, denying the distant watchers hidden across the fields any sight of them.

'Did you get any Christmas presents in Amsterdam, my friends?'

Eamonn smiled broadly and replied, 'Just a box of crackers, Dermot. Just a box of crackers.'

Bridget wanted to laugh, but instead she gestured with her hands and made a sign with her fingers, like an explosion taking place, and mouthed the word 'Puff!'

A fold-up ordnance survey map of northern England was produced with a number of crosses marked in red ink showing wooded areas.

Eamonn smoothed the creases out so that Dermot could inspect the symbols properly.

Bridget held her thumbs up.

Dermot knew then that the explosives and detonators Sean had sent his friends to Amsterdam to collect had been successfully infiltrated back into the United Kingdom. He knew the crosses on the map corresponded with where the explosives were hidden.

Sean smiled, reached for the Jameson whiskey, and poured three large tumblers. He raised his glass and proposed a toast, 'To absent friends at Christmas,' he said, 'Wherever they are.'

Dermot, Eamonn and Bridget turned to the curtains hiding the snow-covered fields outside and in a gesture of mutual arrogance and defiance raised their glasses to the watchers and toasted, 'Absent friends.'

The three drank. There was no further loose talk.

Across the fields, about half a mile from the house, the snow fluttered down on four men who had been digging up the country lane for the last six weeks. They were workmen under contract to the local electricity board and local council. Once the trench at the side of the road had been completed, new plastic pipes containing state of the art wiring could be introduced to the system that served the village of Boston Spa. The wiring would be buried in the trench at the side of the road and another isolated area of Yorkshire would be dragged into the twentieth century. The workmen were in direct line with the detached house where the three Irish people lived. The four labourers had absolutely no idea that the three members of the Provisional Irish Republican Army suspected they were surveillance officers working for the intelligence services. Indeed, the occupants of Boston Spa did not realise that their small village was the centre of a significant counter-terrorist operation.

The detached house at 312 Main Street, Boston Spa, was bordered extensively at the rear and two sides by fields. The topography of the land made it so. The main road passed the front door of the house and connected Boston Spa with the rest of the world. Near to the detached four-bed roomed house lay the old village rectory with its crumbling facade and overgrown shrubbery. A new coat of paint would not have gone amiss. The rectory building was three storeys high and had seen better days. In the top storey, one small window overlooked number 312.

Beyond the ageing curtains, working in virtual silence and with minimum movement, lay two of Boyd's men. Jeans and tee shirts, covered by warm winter survival kit, were the order of the day. They were both experts in surveillance work. One relaxed and took rest whilst the other manned the high-powered binoculars that linked to sophisticated cameras and 'state of the art' technical and surveillance equipment.

When their eyes became strained, they changed places. One worked keeping watch whilst the other one relaxed. This continued for twelve hours. During the night they changed shifts with other members of the team, wrote up their reports and handed them to Anthea so that she could analyse the content for Boyd by eight o'clock every morning. It was going to be a long job, but no one minded that. The trap was beginning to close.

In the nearby police control unit, Boyd took a telephone call from Antonia Harston-Browne. She was speaking from Athlone, in the centre of the Republic of Eire.

'Yes, Toni. It's Boyd. How did you make out?'

'Hi! It's a bad line. Can you hear me?' she asked.

'Yes. Quite clearly,' replied Boyd pressing the scramble mode on the telephone.

'The Garda eventually tracked them up through County Waterford. Our friend Sean has been staying at a quiet little guest house on the coast road between Fennor and Tramore, just outside Waterford. They only left there a week or so ago. It's been a fairly long job. Is your button down?'

Checking the scramble device, Boyd responded, 'Yes.'

'You will not believe who he has been with down here,' remarked.

'Who?' asked Boyd.

'One Shelagh Connelly of Shantallow,' replied Toni.

'Sister of our missing link, Liam?' claimed Boyd.

'Exactly,' responded Toni, 'And very lovey-dovey they both are. Love's young dream, I believe you call it. Unfortunately, the scent ran out at Athlone. Don't bother with the map. I'll save you the trouble. It's slap bang in the middle of the Republic. Anyway, you know how hard it is down here. The whole place is full of country lanes. It's virtually impossible to keep an eye on someone. They look as if they have been on one long honeymoon. I can't quite make it out. What I can tell you is that Sean bought two plane tickets for Amsterdam. He got them from a travel agent in Dublin just before Christmas. He posted them off. I don't know who to. Any ideas, Boyd?'

'I can tell you that. Some mutual friends have just returned from Holland. Are Sean and Shelagh wanted for anything over there?'

Toni reacted, 'The Garda won't touch them since they've done nothing wrong down here. They're both as clean as a whistle, would you believe? One thing is for sure, though,' she coughed and cleared her throat. 'They must be headed back up into the province, presumably to meet up with Liam. They are travelling in a hire car. This could mean that Liam is back in favour.'

'Yes,' agreed Boyd, 'But can you definitely tie Liam to Shelagh and Sean with a positive sighting?'

'No, it is my gut feeling, Boyd. That's all. My presumption makes sense but then you know me. Have Faith, Mister Policeman. It's all we've got left. I'm not one for taking you up the garden path,' said Toni.

Boyd thought for a moment about his friend's remark then said, 'When are you back this way?'

'I need to speak with people here. What's your news?' she enquired.

'You were right, Toni. Well, we both were really. I have the others over here under the eye. There is no change. Just back from a holiday in Amsterdam. The cat man stayed behind. Nothing exciting. We're just waiting for them all to get together again. It has to be sooner rather than later. Don't you agree?'

Toni responded, 'Not necessarily so. We'll have to keep playing it by ear. Speak to you later. By the way, Boyd!'

'Yes!' he answered.

Toni declared, 'Keep warm!'

She cut the connection and walked through the centre of Athlone into the waiting car. Toni drove north into Ulster, skirting Lough Ree and taking in the counties of Roscommon and Sligo. Crossing the border north of Enniskillen, she slept the night in the province once her business had been completed. Business which she would not impart to Boyd.

Not enjoying jurisdiction in the Republic, Toni performed no more than a friendly liaison role with officers attached to the Garda special branch. Eire is a foreign country outside the United Kingdom. The sovereignty of the Republic had to be respected and Toni had ensured that that was the case. However, in some parts of the security forces in the Republic, it was noted that a common enemy to the democratic process was in existence. PIRA!

Eire is a sprawling country with a relaxed road system. Dundalk and Dublin are connected by a forty-four miles long highway known as the Nl. The halfway point is in the general area of Drogheda. It was to this location Seamus Kelty, drove.

Turning off the NI on the outskirts of Drogheda, Seamus parked the car and entered the telephone kiosk. When his call was answered, he listened carefully to the strong Irish accent on the other end of the telephone, memorised the instructions from the leadership of the organisation, and replaced the telephone receiver without comment.

Returning to his vehicle, Seamus continued his journey towards Clogherhead where he used a further telephone kiosk.

Seamus spent the remainder of the day using a variety of telephone kiosks close to the NI highway. On each occasion, and by a variety of phrases and different sayings, he invited selected acquaintances to commence the fishing expedition he had referred to months previously.

Kelty was tired by the time he returned to his home outside Dundalk but it had been worth it. He drank liberally from a bottle of Jameson whiskey and slept the night away.

Seamus had activated a major assault on the English mainland. The following morning he used his own telephone to ring his contact in the organisation's leadership.

'Hello!' said the contact.

'It's the fishing guide,' stated Seamus. 'All the fishing rods have been taken for summer. The bait is good. I have no more lines to let out.'

'Thank you,' said the voice.

The telephone line went dead.

Seamus Kelty donned his waterproofs, selected a suitable rod and went fishing for the day down by the river. It was time for him to relax. The day was overcast, but the fishing was good with the correct fly that glided over the surface and tempted those beneath.

From various parts of the United Kingdom cars and vans were either hired or garaged for impending use. Train seats were booked and ferry passages reserved. Money from secret bank accounts in false names was withdrawn and delivered by the couriers.

The Provos' sleepers had been activated.

Moustaches were grown, hair was dyed and the two-day growth became a beard. Explosives were unearthed from hidden country hides and quietly relocated. Weapons were cleaned and ammunition checked. The agreed targets were discussed and verified for the final time. The planned attacks had been sanctioned from above. The word had been passed. The war of terrorism was reaching a climax. There was no going back. The target was once again the mainland.

The heart of the attack lay in London.

≈
1993

Commander James Herbert was under pressure.

The Metropolitan policeman's desk was covered with the clutter of office work. The trays overflowed and the ink blotter needed changing. The two telephones on his desk continually obstructed him as he tried to sort paperwork into different piles of importance. He liked to sort out the critical things first and then work downwards to the mundane. He busied himself glancing at the reports as he prioritised his morning's work.

Of the two telephones on his desk, one was blue and the other grey. The blue one connected him to the New Scotland Yard network, whilst the grey one acted as a direct line to his counterpart in the intelligence community.

Herbert had spent most of his police service in plain clothes. From a junior detective in the West End of London, he had risen through the ranks of the drug squad, the central robbery squad and the anti-terrorist branch. Now he was in charge of the special crime unit.

Commander Herbert was no ordinary copper. He had got to the top by being the best there was. The criminals feared him and his men would run through a brick wall for him. He was a leader who enjoyed the total respect of his men. There were few in the police service who could make such a claim.

The blue 'phone rang. The Commander answered it immediately.

'Send him in.'

Herbert replaced the telephone and waited for his guest to be shown through the door by his secretary. There were about one hundred intelligence reports a week crossing the Commander's desk. They all told him the same thing. They were coming. No one knew quite where or when, but they were coming, that was for sure. Indeed, some were already here. Herbert had some harsh decisions to make. He had to provide a defensive mechanism for London. He knew, as everyone else in the intelligence world knew, that PIRA would strike at the heart of London. The Commander also knew that he did not have a bottomless pot of money to fund every operation in the United Kingdom.

Boyd was shown in.

'Morning, Commander,' said Boyd.

'Good day, William. Please be seated. I have bad news I'm afraid. Coffee?'

Commander Herbert did not like the pleasantries of a secretary fussing after him. He could tend to himself and poured Boyd coffee before a reply was made.

'Thank you,' acknowledged Boyd as he reached for the coffee and sat down in the plush armchair.

The office was large, with a dark blue carpet extending from wall to wall. In one corner there was a sizeable mahogany table, with six chairs placed around the outside of it. This was the place where the big decisions were made.

Boyd took the spoon, helped himself to two sugars and stirred the coffee thoughtfully.

The Commander continued, 'I'm closing down your operation in the north, Inspector. It's only right that I tell you why ...'

'But...!' Boyd was about to argue when Commander Herbert raised his hand and stopped him.

'I haven't got the money to keep you afloat in Yorkshire, Inspector. The financial year ends on 31st March 1993. It's February next week. I can't sustain you until the first of April and I can't bring forward any money from next year's budget. Don't shout at me, Boyd! It's politicians and finance officers who run the bloody police force now, not coppers.'

The Commander's cynical frustration boiled over. 'Oh yes, I know the Treasury and the Home Office have promised money. I'm sure it will come. Probably too bloody late. I'm closing you down through lack of funds. It's as simple as that.'

'Wrong decision, sir,' suggested Boyd.

'Agreed, Inspector. No money to pay you anymore. You have a ton of intelligence on the group. Now pull the team out. Send them home for a rest and get them down here to bolster the City within the next month. I need to rotate the teams around. Remember, I don't want tired men. They are no good to me. Rest them well. The attacks will be here and they will be soon. I want you out on the ground with that Cumbrian nose sniffing the bastards out. Leave Dermot and his friends to the Yorkshire force. Care and maintenance action, Boyd. Do you understand?'

'Do you mean I wait for Dermot Dougan and his gang to join us from Yorkshire?' remarked Boyd.

'No, I have studied your papers at great length. Sean Brady is the key. The ASU in Yorkshire will not function until he activates them. We will have that covered with the Yorkshire police. Once Brady shows in Boston Spa, we will charge up there and I'll put everything I've got into them and more besides. Let the Yorkshire boys peep out of the window until then, William. Help me here,' said the Commander.

'I'd rather be in Boston Spa, Commander, said Boyd. The coffee cup clinked against the saucer as Boyd raised it to his lips. The liquid was hot and pinched his tongue.

'I know, William. Close it. Leave the locals on a daylight watch only. We must save the money. Look at the map here. This will explain the situation far better than I could. One of the young detectives down the corridor looks after the thing for me. I think he's a Superintendent, but he's definitely younger than me,' said the Commander.

Boyd managed to stifle a laugh at the oldest man in the unit.

The Commander left his seat and ushered Boyd over to the display on the wall. He placed a fatherly hand on Boyd's shoulder and said, 'See this map, William?'

'Yes,' acknowledged Boyd.

'This is the known disposition of every current member of the Provisionals on the mainland. The red drawing pins show our main targets and the blue ones show the known couriers. The black labels show suspected arms caches hidden across the country. Some have been emptied recently. Look at it, William. There are very few people in this organisation who have ever seen this map. It is the state of the war. The stars show every PIRA attack on the mainland since the Troubles started in 1969. God knows what the RUC map looks like. We can't keep up with this with what we have at the moment. We don't have enough resources. Most chief constables out there are looking after their own backyards. They are judged on how many shoplifters they nick. I am judged on how many terrorists I catch. It costs peanuts to nick a shoplifter and sometimes thousands and thousands of pounds to nick a good terrorist.'

Boyd's eyes focused on the map.

The wall was covered with drawing pins and stars. There were dozens and dozens of different coloured drawing pins stretching from Inverness in the north to Newquay in the south. The majority of the pins, probably about eighty per cent, were shown in the Greater London area.

Boyd nodded. 'I'll make the call, sir, and pull them out. I'll arrange for a care and maintenance crew to keep the job on simmer. Day watch only when circumstances allow. Let's hope you're right, sir. I pinned my hopes on Yorkshire.'

The Commander placed his arm on Boyd's shoulder and spoke as a headmaster would address a disappointed pupil. 'I know you did, William, and a good job you've done, too. If they show down here we will have them, believe me. Just explain to Yorkshire that Sean is the key. Believe me, Sean is the key. Take a break, William. Go back to the Lakes. You are a Lakeland man aren't you?'

'No, in Cumbria you are a townie if you don't live in the shadow of the Lakeland Fells. I'm no Lakelander. I'm from the Eden valley. It's Cumbria still, but not the Lake District. That's full of bloody tourists from London. Damn crazy Southerners - yuppies, I believe we call them now.'

Commander Herbert laughed. 'Thank you, William. I appreciate your understanding of the money situation, that's all. Lack of money. No reflection on either yourself or your team. Do me one favour, though?' asked Commander Herbert.

'Yes! If I can.'

'Bring me a Wainwright book back from Cumbria. I'm too damn old to climb the Fells but I can still look at Wainwright's drawings. A great artist, you know. Have you read any of his books? I expect you have. Makes sense, I suppose when you're up there. Here, let me give you some cash. Perhaps ...'

The Commander reached for his wallet inside his jacket pocket, brought it out and rummaged for a banknote.

'No! My treat sir, allow me,' offered Boyd.

'Very kind, William. Very kind,' replied the Commander.

'Miss Harston-Browne, sir?' enquired Boyd.

'Was told by her Director a short time ago. Enjoy your break, William. Goodbye!' delivered the Commander.

Business completed, Boyd was dismissed. He left the office and took the elevator to the underground car park where he located his little two-seater sports car. He found the ignition key and gunned the engine into life. Selecting a gear, he moved the car up the ramp into the London traffic. He travelled to Toni's office where they spent the remainder of the morning on the telephone to Yorkshire.

By the afternoon, Boyd and Toni had closed down the operation in Boston Spa and were travelling north on the Al towards Wetherby. They took the local police out for a drink that night, as well as their own team. Toni accepted Boyd's invitation to spend a weekend in Cumbria. One operation closed down, but one romance blossomed.

During the next few weeks another comprehensive wall map was installed in the Commander's office. The map was similar to that showing the IRA onslaught, but differed in that it charted the history of the Loyalist movement and its activity in the United Kingdom. It reminded people that whilst the Loyalists were not noted for causing bomb explosions, they were known for their ability to mount cold blooded assaults and killings on the Catholic community, particularly in Ulster and parts of Scotland. The differently coloured pins showed that the Loyalists, since 1969, had killed more people than the Provisionals.

Months later, Commander Herbert added more drawing pins and stars to his IRA map. One drawing pin rested on Warrington, where two young boys died when terrorists planted bombs in litter bins in the town centre. Other pins showed the Warrington gas depot bombs. The pin on the map was no more than six inches from another resting over the Baltic Exchange, in London. Here, further deaths and damage had occurred a year earlier. More pins in Bournemouth and the south coast; a further pin over Bishopsgate, in the City of London, where the biggest terrorist bomb

126

ever experienced in the United Kingdom was detonated.

Many Irish Republican terrorists were arrested that year. Some were imprisoned after trial, but in 1993 PIRA ripped the heart out of London.

Boyd delivered the Wainwright book. It was 1994 before Commander James Herbert had time to read it.

≈

PART THREE
THE STORM GATHERS

1993 November

The liner docked at Stranraer and discharged its cargo. Vehicles and pedestrians gradually left the ship, passed through the passenger and cargo security checks, and headed onto the A 75 trunk road connecting Stranraer to the rest of Britain.

It was a glorious autumn day. Sean Brady was a passenger in a heavy goods vehicle destined for Dover and the continent of Europe. The task of the lorry driver was to deliver goods made in Northern Ireland to buyers in France, Spain, Italy and Portugal.

Sean had not enjoyed the troublesome two and a half hour passage over the Irish Sea from Larne. He had vomited uncontrollably. He realised his mistake. He should have taken the 'Sea-cat' hovercraft from Belfast harbour. It cost more, but the journey time was halved. Sean settled down for the journey, stubbed out his cigarette and took a welcome nap. He laid his head against the bulkhead in the passenger compartment of the monstrous vehicle, using his holdall as a pillow.

The A75 meanders through Scotland, touching Dumfries, where the great Scottish poet, Robert Burns, once lived. Burns had been an 'Excise Man' in Dumfries, the jewel of the south of Scotland. The great highway skirts the extensive nuclear complex at Chapel Cross, near Annan, before it passes the world-famous village of Gretna Green, where many a marriage was made across the infamous anvil in the 'Old Blacksmith's Shop'.

Thoughts of marriage to Shelagh Connelly were not part of Sean's thinking as he travelled onwards towards the Borderlands, the Solway Firth and the Lake District. At the end of the A75, the road joined the A74 linking Glasgow with London before crossing the River Esk near the Metal Bridge Inn and graduating into the M6 motorway at intersection forty-four, just north of Carlisle.

Nearby is one of the many truck stops that cater for the heavy goods vehicles.

Liam slid the soft duster, cleaned the pint glasses, and set them in position on the shelves. He made a note of the bottled beers and soft drinks that needed replenishing in the bar and went down into the cellar to get them. He was 'bottling up' and making ready for the evening rush. He tidied the bar, emptied the ash trays and squared the plastic chairs back into position around the low tables. Checking the carpet, he decided it needed a going- over with the vacuum cleaner and plugged it into the wall socket. He began hoovering the debris.

There was plenty of time. The wagon park was quiet, with a handful of drivers taking an afternoon break in the cafeteria adjoining the licensed bar. When he had finished, he went quietly to the small well-appointed room he rented above the premises, climbed the stairwell to his room, and took a carefree doze.

Boyd took Toni out for the day. It was a short break, but the Lakeland Fells were dominant in autumn and there was an added advantage: the Fells were quiet. It was not a recognised holiday time and there were very few tourists about, just a handful of walkers and rock-climbers that Boyd called 'crag rats'.

Crag rats were rock-climbers who scaled the sheer rock face of the Fells in an athletic display of human prowess that often bewildered the more sedentary walkers rambling through the Lakes. Boyd much preferred walking with the attractive Toni.

They covered the ground over the Caldbeck Fells, heading for the summit of Blencathra from Bothel. It was an easy route for the lady from London. Boyd had selected it because there were few sharp inclinations and the area offered solitude and peace, with little danger from the severity often associated with steeper walks.

He had briefed her well and she wore the correct clothing. They sported heavy boots, thick woollen jumpers and hooded anoraks, whilst they carried spare dry clothing and a food reserve for emergencies. Boyd and Brown had walked since the early morning light before they topped Blencathra and were eventually rewarded with a marvellous panoramic view of the Lake District. Boyd told her that locally the Fell was known as Saddleback since, from a distance, in the lowlands, the shape of the mountain resembled a saddle. Boyd reminded her that he could see Saddleback from his own home in the Eden valley.

Antonia Harston-Browne slept well that night. She wasn't used to the steepness of the Fells, nor the rub of hired walking boots. Her long and slender legs ached with stiffness in the morning.

The lazy autumn day progressed and brought sadness to Padraigh O'Toole. He walked from the doctor's surgery into the lush green park near the river, sat on a park bench, and watched the Eden flow gently past him towards the Solway Firth.

The park was quiet with only the distant hum of traffic. Oyster catchers flew low, swooping over the reeds growing defiantly from the sprawling muddy banks lying near the water's edge. Their black and white colourings zipped in and out of the river side as they played their flight of fancy. Autumn sunshine pierced a bright blue sky that had been painted with the occasional cloud. It was a lazy beautiful day: One to remember for a long time to come.

Padraigh would remember that day. He wondered if he should tell his wife what the doctor had told him. He was dying of cancer and had only a little time left.

He decided he had kept secrets all his life. One more secret would be no problem to him. He would keep his impending departure from this Earth a secret from those he loved and would disclose his secret only when he had to, and then only to those who really cared.

Cynical about his death, Padraigh thought it happened to everyone, but 'why me?' he thought.

Sitting alone, silently thinking of his family, it was all Padraigh had left. He thought of his nephew, Liam, and of his wife, Linda. He thought of his only son, Michael, and how, near this very place years ago, in 1982, he nearly lost him. Tears rolled casually down his cheeks as he sat in solitude wondering how long he had to live. He resolved to look Billyboy up and pot the black for old times' sake. He knew Boyd was back in town. Boyd had telephoned him from London earlier in the week. They planned to meet the next evening, before Boyd returned to the capital.

Six o'clock came and Liam locked his room and walked towards the bar. Removing the key from his pocket, he unlocked the deserted licensed premises and was welcomed by the usual musty smell of stale tobacco and flat beer lying in the atmosphere. Liam switched on the extractor fans and heard the motor purring above him. He made ready for the night's proceedings and tidied the beer mats on the bar top.

A big articulated wagon trundled up the slip road at intersection forty-four. The driver roused his passenger and manoeuvred the wagon off the A74 dual carriageway onto the roundabout. The vehicle drew to a standstill and Sean Brady collected his holdall. The two men shook hands and Sean climbed down from the cab.

The driver selected the crawler gear, drove off, pipped the horn in final salute and rejoined the highway to head down the motorway towards the distant port of Dover.

Sean stretched and changed the holdall from his left hand to his right. He was dressed in strong walking shoes, Levi jeans, a roll-neck sweater and a thick fleecy jacket that was zipped up to his chin. He looked over towards the sprawling city of Carlisle and saw the distant signs that were now illuminated. It was the truck stop about half a mile away. Sean set off to meet his man.

Liam stood behind the bar cleaning the optics and deciding whether or not he should replenish the diminishing vodka bottle. The local singer, 'Rita the Lolita', had entertained the boys last night with a borrowed acoustic guitar and a handful of country and western songs. At the end of the night she had done her best to finish off the vodka.

Liam smiled to himself at the thought of her singing voice. It was well received, but terrible in its tone.

The lounge door closed behind him.

Liam didn't look round. There was no need. The caller would realise he was just opening up and return later. Probably a new driver getting his bearings for the night. It was not unusual. Moving the duster over a bowl, Liam cleared the last speck of dust from the optic.

Sean Brady saw Liam standing at the optics with his back to him. The door close behind him and swung on its hinges as it came to settle. He waited for the door to close completely before he dropped his holdall and voiced, 'God made the land and God made the sea, Liam Connelly!'

Recognising the voice immediately, Liam looked up into the mirror behind the optics. Without turning round he found Sean's steel-grey eyes in the mirror watching him. The jet-black hair was fading. Shades of grey crept over the sideburns and adorned the crown of Sean's head. It had been a long time since the two had met.

In the second that passed before he answered, Liam wondered whether friend or foe had called that night. Had his turn to die arrived at long last? Yes, Sean was an old friend from yesteryear, but he was also a killer sent by the Provos. Liam wondered if by some mystical, magical method they had tracked him down at last and contracted Sean to do the killing for them. Time was no friend when money was at stake and he knew Sean was more than capable of killing him for the boys back home.

'I sure hope God shines down on me this night, Sean Brady?' offered Liam, quietly.

Sean read Liam's mind. He knew his friend and anticipated such a reaction.

Neither man moved. They were as statues.

130

Liam continued to dust the optic whilst watching Sean through the mirror. There was no sound save the softness of Liam's duster on the neck of the upturned bottles. The atmosphere was electric. One expecting to die, the other on a mission. The two men were weighing up each other.

Easing the tension, Sean suggested, 'He surely shines down on you, Liam. Have no fear of that. May he shine down on you for many days to come. Will you take a drink with an old Irish friend from the Shantallow?'

'To see you on your way, Sean? Or do you come for me?' suggested Liam defiantly. He remained like a monument, piercing the mirror behind the optics, eagerly seeking the gun that Sean must surely carry.

'I come as a friend, Liam, an old friend. No more, no less. I come to talk.'

Unzipping his fleecy jacket, Sean slowly removed it from his back and dropped it to the floor before holding out his hands, palms upwards, signifying to Liam he carried no gun. He gestured peace.

'Then talk, my friend,' responded Liam turning to look at Sean.

The body had put on a pound of two in weight but Sean had kept himself fit and trim. Only the touch of grey spreading into the hair betrayed the thirty-six years Sean Brady had lived. Thirty-six years of hatred and violence tied up into thirteen stone of physique.

They closed with each other and shook hands vigorously. Then Sean clasped him round the shoulders and hugged him like a brother.

'It's good to see you, Liam. It's been years. How long is it now?'

'Seven years, Sean. 1986. Buncrana. Remember?'

'Like it was yesterday,' replied Sean. 'Good days those. We knew why we were fighting and who we were fighting for. You haven't changed a bit, Liam Connelly. Look at you now. Not changed one bit.'

'Hereabouts, I go by the name of Liam Connors, Sean. I'll thank you to remember that, if you please,' required Liam.

'Aye, that would be you, Liam. Ever careful, never the one to be caught by a stupid act, always one step ahead of the rest.'

'How did you find me?' enquired Liam.

'Shelagh, Liam. She is my woman now. Soon we will be married. Here, pull me a beer. My throat is dry from the dust of the road and we have much to talk about. So much to tell and so little time to tell it.'

Liam brought two pints of beer round from the bar into the spacious room. They selected a table and talked. When the bar opened properly, Sean melted into the background and bided his time watching 'Rita the Lolita'. Eventually, the bar closed and the two talked further, occasionally laughing at a memory from a long-forgotten time. They talked long into the night. By the next morning, when dawn broke, Liam was up to date with the news. They ate breakfast together. Sean asked the question that had been on his lips since Tramore.

'Well! Will you join us again, Liam?'

'It's over, Sean,' suggested Liam. 'Don't you watch the television? Hume is talking to Adams. They talk of peace. Here, look you at the morning paper. It will be all over soon. Neither side can win. They can't beat us and we can't break down their resolve. It's a draw for God's sake! Can't you understand that?'

'There'll be no draw if we can negotiate a peace settlement from a position of strength, Liam. Sure now, if we are to have our way, the way of the movement, we must only talk to the Brits from a position of strength. Do you understand that, my friend?' countered Sean.

'It's different now, Sean. I have my life here. It's not much, I grant you, but it's a good life. I have a job, food in ma belly and drink for the taking. I've also got friends, Sean. English friends. They work here. There are Scots too. They know nothing of the troubles. They have no interest in the 'Troubles'. Sure, Ireland might as well be on a different planet, for all they care. The nearest they get to the Irish is Terry Wogan on the telly. Look you now, you've got Shelagh and good luck to you. Go back home and take the peace, Sean. Take the peace - because it's all we'll get. Aye, and some would say more than we deserve. You say you came in peace, Sean. Then go in peace. Don't do this thing you talk of.'

'That's exactly why we carry the fight on, Liam. Many on the mainland don't care about our cause. We must take the fight to London again. The Brits talk of peace but they need to be reminded that peace comes under our terms. Come with me, Liam. You were the best in Derry. Dermot is making a big one and Eamonn still tells the jokes whilst he's driving. Sure, Bridget is fine, but she's not like you, Liam. You're the best. Join us. I need the extra man. The best man there is. You! Liam!'

'But what of the peace talks?' enquired Liam.

'Remember this, Liam. Your father died in Limavady on active service. Remember? Also remember that last month seven Catholics, our people, you remember them, don't you? They were killed by a Loyalist gunman who blasted them to death at the Rising Sun bar at Greysteel, Derry. Just down the road from our home, Liam. Our home! Where does your loyalty lie? Behind the bar in a place never heard of with strangers for company? Or are you still an Irishman with fire in the belly for the fight? Which is it?' demanded Sean.

'Greysteel was "tit for tat", Sean,' argued Liam. 'You know, to be sure, that the Loyalists hit back because we bombed them out of the Shankill last month. Tit for tat. Twenty-five years and for what? Nothing's changed, Sean. Not a thing.'

'We can change it, Liam. Dermot and I have a good plan. A great plan. One that will go down in history. Forget Bishopsgate, Liam. Our next one will make Bishopsgate pale into insignificance. We will decapitate the British government, Liam, that's fer sure. Join us and be part of it all again. The Loyalists? Their days are numbered, Liam. We must strike at the heart of the Brits. They will capitulate at our strength and we will have our way. But only from a position of strength, Liam.'

Whether it was the drink from the night before, the ever-rising upsurge of Loyalist murders against the Catholics or an impassioned plea from an old friend, Liam would never know. He just knew that much of what Sean said could make sense. Peace might never come. It could just be the talking. That's all. Politicians talking. He sat for a while, listening to the argument that Sean pushed.

Liam decided, 'Okay. I'll join you, but on one condition.'

'What's that then?' asked Sean.

'We cancel the attack if peace is made with the Brits.'

'Agreed!' replied Sean. 'Agreed!'

The two shook hands and made their plans. Sean had no doubts about the peace. It would never come, and if by a chance a ceasefire was announced, then it would be short lived and would not last. The great plan was complicated and would take time to put into place. But it was feasible and if it worked it would bring the Brits to their knees.

Whilst others elsewhere sought a lasting peace, Sean Brady planned a lasting war.

As the weeks passed, the peace settlement took a further tentative step nearer when, in December, 1993, the Downing Street Declaration came about. The proclamation signalled the intention of the respective governments on both sides of the Irish Sea, and those in other lands, to further the search for a long-term peace settlement in the troubled lands of Northern Ireland.

Sean, Dermot, Bridget, Liam and Eamonn continued to work on their deadly plan to bring about chaos on the mainland and, in particular, central London. Dedicated to winning their cause, they held no truck with those in the Republican movement who would willingly abandon the bullet and bomb philosophy for the ballot box. There was much to do! They seldom took time to watch the television situated in the corner of their small living room preferring to spend their days planning the long campaign ahead and discussing the variety of options open to them.

Had they tuned in to one television channel, they might well have been made aware of the great political debate that was gradually unfolding around the United Kingdom, capturing the interest of a divided nation. The television studio was hushed as the popular presenter took centre stage before the assembled guests. Studio lights were dimmed and the invited audience sat back in their comfortable seats. The televised morning talk show was about to begin. The presenter was a prominent member of the network that was continuing a series on the Northern Ireland peace initiative. He wore a single-breasted dark suit, set off by a blue Paisley pattern tie over a lemon-coloured shirt, with a matching silk handkerchief poked loosely from his jacket pocket. He squared his tie, smoothed his hair and took a last sip of a flavoured mineral water as the presentation team finally went live.

'Music,' uttered one of the production team into the studio control microphone.

'Title,' instructed another.

'We're rolling,' offered the producer. 'We're on the air, Action! Over to you! The floor has it! Silence, please!'

The television producer scanned the monitors, selected the camera angle, fingered the controls and perused the script. The cameraman readied his machine. The sound man turned his dials and the morning show was broadcast into the homes of the people living in Great Britain.

Studio lights went up and the cameras went into zoom mode, focusing on the presenter. Acknowledging his introduction, he welcomed the television audience to the morning's proceedings and explained how the programme had charted the peace talks and how today the audience were to discuss their thoughts on the peace initiative. He started by bringing everyone up to date.

The tone of his voice was knowledgeable, sparkling and aggressive. His voice showed no emotion and no sign of nervousness as he waded into the meat of the programme.

'The Loyalist paramilitaries have continued with their campaign of premeditated violence, ruthlessly killing six Catholics at Loughinisland some twenty-five miles north of Kilkeel in County Down. Loughinisland is a small Irish town just outside Downpatrick. Indeed, we have with us today some of the residents of Loughinisland and we may well be able to speak to them shortly. Let us, however, remind ourselves of the last twelve months of the terrorist campaign. Remember the tragic incident that occurred in June, 1994, when a helicopter crashed into a lonely Scottish hillside, killing a number of individuals, men and women, from the intelligence community. They were from the army, the special branch and the security service,' declared the presenter.

Taking a deep breath, knowing that the production team were readjusting the lighting and sound outputs from their computerised control panel, he eyeballed the camera again.

'In July the same year, elements of the Provisional Irish Republican Army landed a heavy goods vehicle at Heysham port in the county of Lancashire. When the vehicle was searched by uniformed police, a large consignment of explosives was recovered and yet another attack on the mainland was foiled.'

The presenter sauntered across to the invited audience showing their faces to the cameras for the first time. A cameraman panned his instrument, following the presenter judiciously on his slow but measured walk as the presenter offered, 'Throughout this entire period it became obvious that the search for peace was still going on. The media continue to speculate on the Hume-Adams initiative, whilst Prime Minister John Major has eventually seized the thorny nettle that we know as the Irish problem. Whether the media focus on Martin McGuinness, Gerry Adams, Sir Patrick Mayhew, Dick Spring, Premiers Reynolds and John Major or John Hume is perhaps now irrelevant. They are all players in the peace game. The point is that during this crucial time the peace initiative, for all its problems and complexities, has not been allowed to die.'

At a standstill, the presenter turned to walk up the aisle dividing the audience. More faces came into the cameraman's picture and were beamed into the homes of the viewers.

'But such well-known men who enjoy the high profile that national, and sometimes international, media coverage brings surely cannot have been the only players in the intriguing game of peace?' he suggested.

'Indeed, it has emerged that on the 7th of July, 1972, secret talks took place between PIRA and William Whitelaw, who was then Secretary of State for Northern Ireland and Member of Parliament for Penrith and the Borders. Cumbrians have affectionately known Lord Whitelaw simply as "Willie" for many years. He is now Viscount Whitelaw, serving his country from the House of Lords. Lord Whitelaw chronicled these secret talks with PIRA in his book The Whitelaw Memoirs as a non-event.

'Whether or not that was so raises the notion that a channel of communication between the Government and PIRA was in being. It is now fairly obvious and reasonable to presume that the potential existed to keep such a channel of communication open between the two sides. Who kept this channel open? When a meeting takes place, one side often speaks and the other side does no more than listen. Meetings can become conversations and negotiations only when both sides listen and both sides talk. Who talked and who listened?' asked the presenter.

He continued, 'Perhaps the task of talking and communicating with the men of violence fell to those grey-suited civil servants in the Home Office or Stormont?' There was a pause but he continued, 'Perhaps the channel was kept open by a female attached to the Whitehall bureaucratic structure. One of the many so-called 'mandarins'? Or perhaps the channel for communication was kept open by the faceless, anonymous men and women who are called to serve but are seldom seen? The 'Intelligence' people?'

Now flowing, he moved further up the stairs that divided the audience. The sound boom above him followed his journey.

'Whoever they were may not matter, but consider that in the beginning of negotiations, whether it be 1972 or 1994, such people would be unlikely to hold high office. They are not the Majors, Humes and Reynolds of the world. They came after the ground work, I suggest. They are more likely to be of a lower order, more likely to be on the shop floor than in the managing director's office, if I can put it that way.'

A wry smile formed at the corner of his eloquent lips when he offered, 'In the pre-media days, the talkers and the listeners had to be from all sides, from both divides, from both religions, from both cultures, from different political persuasions, carrying different ideas for the land that the British know as Northern Ireland.'

Taking a breath, the presenter cleared his throat, 'Those who kept that channel open and kept listening and kept on talking are the unsung heroes in the search for peace. For without such people, whoever they are and wherever they are from, the ability to capture peace would have died.'

Allowing the message to sink in, he paused and then looked straight into camera saying, 'The peoples of the United Kingdom owe to these unsung heroes a debt that cannot be repaid by words alone.'

Another pause. 'What price is a nation's peace?'

The presenter then moved slowly down the stairs, retreating towards the centre of the stage, and said, 'And so it was that at midnight on the thirty-first of August, 1994, the Provisional Irish Republican Army declared a total cessation of military operations. The ceasefire had arrived. It is ironic that on the first day of September, 1994, a child was born of Mairead Docherty in a Belfast hospital. The child was the first to be born under the PIRA ceasefire and accordingly the child embodies the hopes and aspirations of the thousands of good Irish people who are desperate to live in peace. May the child live in peace.'

He stared into the camera, saying, 'And so it was on the fourteenth of October, 1994, Loyalist paramilitaries also announced a ceasefire.'

The presenter had now attracted the audience at home in their armchairs, watching and listening. Those who were bored with it all reached toward their televisions and either changed channels of switched off. Some gathered the daily newspaper and turned reluctantly to the crossword or the latest sporting news. They would spend their day in mild amusement. Others remained tuned in.

The presenter went on, 'It is not a permanent peace. There are no guarantees. Neither side, whether they are the security forces, the Loyalists or the Republicans, have laid down their arms. If the ceasefire is to become a permanent lasting peace, then a long-term dialogue and an uneasy alliance has to be built on. There are those against the peace and those for the peace. Some players want to win outright, whatever their position is, and from whichever side they represent. It is an uneasy peace.'

The invited audience shuffled in their seats. They knew they would soon be asked to offer their thoughts on the peace process. Such thoughts would differ markedly.

The television presenter continued, 'In February, 1995, the British Government and the Government of Eire produced a "joint framework" document. This document carries with it the search for a dialogue and the search for continued talks. It is not binding and enjoys no legislative power. It is not law. The initiative within the joint framework document raises the potential for future rule in Northern Ireland to emanate from Stormont. However, Unionists see the minority Republican movement in Northern Ireland gaining unwelcome advances. Talks are of cross-border co-operation, joint assemblies, joint decision-making bodies in the troubled border area and a reconstituted police force. Everyone will make their own interpretation of the document. What is yours, I wonder? And indeed, what are the thoughts of our invited studio audience?'

The presenter drove to the heart of the matter. 'The issue of sovereignty rises to the surface yet again. Who rules whom? Who rules and from where? Where is the mandate to rule? Where will the power lie? What the joint framework document does achieve is to keep the minds of politicians and leaders on the search for peace,' he said, before clearing his throat again and continuing. 'The political wing of the IRA, Provisional Sinn Fein, offered the Unionists an olive branch on the twenty-fifth day of February, 1995, when at their conference in Dublin, Sinn Fein chairman, Tom Hartley, said, "In our vision of a united independent Ireland there is a place for those who wish to stay British" . . .'

The presenter indicated with his left hand to part of the audience, saying, 'The remark raises questions from the Loyalists in Ulster. How can such a proposition be accepted after all the mayhem of the past? Have the Loyalist terrorists and the Unionist politicians who echo their views, without resorting to violence, been sold down the river by the London Government? Whom can they trust?'

Gesturing to the right of the aisle, he said, 'Will the IRA disarm as a gesture of good intent? Or will the peace process falter and stumble if they retain their weaponry - their arms and their explosives, that is?'

Facing the camera again, he suggested, 'Should Loyalists throw down their arms first or should they disarm at all? Should Republicans disarm at all?'

The questions went on and on. Some people met. Some people spoke. Some people listened. But importantly, some people had conversations and peace grew stronger by the second. The television presenter directed the show and raised the questions, provoking the audience to think and to listen and to exchange views. After an hour the credits rolled and the programme came to an end.

As the audience filed out of the studio to the canteen and refreshment, many agreed that the peace was uneasy, unsettled, wary, almost lazy. It was not surprising. The 'Troubles' had lasted twenty-five years. Peace could take another twenty-five years. It was a fragile peace. The story doesn't end there. It is only the beginning. Who will keep the peace? Will the terrorist leaders maintain discipline within their ranks? It may not be easy. Which way will the game of peace run now?

The television audience numbered about fifty in the studio, but the programme in the early morning session attracted a few million viewers. The debate was on. The ceasefire was up and running. Some asked, 'For how long?'

The television crew closed down, the cameras were housed for the day and the presenter went to his office to read the draft for the next programme. The next issue to be tackled on live television was the issue of animal rights and the carriage of young calves in veal crates. It was a provocative television series. Such programmes often are.

1995

Finishing work early that lunchtime, Liam Connelly made his way from the truck stop bar into the city in search of his uncle Pat. He reckoned on finding one of Derry's former bomb makers in the Carlisle leisure centre and was not disappointed when he eventually located his beloved uncle inside the building.

Padraigh O'Toole occupied a seat in the Sands Leisure Complex overlooking the large sports hall. Like many people with time on their hands and little to do, he had walked into the city, made for the sprawling leisure complex, paid a few pennies to gain entrance to the balcony area and was watching the youngsters being taught the rudiments of gymnastics by an athletic looking young man who sported a plethora of tattoos and a mild northern accent. The complex housed a sports hall, squash courts, gymnasium, fitness room, solarium, bar, cafeteria and theatre. Indeed, the centre was big enough to offer a massive range of leisure facilities and often did.

The centre was bordered to the south by the commercial centre of Carlisle and to the north by the river Eden and the desirable suburb of Stanwix.

Padraigh was enjoying his last few months of life, but his secret was still safe. His family did not know be was dying. He had not told them. He was alone with his thoughts.

Liam found him watching the gymnasts. 'Sure, there you are, Pat. How are you today, then?'

'Goodness be, it's you is it, Liam? I'm well. Come, sit here beside me now. How did you know I was here?' replied Pat.

'I phoned the house but there was no reply. I thought the good lady would be out at the shop. I knew you would be here watching the sports, sure I did,' replied Liam.

'Aye,' nodded Pat. 'Linda's getting her hair done down in the town. She'll join me when she's ready. I like to sit here and watch them all playing the sports.' He motioned to the children. 'It reminds me of when I was young. Sure, that seems a long time ago now. Still, you finished early today then?' asked Pat.

'That's right, uncle. You got it in one. I'm well finished alright.' Liam laughed as he answered.

'And what's that supposed to mean, Liam?' probed Pat.

'I need to speak to you, uncle.'

'What about?' enquired Pat anxiously.

'The organisation across the water want me back, sure they do now!' offered Liam, proudly.

'Jesus be! Don't, Liam! Don't! Do you hear me! Not after all this time.'

'It's time for us to win, uncle. Time for one last push to make sure they know we are here,' challenged Liam.

'Sit down, you young fool. Why do you tell me this?' demanded Pat, shaking his head.

'Because I want my family to know that I go to avenge my father and my mother,' said Liam.

Padraigh O'Toole shook his head again and pulled Liam down into the seat beside him.

'Let me tell you this, Liam. Your father was killed because he didn't handle the bomb right. He made a mistake. There's no one to avenge, you idiot! As for yer mother! She probably died from the shock of what was going on down the stairs the day you killed the boys,' stated Pat.

'The day they kneecapped Shelagh!' interrupted Liam.

The uncle's voice became harsher. 'Be that as it may, Liam, but there is no one to avenge. The Catholic grannies in Belfast and Derry have kept the Troubles going for God knows how many years by handing down the kind of crap that you've just told me. Sure, next you'll be telling me that yer wanting to avenge poor Saint Patrick. It's time for peace, Liam. It's behind you. Leave it behind you. Now, who put you up to this?'

'Can't say that, Pat. You know better than to ask,' said Liam. 'I won't engage in the loose talk, not me.'

'Oh! So someone did come for you then, boy? It's not your own idea to take on the world then?'

'Hold yer tongue, uncle. Others might hear us.'

'Sean Brady?' declared Pat, knowingly.

There was no answer from Liam.

Pat said, 'I knew it. That bastard Sean Brady it is.' Then he shook Liam by the shoulder and continued, 'Am I right then, lad? The killer, Brady?'

Responding by pulling away, Liam snapped, 'Not from me, uncle. No loose talk. I came to tell you so that you would be proud to be Irish again and give me your blessing.'

'Blessing? Blessing is it you want? I'll give you blessing. You sound like a Belfast granny spouting the hate of a century ago. It's some sense you want talked into yer head, sure it is. I am proud of you. You have a life here. What do you want to get involved for? Listen well to me. Blessing indeed! This is not some kind of holy crusade you are on where you ride off into the night on a white charger to save the princess. This is real life, boy!'

'I'm thirty-six! Don't call me boy!' scolded Liam.

'Sure, in my eyes you always will be a boy, Liam. I remember you best as a boy when you used to play on the streets in Shantallow and I used to bounce you on ma knee. You'll always be ma second son after Michael,' said Pat. 'But the world has changed, Liam. Now they talk of peace. There's a ceasefire. They talk of joint assemblies and a new kind of government for the border. Joint decision making and the like they call it. Some say we'll get a new police force and the army will be gone from our streets before the year is out. Give it a chance, Liam. Don't listen to the likes of Sean Brady. They want only violence for themselves so that in the end they will rule the streets through drugs, terror and hate. All they will do is take us back to sixty-nine. Look forward, Liam. Don't look back.'

'I gave my word to them. I go to join them. Be proud, Uncle Pat.'

The old man's eyes grew tired and grey. He twisted awkwardly in his seat and looked sadly down at the ground.

'I don't see the point. How long is it since you were in Derry?'

'You know that. Years!'

'Leave it, Liam,' advised Pat.

'No, I'm a Connelly. I go to join Sean in the south.'

'Wait! I'll wish you luck, but only you, Liam. Remember what we used to say?'

'What do you mean?'

'God made the land!'

'And God made the sea!' finished Liam.

'Aye, and I sure hopes He shines down on you and protects you, Liam. Be gone now. Remember what I said. Give the peace a chance.'

Liam offered his hand, but Padraigh refused it.

The door closed behind him as Liam strode out of the room and stepped purposefully down the winding staircase into the reception area. The red-painted electronic door opened as he approached them. There was a wisp of cold air when he penetrated the winter outside.

Crossing the road, Liam then walked up the side of the dual carriageway before finding the City centre. He made for the bus station and a coach ride to Yorkshire.

Pensive, Padraigh sat for what seemed an eternity, watching the children at play and thinking back to those Derry days when everything was so different. In those days it had all been so easy. There was no question of the right and the wrong. You did just what you did because that was the way of it. When the mob took to the streets, you joined or got left behind. When volunteers were called for to shoot and to bomb, you joined because the neighbour to your left and right had joined. They had known no difference for a lifetime. Padraigh and the generation he belonged to spent the best part of their lives preaching to the youngsters how to mistrust and how to hate. Why should Liam change now? Neither man had ever lived in peace. They could cope with war, but peace? Now peace was a problem. It was new.

Padraigh was not surprised Liam had been the way he was. He was a Connelly. The Connellys had been taught to win all their lives. They were heroes of the Republican movement. Peace did not come easy to men such as these.

Looking down from the balcony, Padraigh saw children putting away the apparatus. Two of the kids pushed each other and squared up to fight. One was taller than the other. It reminded Padraigh of Derry and how Catholic kids had thrown stones and fought with Protestant kids.

Why?

The young man taking the class intervened and sent them on their way.

Padraigh thought to himself, we can't go on like this.

There were two telephone kiosks standing outside the leisure centre. Padraigh entered one of them and reached for the diary inside his pocket. He leafed through the pages and found the number he was looking for. He lifted the telephone, dropped the coins and made the call.

It was time to deliver a promised lesson on Irish history.

That night, Detective Inspector William Miller Boyd, Billyboy to one man, left his office in the capital, took a taxi to Euston, and caught the night sleeper to Carlisle. He read some confidential papers during the journey and captured a couple of cans of beer and a sandwich from the buffet car before he turned in for the night.

At 7.30 the next morning Boyd was awakened by the night service attendant with a cup of coffee and a bacon roll. Boyd was a regular traveller. He knew the staff well. He washed, shaved and dressed quickly before stepping onto the platform at Carlisle railway station.

Boyd crossed the footbridge spanning the railway lines and left the concourse by the main entrance. Within the hour he had collected a hire car and had picked up Padraigh O'Toole from his home. It was nearing nine o'clock in the morning but the Irish history lesson was an important one, at least that's what Pat had said on the telephone.

Padraigh started off by telling Boyd he had once been one of the leading bomb makers for the Provisional Irish Republican Army in the early seventies.

Boyd listened. He wasn't surprised to learn that Pat was a Republican sympathiser. He knew that already, from his many conversations with the Irishman, but he hadn't known that O'Toole had once been one of Derry Brigade's finest. Furthermore, Boyd, the ever tenacious, was mortified when he discovered that one of his dearest and oldest friends had lived a lie to him all those years. He was dumbfounded to learn Pat was the uncle of Liam Connelly, who was the close friend of Brady. The very men Boyd had spent his last few years trying to catch.

Angry and frustrated, Boyd realised twenty-four hours earlier Liam Connelly had been in Carlisle. How many times had he been near to Connelly but hadn't even known he was there? Boyd could have strangled Padraigh as his anger showed.

Regaining his composure, Boyd listened to the Irishman. They spoke of O'Toole's history and of his knowledge of Derry brigade. They talked of the war and they talked of the peace. Boyd took the lesson well. They were still talking way into the afternoon. Boyd had parked the car in the municipal golf club car park.

The two men walked through the park, along the river bank and across the footbridge that was suspended over the Eden. They were nearing the end of their conversation. Boyd had decided there was no time to 'pot the black' that day. Business was now drawing to an end and he knew he needed to get to a telephone.

Pat stopped walking and held Boyd back by the arm.

'Tell me something, Billyboy?' said Pat.

'What's that then, Pat?' answered Boyd.

'Can you do anything for Liam? He is my family when all is said and done.'

Boyd thought for a while before answering. 'No, Pat, I can't. He's on his own.'

'Think well for me, Billyboy,' suggested Pat, stroking his beard. 'I've just told you that the peace settlement is in jeopardy. No one else will have done that for you otherwise you would not have high-tailed it back to Cumbria as quick as you have.'

Boyd pulled the collar of his overcoat closer into his neck. There was a cold breeze whistling through the park.

'That's true, Pat, but how can I keep your nephew out of this thing that they do? According to you he has gone to join Sean Brady and the gang. It will be hard enough to find them all, never mind isolate Liam. What's on your mind?'

Pat offered, 'I'll give it some thought. Never underestimate the Irish, Billyboy. I'll think of something.'

'Don't get involved, Pat,' warned Boyd, turning towards the car.

'I won't, but remember who told you. Don't underestimate them, Billyboy. Dermot Dougan will have something special prepared. He's one of their best. I shouldn't wonder if they haven't kept him in reserve all these years, just in case they needed him for a big one. His time has come, Billyboy. It has to be a massive spectacular and in the capital, London. Sean Brady will be prepared to kill to see it through. Eamonn and Bridget will be expendable in the eyes of Sean. He is a crazy man, I tell you. I tell you no lies, Inspector Boyd. Shelagh still does the letter writing to me and I still have friends in the know in Derry. My friends are older now, those that aren't dead or in prison, but times have changed this last year. It has to stop,' finished Pat.

'It just seems so pointless when you think of it,' suggested Boyd.

'Aye, you're right. They have the chance of peace and they're going to throw it away. It's a pity. The problem is that they have known nothing else but the power that comes from violence, and they can't accept the change. People over there, and I suppose over here for that matter, fear them. They fear the power the men of violence can have. After the peace comes they will be no one. They will have no power like they have now.'

'It's only a ceasefire, Pat.'

Nodding, Pat remarked, 'Aye, but it is the potential you see. The potential for peace. It's all a bit fragile at the moment, is it not?'

'Yes it is, Pat. I suppose it depends on the politicians and the Loyalists as much as anything.'

'And people like you and me, Billyboy. Don't forget that now. I'm Irish. I want the peace and I'll fight for it in my own way.'

'Even if that means dropping your own family in it?'

'Yes,' said Padraigh O'Toole.

The two men turned their backs to the river and the golf course and walked on towards the car.

'Pat?' said Boyd.

'Aye?' replied Pat.

'Why did you call me Inspector? You've never done that before.'

'You're a copper aren't you, Billyboy? Now earn your corn.'

'You're a strange man, Padraigh O'Toole. A strange man,' remarked Boyd searching for the ignition keys in his overcoat pocket.

The two got into the car and travelled into the city. Boyd dropped Pat off near his home and drove to the police station. He parked in the rear yard and entered the station by decoding the electronic door at the rear. He found the office and sat down to gather his thoughts before dialling Commander Herbert's number in New Scotland Yard.

A telephone rang on Commander James Herbert's desk.

The Commander looked scornfully at the instrument, closed the Wainwright book he was reading, reached for the 'phone, and placed it to his ear. 'Commander Herbert speaking.'

'Boyd, sir. I'm up in Carlisle.'

The Commander sat back into his seat and enquired, 'What on earth are you doing up there, William?'

'It's a long story. I'll give you the summary first. Sean Brady is on the mainland. He has made contact with Liam Connelly here in Carlisle. Liam has been here in the City since he was put out of Derry years ago. Liam has moved south to join Sean. They plan a massive spectacular.'

'How do you know this, Boyd?' demanded the Commander, as he made hurried notes on his blotter.

'An old Irish friend just told me, one Padraigh O'Toole,' revealed Boyd. 'What's more, my friend names Dermot Dougan, Eamonn Murphy and Bridget Duffy as the rest of the team.'

'That means they are heading for Boston Spa, William. Wouldn't you agree?' summarised the Commander.

'Exactly,' cracked Boyd. 'We're back in business.'

'Right, William, listen to me, please,' instructed the Commander.

'Go on, sir.'

'How are you travelling?' enquired Commander Herbert.

'By hire car, sir. I have a return booked on the sleeper back to London tonight. I can be in your office in the morning at eight o'clock if you wish?' responded Boyd.

'No, William,' said Commander Herbert. 'As an old boss of mine once said, we'll try and head them off at the pass. Cancel the train and extend the car hire. Drive straight to Yorkshire and take control there. It should take you no more than about three hours drive. I'll tell the Yorkshire boys to extend the watch to cover the full twenty-four hour period. I'll see you in Yorkshire this evening sometime. I just hope we're not too late. You can give me a full report then. I'll arrange clerical support for you.'

'Okay, sir. What about Miss Harston-Browne and her team?'

'Leave them to me, William. I'll update them. Now, get moving, young man. We don't want to miss them. Connelly is a wanted man and Sean a loose cannon by the sound of it. We'll draw firearms in Yorkshire and take them prisoner in the house if we can. There's too much at stake here. We can keep the peace if we're lucky, otherwise those idiots will break it. Send someone to Derry to speak with the RUC. I want Padraigh O'Toole's life story by tomorrow morning at the latest. Hurry, William!'

The lines closed and the two men went about their business. Commander Herbert made three telephone calls: One to Yorkshire, one to the Intelligence service and one to summon his senior advisers for a briefing session. He left for Yorkshire in a helicopter.

Boyd used the 'phone to extend his car hire and cancel the train reservation. He remembered to call his sergeant, Anthea, in order to update her on recent developments. Boyd wanted her to know everything and he wanted her to contact the RUC. There were some questions to ask in Londonderry. Anthea was the right one to ask the questions.

Boyd told Anthea to check out the history of Padraigh O'Toole and his family. He wanted to know everything that could be discovered about the Derry brigade. The RUC would be able to help. They were one of the best police forces in the world, as far as Boyd was concerned.

Anthea made her travel plans. She flew from Heathrow to Belfast that day. By the time the sun had set on the Foyle, she was talking to the RUC and studying old documents, dusty, revealing papers from 1969.

Boyd's last job before the drive to Yorkshire was by far the most important of the day. He called at the canteen and bought a carton of thick, hot, sugary coffee. He was absolutely parched. He couldn't think straight without coffee. He drove out of Carlisle, down the M6 to Penrith and turned left. He crossed Stainmore using the A66 route, before he reached Scotch Corner and the Al dual carriageway. He turned the car south and drove into Yorkshire.

The operation had been reinstated. The chase was on. They were all playing the odds now. The stakes? Peace or war!

The two police officers in the old rectory in Boston Spa, near Wetherby, West Yorkshire, were tired and restless. They had spent many weeks taking turns to watch from their secret perch and they were cold and hungry and beginning to think it was all a big waste of time and money. Their precious time and the poor taxpayer's money!

It approached six o'clock in the evening. It was the same day that Anthea was flying out to Belfast and Boyd was driving south to Yorkshire. Commander Herbert was busy on the telephones back at the office. The Yorkshire detectives were not yet aware of the most recent turn of events.

They were packing up for the day. Soon, they would be home to a warm fire and a hot meal.

'Okay, let's kill it for the day, Jim,' suggested Dave, the older one of the two. His partner stretched his arms above him revealing the fatigue.

'I couldn't agree with you more. I'm absolutely knackered. It's a long boring job, this one,' remarked Jim taking one last look out of the third storey window. He saw the man walking up Main Street towards the targets; house, his only luggage a holdall. Jim alerted his friend.

'Just a second, Dave,' he said. 'We have a visitor. Yes! He's going down the path. Where's the camera? Quick!'

Immediately, Dave was crouched in a kneeling position at the window, clicking away with the camera on automatic focus. The shutter operated swiftly and a number of exposures ran through the camera.

'Got him!' he said, unequivocally. 'They should print up nicely. I wonder who he is? Still, I expect the boys down south will probably know him. They usually do.'

The young man knocked on the door of the house and turned to look back down the street. The detective photographed him again.

Liam Connelly hadn't seen anyone and his suspicions were not aroused. The quick-thinking detective had taken a number of full frontal colour photographs. They would be developed and printed during the night, ready for the photo fax to the London office in the morning, Dermot Dougan heard the rattle, left his seat in the lounge and opened the front door of 312 Main Street, Boston Spa. Recognising Liam, he allowed him in.

'I wouldn't bother about the guy, Dave. He's probably another double-glazing salesman. There's hundreds of them in the area at the moment,' said Jim assuredly.

'Yes, agreed Dave, 'But this one has gone inside.'

'Along with the window cleaner, the coalman, the rent man, the meter reader, the newspaper boy and every other Tom, Dick and Harry north of Watford. Not to worry! Do you recognise him?'

'No! Not in this light. It's too dark. The camera will tell us when the photographs are enlarged. Come on! Time to call it a day.'

They stowed their kit in the bags provided and completed their notes. The two detectives left the rear of the building and walked to their car, which was parked some way off in a public 'pay and display' car park. The men returned to the police station.

Liam, Dermot, Eamonn and Bridget embraced, shook hands and talked of their times together years ago. The team were apprehensive of Liam to start with, but reminded themselves of the comments made by their leader, Sean Brady. Liam was with them, just as he had been before. Wasn't it Liam who had saved the office workers when Loyalists attacked the Sinn Fein office in Derry years ago? Of course! And wasn't it Liam whom Sean had trusted with his life? Liam hadn't betrayed Sean previously, and wouldn't do so in the future. Liam stayed.

By seven o'clock, the team were packing their belongings. They reckoned if they had been under watch then the police had closed down. In any event, the workmen across the fields were gone. They felt safe. Untouched! Untraced! Their leader, Sean Brady, collected them in Wetherby later that night when darkness fell. One by one they left the house, carrying only that which they needed. They travelled light. Dermot wiped the surfaces down and checked their rooms to ensure they didn't leave a tell-tale clue behind. Sean had found new premises in Cheshire. A place called Crewe. It was near the main Glasgow-London railway line. The active service unit was on the move. One step ahead. They would be safe and sound in Crewe by morning.

Sean Brady had one telephone call to make. An important one, for old time's sake, Pulling the minibus into the car park outside Leeds, he used a 'phone box. He'd memorised the telephone number. When he'd sorted the correct coins from his pocket, he rang Seamus in the Republic.

Seamus Kelty heard the 'phone ringing from the garden whilst he cleaned the windows. Placing his cloth down into the bucket of soapy water, he made his way into the house, used a towel from a rail in the kitchen to dry his hands, and took the call

'Hello!' bid Seamus. 'Who's that?'

'It's me, Sean,' revealed Brady in England.

Recognising the voice immediately, Seamus trembled. 'Why are you ringing me here? I told you never to ring me at this number.'

The caller was unperturbed and remained calm as he replied, 'Sure, don't be so annoyed, Seamus. I just thought I would tell you that we're on the move. It's time to wander through that menu you gave me.'

Seamus screamed down the telephone, Jaysus, you fool! It's time for peace. I told you our timescale. If things were going well and the leadership were happy, then fine, no action. We're on the right track, you fool. Peace goes well, Jaysus. Sure and yous are going to spoil it, so you are. Now leave it, Sean! Get back home. Take the discipline. Do as you've been told. Do you hear me?'

'Too slow, old man. You're too slow. Yous boys over there sit and talk to the negotiators. Yous will still be doing the talking in twenty years time. Me? Me and some of the organisation do it our way, Seamus. Now watch me, old man. I'll show yous how to get the peace. We'll cripple the bastard Brits into giving us all that we want now. Now, Seamus. Not tomorrow, not next year, not in twenty years time. Now!'

'No! Wait! Sweet Mary mother of Jesus! Wait! Will ya?'

'Bye, old man! You've passed your sell-by date,' snapped Sean.

The line went dead with Seamus still screaming down the 'phone at Sean who had already made his mind up.

Replacing the telephone, Sean stepped from the kiosk, smiling, happy, and full of mischief. He just loved to upset people in authority. He opened the minibus door, climbed back into the driver's seat and continued his journey through Leeds towards Wetherby. He was doing things his way now. Sean Brady knew it. He was in charge.

"Damn you, Sean Brady! Damn you!' screamed Seamus Kelty into a telephone that only replied with a long monotonous tone.

Smashing the 'phone down, Seamus crashed his clenched fists onto the table top and sat forward with his heart beating at speed. He was stuck in a peat bog and didn't know how to get out. His hands went up to his forehead and his fingers slowly crept down over his face, rubbing his eyelids and stimulating his brain cells. He had never used his own telephone for the organisation's business but this was an emergency.

He dialled the number for his contact with the leadership. The phone rang three times before it was answered.

An Irish voice said, 'Hello! Who calls this number?'

'Me, the man with the fishing rights,' offered Seamus.

'We'll meet then. I don't like the 'phone, as well you know Emergencies only. We agreed, did we not?' spoke the leadership's contact.

Seamus snapped, 'This is an emergency. Goddammit! Sure, one of the rods on the mainland is going his own way. There's a loose cannon in play. Do you hear me, Goddammit?'

There was a considered silence on the other end of the telephone whilst the contact desperately tried to make a quick decision.

'How soon?' came the question.

'Within days. I don't know what he is planning. He has the menu I gave him. They are all massive jobs. Spectaculars! We've got problems.'

The leadership's contact countered, 'No, you've got problems. Find him and close it down. Understand?'

'It's not that easy,' explained Seamus. 'He's on the move and he's taken his team with him. Why don't you tell the negotiators? If we tell the Brits it will be their fault if he goes off the track. Not ours. They have a chance to catch him. Why don't we give them to the Brits?'

'Sure and is it that you are crazy? How can we sit down and talk peace with them? And then say, "Oh, by the way, some of our men are unhappy with the peace process! They are coming to bomb the living daylights out of you!" Do me a favour, Seamus! It doesn't work like that, sure it doesn't. The talks balance on a knife edge every day. It's a very fragile peace you know. The Loyalists will love this one,' argued the contact, and in so doing abandoned twenty-five years of telephone security in the crucial hour when peace and war hung by a thread.

The contact continued, 'No! We can't lose face with the Brits and we can't be the first to break the ceasefire. If it breaks down, then we must hope the Loyalists break it first, not us. We will not tell the negotiating team. Tell me who the cannon is, but don't say the name.'

'Derry,' said Seamus, 'Last one Bond Street Tube years ago.'

'I know the man. He's good, one of our best. I know the team. It's your problem, Seamus. I suggest you contact his brigade commander. The problem must be eliminated immediately without any further ado. Immediately, Seamus! Eliminate the problem,' ordered the contact.

The connection was broken; their discussion complete.

Shaking his head in disbelief, unable to grasp the magnitude of what was happening, Seamus held the telephone for a while, peering into the silent earphone and wondering what to do next. Then he lifted the instrument to his ear, confirmed a new tone, and dialled a Derry number.

'Damien Devenney!' said the Derryman on the other end.

'It's me,' said Kelty, 'Have you heard from your team on the mainland?'

'No, I'm not expecting to either. Why?' probed Damien. 'Should I have?'

'They've gone into action,' revealed Seamus. 'The action is at their discretion, not ours. The peace holds. They've broken it without our authority. I have instructions from the leadership regarding how to deal with them.'

'What! Jesus! There's a ceasefire, for God's sake. Sure, how do you know this?' asked Damien.

'The man from Tramore told me not five minutes ago on the telephone. He has the menu we prepared last year for action only if the talks failed. He has activated the menu. I fear the worst. He must be eliminated as soon as possible. The matter has been discussed with the leadership. The elimination process is sanctioned. Immediate effect! Send your best eliminator. You know who I mean,' advised Seamus.

'But what if we ...' offered Damien.

He was cut short.

'The matter has been discussed. Keep the discipline. Do it! God damn you, Damien! Do it!' screamed Seamus.

Rising to the challenge, Damien responded, 'Consider it done.'

Replacing the telephone, Damien turned to the outer room. 'Eugene! Here a moment. There is work for you to do. You're on your way to London.'

Time hurried on. Damien told Eugene Kelly the story and furnished him with sufficient money for a long trip to London and a quick briefing of the menu sites Seamus had mentioned.

Concentrating hard, Eugene took it all in. The Irishman could remember when he wanted to. Damien drove him speedily to the airport. There was no time for the bodyguard to make the call to the red-head. Only one last slim chance. He tried to take it.

'Damien, I should stay. We could get someone else. Who will look after you if you send me to London?' suggested Eugene.

'No one for the moment. I'll look after myself, that's for sure. Anyway, we're at peace here, you big oaf. It's over there where the problem is. It's a big pay packet, Eugene. Don't mess it up. Make sure they are all well dead by the time you finish.'

The car drew up at the airport terminal and Kelly bade farewell to Damien who sat and watched him enter the concourse.

Eugene looked back and saw his master watching.

Damien stood outside the vehicle, looking over the car roof towards him. His long black coat swirled behind him in the wind.

The call to the red-head would have to wait. Eugene passed through the airport security controls and took the flight to Heathrow. Damien would arrange weaponry at the other end with the London contact, Brendan.

Meanwhile, in Derry, Antonia Harston-Browne sat in her florist's van for an exceptionally long time. After an hour she looked at her wristwatch and decided Eugene wasn't going to make their scheduled meeting. Perhaps he, too, had decided the world was at peace and had had enough. She wondered what had gone wrong. Eugene needed the money. There was something wrong, but she had no choice.

Turning her van away from the River Foyle and the meeting place, Antonia drove to Belfast and took the flight back to London. It was the flight after Eugene's. She had just missed him.

At Heathrow she was met by a dispatch rider from the office and read the note about Liam and Sean being on the mainland. She cursed and did as the note told her. She hired a car and drove to Boston Spa.

Commander Herbert dominated the briefing room. He paced back and forward, muttering about wrong decisions and incompetence to anyone who had the time to spare. The Inspector from the firearms team arrived with his men.

'Are you all set then, Inspector?' enquired the Commander.

'Yes, sir, the uniforms will go in first, followed by your men once we have the house under control. It shouldn't take too long. Let's do it.'

'Good luck, young man,' offered the Commander.

The firearms team travelled to the scene in a large rental van. The Commander and Boyd's team followed in a convoy of plain cars. The observers from the rectory window reported no activity at the house and the teams parked up, dismounted from the vehicles out of sight of the public road, and donned their flak jackets. They checked their weapons and moved the safety catches to the off position.

Dawn broke when the team crept slowly into position like bees around the honey pot.

'Red leader, stand by. Red one?' said the Inspector.

'Red one, ready,' replied one of the unit.

'Red two, ready.'

'Red three, ready.'

'Red four, ready.'

The teams ran through the radio drill. Nothing was left to chance.

The Inspector checked his watch and spoke into the microphone. 'All red units ready. Phase two. Execute!' he ordered.

The four firearms teams acknowledged their leader and moved closer to the house at 312 Main Street, taking up positions at the front and rear doors, with marksmen covering all the windows. Once this was done the red units reported in quietly on the radio band.

'Roger,' acknowledged the Inspector into the microphone. He turned to the Commander and suggested, 'Your men can move up to the outer perimeter, sir. We're going in now.'

Commander Herbert nodded and Boyd's team moved off.

The seconds ticked by. There was no noise save the early morning cockerel, crowing in a far off field. The sun brought a little warmth to the frosty Yorkshire scene. The village was asleep, unaware of the raid about to take place.

The Inspector checked his flak jacket and spoke into the microphone embedded in his NATO-style riot helmet. 'Phase three! Execute! Execute! Execute!'

The air was filled with the sound of splintering wood and breaking glass as the assault took place.

The team took the front and rear doors off their hinges, making a successful and speedy entrance. Whilst one team took the downstairs, another raced upstairs, a well rehearsed move that saw each man covering the other. Within a short space of time the house was secured to the satisfaction of the team leader.

Red leader called it in, 'All secure. Come!'

Boyd's team were the second wave. He emerged within minutes.

'The cupboard's bare, sir!' revealed Boyd to the Commander. 'The birds have flown.'

'We're one step behind again, William,' acknowledged the Commander. 'Search it, wall to wall, top to bottom, inside out.'

'Being done now, sir,' nodded Boyd.

The Commander produced a small hip flask containing brandy, poured two tots into the pewter flask tops, and offered one to Boyd.

The sharp liquid bit the back of the throat but went down well and helped to keep out the wintry cold.

One piece of paper was found in the garden by a young policeman. It was found on the grass bordering the pathway which pointed to the front of the house. The paper was crumpled and wet, having obviously lain in the garden for some time. The typewritten words were hard to distinguish. It was studied intensely and found to be a petrol receipt from a garage near Sandbach, a market town in Cheshire, near Crewe.

The date on the soiled receipt indicated that the purchaser had bought fuel to the value of twenty-five pounds only three days previously in Sandbach. Boyd sat studying the paper evidence for some time, trying to decide whether or not the receipt had merely blown into the unkempt garden from the nearby roadway. The alternative made him think that if the receipt was connected to the house at Boston Spa, then there was a definite Cheshire connection, one to investigate.

Boyd knew the terrorist team had been sighted at the house the previous night, when the stranger had called. He didn't need a photograph to tell him who the caller was. The time-scale from Carlisle fitted the scenario perfectly. It was the wanted man, Liam Connelly.

Grasping it at last, Boyd figured Liam had arrived as planned and Sean, who hadn't been sighted at the house, had, as anonymously as ever, called to collect his team during the night. The terrorists had vacated the premises under darkness with their own personal security uppermost in their minds. The probability existed, in Boyd's mind, that the dishevelled petrol receipt from Sandbach had been discarded by accident by the driver of the terrorists' vehicle. Either that or the receipt had just blown out of the vehicle used by the terrorists in a freak gust of wind.

Boyd decided that it was time his team had a piece of luck for a change. They deserved it. All was not yet lost. Boyd discussed the matter with the Commander.

There was no reason why Boyd should not check out the connection.

Boyd split his team, half to remain, the other half to move. Pulling out the road map, he unfolded it, spreading it out so that he could take a long look. He knew Cheshire and was keen to relate its location to other areas of interest, other possible targets. If he was right, then they were no more than eighteen hours behind the terrorists.

'Soon,' thought Boyd. 'Soon our luck will change.'

They sped across the Pennine Chain, locating the M6 motorway and Cheshire where they booked into a three-star hotel midway between

Chester and Crewe. They unpacked, took a few drinks, and slept the night away. In the morning the hunt would resume.

Naked, his skin taut and damp, crumpled sheets witness to Boyd's long and restless night. He had managed to drift into a hapless sleep eventually, but there was much on his mind and he had not slept well at all. Beads of perspiration hung loosely on his forehead and his chest. The luminous dial on the hotel alarm clock showed the day was already six and a half hours old. The sun was pushing the night clouds asunder.

The telephone rang rousing Boyd from his troubled sleep. He reached across to his bedside table. 'Hello!' he said sleepily.

'Sorry to wake you.' It was Antonia, she apologised, cheekily.

'I wasn't really asleep,' responded Boyd. 'What brings you into my world so early in the morning?'

'I'm just leaving Yorkshire. I've spoken with Commander Herbert. Some of our boys have joined the residue of your team here. The Commander wants the house searched again, just in case anything was missed first time round. We're in the process of sweeping the village dry of any information that might be there. Looks like they've kept themselves to themselves so far. Low profile as usual. There isn't much to add that will help you over there. No sightings of any vehicle here that we can tie into Cheshire. You may be on a wild goose chase for all we know.'

'Thanks, Toni,' answered Boyd. 'And thanks for the assistance with the clear up enquiries over there. I'm sorry it's a fast mover but we need to get ahead of the game instead of being one step behind. The Commander will be right on top of the job, mark my words. I'm his legs, if you want to look at it that way. Talking of legs, we're surfing this morning, estate agents, hotels, the usual. If they're here we'll find them. I promise. What are you doing now?'

'I'm on my way back to London again. God! I just got here. I've been thinking too,' she offered.

Boyd asked, 'What's on your mind?'

'Commander Herbert agrees with me. The best targets we can think of at this time are in London. I've arranged a meeting at New Scotland Yard with just about everyone I can think of. In fact, my secretary is probably getting everyone out of bed at this moment. I'm not giving anyone the choice of whether or not they wish to attend the meeting. They're going to have to reschedule their appointments for the day, I'm afraid. I'm sure the targets will be in London and an attack will be imminent. I'm going to argue like hell that the shutters go up. Round the clock patrols, increased video cameras, armed response vehicles swamping target areas, plain clothes security patrols etc. etc. What do you think?'

'Sounds good, Toni,' offered Boyd. 'Better keep a low profile on the streets, otherwise the politicians will scream that we're deliberately breaking the peace process, an act of provocation and all that. Watch out for the politicians. They live in a different world to the likes of you and me. Get them on your side if you can. Make them listen to you.'

'It's a bit higher up the ladder than me, Boyd, for that one, but I hear you loud and clear. Look, I'll ring you tonight Same number?'

'Don't know about that. I just don't know what's going to happen in the next twelve hours. Try my mobile or the pager. Take care in the big city. It's full of southerners,' counselled Boyd.

'Good!' responded the lady.

Boyd replaced his handset and ran his hand across his chin. The stubble was awake. He decided he needed to shave, but he wasn't sure if his face could take the strain.

Climbing weakly out of bed, Boyd made for the bathroom. He bent down, turned the taps, and ran his bath, adding some bubble mixture from a bottle in the wall cabinet. The bathroom was well appointed, with an electric shaving point near the basin and adjacent to a convenient mirror. He rummaged in his holdall for the electric razor.

The telephone sounded again.

What now, thought Boyd when he answered the 'phone.

'It's me! Anthea!' said the sergeant. 'It's time to wake up, oh my leader. Rise and shine, Inspector!'

'You're early, my girl. Are you still in Londonderry?' enquired Boyd, smiling at the cheery voice.

'I was. I've just got back. It was an interesting visit. I've arranged breakfast downstairs in fifteen minutes, Inspector. Get your backside out of bed and be there,' ordered the detective.

'How did you know I was here?' quizzed Boyd.

'I'm a detective!' she answered.

'So!'

'I rang Yorkshire. They told me where to find you. Toni has a tout in Derry!' said Anthea, triumphantly.

'What?' responded Boyd.

'You heard me the first time, Inspector,' said Anthea, 'A tout in Derry and a good one too. I'll see you at the breakfast table. You're buying. Hurry up! I'm starving.'

The telephone conversation, the second of the day, was again ended by the female. Boyd was getting fed up with this. It had been a bad day so far and he wasn't even dressed yet.

Cancelling the bath taps, Boyd quickly glided his razor over the stubble on his chin and dressed in record time. He took the elevator down to the breakfast room as he wondered why Miss Harston-Browne had not told him of her tout in Derry. Perhaps the tout was a new one. All would be revealed in due course. The lady from the big city would have her reasons, no doubt. But what had happened to the partnership?

Joining Anthea, he listened to her story. Yet another history of the Derry brigade unfolded before him. The early morning breakfast meeting went on until eight o'clock. The visit to the province had been worthwhile. She had recorded Padraigh's history and discovered Toni had a tout! Anthea had done well. Boyd told her so and, what's more, paid for breakfast. She ate like a horse.

Padraigh O'Toole watched the children playing in the Sands Leisure Centre in Carlisle. The omnipresent Commander Herbert wrapped up the remaining enquiries in Yorkshire. Boyd put his team to work in Cheshire, whilst Toni convinced those in London that an attack was imminent. There was no sign of the elusive active service unit. They had disappeared from the face of the earth once again.

They had gone to ground.

Boyd had a reputation for being tenacious. His team of detectives had the photographs of the terrorists they were looking for in their possession. They refreshed their memories, committing each face to their eager minds.

Boyd made another plan. Part of the plan was to mount a watch on the railway station in Crewe. The other part of the plan was to watch the link roads onto the motorway from Crewe town. Sandbach was at the centre of the plan. They were in there somewhere, according to Boyd. He could feel it in his bones. The active service unit had to travel somehow.

It was the usual ill-considered Boyd plan. Half a hunch and a gut feeling were all he ever needed. He survived on instinct. Boyd was trying to do everything with very little at his disposal, scarce resources at every corner. No one in Boyd's team argued with him. He was right more often than he was wrong. He reminded them that the key to Cheshire was the transport link with London.

In the county of Cheshire, Chester was the old Roman city, but Crewe was the old railway town. Immediately after the war years, Crewe grew in significance in the north of England when Rolls-Royce located there and mushroomed into a major manufacturing company.

The town was well placed to serve the rail traveller from the north-west of England. The M6 motorway was no more than a dozen miles from the town centre. All roads lead to the city of London.

The watchers watched and waited. Another long job ground into gear and got off to a slow start. Patience was needed once again.

Toni's meeting with the hierarchy went well. The shutters went up in the capital city. Vigilance became the order of the day, the key to success, the watchword for victory.

Commander Herbert praised his men, inspired the weary and jostled the lethargic. The game of peace had become a game of waiting. Watching and waiting.

Toni's team were in one of the surveillance response vehicles touring the Chinese sector of the Soho district, central London. Their job was to follow up on possible sightings of the suspects received from their colleagues on foot. The area was bordered by Oxford Street, Regent Street, Shaftesbury Avenue and Charing Cross Road.

She sat in the rear compartment whilst her colleague, Eric, drove the black London taxi through Greek Street and into Shaftesbury Avenue, before turning left into Gerrard Street. The Intelligence service's team were peering through the cab windows in the ceaseless search for the terrorists. They were literally touring the shady Soho streets, carefully studying the multitude of faces and comparing them with the photographs which were imprinted on their mind's eye.

The job was arduous and unrewarding, occasionally boring, it needed to be done. If they were out there, the terrorists would be checking out the selected targets, making their last minute preparations for the lethal attacks that would surely follow. The trick in the game was trying to catch the active service unit, on the streets of London, in the final throes of their deadly reconnaissance. Thereafter, the master plan was fairly simple and easily operated. One merely had to follow the faces back to wherever their base had been established and bag them all together at the same time.

Easier said than done, particularly when the person you are following has spent half a lifetime looking over his or her shoulder. The hope existed, however, that when the terrorist base was raided by police, bomb making equipment, explosives and weaponry would be found. The gang would be questioned under the terms of the Prevention of Terrorism Act. If terrorist paraphernalia were found at the base, then charges would follow. If insufficient evidence could be adduced to prefer charges against them, then the terrorists would be expelled from the mainland by the Home Secretary and returned to the province under escort.

In any event, there was no doubt that the wanted man, Liam Connelly, would be returned to Londonderry and the custody of the RUC to stand trial on the two infamous Shantallow murders and the associated arson. The intensive search continued.

Meandering incessantly in and out of the busy London traffic, the black taxi criss-crossed the area and melted into the background with the scores of other taxis on the streets. They circled for a while before moving south, navigating Piccadilly Circus and passing the statue of Eros. The taxi cab located the Haymarket and lazily followed the traffic round until it found itself in Whitehall and the heart of government. The traffic here was heavy and moving fast.

Stupendous! She saw him. He was on her right-hand side near the entrance to Horse Guards Parade. At first it was just a glimpse, but then as she focused in and moved across the rear of the taxi seat to the offside window, she confirmed her suspicions.

It was his unmistakable shaven head, bobbing majestically above the crowd. His broad features and a heavy woollen overcoat confirmed her opinion. She pressed her face to the glass window to make sure.

Yes! It was the Derry man, Eugene Kelly. Here in London.

'Eric! Stop the cab quickly,' Antonia yelled.

Eric willingly obliged, pulling into the nearside kerb midway between Downing Street and the Cenotaph. The tyre scrubbed the kerbside slightly as the vehicle came to a standstill near a lamp standard.

Toni snapped, 'Drop me off. It's Eugene. Travel back up Whitehall and pick me up on Horse Guards near the Mall. I'll be somewhere round there. Look!' She pointed towards the Ministry of Defence.

'He's gone into Horse Guards Parade. Shout it in. Code Amber. Let's not upset him.'

'He's not on my list. Who is he?' asked Eric scanning his papers.

'My man from Derry, and the man who will probably lead us to the ASU, Eric. Call it in, quickly, while I catch up with him,' ordered Toni.

She was out of the vehicle.

Eric busied himself with the radio network whilst Toni made as if she was paying the fare and set off in hot pursuit of Eugene Kelly.

Her mind was racing as fast as the London traffic. What was Eugene doing in London? Why hadn't he shown up at their last planned meeting in Derry? What was so important to have brought him so far? Was he involved with the other terrorists? Had he double-crossed her all those years ago and told her nothing but lies? Why was he in London?

A hundred questions flooded her mind as she walked briskly, gaining ground on the object of her interest. Toni decided to follow him and see what developed. The lady was exceptionally intrigued at the unexpected presence of Eugene Kelly on the streets of London.

Puffing in the heat of the day, Eugene failed to heed a friend's advice and had not taken kindly to reducing his intake of cigarettes, food or alcohol. He was, however, still a large, brutish looking man, overweight with a square chin and a shaven head. A look from Eugene could bring terror to the eyes of those who knew of him and his terrible reputation.

Making his way through Horse Guards Parade towards St James Park, Eugene came to an abrupt standstill at the edge of the footpath. He stopped momentarily at the kerbside and eyed the traffic flow.

Eugene waited for a break in the traffic. He failed to see the red-head following him and wasn't expecting to be followed in London.

A black London taxi crossed his path and pulled up further along the street from where he was standing. He ignored the vehicle, probably because he was used to seeing so many black taxis in Northern Ireland. The black taxis were a favourite mode of transport for PIRA in Londonderry, Belfast and the rest of the province.

The traffic cleared for a brief spell and he crossed the road, entering the park by one of its many gateways. Once inside the park, he had no hesitation in turning left and walked hurriedly towards Duck Island. The taxi cab stopped in such a position that Eugene could not possibly see Toni as he crossed over into the park.

She spoke briefly to Eric, updating him and using the radio to bring her squad towards their location then watched Eugene through the rear window of the cab whilst passing his description over the radio. Toni gradually positioned her people so that the main park entrances on the Mall and Birdcage Walk were under the watch of the trained eye. The net closed in around Eugene.

They watched and waited, wondering what was to happen next.

Toni explained she was unsure of the tout. She didn't know whether to approach him or lay off him and see if he led them to the active service unit.

The traffic cleared and she too crossed into the park to find out what the tout was up to! Making ground quickly on her quarry, espying him briefly, he made towards Duck Island.

Eugene found the sales kiosk situated nearby and bought a carry-out drink and a pre-packed sandwich. He took a seat near the waterside and casually flipped the aluminium ring top from his drink. Unwrapping the cellophane package, greedily, he ate the sandwich and threw the occasional titbit into the water for the ducks to feed on. Twenty minutes elapsed before he finished the soft drink. He threw the can towards a litter bin and projected it in a perfect arc into the centre of the bin. Surprise! Without warning, he was up and moving once again.

Retracing his steps, Eugene arrived back at Whitehall near the entrance to Horse Guards Parade where he stood waiting and watching.

Puzzled! Was he waiting for someone? Toni moved onto the footpath and occupied a position about forty yards from him, partly concealing herself from the brute by stepping into a convenient doorway. She radioed in, giving the current location of the man who she believed had the potential to lead them to the jackpot.

Watching and waiting again. Patience is a virtue to be encouraged in the game. An hour passed without mishap.

Eugene walked up and down the pavement between Horse Guards Parade and the Downing Street entrance. At one point he stopped near the massive black security grille that sealed off Downing Street from Whitehall. He avoided the stares of the uniformed personnel on duty in the area and acted like a tourist producing a small pocket camera from inside his overcoat and taking photographs of the Household Cavalry standing on ceremonial guard in the area.

Eugene then photographed the Cenotaph.

Toni was convinced he was waiting for someone to arrive in the area and decided he was filling in the time by pretending to be one of London's many tourists. The minutes grew into another hour and saw Eugene return through Horse Guards Parade to Duck Island. Here, he again bought a sandwich but this time selected a hot drink before returning to Whitehall.

Eugene stood sentry again as the mystery surrounding his presence in London deepened.

The lady still couldn't fathom it out. Toni joined Eric in the black taxi as Eugene walked round the nearby Ministry of Defence building on the corner of Whitehall.

He was not paying any particular attention to the building. He seemed to be more interested in checking out the pedestrians in the area.

She grasped it finally. Eugene was doing exactly the same as her own team. He was looking for someone.

Again, Eugene grew bored with looking at the people and made his way back across the road towards Duck Island.

Eric dropped Toni off from the taxi prior to Eugene's arrival.

Toni walked into the park and sat on a bench near the fast food kiosk, waiting for Eugene's arrival. Minutes passed before Eugene appeared, puffing along like an over laden train, desperate to find a railway siding for a rest.

Pulling up, Eugene bought another drink using money from a fat leather wallet. He looked for an empty seat before his eyes fell on the dangerous red-head and he nearly choked on the hot coffee about to cross his lips.

'What the...?' He said, as he looked around him. 'What are you...?'

Eugene was lost for words, finishing neither sentence, as the shock of the encounter registered on his brain and numbed his vocal cords.

'Sit down beside me,' beckoned Toni, casually.

Her voice was neither commanding nor arrogant, speaking softly to him at first, using skills she had amassed over the years. Like a pet lamb, he walked towards her, visibly shaken by her presence.

Standing in front of her, Eugene took a long look around the park before finally taking the empty seat next to Toni. He drank his coffee in such a way that he virtually tried to hide himself behind the paper mug.

'It's a small world, Eugene. What brings you to London?'

'Where did you spring from, woman?' replied Eugene.

'I heard you were in town, so I thought I'd look, you up.'

Eugene didn't answer, but shook his head in a negative fashion, from side to side.

'Okay, so I saw you in Whitehall. Have you developed an interest in historic buildings? Or is it one of the big boys in the Household Cavalry that's tickled your Irish fancy?' suggested Toni, sarcastically.

'Very funny,' he countered, not amused.

'What happened in Derry, Eugene?' she enquired. 'You stood me up last time out. Why?' she asked.

'I tried to ring you but I couldn't get to a 'phone. You won't believe me, woman! You just won't believe me!'

'Try me,' she suggested. 'The floor is yours, Eugene, try me.'

'Sure, I intended to make the last meet in Derry as arranged, but Damien sent me over here instead. I couldn't get to the 'phone because he took me straight to the airport in Belfast from Derry. I thought about walking up to the police at Heathrow when I arrived, but then I decided that would be a bit risky. I don't know how to contact you over here and I sure as hell wasn't going to ring the bastard RUC, that's for sure.'

'Good decision at Heathrow,' she offered. 'What's the score at the moment then?' questioned Toni.

Eugene sat looking out towards the ducks, watching an elderly couple throw handfuls of corn into the water. The lake became alive with birdlife, competing with each other for the best morsels.

'Come on, Eugene,' she said, 'Don't be shy.'

'Don't play with me, woman. I can't win whatever I do. Don't you understand that?' replied Eugene.

Toni tried the sympathetic approach with, 'Yes, I understand your position better than you may realise. You are in danger if you help me and in danger if you don't. Am I right?'

'That's about the strength of it, to be sure,' he said.

Toni engaged his fierce eyes and looked anxiously into that ragged Derry face. The soft sympathy in her southern voice hid the cold hard determination of her professional nature.

'One more time, for old time's sake?' she ventured.

'The last time?' he probed.

'I don't know what can be done until you tell me what you've got, Eugene,' delivered Toni. 'But you should know by now I that I will see you right.'

'Sure, and when do I get my big pay-off, woman? Don't mess me about now, that's fer sure. I'm here for an important reason and yous know it. When do yous pay me off? I've had enough of it all.'

'When it's over,' she said teasing him with her words.

'It might all start again if I don't find them first, woman.'

'Tell me what you mean by that then?'

'The day I was to meet you in Derry Damien got a 'phone call from Seamus Kelty in the south. Apparently some of the organisation don't agree with the peace process. I don't know if it's going too slow for them or if it's just not acceptable to have any kind of peace. What I do know is that there is a rogue ASU here in London at the moment.'

Eugene waited for the gist of what he was saying to sink in. Toni did not reply, but nodded and waited for him to continue.

Shuffling his big feet, Eugene placed the cup of coffee on the ground, reached into his jacket pocket, and pulled out a piece of paper. It was A4 size, folded twice and well worn. The piece of paper contained a list of public buildings and places of supreme interest in the capital city.

He played with the paper offering, turning it over and over with his fingers before announcing, 'Last year, according to Damien, Seamus gave Sean Brady instructions to carry out some massive bomb attacks here in London. The attacks were only to take place if the peace talks were not working out and the leadership wanted to exert further pressure on the government. A menu of attacks, Seamus called it, only to be actioned when the leadership sanctioned them. To be sure, Sean can more or less pick out what he wants to bomb whenever he wants. Sure, that's why Seamus called it a menu, so Sean could pick and choose!'

Pausing for breath, he took the opportunity to look round the park again. They were still alone and he allowed his voice to gain in authority as he guided the woman through his maze of mystery, 'Some of our people have never been touched over here. For every ten you've put inside, another one has been sent over from Ireland. We had such people here, sleepers yous call them. They're not all sleepers, woman. Some, you just never caught! Dedicated and hard people who would stop at nothing to achieve their objective in their own time. Sure, they've been told to do nothing while the peace talks are on. Now the rogues are out, that's for sure,' said Eugene.

'Who?' asked Toni, almost anticipating the answer.

'Sean Brady I've already mentioned. The others are Bridget Duffy, Eamonn Murphy and Dermot Dougan. My job is to find them.'

'What about Liam Connelly?' enquired Toni. 'You've mentioned him once before.'

'Did I? Yes, him too, then,' responded Eugene.

'What have you to do when you find them?' asked Toni.

'Kill them!' came the cold reply.

'Are you armed, Eugene?'

Eugene could feel the heavy weight of the gun resting in the holster under his armpit. He lied, 'No, but I can be when the time is right.'

'How?' she asked.

'My business, woman. I have contacts here, or at least the organisation has,' admitted Eugene.

'How will you find them, Eugene?'

Eugene looked down at the piece of paper and handed it to her.

'This is Seamus Kelty's menu. I've memorised it. Keep it. I don't need it anymore. Brady and the team moved down here some time ago. I suppose a week since, something like that. Anyway, it's a while since they were in London. They'll come and take a look at the targets again just to see what the security is. I don't know how they will attack, probably a bomb from some kind of vehicle, but I know that they will come.'

Eugene ran his hands over his shaven head and continued, 'When they come, I will follow them to their lair and kill them.'

His voice was cold, final, business like.

Pausing, Eugene then turned to look at Toni. Peering directly into her eyes, he declared, 'The organisation is embarrassed. The leadership has instructed Seamus Kelty to save the peace talks by eliminating the problem of the rogue ASU. Seamus sub-contracted the job to Damien who in turn has sub-contracted the killings to me. I use the organisation's eyes and ears over here on the mainland to locate them. The organisation will not tell you of this in the negotiations for peace. There is only a small percentage of the organisation against the peace. Those against the peace have the ability to wreck it if they so desire. The leadership cannot be seen to be killing its own people. After the murders I leave for warmer climes until it is safe to return, a month or two I expect. The organisation pin their hopes on me. Would you believe that?'

'You and who else?' she asked.

'The friends we have in London are also looking out for me. I control them. They work to me and no one else. Don't ask me who they are. I will not tell you. They also control my getaway route from London. I'm not stupid enough to tell you everything, woman,' said Eugene.

Toni studied the details in the so-called menu. The list contained names of public buildings. It gave their locations and, in some instances, opening times to members of the public. The list took in twenty different locations. Toni knew immediately that there was nowhere on the list that would be a surprise to anyone in Intelligence circles. Downing Street, Whitehall, the financial centre of the City, Parliament, they had all been attacked before. It would not take a great investigator to work out why they were on the target list.

The names represented the public face of the 'Establishment', the public face of the government and the public face of British political life. But if the menu were true then her entire resources could be channelled towards protecting the twenty targets on the menu.

The menu was a major find in her eyes. They were presently trying to provide security at over seventy sites in the city. Her mind consciously redeployed her staff as she read through the list. Most targets were already covered, but some hadn't figured previously. Either way she had the power to change her defensive attack plan. There was no further need for patrols in areas that were not mentioned on this menu.

The alternative crossed her mind. Eugene could have been deliberately sent over by Seamus Kelty with a red herring. Could the list be deliberately false? Had it been planted by PIRA in order to cause her to divert resources away from the true targets? Had PIRA decided to abandon the peace talks altogether and steal a march in a new offensive? Was Eugene on a fool's errand, designed to fool himself and to fool her? Did PIRA know that Eugene had been her tout all these years? Was that why they had sent him?

She needed time to consider this. The questions came and flooded her mind again. Folding the menu into her handbag, Toni looked at Eugene. It was some hours since she had first sighted him at Horse Guards Parade and now it was growing dark.

'This menu, Eugene, is it straight or a figment of your imagination?'

Eugene snapped, 'I'm tired, woman. I want out. I want it to end. The menu is straight. I saw Damien's face. He is a worried man. He will lose command of Derry if I fail him and, what's more, the leadership will eliminate him if I fail. People like Damien run the rackets in Derry for the organisation. Once the peace comes, people like Damien will run the rackets themselves, drugs and the like. The menu is straight, believe me.'

Looking him in the eye, Toni threatened, 'I could have you arrested by the policemen hiding in the bushes for possession of this list. It's enough to deal with you under the Prevention of Terrorism Act. What do you think of that, Eugene?'

'Do it then,' he challenged, holding out his wrists, waiting for the handcuffs.

'I could also add the firearms charge for the gun you have, Where is it? Shoulder holster or ankle?' asked Toni. 'You could get ten long years, minimum, Eugene.'

'I know, but you won't. You need me on the street. You know, fer sure, that I will find them before you. You could have an army on the street, but I need only a handful of Irish friends looking out for me. You won't arrest me. I can solve the problem for the IRA and the British government. All you have to do is give me immunity,' suggested Eugene.

'I can't give you immunity for murder, Eugene, but you can find them for me,' she declared.

'Do I have a choice?'

'If you find them and tell me, then I will give you the big pay-off and arrange for your disappearance to a country of your choice. I can make it so that you look as if you died in a road accident, false passport and the works! But you must find them for me and tell me where they are. If I find them before you, then tough, you've lost out. So find them quickly and tell me where. Once that is done, I will never bother you again. If you find the ASU and kill them, then you will have to look over your shoulder for the rest of your life, wondering if those against the peace have made you the subject of a contract,' said Toni, 'Or, for that matter, whether or not the police want you for murder. No immunity, Eugene, I don't trust you enough. I don't want you dribbling off at the mouth to the press in years to come that I put you up to murder. It doesn't work that way. Understand?'

Allowing her words to be taken in by Eugene, Toni shuffled into a more comfortable sitting position and said, 'Remember, your Irish friends here in England will know what you did. Can you trust them?'

Eugene sat quietly studying the tarmac in front of him. He heard traffic noise and realised he had sat too long with her. He also knew that this was his time. Time to make a killing for the Queen's shilling.

'I'll take your offer, the money in the bank account that's due, plus a big bonus for this last job, a false passport and anywhere hot that speaks English, say New Zealand, Australia, even South America, I suppose.'

Eugene began to chuckle. Somehow the pressure on his shoulders had just been lifted. For the first time Eugene, the tout, could see the light at the end of the tunnel. The big pay day was coming soon.

'Every day you will meet me here at Duck Island at two o'clock in the afternoon,' explained Toni. 'You will then give me a progress report on how the search is going. We can eventually discuss how the money can be diverted to you. I suggest part cash up front, in a relevant currency for travel purposes, followed by a credit transfer into a bank account once you're settled in wherever it is we decide to put you. After that you are on your own. I'll arrange the passport and everything else. You'd better arrange two passport photographs from one of those little kiosks as soon as possible. Have them here tomorrow so that I can work on the passport. Understand?'

'Be quick with the money. I'll have passport photographs tomorrow. Yous be sure the money is ready. Don't expect to wait long before I find them. My friends work quickly. They will turn up soon.'

'Just one more thing then, Eugene,' Toni advised.

'What's that?' he asked.

Taking a small business card and a ballpoint pen out of her purse, Toni flipped the card over, scribbled a telephone number onto the back, and handed it to Eugene.

'This is a telephone number at which you will be able to reach me at all times. If I don't answer the phone, you must pass on the information you have to the person who answers your call. It's for emergency use only. Understood?'

'I understand that, sure enough I do,' replied Eugene.

Toni smiled at him for the first time that he could ever remember and suggested, 'It's a deal then?'

'To be sure! came the reply as he studied the business card. He carefully folded the card and secreted it into his jacket pocket.

She nodded at Eugene, signifying the meeting was over. A breeze was starting to blow.

Eugene drew the collar of his coat closer into his neck.

Toni dug her hands into her anorak pockets. The artificial fur hood warmed her ears.

They both stood up and walked off in different directions.

Eric spotted Eugene emerging from the park. He started up the taxi and switched the light off indicating he was en route for a fare. Eric confirmed in his own mind that it was Eugene and looked for his boss, Toni.

He saw her walking northwards, still in the park, making for another exit. She was alright. No harm had come to her during the meeting with the man from Derry. Eric concentrated on Eugene. He called in the sighting through the radio network and the team began the long follow on Eugene Kelly. Men like Eugene Kelly were never totally trusted. They played the cautious game and followed him home that night.

Eugene walked to Westminster tube station and bought a ticket from an automatic machine. He rode the underground for what seemed an eternity, perhaps expecting to be followed. Eric's team reported Eugene eventually left the tube system some two hours later at Sloane Square station. They followed him on foot to a flat he had rented in Chelsea, just north of the River Thames.

Toni left the park about five minutes after Eugene and from an entirely different exit, just in case any of Eugene's friends had been watching. She was deep in thought. Toni knew that Eric would now take control and follow Eugene to his destination. She was happy. Boyd was out looking for the ASU up north whilst she had the centre of London to cover. Eugene was a bonus. He had been correct when he had said that he would find out where the ASU were quicker than any army that Toni could muster.

It was time to play the bonus card. Eugene had been given his head. Toni also reckoned that her bosses would be happy, as would the politicians. It appeared that the PIRA leadership wanted to maintain the peace. If all else failed, Eugene would kill the ASU and save them all the trouble. A few thousand pounds and a trip to South America for the tout. If, on the other hand, Eugene led them to the ASU and reported back to her, then the game was won. They would be able to keep the peace and manipulate the PIRA leadership. PIRA would be weakened at the negotiating table, unable to maintain discipline until the weapons and explosives had been handed in.

Terrorists in waiting, she called them. Circumstances were improving. They were getting nearer to their objective when only a week earlier they had drawn a blank at Boston Spa. She couldn't really fail now, but she still needed to find Sean Brady and his friends. They had to be located. However, the net was closing in.

Toni decided to telephone Boyd; still no need to speak of Eugene Kelly. Boyd might never need to know about Eugene if they were lucky enough to find the ASU in London whilst Boyd continued to waste his time in Cheshire. It was all going rather well for Toni.

Returning to the office, she picked up the telephone, dialled, and waited for Boyd to answer. The 'phone rang for a long time before a woman's voice answered. Toni recognised the female voice immediately.

'Hello! Incident room,' announced Anthea.

'Hello, Anthea,' said Toni. 'Where's Inspector Boyd?'

Anthea said, 'He's up north in Cumbria. He goes up once a month to see his parents and take time out. He'll be back with us tomorrow morning. Actually, I think he's going to see some relation or other in hospital. I don't know the full details. Anyway! How are things with you?'

'I'm fine, Anthea, just fine,' replied Toni. The two red-heads talked through the enquiries made so far. Both spoke of Boston Spa and Cheshire. Neither mentioned Londonderry. And neither mentioned the tout, Eugene Kelly.

≈

Boyd waved and sounded the horn as he drove the sports car down the narrow lane over the pot-holes to the main road. He bounced over the final cavity, reached the junction, and turned towards the city. He remembered to turn the sidelights on as he engaged the traffic and accelerated into the traffic flow. He swiftly changed up through the gears and sought the best from the car.

Fingering the heater system, he found warm air responding at his feet. A slight manoeuvre with his hand found the stereo and jazz music

166

filled the car. The sound of Johnny Hooper's saxophone accompanied a female singing 'Street Life'. Cool music on a chilly night.

The car accelerated and he came over the brow of the road to drop down towards the motorway. Ahead of him, he saw the broad sweep of the Solway Plain opening up in distance. The Scottish Lowlands stood proud across the Solway divide. To the south, and clearly visible in the daylight, stood Saddleback, guardian to the Lakeland Fells. Pretty lights shone like crystals across the full extent of the darkening sky, showing God's handiwork. He had done well. Wordsworth wrote poetry about Cumbria, Lowry had painted parts and Wainwright drew it. But some Cumbrians reckoned God had made it - with a little help from a Cumbrian farmer or two!

It was the evening of Tuesday, 14th March, 1995. The night on which British television announced that John Major had met Yasser Arafat at the Gaza Strip in the Middle East, Gerry Adams had travelled to the United States of America to meet President Clinton, four hundred troops from the Artillery Regiment were to be withdrawn from Ulster, and the Loyalist prisoners at the Maze had run riot setting fire to the prison and causing extensive injuries amongst some fifty prison wardens. It was an important day. A day that just might determine the course of history.

It was also the evening on which Carlisle United Football Club would beat Rochdale in the semi-final of a cup match.

The British army were withdrawing slowly and carefully from Ulster, but Michael Knighton's blue-and-white Army were preparing to invade Wembley for the Auto-Glass Cup Final, the first visit to Wembley in the history of Carlisle.

Boyd gunned the sleek black sports car over the motorway bridge and entered the city at speed. He crossed the Eden, negotiated the roundabout, turned west and drove towards the hospital. He slowed the vehicle as it negotiated the speed ramps, found a space and parked the car.

His pager sounded and he saw from the window display that Toni wanted him urgently. Locking the car under a convenient security light, he made his way briskly into the hospital, climbed the staircase, passing the white-coated medical staff, and duly located the ward. He gently pushed the two-way doors and entered the ward.

His heart beat faster, pounding. She was reaching up for some files on the top of a cabinet. He eyed her legs. He would never forget them.

'Excuse me, nurse, have I got the right ward?' asked Boyd, standing at the doorway, 'I'm looking for Pat O'Toole.'

The nurse turned and eyed the visitor carefully. 'It's Sister, actually. Sister Meg, and yes, you have got the right ward. No more than five minutes at this time of night. Who are you anyway? Not another one of those drunks from the Catholic club?' she joked.

'Billy Boyd, Sister! Friend of Pat from years gone by. Which bed is he in?' smiled Boyd.

'Boyd! Oh yes, the policeman. Pat speaks of you all the time. He'll be pleased to see you. Michael, his son, has just gone,' she said.

'Yes, Michael rang my house this afternoon. He's a smashing lad. I didn't know Pat was here until then. Pat's kept that close to his chest. Tell me, how is he?'

'Good days and bad!' replied Sister. 'He's only been with us a couple of days but it feels like weeks. He's a character I can tell you, but you probably already know that. He keeps on wittering about some cousin or relation of some kind or other who you're looking for. He keeps telling us you're the only one who can find him, so I expect he'll be at you about that.' She paused. 'I think he wants to see whoever it is sooner rather than later. Other times? Well, he sleeps mostly,' she offered.

'Not good then?' suggested Boyd, his bleeper sounded as he spoke.

'Bottom line, Mister Boyd, is that it won't be long. We can make him comfortable and we can reduce his pain to a minimum, but we can't give him back the life he so desperately wants to continue and we can't give him happiness. Only his friends can make him happy. Fortunately, he has hundreds. They've all been here this week, I think. Not too long, please. He needs the rest,' said Sister Meg.

'I wonder,' muttered Boyd. 'I've just been paged. Could I possibly use your 'phone to ring my office? It must be important.'

'No, it's not usual for visitors to use hospital 'phones.' She considered the request. 'On the other hand, your lot are never out of this place, either visiting or being treated for some fight or other. What's it worth to use the 'phone? You out of here within ten minutes so I can get them all bedded down for the night before I finish?' asked Sister. 'I should have finished hours ago. It's late enough now.'

'You're an angel,' said Boyd, trying to flatter her. 'A lift home after work for one 'phone call and a ten-minute visit to Pat?'

Sister thought about it. Pat had said he was a cheeky chappy. He was handsome. He was tall. Why not? She knew lots about the man from Pat. She decided, 'I warn you. I don't come cheap and I don't need a lift home. I have my own transport, thank you very much,' she replied.

He looked slightly hurt but was interested in her, she could tell.

She studied his face as they moved from her legs to her eyes, It was a kind-looking face. A little tired, but kindly-looking with a softness around the eyes.

'Mind you,' she added, 'You can buy me a coffee downstairs in the canteen before I go home. It's open all night.'

The man smiled at her. 'I'd like that, Sister, thank you.'

'It's Meg. Now hurry up and get on with your life and don't get under my feet.'

Gesturing to the telephone, she tidied some papers into a cabinet, and closed the door behind her as she left the small office and returned to the other patients.

'And make sure it's no longer than ten minutes at this time of night,' she shouted back at him.

'Wow!' thought Boyd. 'Some woman!'

He shook his head, still reeling under the soft odour of her perfume. She was certainly a good looker, probably early thirties, nicely built, with the curves in the right place, mousy hair and no wedding ring. He wondered about her as he lifted the telephone and dialled Toni.

'Hello, can I help you?' said Toni.

'Probably,' replied Boyd. 'You called, I answered, oh mistress of the genie.'

'Ah, Boyd! We have developments down here in the capital. I think you are in the wrong place again. Cheshire is the wrong playground. Commander Herbert met with my boss today. They have an agreement. It's a new game plan. We need to concentrate down here. We're pulling everything into the capital and I wondered if you could make a meeting with me tomorrow afternoon, say five o'clock in this office?'

It could have been an order, not a request.

'And a good evening to you. Yes, I've had a nice break at home with the family and they are all well. Yes, I'm setting off soon. I'll be in the Incident Room at Cheshire by seven in the morning. Once I've caught up with events there I'll travel south, probably train,' said Boyd.

'Sorry, Boyd. I didn't mean to get into you right away. Must be the pressure getting to me, need a good night's sleep, I expect. Glad everything is all right up there. It's just that we may need to talk soon. I think there's something you should know. I'll tell you when I see you. Not important, but I'll feel better when you know,' she said.

'I'll look forward to that, Toni. I'm setting off soon and I'll be in Cheshire by midnight. Nothing for me to think about on the way down then?' ventured Boyd.

'No, see you tomorrow, Inspector,' said Toni. The conversation ended.

Boyd replaced the 'phone and shook his head wistfully. He was getting tired of running round the country like a hound after a fox. He went to see Padraigh O'Toole.

'Time to pot the black then, Pat?' offered Boyd, for openers.

'To be sure, if it isn't the boy wonder himself,' replied Pat as he raised himself up. 'Now, how would you be this fine day?'

'Fine! More importantly, how are you? You've been keeping things to yourself, haven't you?' suggested Boyd.

'Now listen, Billyboy, don't you be going listening to all them doctor people. What do they know? The cemetery is full of people they couldn't cure, sure it is.'

Pat eased himself into a semi-seated position with the aid of Boyd's strong arms.

'Tell me, Billyboy, have you found him yet then?' He whispered, 'Our Liam I mean, that's fer sure.'

Boyd answered, 'I didn't come to talk about Liam, Pat. I came to see my old friend. Where is the good lady wife? Sister tells me Michael has just left. By the way, it was Michael who 'phoned the house to tell me you were here. Thank him for me, will you?'

'That I will,' said Pat. 'Linda! She's been here all day has the wife. Worried, you understand! She went. Michael came. You've just missed him. He's turned into a fine young man, Billyboy. 'Bout time you took a wife. You never married, Billyboy?'

'No,' answered Boyd. 'Never found the right one!'

'Why not then?' asked Pat.

'There's been plenty from the opposite sex but ...'

'But not the right one yet, Billyboy?'

'No! There was someone once,' replied Boyd, turning his mind to a redhead in London, 'But you need total trust in a partnership and it wasn't there. I thought it was then something happened. I found something out, something I thought she'd tell me. Hey! Enough of my love life, it just didn't work out, Pat. Let's leave it at that. How are they treating you here?'

'They're great. The nurses are fine. There's a little Indian one called Sindy, she's terrific, and a Carlisle girl called Vikki. Two great girls. Staff nurses, I think. You've met Florence Nightingale?'

'Sister?'

'Now there's a woman, Billyboy, a woman to make me a younger man, I think,' chuckled Pat.

'She's certainly that alright, Pat, but I think you should concentrate on getting better and getting out of here. Don't you?.

Pat's eyes dropped and he shook his head. 'Not much time. Billyboy. They tell me that every day, but I know it's got me deep inside, that's fer sure, Billyboy,' said Pat sadly. 'I know what the doctor told me months ago. The pain at first is bearable, but then it gets worse and eventually, well...' Pat's voice trailed off.

'Keep fighting, Pat. Keep fighting.'

'You mentioned partnership, Billyboy, when you were talking about marriage, remember?'

'Yes,' replied Boyd.

'I've never told you a lie since the day you saved Michael. Have you found Liam yet?'

'No,' answered Boyd.

'Then it's a bit of business we have to do this night, Billyboy. Can you get him out of it for me when you find him?' asked Pat.

'You know the answer to that, Pat. I can't get him out if he's in as deep as it looks like,' replied Boyd.

'Sure, but what if he wasn't so deep, Billyboy?'

'Then it might be different. Why?' asked Boyd.

'Sit down and listen to what I have to say then, Billyboy.'

Boyd pulled up a chair and brought it closer to the Irishman.

Pat struggled a little for air and coughed for a second or two before he regained his composure. It was going to be a long and slow death.

Boyd listened intently whilst Pat quietly explained his plan. The clock ticked on.

The final whistle went and Carlisle United went into the cup final. The Loyalists took the Maze and the televisions made their announcements. The printing presses were busy that night, preparing the news for the nation the following morning.

Boyd listened. Pat had the cheek of it, but then he was Irish.

'Hey, you two, time up. You've had more than ten minutes, Mister Boyd, now off with you and let my patient sleep,' ordered Sister Meg as she bristled into the ward.

'Sorry, Sister, I didn't see the time,' apologised Boyd.

'Don't go getting all bossy now, woman. The man's just going, that he is,' responded Pat. 'She's a Protestant that one, Billyboy, mark my words, a Protestant.'

'And that's a typical Irish remark, Mister O'Toole,' said Sister. 'It just explains why the Irish can't go forward for looking backwards. Now you, off to sleep, and you,' she pointed to Boyd, 'Off out from under my feet before I put you out myself.'

'Bye, Pat. I'll think on what you said. See you next week,' said Boyd, shaking hands with his friend. He smiled pleasantly at the nurse in the blue uniform thinking that she must have an understanding of things outside hospital life.

'Aye, I'll still be here, Billyboy. Goodnight,' said Pat.

The two men parted, with Sister ushering Boyd from the ward.

She remembered the coffee date. Boyd took the lift down to the canteen and Meg joined him within minutes. One coffee led to another and then another before they touched hands casually and Boyd managed to get a date from her during his next visit. He didn't even look at her legs, he only had eyes for her. What a find!

Meg listened. She talked and weighed him up, wondering if he were her match. When he smiled, she frowned, and when she smiled, he smiled. He threw the line, but Meg played the fish. He was chasing her, but she was catching him.

Boyd arrived in Cheshire well past midnight, was late into the office and only just caught the London train.

In the afternoon, Toni, on the instructions of her boss, told Boyd all about Eugene Kelly, the tout from Londonderry that she had been operating for all those years.

In some respects, the revelation had come too late in the day. Boyd suddenly developed an interest in nursing.

The meeting wore on laboriously. The two policemen sat on opposite sides of the large polished walnut desk, only the tabletop and a bank of telephones between them.

So! Toni has a tout in London,' said Boyd. 'It doesn't really change things to any great extent in Cheshire, sir. I mean, it isn't stopping us from carrying on our search.'

'But she's right,' answered Commander Herbert. 'The tout is there because he knows that is where he will find them.'

'Or I might strike lucky before then in Cheshire, sir,' suggested Boyd. 'Who knows what we'll turn up if we get lucky?'

'On the strength of one petrol receipt, William?' asked Commander Herbert. 'Come! Come!'

Leaning forward in the chair, Boyd poured more coffee into his cup. He gestured to top up the Commander's drink, but the older man shook his head and moved to cover his cup with his hand.

'Don't close me down again, sir. I feel it in my bones, and in any case, we haven't finished all our enquiries up there,' replied Boyd.

Commander Herbert stared directly at Boyd. 'How long will that take?' asked the Commander.

'Who knows? Perhaps a week or two at most,' suggested Boyd. 'We're working round the clock now.'

'Yes, I understand, but by that time it might all be over.'

'That depends on the time scale of things, sir. We don't know what their game plan is,' revealed Boyd.

'Do we ever?' ventured the Commander swivelling his chair round. He studied the wall charts showing all the coloured paper flags and atrocities of the past. It wasn't computerised high grade technology on the wall charts - paper flags are far from that- but it did adequately portray the problem they faced. When would it end and how would it end? He thought his strategy through carefully as he tapped a pencil against the end of his nose. He quickly turned back to face Boyd.

'This list given to Toni by her tout might be designed to take us down the wrong road. We could run around forever, up and down blind alleys, William!' stated the Commander.

'That wouldn't be new to us, sir. It's what we get paid for, isn't it?'

'Amongst other things, yes. But I'm not going to close you down, William,' decided the Commander 'You're both right. We must cover London and we must complete our enquiries in Cheshire. I have enough undercovers in London at the moment to eat the job. Did you know that I have over a hundred armed officers in plain clothes quietly patrolling these target areas, just watching?'

'And waiting,' said Boyd

The Commander said, 'Yes, William. Nothing has changed. Watching and waiting. It's like a big game of chess, isn't it? Who is next to move, I wonder?'

Commander Herbert held the silence as he considered the options.

Boyd held his tongue.

'No!' decided the Commander. 'Go back to Cheshire and turn the screws on the job up there. Get it done as quickly as possible and give my very best to the local Cheshire squad. They've had a big part to play these last few years, Warrington and all that, you know? You couldn't have better people to work with.'

'I know that, sir,' agreed Boyd.

'Sometimes, William, people at the top like me should listen to people on the streets like you. That way, we'd probably be ahead of the game instead of behind it. I made a mistake. I should have kept the operation at Boston Spa going on a twenty-four hour basis. But I played politics and saved money. If I had kept you going, then who knows? We would probably have them in the bag now,' said Commander Herbert.

Boyd nodded, but didn't respond. It wasn't easy to agree with someone that they had probably made a mistake, particularly when loss of life was always a distinct possibility.

'Anything else come out of yesterdays meeting with Toni?'

'No, sir, nothing new,' replied Boyd.

'Good! One thing, William?'

'What's that, sir?' enquired Boyd.

'Are you hurt? All this time and not knowing about the tout.'

'Slightly, but I understand why I wasn't told. Loose talk comes from everywhere, doesn't it? Even policemen,' suggested Boyd.

'Yes,' replied Commander Herbert, 'Touts are important to us. We couldn't do our job without them, so we keep their identities a secret. Thank you for being so understanding, William. I won't forget.'

'It's not a great problem, sir, but it does make you wonder at times, doesn't it?' said Boyd.

'How do you mean?'

'Well, we are all doing the same job. I suspected a tout, but I hadn't worked out who it was until Anthea returned from Derry. I thought it could have been any one of the ASU, even Sean or Liam. You never know, do you?' said Boyd.

'We've lost nothing, William. When the time was right, we told you,' said the Commander.

'You mean you knew?' asked Boyd.

'Yes, William, I knew. Now you know. Cheshire, William, time for you to go to Cheshire. Don't think it's because we don't trust you. Just remember the game is sometimes about keeping touts alive. Touts expect to be trusted, okay?'

'Yes,' responded Boyd as he rose from his seat. 'I'll be on my way north again then, sir.'

'Good luck, William,' offered Commander Herbert.

Boyd left the Commander's office and walked down the passage to his own sanctuary. He sat silently by his desk and surveyed the contents. The desk was cluttered with paperwork and roughly scribbled notes. On the desk top sat two framed photographs, one of his parents and another which was a smaller cameo of Toni on the top of Saddleback. It was a colour photograph, obviously taken on a sunny day. Any thoughts of a long-term romance were over.

Opening a drawer, Boyd shuffled the cameo of Toni inside, closed the desk, and locked it as usual.

He was an old-fashioned man in a funny sort of way. Lack of trust between the two was no basis for a long-term relationship. His thoughts wandered to the north.

Boyd lifted the telephone and rang the hospital in Carlisle to find out how his Irish friend, Pat, was bearing up. The switchboard was jammed with calls, but he eventually got through to the terminal ward.

Sister Meg answered in a chirpy fashion. Ten minutes later she told Boyd that Pat was holding up well. In between time, Boyd tried to flatter and impress. She would have none of his cheeky telephone antics but reminded him of their date for his next visit home. She was looking forward to it. He felt good, a lot happier. He replaced the telephone.

As soon as it touched the cradle, the 'phone rang. He reached for pen and paper, in case he needed to make a note. It was Anthea's voice. He detected the excitement creeping into her tongue once she spoke.

One of Boyd's men had made a possible sighting of Eamonn Murphy driving a furniture van on the motorway into Cheshire. The officer had turned to follow the vehicle but had lost it in the heavy traffic.

The owner of the furniture van, however, had been traced locally, to a firm trading as Clive Montague and Partners of Sandbach, Cheshire.

Enquiries had been instigated immediately by Anthea. Clive Montague's firm was a small concern specialising in furniture removals. Their premises were two and a half miles from a garage where a petrol receipt had been obtained some weeks earlier and recovered from the front path of a certain house in Boston Spa, Yorkshire. The only other thing that they had been able to find out in the time available, was that Clive Montague himself was an Englishman of Irish parentage.

Clive Montague was not known to either the local police or the local special branch. He was a mystery man, apparently. Anthea was organising a close watch on the Clive Montague business. It could be the breakthrough they had worked for. Boyd cheered out loud, told Anthea she was wonderful, banged the 'phone down and made for Cheshire.

As he pulled the office door behind him he was heard to shout loudly, 'Yes!' before clenching his fist in the air.

Anthea spread out the ordnance survey map before her, bent over to take a closer look and focused on the target area using a magnifying glass. One of the local detectives located the Montague premises on the grid and drew a big red circle round the area. The coordinates were taken and passed by telephone to a spotter in a police aeroplane.

The premises were in the country, partially hidden from the main highway. There was one road, in and out. The site was at the end of a cul-de-sac. A large wooded area, criss-crossed by a number of small streams, bordered the rear with an abandoned rock quarry lying no more than a mile from the Montague business.

Studying the map, Anthea carefully made a plan. She plotted surveillance positions for the team of hand-picked watchers. When she had finished, she pinned the map to the wall and realised there was no time to celebrate. They hadn't won yet. Anthea studied the map on the wall again, mentally calculating distances between the key towns and villages as well as picking out the high ground and the waterways in the area. She needed to know the location well.

Anthea committed the map to her memory. The team she had summoned walked into the compact police office and sat down. Anthea drew their attention to the map on the wall and briefed them up on the suspected sighting of Eamonn Murphy. She knew her men well. When one of them reported such a thing, her experience was to follow it through. The team were not famous for red herrings. If one of the team said, 'I think it was Eamonn,' then that was enough for Anthea. The trust came from working with the same people day in and day out.

The team started to gather together the equipment they would need for the operation. The hustle and bustle intensified. The atmosphere was one of anticipation. They carried empty holdalls and went to the shelves at the rear of the office. They selected the encrypted radios, the maps, the binoculars and all the paraphernalia required for the arduous task in hand.

The team laughed and joked. They had the bit between their teeth now. Something felt right about this new lead. The investigation was at last starting to move on, to take shape, to reach a climax.

The team collected the car keys from the disposition board bolted to the wall and filed out of the office with their briefing sheets, note pads, vacuum flasks and bags, and set off for their predetermined positions.

Another job twisted and turned yet again.

The centre of intrigue was one Clive Montague. He was a wheeler and a dealer. Clive was an Englishman born of Irish parents, both of whom hailed from Londonderry, in the province of Ulster.

Clive Montague had been born in London, where his father had been employed in the construction trade doing subcontractor work as a builder, a plumber and a labourer. Indeed, his father was the type of man who could turn his hand to just about anything, and often did. It rubbed off on Clive.

When the parents returned to Londonderry to settle into old age and a deserved retirement, Clive started a haulage business on the outskirts of Sandbach. From this location he spent his days feeding the motorway and the great conurbations of Manchester, Liverpool, Cheshire and the Wirral peninsula. Clive was the kind of man who could turn a penny into a pound.

He was a married man living in a split-level bungalow he had built himself next to the warehouse facility in which he now conducted his small, but expanding, removal business. Clive was really a self-employed entrepreneur with a sharp business brain who owned three furniture vans but made much of his income by renting out the warehouse for goods in transit. He also owned a small, but profitable, business in central London.

Living near Sandbach for over eighteen months, Clive was a hard worker but quick to spot a fast buck and somewhat shady in the manner in which he dealt with the many gypsies, itinerant travellers and dealers who regularly crossed his path. He took an Irish wife and loved her dearly.

Mrs Montague was a Derry woman, born and bred on the Galliagh estate, north of the Foyle. Clive had not been unduly suspicious when two Irishmen called at the warehouse to leave the dark blue, hand painted, furniture van. One of the men carried a cat perched on his shoulder and was a softly spoken individual who did not give much away about himself. The other, the driver, had been much more open, joking and paying Clive in advance in English five pound notes for the rental agreement. It was after they had gone he had started to worry.

Eamonn Murphy parked the furniture van near the entrance to the warehouse and made sure all the doors were locked and the rear padlocked. They left the minibus at the warehouse and boarded the bus to drive back to their base in Crewe. Dermot sat in the front passenger seat with the cat on his lap. Scrappy licked Dermot's fingers and purred contentedly as Dermot occasionally tickled the cat under the throat.

Negotiating the Crewe streets, Eamonn found the flat and parked on the wasteland at the rear. The two men locked the minibus and climbed the stairs. They entered the flat using the front door key and walked in to see Sean and Bridget on the sofa.

Cold, Liam switched the electric fire up onto a higher setting.

'Parked up on the truck stop, is she then, boys?' asked Sean.

'No, we couldn't get it on. The wagon park is full, so it is,' replied Eamonn.

'What!' snapped Sean. 'I told you to put it on the truck stop with the rest of them, so I did! Where is it for God's sake?'

'Just outside Sandbach in a warehouse,' volunteered Eamonn.

'Tell me about the warehouse,' ordered Sean.

'No sweat, Sean, it's near that petrol station just outside the town,' replied Dermot.

'You fools,' argued Sean, 'I told you to put it on the park with the other lorries. It's far too near the garage, you idiots! On a lorry park it's one of hundreds, in a warehouse it's one of a few. Who's looking after it?'

Eamonn looked sheepish and replied, 'It's okay, sure it is.' It's the Englishman, Clive Montague. It will save us time when we go. It's just a small concern. He'll never know, believe me, Sean.'

'This Englishman, what do you know about him?' asked Sean.

'His parents are Irish, sure they are, from Derry, would you believe?' explained Dermot.

'And you should have more sense, Dermot,' countered Sean. 'So this Irishman will know your faces then?'

'Aye,' acknowledged Eamonn.

'And your Derry accents?' queried Sean.

'I suppose,' confirmed Eamonn.

'Did you pay him well?' probed Sean.

'Aye, the going rate in English pound notes,' countered Dermot.

'It's too near the garage. Never the same place twice, you fools! You should know that by now,' said Sean. 'Come on, we'll move it now. Clive doesn't know we intend to use his London business for the hit. There's no sense in leaving your calling card all over the place.'

'There's no need, Sean,' argued Eamonn.

'I'll decide on that, Eamonn, and I say we move it now. Let's put it where we agreed. Clive's business in London is our business, but he doesn't know what we're up to and he's not going to get the chance. Come on, Liam,' said Sean.

With that, Sean and Liam left the flat, taking both the mini, bus keys and the furniture van keys from Eamonn as they rushed out of the door. They jumped into the minibus and headed for Sandbach.

'I can't believe it, Liam,' said Sean. 'I planned to break into Clive's house and take the spare keys for the London shed and those clowns go and park the furniture van there. Unbelievable! Clive's warehouse in Battersea is part of the plan. He knows nothing of it. I planned to take his keys, collect the furniture van from the lorry park and go down and do the job, all within twenty-four hours.' Sean continued to talk as he drove with his fingers drumming the steering wheel nervously. 'I don't like it. I don't want him looking at the big van so we'll try and move it without him realising it's gone. Who knows? He might not even be there when we arrive. If he is then we'll tell him we've been told to collect the van ahead of schedule and take it up to Scotland. That way we get the van, he keeps the money and he'll be none the wiser when his house gets screwed. I know it's not brilliant, but I don't want him nosing about the van. Out there in the country, he could do just that. If they'd put it on the lorry park where I'd told them, no one would give it a second look. I can't afford him to put two and two together before we're ready.'

'What do you mean? Is it the barge that bothers you?' asked Liam.

'Aye, that it is,' said Sean.

'Jesus!' said Liam. 'Just move the van then, quick as you like. He'd never know, would he? And if he did report it to the police, and I doubt it since he's been paid, then it'll all be over. Jesus, if we take it now, he'll just think the boys have had to come back for it, just like you said. You're right though, Sean, the lorry park would have been better. Hundreds instead of only a few. Less attention to it and all that. Get a move on.'

The minibus sped towards Sandbach, threading through the traffic towards the warehouse.

Clive Montague took another look at the furniture van. The paint on the bodywork seemed fresh. Intrigued, of course, he remembered now. He was looking at a vehicle that once belonged to him. He had bought the van months ago at an auction and registered it in his name before selling it to a dealer in the Midlands, making £100 in the process.

Clive wondered whether the van was still registered in his name as he considered the ironic circumstances that had returned it to his care. The vehicle was locked. He went to the office and collected a bunch of spare keys. The shady business he found himself in had taught him to collect keys for a host of different vehicles. He would often plunder loads from lorries, guessing that drivers would be blamed for shortages when the cargo arrived at the delivery point.

Walking back towards the warehouse, carrying the large bunch of keys with him, he felt them rattle by his side as he made his way over the smooth tarmac.

Sean and Liam passed through Sandbach.

Anthea's team had been briefed. They left the office and were climbing into their vehicles to make for the watching ground.

A police aeroplane made its way down the runway. The navigator plotted the course and loaded the cameras with new film. The pilot radioed for clearance to take off. It was granted. They would be in the air within minutes. The pilot increased his ground speed and began to ease back the stick.

Selecting the right key, Clive entered the cabin of the furniture van and rummaged in the front of the vehicle before checking under the seats. He hoped to find either a forgotten wallet, a discarded cheque book, or some other titbit that would make his day and increase his income.

Sean found the lane and turned down the tarmac strip towards the warehouse. The site was bordered by trees, but he took no notice as the vehicle sped along over the newly laid entrance.

Anthea manoeuvred the saloon car through the Crewe traffic as a police aeroplane penetrated the airspace over Crewe, banked and turned towards Sandbach.

The pilot reported his position and made his course to the grid references given earlier. The clouds parted and the police spotter saw the green countryside of Cheshire resplendent beneath him.

Linda Montague busied herself in the kitchen, wondering what her husband was up to. She dusted the worktops and rearranged the collection of dolls resting in the pine kitchen display cabinet. All the dolls were in Irish dress and reminded her of home. One day they would make a fine present for the daughter she longed for.

Clive abandoned his search of the cab. It had been fruitless. There was nothing worth stealing on this occasion, not even a credit card to sell to his dubious contacts. The vehicle was covered by the roof and parked no more than ten feet from the entrance. There was no one else nearby, save his dutiful wife, doing the housework.

He didn't hear the minibus approach.

The rear window of the cab was covered by an old curtain.

Clive drew it back and looked into the locked compartment that carried the load. The window was dirty and covered with grease. Unable to make out the cargo, Clive took a rag from his overall pocket and cleaned the window so he could see into the rear. There had to be something worth stealing. Furniture vans always carried a good bounty.

'Good God!' Clive's heart missed a beat and he started to sweat.

Parking the minibus at the entrance to the warehouse, Sean saw Clive's legs dangling from the open cabin door. He saw Clive cleaning the rear window of the cab. The curtain across the back of the cab had been withdrawn.

Clive didn't see the man who killed him. He merely felt his legs being dragged backwards onto the concrete floor. His knees bounced on the tarmac as he unceremoniously hit the ground and he felt the pain shoot up his legs towards his hips. Then he felt the cold muzzle of the handgun against his temple.

Sean pulled the trigger and blew Clive's brains onto the floor.

A pool of blood slowly seeped into the concrete.

Clive Montague died instantly. A victim of his own curiosity and another victim of the terrorist war. He was in the wrong place at the wrong time.

'Inside, Liam! Quick! Drive! Here's the keys,' said Sean, as he handed over the ignition keys.

'Wait!' said Sean. 'Let me have a look here. We might be lucky. You never know, do you?'

Turning Clive's body over, Sean knelt beside the body, rifled the overall pockets, and found what appeared to be Clive's own private keys.

Examining the keys, he smiled and said, 'That's the one, Liam. The one with the blue tag. Pocket it and drive to the yard near Battersea. Go to the safe house there. I'll collect the rest and join you soon. We'll have to bring it forward, but no matter.'

Liam took the keys, settled into the cab, started the diesel engine, and looked down at the motionless body of Clive Montague. It bothered him the killing had been so cold and calculated. No time for questions, no bargaining, no explanations, just a short sharp bullet to the brain. Life snuffed out in an instant, without either remorse or pity.

Mrs Montague heard the gunshot. At first she thought it was one of the vehicles backfiring, but then she couldn't hear an engine noise to go with it. She dried her hands with a tea-towel as she walked out of the back door towards the warehouse. She saw the body of a man lying on the ground near a furniture van. She didn't realise it was her husband until she walked closer and saw the overalls.

Dark red blood trickled slowly down from his temple onto the vast concrete floor. He was lying inside the warehouse with the doors opened.

Linda remembered seeing a man in the cab of the furniture van with his hands on the steering wheel, looking down at the body of her husband then she saw Sean Brady.

180

She didn't have time to scream or rush to her husband's side.

Sean Brady saw her coming and put a bullet between her eyes, just above the bridge of her nose.

Linda Montague fell backwards to the ground, thrown there by the powerful force of the bullet. She still held the damp Irish linen tea-towel in her hands as Sean walked over to her.

He listened to her murmuring, pushed the dying woman over with his foot, looked into her pretty Irish face, bent down, and callously drilled another bullet into her head at close range.

Linda died immediately, her brain powerless to either stimulate or activate her young lithe body.

The blood splattered and covered the tea-towel

'Look you, Liam!' cracked Sean, 'Sure, a tea-towel made in Ireland, but dyed red with blood in Sandbach.'

Placing the handgun into the rear waist band of his trousers, Sean heard an aeroplane approaching and casually glanced up into the sky to see only clouds.

Laughing, he asked, 'I wonder if she was Irish? Still, no matter. It had to be done. We don't want any witnesses. On yer way, Liam. No more time to waste.'

Slowly manoeuvring the furniture van out of the warehouse, past the two corpses and into the lane that would take him to Sandbach and the motorway, Liam looked down at the bodies.

Where once there had been life, there was now death. Life had been taken without a thought and without a care.

Liam felt sickened by the outrage. It was one thing to fight for the cause and another to kill for the sake of it. That had never been Liam's way. He wondered if the woman had been Irish. Whether she was Irish or not didn't matter anymore. She was dead, so was the husband. Neither of those murdered could be argued as legitimate targets to the organisation's cause. The murders had been carried out by a man driven by an unquenchable thirst for violence and mayhem. Murders that did nothing for the cause, not even a step towards a peace or a victory of some kind. Death at the hand of Sean Brady was no more than a savage and brutal ritual. A ritual that Sean appeared to enjoy when it suited him, and when he needed to protect his own skin.

Driving through the picturesque towns scattered throughout Cheshire, Liam eventually took the motorway south to London.

Sean Brady didn't blink an eyelid at the carnage he had caused. Remorseless, he climbed into the minibus and returned to Crewe, collected the remainder of the ASU, and set off after Liam. No mention of the killings was made to Dermot, Eamonn and Bridget.

'It's just a change of plan,' explained Sean.

The police aeroplane overflew the warehouse as the cameras filmed at the ground below them. The occupants of the 'plane could not see the corpses lying inside the warehouse nor did they see the furniture van and the minibus as they sped away from the scene.

Slowly and carefully, Anthea's team surrounded the site and began the watch.

It was some hours before one of the detectives stealthily took up a position near enough to see directly into the premises. They were cautious and they were careful, because they didn't know what to expect and they didn't know whether there was a relationship between the Montague family and the active service unit. There was a chance this could be the lair they had been searching for. A chance to wait and to watch and to arrest them all in one well planned raid.

The detective who cleverly secreted himself in the woods used high powered binoculars to scan the site, looking for signs of Montague and the targets they so desperately sought. He reported on the radio that the site looked deserted, almost dead. A short time later he saw the dead.

He called it in before his stomach heaved its contents onto the concrete floor next to the pool of blood. Clive Montague's warehouse became a murder scene.

Anthea blamed herself for being too slow but Boyd arrived and reminded her she couldn't have acted any faster.

The men in white coats arrived and started to gather forensic evidence.

Mr and Mrs Montague were placed into body bags and taken to the mortuary. The police slowly started to piece together their lifestyles, private lives and public businesses. There was no sign of the furniture van that had led everybody to the quiet Sandbach countryside.

The luck of the Irish held again, with the exception of a family on the Galliagh estate in Londonderry. They would mourn the death of their daughter and son-in-law to their final days. Clive's parents watched the television, read the newspapers and learnt about a bomb planted in a Texas retail store in Newry. A warning had been given, so there had been time to defuse the device and save loss of life. Another bomb disposal officer had earned his daily bread. They grieved for the loss of their son and daughter-in-law and wondered how peace could be achieved. Even in the quiet Cheshire countryside, there was no escape from 'The Troubles'.

A long black coat swirled round the man's knees. The gale swept across the busy Derry street, billowing the man's trousers behind him and blowing litter up into the air. He waited for a safe gap in the traffic and crossed the road towards the telephone kiosk. Casually, he checked his wrist-watch. Damien Devenney awaited his contact with Eugene Kelly.

The agreed time approached. Damien waited for a few moments, moving closer to the designated kiosk as the street gradually filled with morning shoppers looking for the latest bargains in the windy streets.

A RUC Land Rover moved slowly down the street, its occupants studying the people as they went about their business. The vehicle was coloured battleship grey and the windscreen was covered with a protective wire mesh. Only weeks earlier it would have been accompanied by an army patrol, with young soldiers bobbing and weaving along the streets, some crouching low, some turning and pointing their rifles at the direction from which they had come. Ever cautious, ever vigilant. The constant patrols in support of the police had recently been the norm.

Now the fear of the past had been replaced by an uneasy anticipation. An anticipation rooted in the belief that there was an uneasy peace, a peace that needed to be respected, almost revered, but certainly monitored. Peace would not happen overnight It took time.

The telephone rang and Damien stepped into the kiosk with one eye on the disappearing Land Rover as he picked up the instrument. In London, Eugene Kelly kept his appointment as he looked through the windows of the 'phone box out onto the Thames.

'Sure, it's me,' announced Eugene. 'No sign of the packages yet, though I'm still searching the mail, so I am.'

'Keep looking, the packages can't be far away. I thought you might like some more help if you can't find them, so I did,' offered Damien.

'Not yet, plenty of good friends here helping. I just need more time. Nothing has happened down here yet, but I expect the packages to arrive any day now. Don't you agree?' suggested Eugene.

'Sure, that's about right. I thought they would have arrived by now.'

'I'm a bit concerned, mind you!' said Eugene.

'Why's that then?' asked Damien, as he eyed the Derry streets.

'What happened down in Newry?' asked Eugene.

'Nothing to get concerned about. Looks like some friends of ours who are a little disheartened at the way things are going. Just a reminder, I think, don't you?'

'A reminder to who, from who?' asked Eugene.

'Don't concern yourself with such matters. You have your instructions, attend to them now and don't ask questions that don't concern you.'

'That's fine then. I was wondering, so I was, and being so far away I didn't quite know what to make of it all,' answered Eugene hopefully.

'Sure, I can understand that, my friend, so I can. Thanks for the call. Are you alright for money?'

'Aye,' replied Eugene.

'I like to know how you're going on. Ring me same time, day after tomorrow. You may have sorted the mail out by then?' suggested Damien.

'You'll know when I do,' replied Eugene replacing the telephone.

Damien smiled to himself, cut the connection, and stepped out of the kiosk into the windswept street. He made his way to the Dun Low public house for an early drink.

The bar was starting to slowly fill up with the locals. Damien was glad of the shelter from the unfriendly elements outside. He was also very pleased to learn that his man in London had kept the telephone contact. It reassured him Eugene was still out there looking for the rogues and still thinking about the negotiating process going on behind the scenes.

'Soon!' thought Damien. 'Soon!'

Eugene Kelly stepped out of the London 'phone box and walked along the Embankment. London was experiencing a different kind of weather. The capital was in springtime bloom with bright sunshine, although there was a typical March breeze. Today Eugene was checking out the riverside area in central London. His friends were in the City, searching the financial areas that drove the British economy, but Eugene chose a quiet walk by the river.

As Eugene turned into Bridge Street to find Millbank and the Houses of Parliament, a black taxi changed position to cover the man's anticipated movements.

Eric pressed the button on the wireless set and radioed in the change of circumstances. The followers were on the move again.

The saloon cars engaged the hectic London traffic and those on foot mingled discreetly with the London crowds.

Eugene huffed and puffed, like a steam engine, slowly down Millbank towards Lambeth Bridge, the famous Tate Gallery and Pimlico. All this exercise was good for him. He was shedding a few pounds and firming up the odd muscle here and there though he wasn't consciously aware of that.

The followers followed.

Eugene remained unaware of their presence.

The followers were professionals. They kept their target in sight using the street furniture to best advantage. The soldiers in Derry had once bobbed and weaved on their armed patrols. On the streets of London the Intelligence services still bobbed and weaved behind the vehicles, the advertisement boards, the newspaper stands and the bus shelters. A different organisation, waging war against the enemy in a different manner.

Meanwhile, Eamonn Murphy carefully negotiated the Kennington traffic and headed directly towards the Oval. He made the massive roundabout and steered the minibus past the renowned cricket ground and along Harleyford Road towards Vauxhall Bridge.

A dispatch rider on a powerful red motorcycle tore past the minibus at speed, narrowly missing the front offside wing as the young leather-clad rider swerved to the nearside of the carriageway to avoid a pedestrian, who had unwisely strayed into the street.

Sean Brady sat in the front passenger seat, with Dermot Dougan and Liam Connelly in the rear. The radio was tuned to a local station and the music was playing softly in the background. Liam was looking at the London sights from his vantage point. Sean held a key in his hand and was tapping it against the vehicle dashboard. Attached to the key was a blue keyfob the property of the late Clive Montague of Sandbach, Cheshire. The nearside window was rolled down, allowing Sean to casually rest his left arm on the open window ledge.

Holding the key aloft in his left hand, Sean turned to face the rear passenger compartment and waved the blue tag at Dermot.

'So, what do you think, Dermot? Everything alright or is there something I forgot?' probed Sean.

'No problem, Sean,' replied Dermot. 'Just yous be leaving it all to me from now on. Once I've got the timing sorted out we're in business, that's fer sure now.'

'Good,' smiled Sean. 'That's what I like to hear.'

Sean turned to face the front and played with the keyfob, his fingers fiddling with the blue leather tag. Looking to his left, upstream, the Thames was as grey and forbidding as ever. They were halfway across Vauxhall Bridge with the river beneath them slowly creeping down to the sea. At the midway point on the bridge the road is characterised by the brow of a hill. Six traffic lanes make up the road surface and there is a footpath on either side of the road. One lane is designated a bus lane to cater for the early morning rush hour. The old bridge is painted red, navy blue and gold, with its name etched neatly in the stonework. Millbank Tower dominates the area and looks sternly down on the river below.

Eugene Kelly stood at the bus stop near the junction with Millbank and Vauxhall Bridge Road waiting to cross into Grosvenor Road and continue his riverside quest towards Chelsea. The traffic was heavy and he had been scanning the faces of vehicle occupants as they passed him by. There was always the chance he might just see them. His followers renegotiated their positions as he stood waiting for the traffic to part so he could cross over the busy road.

Eugene was, in fact, virtually surrounded by a well hidden, ever changing, sea of faces and drivers who remained near enough to see him without been seen themselves.

Suddenly, without warning, the red motorcycle ploughed into the rear of a black London taxi. There was a loud crushing noise. The dispatch rider was thrown upwards and slightly to the offside as the front wheel of the motorcycle buried itself into the rear of the taxi, spoiling both the bumper bar and the luggage compartment. Immediately in front of the taxi was a flat-backed heavy goods vehicle laden with long steel pipes of various lengths which protruded over the rear of the flat lorry bed. The taxi lurched forward, colliding with the rearmost pipe.

The windscreen of the taxi exploded as the first few feet of pipe work rushed across the taxi bonnet and penetrated the windscreen. The remainder of the shorter steel pipes followed and projected themselves towards the drivers head.

Eric was the taxi driver. His quick brain saved him from certain death as he threw himself to the nearside floor of the taxi and the pipes shot across the space where his head had once been. He was trapped grotesquely underneath a row of steel pipes that drilled themselves further into the taxi. Semi-conscious, Eric lost control of the radio network.

The followers, whom he supervised, did not realise he was out of the game. They wrongly presumed he had his eye on the target, Eugene.

Mayhem continued when the steel tether holding the pipe work onto the lorry snapped under the pressure of the impact. The pipes spilled onto the roadway and bounced uncontrollably towards the pavements on both sides of the road.

An oncoming estate car was hit on its offside by the first steel pipe to fall from the load. The car mounted the pavement and careered into a lamp standard slewing broadside and blocking the carriageway.

The driver lost consciousness when his head crashed into the steering wheel and he was thrown backwards like a rag doll into an unexpected sleep.

The motorcyclist who had caused the accident lay motionless on the roadway with his leathers torn by the tarmac surface. The black full-face crash helmet probably saved his life. The visor covering the rider's face splintered as his head rolled to one side.

Hitting the brakes as hard as he could, Eamonn locked all four wheels. The minibus skidded to a halt with the rear of the vehicle slewing to the offside of the carriageway. The three passengers catapulted forward as Eamonn gripped the steering wheel and brought the minibus to a standstill only a few inches from the motor cycle.

The road ahead into Westminster was blocked.

Hearing the commotion, Eugene walked slowly towards the accident situated at the brow of the hill near the centre of the bridge. He walked past the stonemasonry inscribed 'Vauxhall Bridge' and climbed the very slight incline towards the midway point.

The followers radioed to Eric that the subject was crossing the bridge. They knew Eric was travelling over the Thames but it was some minutes before they realised what had happened. In the chaos that followed, they did not record the actions of Eugene Kelly who walked towards the scene of the accident.

There were pipes all over the highway with the motor cyclist lying unconscious on the road. A taxi was married to the rear of a lorry and an estate car was lying at right angles to the road. A minibus in the distance had narrowly missed the carnage but had ended up facing neither north nor south, resting in a haphazard position in the centre of the roadway. The traffic was gradually backing up behind the accident.

The shaken occupants of the minibus slowly got out of the vehicle.

Eugene recognised his quarry.

'Keys, I've lost the key. Where's the key?' cried Sean holding his head with both hands. Patting himself down, he remembered where they were. 'No! No! The key! It's on the road somewhere, fell out of the window, must have! Bang! Smash! Key out the window, where?' said the confused and shaken Sean Brady.

Falling to the ground onto all fours, Sean frantically looked for the key fob.

Eamonn walked towards the motor cyclist but stopped on the way. No, he thought, we can't help, must get away, move, keep moving, where to? The road, it's blocked. And then he shouted, 'Sean! Sean!'

Seizing the moment, Eugene rushed towards the pipe work and dropped to one knee. Smoothly, he removed the weapon from his shoulder holster and fingered the money belt inside his waistline. It wasn't money he was looking for. He found the silencer and quickly screwed it to the barrel of the gun. Peering cautiously over the pipes, Eugene moved to his right to adopt a better firing position.

A motor cyclist was murmuring and trying to get to his feet.

Taxi occupants were nowhere to be seen.

And the lorry driver was irrelevant.

Eugene shot Eamonn dead with two bullets that penetrated the heart through the chest cavity and exited Eamonn's back, fracturing his spinal cord en route.

As Eamonn fell to the ground, Eugene took up another firing position while still bent on one knee. He chose his next target, Liam.

Liam watched Eamonn stagger towards the motor cyclist but couldn't understand why Eamonn had suddenly been thrown backwards.

Why? Then he saw the hole in Eamonn's chest and knew exactly what the score was.

Turning, Liam ran for cover as a low sounding 'zip' scorched the air above him.

'Move!' yelled Liam. 'Eamonn's dead! Shots fired! Move! Run!'

'Shots! What shots?' asked Sean. 'Keys, must find the key.'

'Get in, Sean, get in the bus,' snapped Dermot running towards the driver's seat. Another quiet 'zip' rifled through the air and smashed into the side of the minibus only a foot away from Dermot and Liam. A jagged hole appeared in the vehicle bodywork.

How could he miss thought Liam, glancing over his shoulder.

But Eugene was wrestling with the motor cyclist who was badly injured. Eugene pushed him away and threatened him with the handgun. But the motor cyclist threw himself onto Eugene's outstretched arm, pushing him off balance and ruining his aim. The motor cyclist fell to the ground again, barely able to maintain his stand.

Eugene bludgeoned him on the neck with the butt of his gun and turned back towards the minibus. He approached the minibus with the weapon held menacingly before him.

Drivers in the waiting traffic queue slowly came to terms with the scene developing before them. The nearest drivers, on seeing the shaven-headed gunman dominating the roadway, either shrank into their seats or abandoned their vehicles and ran off. Fear filled the air.

Stood out from the pipes in full view of an audience, Eugene held the gun in front of him and fired again at the retreating Irishmen.

A hint of burning flame spat from the end of the silencer.

Using the weapon to good effect, Eugene ran out of bullets but merely dropped to one knee, reloaded, stood up, tall and daunting, and fired again. He was a man possessed with no one around to stop him. The air was alive with the soft and hushed sound of bullets being discharged from a silenced muzzle.

Dermot took a bullet in the top of the thigh and fell against the minibus. The pain seized him when a bullet rifled through his muscle tissue and scorched his innards on its callous journey that saw the bullet exit the limb above the kneecap and wallop into the side of the bus.

Liam rushed past Dermot but then turned and dragged him inside, hastily pulling the minibus door closed.

Dermot screamed in agony when Liam pulled him unceremoniously into comparative safety. The blood spilled onto the highway and covered the front seats of the minibus.

Still on his knees, Sean explored the road surface. He splayed his searching hands out before him like a blind panic-stricken man frantic in his desire to regain the keyfob that meant so much to their evil operation.

Eugene fired again, smashing the minibus windscreen as a bullet whistled only inches above Liam's head.

Liam started the engine and it burst into life. He depressed the clutch and frantically sought reverse gear. The gears crunched noisily before Liam dropped the handbrake and accelerated backwards towards the approaching Eugene.

The tyres screeched from the ferocity of Liam's driving.

Eugene stepped away from the reversing bus, narrowly escaping a collision course that nearly found its mark.

Liam skilfully manoeuvred the minibus into a frenzied three-point turn. The bullets ripped into the minibus from all angles. Tyres screeched and gears clattered. Panic and fear struck deep into the heart of Liam Connelly. The side of the minibus was peppered with killer bullets, each eager to hunt down and end their quarry's life.

A second crippling bullet entered Dermot's thigh near the initial wound. Dermot uttered a piercing cry of pain, filling the heavens for all to hear: A scream of sheer agony.

'Where is it? I can't find the key!' shouted Sean.

'Get in, Sean,' begged Liam.

Eugene ran towards them. Two down and two to go, he thought.

Liam slammed the accelerator to the floor as Sean Brady threw himself bodily into the open passenger door and to the relatively safe confines of the peppered vehicle.

The madman continued to heap fire on the minibus; the ricochets pinging against the bridge and flying in all directions. At last, safety became a reality. Liam dodged the stationary traffic, striking a glancing blow to a Ford Escort as he fought desperately to escape the cauldron of gunfire. The mini-bus swept down the road towards the Oval and into South London.

Eugene realised his quarry was disappearing from view but there was something shining on the road, near to where Sean Brady had been searching. It was glistening in the sunshine. He bent down and pocketed the object.

Looking for his own escape, Eugene jogged along the line of traffic, opened a car door, and roughly dragged the driver from his seat. He bundled the driver onto the ground and pressed the end of the silencer into the man's cheekbone.

The man ran off, terror in his face, onto the nearby pavement and behind the sprawling pipes.

Turning the car swiftly in the line of traffic, Eugene set off after the minibus. He raced through the gearbox and the car tyres prayed for grip on the streets of London. The minibus was four hundred yards ahead of him when Eugene reached fifty miles an hour. The car continued to hurtle after the bus, accelerating harshly for all it was worth.

Checking the rear view mirror, Liam saw the high-speed car gaining on him and could see the ugly shaven head resting on the big broad shoulders of the lethal Eugene Kelly.

Taking a right, then turning to the left, Liam was oblivious to the traffic signs as he fought to keep the vehicle under control and outwit Eugene at the same time.

The Ford Escort clung on, gaining slowly.

The two vehicles careered through the streets into South London like two wild horses in a frenzied chase of passion, hate and fear. Two chariots of enigma; one bound on a mission of death and one dedicated, for the moment, to escape the mad killer of Londonderry.

The merchant of death from Derry had descended on deepest London.

Toni heard the loss of radio contact from her office and took control calling for updates and repositioning the followers. Minutes ticked by before the first follower reached the middle of the bridge and examined the war zone Eugene and an unfortunate young motor cyclist had created.

The followers reported the scene and quickly put two and two together.

Pressing the alarm button, Toni alerted the Metropolitan police who swung into action. She reached for the map and tried to second-guess the destination of the fleeing cars. The followers used their radios, reporting what they had been told by eye-witnesses on Vauxhall Bridge.

Another rogue had joined the club. Eugene had preferred to put his faith in Damien in preference to Toni - or so it appeared.

Guiding the minibus on its speeding path, Liam twice mounting the pavement to avoid trucks and taxis. Dermot cried in pain when the blood ran unchecked from his wounds. Sean watched through the rear windows but crouched low, relaying the position of the chasing Ford to Liam. Eugene had the faster vehicle but couldn't outrun Liam as they fought their duel in the busy streets.

Liam constantly changed lanes and took both left and right-hand turns, slowing the Ford down and moving from the nearside to the offside to prevent Eugene from overtaking.

Within minutes it was all over when the minibus slid round a tight left-hand bend.

The Ford moved out to the offside and tried to overtake the minibus on the blind side. Eugene lost control when the Ford mounted the pavement yet again and collided with the building line.

The minibus drove on out of sight, with Liam and Sean shouting to each other that Eugene had crashed.

Steam rose from the bonnet of the car and Eugene recognised the sign of a dead Ford. He cursed as the minibus disappeared from view.

Sliding across into the nearside passenger seat, he opened the door and left the Ford stranded on the footpath before he vanished into the London streets, still armed with the deadly handgun and the silencer.

Feeling in his pocket, Eugene removed the keyfob. The key looked like an ordinary padlock key and was attached to a circular metal ring and a blue leather tag. The key meant nothing to Eugene. There was not one piece of evidence on the keyfob to betray its origin. Pocketing the key, Eugene entered the tube station to complete his escape.

'Jesus, would you believe it, Bridget?' offered Liam. 'He appeared out of nowhere, sure he did, just started firing at us like a man possessed. We couldn't get out of his way fast enough. Poor Eamonn went down and didn't get up.' Liam paused and continued, 'Sorry, Bridget, but Eamonn didn't make it. His chest was split in two. He had no chance.'

The room was quiet as they waited for Bridget to contain herself.

Bridget sat quietly weeping over Eamonn Murphy. Liam and Sean had been back at the safe house for over two hours. The terrible events of the day had been explained to her.

Pacing back and forwards in front of the window, Sean was edgy, nervous and very worried. Every few minutes he peeked cautiously out from between the navy blue curtains and checked the London streets. It was as quiet as a grave. They were safe for the time being.

Sean's mind conjured up thoughts of Shelagh, home and the comparative safety of Northern Ireland. He missed his love, but he would be with her soon when they had run their course.

Dermot was lying uncomfortably on the sofa with a massive bloodstained bandage applied around his thigh. It was the quickest method they could think of to treat the wounds and stop the bleeding.

Liam wondered how to get a doctor. The approaching night would soon bring darkness and the shadows in which he could move safely. It had been a long day for the terrorists. Just after Eugene had crashed the Ford Escort, Liam had driven into the Jamaica Road area and hidden the peppered minibus in a derelict warehouse. They knew of the place from an earlier inspection of the Thames area. They were very interested in the Thames and the property bordering the river. It was all part of the plan. Or at least it had been, until Eugene upset the apple cart.

Sean set fire to the minibus after walking into Bermondsey, stole a car, and returned to the wounded Dermot and troubled Liam. The two men had loaded Dermot into the rear of the stolen car and dropped him off at the safe house in Battersea as the light was beginning to fade. Sean then drove to Waterloo Station where he had abandoned the stolen car and returned to Battersea on foot. Now he longed for darkness so that he could take Dermot for that much-needed medical attention.

'Dermot, can you hear me?' asked Sean.

Dermot was semi-conscious.

Bridget shook his shoulder gently, trying to rouse him from his stupor.

'Dermot. Speak to me, Dermot,' said Sean.

'What? What's that then, Sean?' murmured Dermot.

'Good man! Don't you go dying on me now, Dermot,' ordered Sean.

Worried, the events of the day had penetrated Liam's conscience. Now he realised that not only were the police after him, but his own side from the Provos were also intent on not just catching him, but killing them all.

'Liam!' remarked Sean.

'Yes,' replied Liam.

'It'll be dark soon. Once the light has faded I'll go out and make some 'phone calls. I have contacts in a pub down here. Do you remember me telling you that?'

'A long time ago, sure I do, a long time ago,' acknowledged Liam. 'Things were different then, Sean. We knew what we were about until I was put out of the country. Since then we've just gone from one hiding place to the other. What happened to us all, I wonder?' offered Liam.

'Hush you now, Liam,' said Sean. 'It's the excitement of the day that has caught up with us all. We'll move Dermot and make sure he's taken care of then we'll be getting back on the right track. Understand?'

'Sure, Sean, sure,' replied Liam.

Propping Dermot up, Sean placed a cushion underneath the bomb maker's back and then brought him round by dampening his forehead with a handkerchief until Dermot was properly attentive. Sean questioned Dermot eagerly and, as he did so, the onlookers could see that Sean was picking up the pieces and putting the show back on the road.

'Now then, Dermot,' said Sean. 'I need to know about the timing device, the run, the speed, the detonation time and the damage area your little bomb will produce. You must understand me now. You've done us proud but the game is over for you. I'll take care of you and deliver you into good hands. Trust me, Dermot. I will not leave you to the wolves.'

Dermot knew he was now surplus to requirements and feared the worst when he replied, 'I know I'm no good to you now, Sean. I also know if I'm taken by the police then you will think I'll do a deal with them and sell you down the river. Sure now, that's damn right is it not? Sell you down the river. Indeed I could, Sean.'

'Sure, Dermot, not many people know how to make bombs like you. I'll take a chance, so I will. I say you'll not talk, Dermot.'

'If you're going to kill me, stop the talking, do it now. Have done with it, Sean. I understand. Do it now and be gone.'

'No! You live,' replied Sean, 'But, before I make you safe I must know all you know about the device.'

'Sure, Sean, I understand. Listen to me now, the device will only work if the speed is right. Sure, it'll go off anyway, but its maximum damage will occur if you calculate the time of the explosion exactly. Understand me now?' questioned Dermot.

Responding, Sean suggested, 'Go through it carefully, Dermot, and slowly, so that I understand everything. Once I have understood it all, my only problem will be the key. We can overcome that on the day. Slowly now, Dermot, right from the start.'

Weak and in tremendous pain, Dermot struggled with the details as his blood continued to seep unabated through the hastily applied bandage.

Sean listened intently and for the first time the final masterstroke of the plan reached the ears of Bridget and Liam. He was pleased. Dermot had successfully traded his knowledge of the bomb for his own life. Sean knew what he wanted.

Dermot lived.

That night Sean and Liam carefully transferred Dermot into the hands of an Irish couple living above a public house in central London where they tended to Dermot. The man was a surgeon who had been struck off the register many years earlier. Fortunately for Dermot, the surgeon retained many of his skills and much of his knowledge.

Collecting Bridget, they were soon on the move again. Dermot wouldn't talk. He seldom spoke when he was well. He travelled light; only a cat called 'Scrappy' accompanied him on his journey.

Sean suspended the bomb attack needing time to practise with the timing mechanism. He acquired charts showing the Thames and refined his master plan when he made the final preparations.

The pressure was on.

Eugene's attack on Vauxhall Bridge rocked the Intelligence community and Toni felt the world was about to fall in on her. It seemed that everywhere she went and everyone she spoke to was holding her personally responsible for the mayhem in the centre of London. There was no escaping the torment. It was, after all, her tout who had fired off his weapon at everyone in sight.

Some even said Toni planned it that way, giving the tout immunity from arrest. The truth was, of course, completely different. Eugene must have had a better offer from his own organisation. He had killed when he should have been reporting the sighting of the ASU to Toni. She couldn't understand why and presumed it might be money. There was no other reason for it since Eugene did everything for money. He was a greedy man and she knew him too well for there to be any other explanation.

Antonia Harston-Browne was the centre of attention; a cause for concern, a case of bad management. Rogues were afoot in London. A loose cannon was on the streets because she had got it wrong. She had failed to exercise control over her tout.

The bosses were unhappy, the politicians angry, the police livid.

The old sage, Commander Herbert, was slightly different. He rested his hand on young Toni's shoulder, consoling her in her time of distress. The Commander was a practical man. He had walked the same way once before. When the tout acted 'out of order' it was always the tout's handler who was called to account for his actions.

It was a messy business. When things went well, you were a hero in the organisation. When things went badly, no one wanted to know. It was the same the world over. Toni found it impossible to explain why Eugene Kelly had killed one man and wounded another. He had lost his head. It was probably as simple as that.

Commander Herbert declared, 'It explains why he didn't keep the appointments at Duck Island. He had no intention of meeting you again, did he?'

Toni ran her fingers over her forehead and pinched the bridge of her nose with the finger and thumb of her left hand. She was tired and under stress. A good night's sleep would not have gone amiss but she replied, 'I was sure he would. I've known him too long. He must have been given a much bigger sum of money in order to carry out the killings. Something or someone got to him, perhaps he didn't hear me right, or ..'

'Or what?' asked the Commander.

'Well, I don't know. Perhaps he was on to them and couldn't make the meetings. Perhaps he lost my number or forgot where to meet. Perhaps...'

Commander Herbert intervened, 'Perhaps you're making excuses for him. It happens, Toni. Put it aside and start again. That's all you can do.'

Nodding, Toni sat back in her chair.

Commander Herbert advised, 'In any event, he's ours now. Tout or no tout, when we find him he'll be inside quick as a flash.'

'What makes you think he'll come quietly?' asked the redhead.

'That's his choice to make, Toni. We have to find him first.'

'At least he's saved us one problem, Commander. We needn't look for Eamonn anymore. One less to worry about,' declared Toni.

'I wouldn't say that too loud in some places, Toni. Take a tip from an old friend,' offered the Commander, 'Keep that thought to yourself. Politicians and senior civil servants don't see things like us. They don't understand how the system works. They don't realise how difficult it is to work someone from the inside of an organisation and make it all come out right. Okay, some people might be happy that we have a couple less to worry about but, just remember, for every politician who thinks "Well done" there's another thinking the opposite and waiting to take his place. It's a dangerous world, Toni, but it's a damn sight more dangerous in the office. They shoot you in the face on the streets. In the office they stab you in the back. Take a break Get away from it all. See Boyd.'

'Boyd! Does he know?' asked Toni.

'Yes,' replied the Commander. 'I have told him. He's still up in Cheshire working on the Montague case. He tells me there are apparent connections between Montague and London and he wants to bottom them out. I seldom argue with Boyd. He's a good man is William. He may be on to something. It may well turn out that we can link the Montague murder with the Vauxhall Bridge incident and the Sean Brady ASU. Evidentially, I mean, Toni, knowing things or believing them is a long way from proving them in a court of law.'

'Yes, I understand you,' admitted Toni. 'I suppose I'd better get out there and find the great Eugene?'

Commander Herbert suggested, 'Leave him to the police. Don't get involved any more. He's ours now, once we find him.'

Sitting in the back bar of a public house just off the Old Kent Road, Eugene Kelly drank down from a half pint of beer and studied the racing pages of the evening newspaper. Tomorrow's going would be soft, but he had a fancy or two which he pencilled in at the side of the newspaper.

His friend approached.

'Evening,' greeted Brendan O'Connor.

'Take a seat, Brendan,' acknowledged Eugene.

'I've good news, Eugene, so I have,' suggested Brendan taking a seat opposite Eugene.

'Good! Tell me!'

'The man they call the bomb maker, sure it is,' stated Brendan O'Connor, sipping the froth from his pint glass.

Eugene eyed his friend and said, 'Brendan! Damien told me you would help me out in London. I have no time to talk in riddles and I have no need to be about the town just now. Now tell me, my little Derry boy, what about the bomb maker?'

Running his hand across his chin, Brendan eased himself forward, lowered his voice, and stared into Eugene's eyes. He had no intention of upsetting Eugene Kelly whose reputation had extended to London.

'Across town an old friend looks after Dermot Dougan. Gunshot wounds it is. My friend used to be a surgeon or a vet, something to do with doctors and the like, whatever! Anyway, I'm told he looks after Dermot. No hospital, you understand why? Two men took him in the dead of night. Dermot rests well,' announced Brendan.

'Address?' ordered Eugene.

Taking a biro from his anorak pocket, Brendan pressed the top. The ballpoint poked out as Brendan flipped over a beer mat and wrote on it. He handed the mat over and returned the pen to his pocket.

'Sure, there's the address, Eugene. Remember to tell Damien who told you where to look,' said Brendan.

'The others?' probed Eugene.

'No word yet, Eugene. Perhaps Dermot can tell you.'

'Perhaps,' offered Eugene thoughtfully. 'Brendan!'

'Yes?'

'It's a drink I owe you then, is it?' suggested Eugene.

Brendan replied, 'No, this one's free. Be sure to tell Damien now.'

'I will,' acknowledged Eugene who slowly sank the remainder of his drink before saying, 'Just one more thing, Brendan, if you please?'

'What would that be?'

'What do you make of this?' asked Eugene, passing over a blue leather keyfob.

Accepting the key, Brendan examined it, turning it over in a search for clues.

'Not a thing, Eugene. Looks like a padlock key with that hole in the end of the stock, so it does.'

'That's what I thought, Brendan. Thanks, I'll remember you to Damien when I see him next,' said Eugene. He took a couple of fifty pound notes out of a thick wallet and left them on the table as he retrieved the key from Brendan.

'I had a big win today, Brendan. I like to share with my friends. You never know when you're going to need them. Take a drink, Brendan. You've earned it,' quipped Eugene.

Brendan's big fist covered the banknotes as Eugene stood up, adjusted his collar and walked from the pub. The keyfob jingled against the loose coins in Eugene's pocket as the Demon from Derry crossed the road and disappeared into the crowds.

There was a soft crumple of banknotes when Brendan eased the cash from the table and folded them into his back pocket.

Two hours later Eugene stepped into a tube station and bought a ticket for the Central line. He then phoned Toni.

Once the telephone rang, Toni knew immediately who it was. No one else had the number. She gestured for silence, pressed the switches and said, 'I'll keep him talking, if I can. Ready for the trace? Here we go.'

Commander Herbert signalled for complete silence as Toni picked up the telephone.

'It's me,' admitted Eugene.

'Where are you?' queried Toni.

'Safe,' admitted Eugene, 'I have news for you, so I have.'

'You've been making the news lately yourself, Eugene.'

'Just helping the peace process along, sure I am,' chuckled Eugene.

'Hardly that, Eugene. You've landed yourself deep in trouble. You must know that, surely?'

'Now then, lady, I'm helping you along, sure I am. One less to worry about, I say. Don't you agree?' suggested Eugene.

'You're wanted for murder, you idiot!'

'Is that a fact now? I got one! Sure, that's right, but I can give you one of the others, so I can. Are you interested in that now?'

'It makes no difference to me, woman. It's your choice.'

Toni reached for a pencil and paper and poised herself ready to write down the details.

'You know I'm interested, Eugene. Where? Who?'

'Dermot Dougan,' offered Eugene.

'Which one is that?' probed Toni, as she tried to spin out the conversation.

Commander Herbert gestured with his hands. His fingertips were touching. He moved his hands apart, indicating to Toni that more time was needed to trace the telephone call.

'Sure, you know the man. Bomb maker, so he is. He'll know all about the little job Sean and his friends are putting together. Much more than you and I. I'll give him to you, so I will,' said Eugene.

'I'd rather you left them all to us, Eugene,' replied Toni. 'The deal was that you would report sightings to us, you know, find them and report in, not engage in a duck shoot in the middle of London. What do you think this is? A shooting range at the funfair?'

'No, lady, you got it wrong. I can't lose. If I take one or two out for the organisation, they will look after me and I will collect a nice earner, as you call it. If, on the other hand, I give you one or two as well, then you will pay me as agreed. You'll look after me. I can't lose, can I?'

'I don't follow you, Eugene,' suggested Toni.

'By doing it my way, woman, I stay safe. A foot in both camps,' argued Eugene. 'If the peace fails, then the organisation will know that I did my bit for them. By yous taking out Dermot then the organisation can blame yous for restarting the war. You'll get the blame for breaking the peace, just as I'll be looked on as a man who did as he was told and tried to keep the peace going. Do yous see that?'

'That's some kind of crazy perverted attempt at blackmail, if you ask me,' she replied.

'I'm not asking you for permission, but yer right there, woman,' said Eugene. 'Just what yous have been doing to me all these years. Blackmail, so it is.'

Toni offered, 'No one ever blackmailed you, Eugene. You did what you did because you wanted the money. No one made you do it.'

'That's as maybe, but now I'm in charge, woman.'

Cradling the telephone on his shoulder, Eugene cocked his head onto the side with his ear, listening. The 'phone was trapped on the side of his neck. Reaching into his pocket, he removed the beer mat, placing it on the ledge inside the telephone kiosk. Next, he removed the key and placed the blue leather keyfob on top of the beer mat. Then he placed the two items inside a brown envelope which he sealed but did not address.

Lifting the 'phone to his ear, Eugene waited for her to speak.

'Where are you, Eugene? We need to talk,' ventured Toni.

'Liverpool Street tube station,' revealed Eugene. 'Try the post box outside. Brown envelope. Dermot's address is inside it, along with a key that I picked up off the road on Vauxhall Bridge. Sure, the man, Sean Brady, dropped the key, so he did. You wouldn't believe his face when he couldn't find it. He was mortified, all over the place on his hands and knees looking for it, so he was.'

Eugene laughed out loud at the thought of Sean Brady looking for the key on all fours on the roadway, and then said, 'Find where the key fits and you've cracked it, so you have now. I've no time for running around the town with a key in ma pocket. It was Sean's key, now it's yours. Remember now, Liverpool Street tube station. You'd best be quick before the mail man comes.'

Eugene Kelly hung up and walked towards the post box set into the station wall. He slid the envelope into the open mouth and heard it fall and rattle on the bottom. It sounded as if the post box had recently been emptied. Eugene calmly took the escalator, found the platform, and boarded the next train.

'Damn!' said Toni as the line went dead.

Commander Herbert lifted the radio handset. 'Liverpool Street tube station! Hit it now. Remember, he's armed and dangerous.'

The waiting cars swung into action and closed on the tube station, sirens blaring and lights flashing.

'Seal all the post boxes at the tube station,' radioed the Commander. 'We're in touch with British Transport police now.' Then he quickly spoke into a telephone and his counterpart in the British Transport police swiftly deployed all available resources.

They were too late. It was no surprise to find the cupboard bare. Eugene Kelly was long gone.

Within the hour the post boxes at Liverpool Street had been rummaged by the police and the plain brown envelope recovered. The contents spilled across the desk, leaving Commander Herbert and Antonia Harston-Browne to inspect the bounty.

One beer mat and one blue leather keyfob with a strange looking padlock key attached. The two objects were studied at length.

The Commander made preparations for a raid on Dermot Dougan's hide-out. They would go in at dawn.

The apartment above the public house was in total darkness. There were no lights at all visible to the casual observer in the street and dirty green curtains were drawn tightly across the first floor window of the anonymous dwelling.

The occupants slept soundly with Dermot Dougan occupying one room and his hosts the other. The outside steps to the rear entrance of the apartment were deserted. Three empty milk bottles gave the only clue to the occupants. And late night drunken revellers who had jollied the night away in the public house downstairs had long since retired to their homes.

The pub was silent. The till had been emptied and the lounge had been tidied briefly to await the morning cleaning staff who would chase their vacuum cleaners around the bar and spray aerosol polish before the mid-morning drinking session commenced.

In the roadway outside, halogen street lamps cast long shadows across the pavement as the inner city slumbered through the night. A neat row of parked cars were still and traffic lights at the end of the road, near the junction, flickered through a colourful sequence.

One of the police raiding team vehicles pulled up short of the junction. Its driver applied the handbrake and switched the engine off. Police prepared for the assault and assembled on the footpath.

Simultaneously, a second police personnel carrier cruised into the street, stopped near the kerb, and waited.

There were dark blue coveralls with a logo 'Police' embroidered above the left side of the chest. And a mixture of nine-millimetre carbines and double-barrelled shotguns. There was body armour and dark blue baseball caps with 'Police' printed boldly across the front. And the baseball caps sported a chequered black and white band around the base.

They checked their weapons nervously and waited. The appointed time arrived at last.

'Red One to the teams. Phase one, execute,' said the firearms leader.

The radio systems came live.

Simultaneously, the two raiding teams crept stealthily towards the target. One team covered the front of the public house, in order to block any escape route from inside the apartment to the bar, while the other team moved near to the steps at the rear entrance. Seconds ticked by. Adrenalin flowed fast and pulse rates increased. Lungs drew in gulps of fresh air to offset the increased respiration rates. Safety catches were moved to the off position by nervous tingling fingers.

Two patrol cars swung lazily into the street and adopted stand off positions a few hundred yards from the scene, their occupants monitoring proceedings, preparing to block off the surrounding road system immediately if things didn't go according to plan.

'Red team, ready,' said the team leader at the rear. He was crouched low, brandishing his firearm menacingly at the rear bedroom window.

'Green team, ready,' said the firearms leader at the front. Their weapons engaged the deserted doors and windows of the public house.

'Red One to control. We are in position. Confirm requirement,' said the firearms leader into the radio.

Commander James Herbert stood in the specialist operations room at New Scotland Yard. Pressing the switch on his radio microphone, he said, 'Confirmed! You have control.'

Stepping back, Commander Herbert crossed his fingers. Let's hope we get lucky this time, he thought to himself.

'Roger,' returned Red One. 'I have control. All teams, stand by. I have control.'

Turning over in his sleep, Dermot felt a pain shoot up the inside of his thigh. Suddenly and violently, he was awake, clenching his teeth in anguish and grasping his wounded thigh as he fought a mental battle to beat the excruciating pain barrier he had to overcome.

In the darkness outside, a milk bottle chinked against another on the steps leading to the back door.

A black cat jumped from its bed and made towards the door

The creature purred against the bedroom door, cleverly sensing something was out of place but unable to communicate to her master.

Milkman's early, thought Dermot. What time is it?

Carefully rolling over, still clutching his thigh, Dermot sleepily checked the alarm clock as he gradually came out of his troubled and painful trance into the wakening world.

Outside, the decision had been taken.

'This is Red One. All teams. Phase two, execute. Go, Go, Go!'

As Dermot checked the alarm clock, the rear door to the flat was taken off its hinges by a large London policeman using a specially designed steel door opener.

The first three police officers into the apartment carried handguns held menacingly in front of them.

Dermot heard the door splinter and the muffled sound of boots stamping on the staircase. He reached under his pillow.

It was his time.

The killing time struck as an alarm clock sounded its piercing cry.

The first officer, on reaching the top of the stairs, moved to the left of Dermot's door. The second took up a position to the right. The third officer booted Dermot's door open and saw the back of the Irishman's head. With his right hand underneath the pillow, the Irishman's left arm was under the bed clothes.

The alarm clock screamed.

The officers entered the room crouching low, one to the left, the other to the right, panning their weapons round. Dermot was the only occupant visible to them.

'Armed police! Freeze!' filled the air. The police bundled into the apartment, to the sound of the alarm clock attacking their ears.

Downstairs further footsteps could be heard rushing up the concrete staircase. The sound of splintering wood was heard as another door was taken off its hinges and the firearms team entered the premises.

Two broken milk bottles rested on the steps, the glass fragments splintered by the assault team.

As the police rushed into the building a cat called Scrappy decided it was time to go. The little black cat waited for a suitable moment and stealthily crept out of the bedroom and downstairs. The cat found the alley and ambled off into the London streets.

Dermot found the loaded handgun secreted conveniently under the pillow. He did not turn to face the policemen. There was no need and only a little time. He knew it was the killing time, his time.

Withdrawing the gun, he cocked it, opened his mouth, and fired one lethal round into his head.

The bullet streaked through his skull and exited the top of his head as the contents of his brain made red and grey coloured patterns on the back board of the bed and the yellowing wallpaper adorning the apartment.

Dermot died before his head touched the sheets. He had lived his life and had decided if he was ever cornered, then only he would end it.

Dermot was not the kind to engage in loose talk. He took his own life in a sordid little apartment above a back street pub in central London having been betrayed by his own people for the despicable sum of one hundred pounds. He had told Sean Brady he would not speak and didn't, but others had.

Dermot uttered not one word as he died for the cause. He took the secret of his special bomb and all those previous bombings to the grave.

The fatal gun rested limply in the dead Irishman's hand.

The policeman moved it from the lifeless fingers then vomited at the sight of the virtually headless corpse of Dermot Dougan.

The high-pitched alarm clock rang on, penetrating the ears of all in the vicinity.

The young policeman sat on the end of the bed to regain his composure. He was shaking. When he was calmer and in possession of his faculties, he knocked the screeching alarm clock from the bedside table and silenced it with the heel of his boot.

Leaning against the iron railings overlooking the River Thames, Liam's hands took his body weight. His knuckles were white. There was a slight breeze blowing up from the river below and the artificial fur lining on his black anorak soothed his stubble chin in the chill when he heard the faint sound of sirens rushing through the distant streets of London.

He wasn't to know the wailing sirens were police vehicles rushing to a pub where a gunshot had been heard and a suicide had taken place.

It was early in the morning, Liam had studied the river all night. He was tired having volunteered to report on the night movements on the river. But more importantly, he'd taken the opportunity to leave the safe house for a breath of fresh air and a taste of freedom., and time to think.

Sean asked him to study the river at night but Liam took his moment of solitude to consider his position. Earlier that night, Liam had left the house in order to carry out his deed for Sean. A simple deed that took patience rather than skill. Liam made his way to the river through the streets of London. It was the man in the Turkish kebab house who had frightened him. Liam looked into the window of the kebab house as he casually passed it by and jolted in shock when he saw the unmistakable face of Eugene Kelly waiting in the queue inside the shop.

Walking away quickly, Liam then ran when he reminded himself of the killing potential of Eugene Kelly. It was some moments before he glanced over his shoulder, checking he wasn't being followed, slowing to a normal walking pace. Thankful he had not been followed, Liam realised Eugene did not see him at the kebab house.

The brief encounter only added to Liam's concerns. He wondered what Eugene would have done had he been spotted outside looking through the window. Would Eugene have shot him dead there in the street outside the kebab house? Probably!

Now Liam Connelly turned his problems over in his mind. The Derry man deliberated as he spied the dark and murky river. Water flowed serenely under the bridge as his mind turned back through the years. He remembered his mother and their home in the Shantallow, a father taken before his prime and a sister who deserved a better way to live. His family had devoted their lives to the cause in one way and another. It had got them nowhere. Devotion to the Republican cause had brought the Connelly family only sadness and despair. Things were so different now. Despite all that had happened, it seemed they were no further forward than before. Killings and bombings were said to be at an end with the ceasefire, but Liam could not find his peace. He knew in his own mind it was only a question of time. The RUC wanted him, the organisation wanted him and Eugene had been sent to neutralise him.

For all Liam knew, the English police were breathing down his neck. Scan Brady had offered him the chance to return to Northern Ireland and the organisation, in exchange for a war on the mainland and a spectacular attack in central London.

Be this right, or be it wrong, the organisation had sent Eugene after him. There was no safe place, nowhere to run, only places to hide. The best Liam could hope for was his own kind of fragile peace.

Closing his eyes tight, Liam forced a blood rush into his forehead to help him stay awake.

The city was moving.

Muffled sounds from early morning workers could be heard, starting their vehicles ready for the drive to beat the rush hour. Opening his eyes, Liam worried about Sean Brady. Why had Sean killed the Montagues in Cheshire? There was no need! Why did they plan this spectacular bomb attack when the organisation had sent someone to kill them all? It didn't make sense.

Turning from the river, Liam made inland.

Skirting the high rise flats he saw the twin telephone kiosks. They were back to back. He chose the coin-operated box, selected a handful of small coins from his jeans pocket, and reached for the 'phone.

Sister Meg worked rapidly at her desk, moving the paperwork and tidying the ward files. She concentrated on one tray of reports and glanced through the documents, signing and amending papers as she displaced the contents of one tray into another. Meg was a speed-reader and wasted no time since she hated clerical work.

Sister brought the coffee mug to her lips before realising the contents were cold. Grimacing, she replaced the mug on its saucer. The pen flowed again.

A 'phone sounded in the corridor and Vikki, the staff nurse, answered it.

'Sister Meg,' called the staff nurse. 'It's for Pat. I told him it was far too early to be taking calls, but the man insists. He says he's a nephew and must speak to his uncle. I'd better tell him to 'phone later, don't you think?'

Sister's pen lifted from the paper when she replied, 'Certainly, no calls at this time of day. The patients are still asleep.'

Vikki turned to deliver the message.

'Wait!' called Sister. 'A nephew, you say? I tell you what, put it through and I'll take the trolley 'phone through to Pat. I remember now, he's been expecting his nephew for a long time.'

Vikki told the caller to hang on whilst the call was transferred.

Entering the private ward into which Padraigh O'Toole had been moved, shaking him carefully, Sister opened his eyes and explained it was his nephew on the telephone.

Pat woke up and nodded vigorously. He would take the call.

Meg wheeled in the trolley, plugged it to the socket in the wall, and made the transfer.

Pat took the telephone as Sister Meg left the room.

'Hello, it's me, Pat.' He eased himself up onto his elbow.

'Sure, it's me, Liam, Uncle. How are you?' enquired Liam.

'Better for the hearing of you Liam, that's for sure,' replied Pat, 'And yourself?'

'Well! Uncle, can you do me a favour?' asked Liam.

Pat answered, 'What do you want? How can I help?'

Liam replied, 'I want out!'

'Is it bad, Liam?' enquired Pat.

'It's a long story and not for now. Can you help?' pleaded Liam.

'What makes you think I can help, Liam?' queried Pat.

Liam reminded Pat, 'You used to talk about a policeman. The one who saved Michael, remember?'

'So!' replied Pat cautiously.

'I'll take a chance on my uncle that I will. Are you still in touch with him?' probed Liam.

'Just as a friend you understand, Liam, just as a friend,' revealed Pat.

'Give the policeman a message, Uncle, will you?' asked Liam

'Go on,' replied Pat.

Pat listened carefully to his nephew and memorised the message. 'I'll see what can be done, Liam,' said Pat.

Liam declared, 'It's over for me, Uncle. I messed it up. I had a half chance when I came over here. I have no chance now. Don't ask me how or why. I just know in my mind that it's all over for me. I'll go down fighting though. God forgot to shine down on me, so He did. Sleep well on that now!'

Liam hung up, left the telephone kiosk, and walked back to the safe house. Dawn was breaking over London. Spring had arrived.

'That was a short call considering all the time it's taken him to find you, Pat?' ventured Sister Meg.

Handing her the telephone, Pat replied, 'Billy! Do you know how I can get in touch with him?'

'Ring his home number,' suggested Sister.

'No! It's important. I mean, where can I get him today? Now! Where is he?' demanded Pat.

'Cheshire,' stated Sister Meg. 'I can call him for you if you like.'

'Cheshire! Yes, Sister, please. Tell him I must speak to him urgently. Tell him Liam has contacted me. He'll know what I mean.'

Settling Pat down, Sister and eased him onto his back. She returned the telephone trolley and resolved to endure the never-ending amount of paperwork that came with nursing administration. Padraigh O'Toole could wait a while. Once she had finished her clerical work, she would ring Boyd. But, for now, the Irish problem and the policeman could wait their turn. She would deal with them when she was ready and not before.

Sister Meg reached for the tray and took up her pen once again.

≈

Boyd returned the telephone to its cradle following the call from Commander Herbert and replaced the fountain pen he had been doodling with in the wooden dispenser on the desk. Shaking his head sadly from side to side, he raised his eyebrows, yawned, and reached for the papers lying in his 'In' tray. His mind swiftly tuned in to the necessary clerical nature of his occupation. The dawn raid in central London had been unsuccessful. The well planned armed expedition produced one dead terrorist but no other members of the Active Service Unit in the apartment. A unique bonus realised a shocked and tired elderly Irish couple detained by the police firearms team for questioning.

The couple told the anti-terrorist squad Sean Brady had taken Dermot Dougan to them. They had agreed to help the wanted terrorist because they were more frightened of Sean than they were of Scotland Yard. Unfortunately, an all too familiar story to Boyd.

However, now that the fear of Sean Brady had been removed, albeit temporarily, from the Irish couple, an intriguing story of connections between Londonderry, Belfast and the English mainland was slowly emerging from the two elderly prisoners. They were eager to talk and talk they did.

It transpired various terrorists from Northern Ireland and, on occasions, the Republic of Eire, made regular clandestine use of the ageing Irish couple and their discreet apartment whilst they had been based in London on short-term terrorist activities. Safe houses, safe vehicles, safe money and a trusted former doctor of Irish descent were important elements in the terrorist arsenal. The frightened and apprehensive couple supplied all that had been required of them.

Adding recent fax transmissions from London to his increasing pile of papers, Boyd freshened his coffee mug once again and carefully re-read the large bundle of enquiry documents, trying to find the elusive missing link: The link Boyd suggested was all-important and central to the terrorist's campaign. His team in Cheshire had worked steadily through the complex affairs of the late Clive Montague and uncovered the profile of a wheeler-dealer type of man with fingers in business deals all over the country. 'A penny here and a pound there' was a favourite motto Clive Montague adopted with his business contacts.

One thing was quite obvious, though. Clive Montague had many dubious associates in the travelling fraternity. They ranged from gipsies currently camped in Inverness, to door-to-door salesmen working in the Isle of Wight. Indeed, Boyd's team interviewed literally hundreds of people who were known to the Montagues in an attempt to piece together the lifestyle of the murdered couple. It was one thing to be sure in your own mind that Brady and company were either somehow responsible for, or involved in, two murders. It was quite another to be able to prove the hypothesis conclusively in a court of criminal law.

Separating proof from assumption, Boyd scribbled his thoughts onto a writing pad. A handful of bullets taken from the bodies of the dead; a partial tyre print from a large vehicle at the entrance to

Montague's drive, and a possible sighting of Eamonn Murphy driving a furniture van into Cheshire were the main items of tangible evidence.

These were the only pieces of the jigsaw that could be taken to court. Clearly, Boyd needed to link the active service unit to the atrocious Cheshire killings much more positively. It had to be Brady and company, reasoned Boyd. There had been no sign of a break-in and nothing appeared to have been stolen from either the house or the warehouse. There was no evidence to indicate blackmail, fraud or drug dealing. Yes! The furniture van had been spotted heading towards the Montague warehouse near Sandbach, but there was no sign of the vehicle anywhere else. What happened to the furniture van? It couldn't just vanish into thin air! But it had! Where was this mysterious van and why was it so important, so seemingly crucial to the active service unit? It had been important enough to kill for, but why?

It was a puzzler and Boyd strove to make sense of it. His simple theory was built around the intrigue of Clive Montague's business. The fragmented theory argued that, somewhere along the line, a furniture van was involved with the Montague warehouse in Sandbach. Boyd reasoned the furniture van had been at the premises but was not there now. This would explain the sighting of the furniture van which had led them to the area in the first place and its absence ever since. However, there was no evidence to prove the furniture van had been at the warehouse, only the gut feeling of a tired and restless policeman.

The tyre print at the entrance to Montague's drive could have originated from any one of a number of vehicles. The tyre print was attractive to Boyd because it was freshly made in the loose soil bordering the Montague drive. He needed the furniture van, however, in order to match the tyre print found at the warehouse with the vehicle in question. This was evidence that would provide the basis of a case against the terrorists. If the furniture van had been at the Montague warehouse, why? What was in the van? Where was it now?

The questions without answers continued round and round in Boyd's head as he dragged his mind through the enigma, fathoming constantly on the whys and wherefores of the Montague connection.

Anthea had better luck locating the garage nearby where a man fitting the description of Sean Brady purchased fuel some weeks earlier from the garage attendant. The man had been in a minibus.

The garage attendant was a part-time art student working at the garage to supplement his student income. He remembered the Irishman and presented a drawing of the man who had bought the petrol some weeks earlier. His drawing was in pencil and resembled Sean Brady.

Anthea made further enquiries and discovered the minibus had been found burnt out in London by the Metropolitan police. Apparently there had been some kind of gun battle on Vauxhall Bridge! The body of Eamonn Murphy had been recovered on Vauxhall Bridge. Dermot Dougan escaped with gunshot wounds but when cornered in an apartment in central London, this morning, he chose to blow his brains out rather than betray his secrets.

Anthea read the notes Boyd had written and read the flimsy from the fax machine. She joined the 'think tank'. It was a puzzle. She briefed the team on the latest developments whilst Boyd put his thinking cap on.

Boyd thought the furniture van had to be involved but couldn't prove it. Many people in the Cheshire area said Montague spoke of travelling to and from London on business, but no one could explain why or where. Sure, there were lots of papers and documents relevant to the transport business in London recovered from his personal possessions, but somehow there was no indication of where Clive Montague had run his London business. Battersea had been mentioned in statements taken from people who knew him well, but so too had Surrey, Southwark, Waterloo, Lambeth and even Gravesend.

Perhaps it was a figment of the man's imagination. Perhaps there was no such business. Perhaps it was just bravado, said to impress, perhaps...

Boyd lifted the telephone and rang Toni. It was time for a different type of brain to be applied to the problem, time to share a puzzle. Perhaps she could help.

Toni answered the telephone immediately from her desk in London, chirpy and eager to mull over the events of recent days. The conversation between the two merely went over and over the same ground, but Toni had a different puzzle to play with, the keyfob!

Whilst Boyd considered the furniture van, Toni studied the blue leather fob and the padlock key. Why did Sean Brady risk his life looking for the key on Vauxhall Bridge when Eugene Kelly had been taking pot shots at everyone who moved? It didn't make sense! What was going on? What was so important about the key that caused Brady to crawl all over the road looking for it? There was no mistake. So many witnesses had sat frightened in their cars on Vauxhall Bridge during Eugene's shooting gallery and watched the man the security forces knew as Sean Brady searching for something on the tarmac. He had been sighted crawling on his hands and knees looking for something on the road. Why? Those same frightened drivers watched Eugene Kelly pick up an article from the roadway and place it in his pocket before commandeering a vehicle at gunpoint and setting off in pursuit of the minibus. Later, Eugene left the beer mat in the post box at Liverpool Street tube station. As a result they located Dermot Dougan. Eugene then put the leather keyfob in the same envelope and told Toni it was the key he picked up from the roadway on

Vauxhall Bridge. The article the terrified motorists spoke of on Vauxhall Bridge turned out to be a key. The padlock key hung on the leather keyfob like a silent witness, unable to talk and unwilling to help. Toni knew Eugene too well. There was an important connection to be made between the keyfob, the furniture van and the Cheshire warehouse, but what connection? Eugene was playing the odds again. This time, she had to figure it out. . .

Toni reckoned if Eugene knew where the key was from, then he would have told her at the time he left the beer mat in the tube station at Liverpool Street. Toni decided Eugene didn't know how the key figured in the plot and had given up the keyfob in an attempt to take the steam out of his attack on Vauxhall Bridge and climb back into her good books. He needed to achieve a balance with her. This was his way of meeting his shortfall, she thought. Eugene was a devious creature with a cunning and perverted mind: A sick mind that had gradually evolved from the streetwise Derry tout to a politically astute and dangerous demon. Eugene Kelly was proving he was capable of holding the peace process to ransom by trying to control the various factions in play.

Toni and Boyd discussed the puzzle at length on the telephone, unable to come to grips with the clues. Between them, they could put forward plenty of suggestions and a dozen or so theories, but at the end of the day they had no hard evidence, just a handful of suppositions. They agreed, however, that Eugene Kelly had overstepped the mark.

Boyd returned the 'phone to its cradle as Anthea walked into the office, smiling as usual, her red hair this time perched high in a bundle at the back of her head. A dark maroon coloured trouser suit, cut neat to the lapels, complemented her hairstyle and accentuated her lithe figure.

'Inspector! It's Mr Montague from Derry. He's come over for the personal possessions of his son, Clive,' she said.

'Thanks, Anthea, show him in,' replied Boyd.

Glad of the distraction from his papers, Boyd prepared to meet Montague senior and readied a chair for his guest.

The sergeant disappeared returning within a few moments with Clive's father. He wore a dark checked suit and sported a trilby, fashioned with a plume at the side. He removed his hat on entering Boyd's office

Mr Montague senior was an elderly, white-haired man who sported a walking stick for support as well as for show, thought Boyd. Indeed, he considered one might be forgiven for thinking that if you were to upset Montague senior, then he might just boldly introduce you to the walking stick by his side.

Shaking hands, Boyd beckoned his guest to take a seat.

Placing the walking stick by his feet and the trilby on his knee, Montague senior obliged by sinking back into the armchair provided.

'Thanks again for coming over, Mister Montague. It's a long trip across the water and I feel I must offer you my sincere condolences.'

Nodding at Boyd, Montague suggested, 'Cedric, call me Cedric, Mister Boyd. Thank you for your kind words but they will not find the killers. Can I help at all? Perhaps a reward? What would you have me do?'

Boyd advised, 'There's no need to even consider offering a reward at this stage, Cedric. There is still a lot of police work to be done. We'll find the killers, don't worry about that. But I need time and, to be honest, a bit of luck.'

'You make your own luck. Mister Boyd,' offered Cedric playing with the trilby in his hands, rolling it round between is fingers and grooming the feathered plume at the side.

'Coffee?' enquired Boyd.

'No, thank you,' replied Cedric, settling the hat once again on his knee.

'And you seem intent on helping us bring the killers to justice?'

'I've cried for my loss, Inspector. I expect I shall weep again when I have time. At the moment, there seems so much to do, what with funerals to organise, death certificates, insurances and all that. I expect it hasn't quite sunk in yet,' reflected Cedric.

'If we can help at all, transport for instance? Where are you staying? Locally, I presume?' offered Boyd.

Cedric answered, 'Thank you, but I will be alright on my own. I'm staying at a hotel your sergeant recommended and as soon as all the formalities have been completed. I will be on my way back to the province to look after my wife. She's very upset at the moment. I don't want to stay any longer than is necessary. I'm booked on the night crossing, so I trust I will make it.'

Boyd replied, 'Fine! Thank you for going through the house and the grounds etc. No easy task in the circumstances. I know you've double checked everything, so I expect we will not need to detain you for very much longer. Tell me, is there anything at all in the house that is missing? Anything out of place? Indeed, is there anything at all that you want to say to me? Anything we have missed?'

'I've already been asked that question but I understand you have to be sure. I've turned everything upside down twice, Mister Boyd. There is no money missing, the floor safe for instance has not been touched. Clive had a nest egg there, to avoid the tax people, you understand?'

'No concern of mine, Cedric,' offered Boyd. 'Obviously by now I am aware of it, but the safe doesn't look as if it had been tampered with in any way whatsoever.'

'Indeed,' responded Cedric. 'Thank you! Not even that has been touched, no paintings removed, no ornaments, no cheque books, nothing, as far as I can see.'

'Strange, very strange,' remarked Boyd.

'Quite,' muttered Cedric. 'I expect some would-be robbers pushed their luck too far and lost their bottle, as it were. I suppose they threw the keys away.'

Boyd queried, 'Keys! What keys are those Mister Montague?'

'Clive always carried his keys with him. The keys for the house and the warehouse were in the back kitchen, so I am quite sure he had no intention of leaving the premises on the day he was murdered, otherwise he would have had the keys on him.'

Cedric Montague wiped a tear from the corner of his eye at the mention of the word murder. He was putting a good front on but Boyd knew that deep inside the deaths had come as a complete shock to him.

Boyd ventured, 'Do you mean he had arranged to meet someone at the premises so he didn't have his keys in his pocket because he wasn't going off anywhere?'

'Perhaps,' offered Cedric.

'I don't quite follow you, Cedric. Are there any keys missing?'

'No, Mister Boyd, all the house and warehouse keys are intact with his wallet,' answered Cedric.

'Good,' offered Boyd.

'But the warehouse key for London is missing, not that that is important anymore,' revealed Cedric.

Boyd's eyes narrowed as he sensed the importance of what was being said. 'Tell me about the London warehouse, Cedric, please.'

'Oh, there's nothing to tell really. It's just that I've racked my brains as to where Clive might have put the key. You see, many years ago Clive bought an old disused warehouse in Lambeth. Clive was the type of man who could spot a potential bargain, you see. He worked out in his own mind that one day the warehouse would be bought up in a compulsory purchase order or someone would want to buy the damn place and develop the area, something like that. Anyway, he bought this warehouse, well it's a shed really, in the hope that one day he would make a profit on the sale,' said Cedric.

Cedric Montague ran his hands through his white hair and checked the time on his wristwatch.

'And did he?' questioned Boyd.

'Couldn't tell you, Mister Boyd, never been there myself. I only mention it, irrelevant really, since it's the only thing that's missing. Could be, of course, that he sold the warehouse, in which case there would be no key, would there?' offered Cedric.

'Did you ever visit this place in Lambeth yourself?' queried Boyd.

'Good gracious no!' replied Cedric.

'Do you know where it is then?' asked Boyd.

Cedric answered, 'No! Somewhere near the Thames. He had this harebrained idea that if the property prices didn't take off, then he would use it as a depository for the docks nearby.'

'But you don't know if he still owns such property?' suggested Boyd.

'Couldn't tell you, Mister Boyd, that's why it's all irrelevant. Who wants to be landed with a disused warehouse, or shed, to sell? More trouble than it's worth, I can tell you,' suggested Cedric.

'The keys, Cedric. What type were they?' queried Boyd.

'Just the one,' revealed Cedric. 'I remember he bought the damn place in a pub in London from a gipsy type. Clive paid up a few hundred pounds, signed a slip of paper and pocketed the key. I don't know what happened after that. Where is all this leading to, Mister Boyd? I really don't think he could have been killed for a ramshackle old shed, Mister Boyd. Do you?'

'You're probably right, Cedric, but let me worry about that. You saw this key then? The one Clive got in London?' probed Boyd.

'Padlock key on a blue leather tag. I remember telling him that he'd probably spent a few hundred pounds for a key rather than a warehouse. I laughed. Clive wasn't impressed with my sense of humour. I told him it was one of the worst deals he had made, that's why I remember it so well. I often pulled his leg about it. It was the subject of father-son banter between us.'

'Excuse me a moment, Cedric. This may be important. You never know. I must check something out,' offered Boyd.

Vacating his desk, Boyd went into the adjoining office where he located Anthea and relayed the facts to her. Within minutes Anthea had received, from Toni in London, a photo fax of the key recovered from Liverpool Street tube station.

Anthea handed the document to the Inspector.

Boyd returned to Cedric carrying the flimsy in his fingers and asking, 'Is this it, Mister Montague? The key?'

Boyd showed the photo fax to Cedric Montague.

Taking it in his hand, Cedric studied it carefully and removed an old pair of spectacles from a battered case inside his suit pocket. He held the photo fax to the light, making his pronouncement.

'Well, well, well! I can't believe it. I'll tell you this, Mister Boyd, it's a long time ago but I would say you've just shown me a photograph of a key that my son Clive bought some years ago. Are you onto something then, Mister Boyd?' enquired Cedric.

'Perhaps,' ventured Inspector Boyd, thoughtfully. 'Perhaps we are at last. You'll need to see the real thing, though as soon as possible. I'll try and get a fast car to bring the key up for you to look at. It's in London at the moment but it's important to us. Let me see, a three-hour drive, I suppose, maybe three and a half? A traffic motor cycle would be even quicker! I promise I'll have you on the night crossing. If not, I'll get a police helicopter to fly you over the Irish Sea.'

'A helicopter! Oh, my! I've never been in a helicopter before. Cancel the ferry! I'll take the helicopter,' chuckled Cedric.

'It just might be the bit of luck we need, Cedric. Now, can you tell me about Lambeth and the man Clive bought the key from?' asked Boyd.

'Nothing to tell, really. A down and out, I suppose. I can't tell you much more about it. The warehouse probably isn't even standing now. Mind you, it's just like Clive,' said Cedric.

'How do you mean?' enquire Boyd.

'A hoarder, Mister Boyd. Once he owned something he never let go. It doesn't surprise me he kept the key all these years, that was Clive. Spend a penny to make a pound! Where did you get the key?'

'Not far from Lambeth, Cedric,' responded Boyd.

'Really!' said Cedric.

'And you've no idea where the warehouse stood, Cedric?' queried Boyd. 'No idea at all?'

There was a sense of urgency, a sense of pleading in Boyd's voice that Cedric detected.

'None whatsoever,' replied the elderly Montague. 'Near the Thames on the riverbank, that's all I ever knew. Try the docks down by the river. I don't really know what to suggest, Mister Boyd, other than that.'

The two men talked on. The minutes ran into hours.

Toni arrived with the key from London and displayed the silent witness in all its glory on Boyd's desk. A padlock key attached to a small key ring and an old blue leather keyfob lay on Boyd's spacious white ink blotter.

Cedric Montague positively identified the article as the property of his son, Clive Montague.

The link between the Cheshire murders and the terrorists on Vauxhall Under had been positively made, decided Boyd. The pieces of evidence would follow as sure as the Eden flows into the Solway. It was just a question of time and a matter of patience.

That night Meg telephoned Boyd and told him that Padraigh O'Toole had been asking to speak with him urgently. She apologised for not passing the message sooner. Pressure of work she said.

Boyd didn't argue with her. He hurriedly packed an overnight bag and travelled to Carlisle. It was a good excuse for a quick break and a time to gather his thoughts together. Moreover, his oldest friend, Padraigh O'Toole, had spoken of his nephew, Liam Connelly.

Making all haste, leaving the trusty sergeant Anthea in charge of the team, Boyd wondered if he could make Brunton Park in time for the game between the 'Blues' and the southerners from Chesterfield, but he was too late leaving Cheshire and had to content himself with listening to the game on Radio Cumbria as he drove north.

By the time he had reached home, it was too late to visit the hospital. Boyd made an unexpected visit to his parent's home where he stayed over and talked well into the night.

It was the evening of Tuesday, 4th April, 1995. In the morning he would see Sister Meg and satisfy his burning curiosity with an early visit to Padraigh O'Toole.

Boyd sank a Bushmills or two with his father, telephoned the late duty officer in the incident room for an update, captured his bed and slept well that night.

PART FOUR
THE MEETING

Sunshine on the Fells. It was a warm day. Snow that had sprinkled down on Cumbria, on and off since Christmas, had vanished. It hadn't been a particularly cold, hard winter in the county. There'd been worse winters, but it had certainly been a long cold season.

Rearranging the sunglasses perched on the bridge of his nose, Boyd drove leisurely into the city of Carlisle, tilting the visor down as the bright sunshine penetrated the windscreen and dazzled him. It was an exceptionally bright day.

Negotiating traffic, he arrived at the hospital early. Parking near the entrance to the car park, Boyd locked the vehicle and tapped the roof 'adieu' before walking away.

The hospital clock struck nine in the morning as he walked into the ward and sneaked up on Meg who sat head down, lost in a world of documents. Her pen nib scribbled across papers. It was the only sound in the office save for the ticking of a small clock on a filing cabinet.

Boyd produced daffodils from behind his back and slid them in front of Meg's eyes, making much of the presentation.

'Present from the garden,' declared Boyd.

'Lovely! Oh, they're gorgeous,' replied Meg, laying her pen down. She recognised the voice immediately. Umpteen shared telephone calls had helped cement their relationship.

Meg took the flowers into her hands and cradled them, then she stood back from the chair and kissed Boyd tenderly.

'Mother's idea, I suppose?' she suggested.

'No way!' cracked Boyd. 'I picked them myself this morning as soon as the sun came up.'

Meg chuckled, 'I doubt it, but thanks anyway. They are beautiful. If you don't mind, I'll keep them here in the ward.'

'Of course not,' replied Boyd. 'When I saw them blooming in the garden this morning I immediately thought of your golden hair and couldn't resist picking them for you.'

She'd heard the patter before and inspected the flowers again. She loved daffodils but acknowledged, 'Okay, enough of the flattery, what do you want? Pat, I presume?'

'Yes, please, Meg. Thanks for the call. I came as soon as I could. I'm busy, so I'll be on my way again soon.'

'He'll be glad to see you,' said Meg. 'He's in a side ward.'

Placing the flowers to one side, and in a much softer voice, she offered, 'Actually he's sinking fast and in a fair bit of pain, Billy, so don't be too long with him. Okay?'

'Of course, whatever you say, Meg, thanks,' replied Boyd.

Escorting Boyd to a nearby side ward, Sister Meg opened the door and ushered Boyd in. She helped Pat into a comfortable position then left the two men together. Sister returned to her office, found a vase, collected the flowers, and arranged them for display.

Boyd closed with Pat and hugged his old friend. He took his hand and held it firmly, feeling the weak grip.

Pat was looking tired and haggard. There was a tremendous and obvious difference in the Irishman since Boyd had seen him last. Padraigh O'Toole did not look well at all.

'You called for me. I came to you,' said Boyd quietly.

'Ah, Billyboy! I knew you would come, reliable that you are.'

'Where's the family, Pat?' enquired Boyd.

'Eleven o'clock, Billyboy! They'll be in at eleven this morning. They come every day now. I think I know why,' muttered Pat sadly.

The Irishman cleared his throat and ended up coughing deeply from the chest.

'It won't be long before you're up and about, Pat, mark my words,' ventured Boyd.

'No, Billyboy, you've never told me lies before, don't start now,' chided Pat, wiping his lips with a cotton handkerchief.

Boyd poured a drink of water from a jug on the bedside able and stationed it near the Irishman.

'Didn't mean it like that, Pat. You know me better than that. I'd sooner pot the black with you in the club than here.'

The Irishman beamed and nodded his head in agreement. His beard bounced against his chest as he talked to Boyd.

'If there's a bar in heaven. Billyboy, I'll get the first round in, but you'd best leave the money on the side for me now I've stopped work. What will it be now? Vodka, Campari and a pint of Murphy's?' asked Pat.

Boyd smiled at the humour in Pat's quiet, almost stifled voice. Where once a great giant of a man had walked, a dying man clung to life.

'Sure, if God's a Protestant he won't serve you, Pat,' joked Boyd.

'Sure, and that he will now,' cracked the Irishman. 'I happen to know that God's a brother of the Pope, so you'd best watch your tongue or I'll make sure he doesn't serve you when it's your turn.'

There was a hint of sadness in the conversation.

'Have them lined up on the bar for me then, Pat,' said Boyd.

'To be sure, I will, Billyboy. To be sure, I will.'

They looked into each other's eyes and said nothing. The two friends didn't feel the need to discuss the matter at great length. They could read each other's mind.

'How long, Pat?' asked Boyd.

Pat shuffled, trying to make himself comfortable. 'I hope to get the Wembley result. Billyboy,' said Pat.

'Are you going to see the Blues beat Birmingham at Wembley then, Pat, or are you staying behind to watch it on the telly?' enquired Boyd.

'Watch it here, I think. It's a lot of hassle going to London and, anyway, they make the beer with water down there. No taste in that southern water,' observed Pat. 'Do you think that Sister would notice if I went down to Wembley with yous?'

'She'd notice, Pat, and by God you'd catch it.'

'Best stay behind then, Billyboy!'

Boyd smiled and said, 'Do you mind?'

'I've been alone before. Now Liam is on his own,' said Pat.

Boyd replied, 'He's been in touch then, has he?'

'Yes,' confirmed Pat.

'How?' asked Boyd.

The Irishman encountered Boyd's eyes and advised, 'He telephoned. He wants out. He's in trouble, Billyboy, and he doesn't know what to do. He says he has no escape. Sure now, Billyboy, can you help an old friend here?'

'I just might at that,' said Boyd, pulling up a chair beside the bed. 'What did he have to say then, Pat?'

'He's in London, so he is,' confirmed Pat.

'I know that, Pat. Whereabouts?'

Pat answered, 'They keep moving about. He's being chased by a mad man, but I expect you know that too, do you?'

216

'Yes!'

'He told me, Billyboy,' said Pat. 'The warehouse?'

'What warehouse would that be, Pat?'

'Lambeth!' answered Pat.

'It's time for you and me to be straight with each other in the matter of your nephew, Pat,' suggested Boyd. 'I know that Sean Brady, Bridget Duffy and Liam Connelly are all down there in London. I also know they are planning a big job, a spectacular they call it, one that will receive massive attention from the media. It might even affect the peace process, that's the whole point of the attack. My problem, Pat, is that I don't know everything. Do you?'

Reaching into his bedside locker, Pat rummaged inside and removed a plain brown envelope which was unsealed and bore no writing on its sides. It appeared bulky as if it contained something other than papers or an ordinary letter.

'What have you got there?' asked Boyd, spying the package.

'The deal!' replied Pat quietly.

'What deal is that then?' asked Boyd.

Pat moved his fingers and spread out the top of the envelope, peering into the body of the package, checking the contents.

'I can give you this, Billyboy, but only if you honour the contract.'

'When do the riddles stop, Pat? What contract?' enquired Boyd. 'We have to trust each other sometime, don't we? How about now? Or do we go on and on round the houses?'

'Are you the same man who dived in the Eden and saved Michael's life?' asked Pat.

'One and the same, yes. Why?' asked Boyd.

'Because once you saved my son. but now I ask you to save my nephew,' said Pat.

'Old friend, we are from different nationalities and different generations. We're from different religions and different upbringings, in fact, when you are in the Gaelic, we don't even speak the same language.'

Drawing his chair closer to the frail, failing Irishman, Boyd sought his feeble hand and noticed how weak the pulse in his wrist had become.

'Speak the same language to me now, Pat,' said Boyd. 'Whether we like it or not, Padraigh O'Toole, that day years ago down on the Eden bound us together as sure as if we had been married. Am I right?'

'Sure, that's right. Billyboy. I'll tell you this, though, whether you think it true or not! You're still a local boy at heart, are you not?'

'I like to think so, Pat,' said Boyd. 'But others are the judge of that.'

'Billyboy, I'm still a Derryman myself and I will be until the day I die. Can you understand that, after all these days here on the mainland, in England?' said Pat.

'Takes no working out, Pat,' suggested Boyd. 'If you've no pride in your roots then you've no pride in your life.'

The two men had established common ground once more.

'Look in the envelope, Billyboy,' offered Pat.

The Irishman gestured the envelope forward.

Taking the package from Pat, Boyd carefully spilled the contents onto the bed sheets and rummaged through the pile, scrutinising the contents before his eyes lit up in surprise at what he saw. His brain went into top gear as another piece of the infernal jigsaw puzzle lay exposed before him.

'But...' offered Boyd.

Pat raised the index finger of his left hand and pressed it firmly against the lips of William Miller Boyd, preventing him from speaking. Pat moved closer to the detective and engaged Boyd's eyes.

'No buts, Billyboy, you promised me now,' said Pat. 'If it was possible, you would help, you said. I know it's difficult for you in your position, but Michael and I, well Michael and I got to thinking and that's the result. What do you think?'

Boyd surveyed the contents of the envelope and smiled wryly at the thought of the Irishman's cheek. He mulled the proposition over in his mind before he said, 'Anything's possible, Pat. Now, what do you have in mind?'

'Is it a deal, Billyboy?' asked Par.

'You have my word, Pat. Consider it a contract between us.'

Smiling broadly, the Irishman nodded his head which splayed outwards as it bobbed on his chest. Easing himself up onto one elbow, he leaned towards Boyd.

'Take the warehouse first, Billyboy. Find it and you win, otherwise you lose,' advised Pat. 'You have a few days, maybe a week or so. Now that Dermot is gone from the scene they will need to time it all out and practise. They must do it right or it won't work. Can you see that, Billyboy?'

'It's funny isn't it, Pat?' said Boyd. An ironic smile formed on his cheeks and he started to laugh out loud. He was sure the other patients would hear him down in the main ward.

'What do you mean, funny?' replied Pat. 'You'll have to explain what you mean. Billyboy. Don't keep it to yourself now.'

'All these years and we're back on the river bank,' offered Boyd, laughing. He leaned backwards, placing his hands behind his head in a resigned fashion.

Pat joined in the laughter and, as he did so, took Boyd's hand and shook it as heartily as he could.

Eventually Pat's laughter died down into a rough chesty cough which caused him to splutter and wheeze. Slipping back against the pillows, tired with the effort, Pat breathed heavily and gradually regained control of his faculties.

Boyd poured the Irishman a drink of water and handed him the glass. He helped Pat drink it and passed him the hand towel to dry his lips and chin from the droplets that had escaped the Irishman's mouth. The two men talked on in hushed and secretive voices, occasionally joking and laughing in a private conspiratorial manner. They spent their time planning their council of war.

Boyd left the hospital well before Pat's family had arrived. Before leaving, he sought out Meg and pledged eternal love for her. She responded by making a mockery of Boyd's flattery but confirming a dinner date in the future. With Pat's failing health, a long friendship which spanned the generations and ignored the barriers of age and religion turned fragile. With Meg's bright and sunny smile, another friendship grew and blossomed with the late daffodils of spring.

Routing himself through the city centre, Boyd passed the railway station with its newly refurbished facade and glanced at the gardens by the old court building. Once through the junction he then rushed through the gearbox and accelerated down the main street, luckily catching the traffic lights at green. He left the city behind him.

Within minutes he had found the motorway and the road south. His nimble fingers pressed the buttons and Johnny Hooper's sophisticated jazz saxophone seeped into the car. The radio played softly as Boyd pressed on towards Cheshire in the overtaking lane.

He hummed the tune along with Johnny and the saxophone, drumming his fingers on the car steering wheel in time with the music. The sleek sports car sped down the motorway, passing the heavy goods vehicles and enjoying the quiet open road.

It was a good day, a winner's day. A day to think again and plan for the future. Next to Boyd in the passenger seat of the car lay a black executive style briefcase. The smart briefcase was made of the finest leather and was controlled by a twin combination lock. The numerical sequence required to open the briefcase and reveal its secrets was known only to Boyd. Inside the locked briefcase lay two sealed brown manila envelopes.

One envelope contained tickets for a football match at Wembley stadium, the other contained a surprise: a gift from an Irishman to an Englishman, a gift from a Catholic to a Protestant. Boyd balanced his sunglasses on top of the stylish briefcase as the sun scurried temporarily behind a cloud.

He started to chuckle at the irony of it all. As he drove, he could help himself no longer. He giggled at the circumstances laid out before him and the position he had been manoeuvred into by his old friend, Pat. Then, as he continued south at speed, he burst into a fit of uncontrollable laughter.

Liam Connelly lived in total fear. Wherever he went, whatever he did, he imagined Eugene Kelly was watching and waiting. Waiting for the right time and the right place to finish the killing that had been started on Vauxhall Bridge. He just couldn't get Eugene out of his mind. Come morning, noon or night, he looked over his shoulder for Eugene, the demon from Derry. Liam was a man stalked by death.

It was for that reason Bridget Duffy could sense there was something wrong with Liam. She was unable to put her finger on it and tie it down to a specific reason, but she had known her friend a long time. She sensed the strange, inexplicable atmosphere whenever Liam was around. She could feel it in her bones. Something wasn't quite right about Liam. The chinks in the armour were starting to show.

Bridget tried to discuss her concerns with the only other survivor of the active service unit, their leader, Sean Brady. She sought him out for counsel but he denied her the time she needed. Sean acted like a new man with a lot on his mind. The adrenalin flowed in Sean's body. He bounced with anticipation. He was alive with the thrill of the fight ahead. His eyes were blinkered, his mind focused, his desire unwavering. The battle of Vauxhall Bridge had dulled into insignificance, as far as Sean was concerned. Indeed, he was more determined than ever to carry the battle plan forward. He had no time for doubters. Only time to hate, to seethe in anger and plan his terrible revenge. Bridget's fears were relegated.

While Bridget Duffy worried over Liam, Sean dismissed the matter from his mind and blamed the excitement of the chase. Sean decided the old enemy, fatigue, had set in. It was a good time to move again, up and away, take a break, practise the timing and return once more for the final lethal assault. They packed their bags.

By dawn's early light, the three remaining terrorists had decamped and left London for the Home Counties. They travelled south through Brixton and eventually found the busy A2 highway. Soon the congested road system thankfully broadened and changed into a dual carriageway.

By nightfall they had resettled in their new surroundings. Their heads hit the pillow in another rented house. Another hiding place in the country. The new building was set back in its own grounds, just off the busy Dover to London road. Sited in two acres of sprawling green countryside with a walled border, they knew they would be undisturbed and well protected. They were located at Northfleet, near Gravesend, in the county of Kent, the so aptly named 'Garden of England'.

Sean chose this locality for strategic reasons, not for reasons of grandeur or beauty. They were within striking distance of the centre of London, no more than a couple of hours' drive from the target. In the morning they slept late in the rented accommodation that Bridget had secured from a central London estate agent.

Sean was many things, but he was no fool. He was a committed terrorist who had carefully planned and placed his boltholes across the country many months previously. With the organisation's money and Bridget's expertise at disguise, the premises had been quietly rented by a rich old lady with a walking stick and an air of eccentricity that caused no grave concerns in the estate agent's office. Sean needed time to check the flow, practise setting the all-important timing mechanism and select the best escape route. Dermot's loss had moved the onus of the attack onto himself. Liam would drive; Bridget would carry out reconnaissance and watch their backs whilst he would prime the bomb.

The bomb? A device that would eventually comprise one ton of explosives. A device that would shake the very foundations of the British Government.

It was mid-April, 1995. The Republican terrorists would strike at the heart of the British Establishment by the end of the month.

Sean checked his team, fed them, rested them and prepared for the final onslaught. The killing time was approaching and Sean's itchy finger moved towards the trigger.

Relaxing alone in the Kent garden amidst the early bloom of spring, Liam listened to traffic moving quietly along the main road in the background. Daffodils peeped through the soil, striving to hold the embrace of the rays of the sun heralding the young season.

Bridget joined Liam and took a seat on the patio near the rockery. Her blonde hair flowed down her back in long tresses as she took a brush and preened herself.

'How are you today, Liam?' The hairbrush worked overtime.

'Sure, I'm well, Bridget. Tired but well, so I am,' replied Liam.

'You've not been yourself, Liam,' suggested Bridget.

'Don't concern yourself, woman,' replied Liam. 'Just remember that the bald-headed swine from Derry didn't come after you. You were safe in the house, so you were. We were lucky that day, Bridget. I thought my end had come, that's for sure woman.'

'Eugene!' snapped Bridget. 'I wonder why he came after us in the way he did?'

Throwing her hair to one side, the blonde locks relocated themselves. She took the brush again and made a parting in her hair.

'Haven't you thought about it, Bridget?' suggested Liam. 'Why indeed? Do you think our own side is trying to stop us then?'

'Sean would have said, if that was the case,' offered Bridget.

'Would he now?' replied Liam.

She dropped the hairbrush and Liam stooped to retrieve it from the floor and handed the brush back to her.

Bridget said, 'Do you doubt him?'

Realising he shouldn't have introduced doubt about Sean Brady into the conversation, Liam turned his head away from the blonde woman when he replied, 'I suppose you're right, Bridget. Sean would know if the leadership had withdrawn the sanction for the attack. Sean will look after us. It's just that I can't understand why Eugene came for us.'

Bridget said, 'Probably because the peacemakers back home are happy to settle with a draw.'

'How do you mean?' asked Liam. 'No one likes a draw.'

'The peacemakers in the organisation are tired of the fight. They'll settle for peace if the terms are reasonable,' said Bridget, convincingly.

'But they won't get their own way on everything, surely?' offered Liam.

'They want the British army out. Today's paper says the Artillery Regiment are pulling out. Sure and do you see now, the Bessbrook Barracks are closing down, Liam?'

'Wasn't that the SAS base, then?' enquired Liam.

'One of many, Liam,' replied Bridget knowingly. 'You never knew where they were.'

'What about the RUC?' asked Liam.

'I can't see the Brits giving up the RUC for either a Catholic or a Republican police force, but you never know. What we need is a land of our own, policed by our own and run by our own. The peacemakers think they'll get it, or part of it. Though I doubt it myself,' said Bridget.

'Where does that leave us then?' enquired Liam.

Bridget gave the question serious thought as she returned to combing her hair in earnest. Eventually she said, 'The peacemakers sent Eugene, Liam. They see themselves as the new politicians with power and respect in the community. They sent Eugene after us because they want to hold onto power, their kind of power.'

Dispatching the hairbrush to the nearby table, Bridget stretched her legs out and leaned back into the white plastic garden seat. She felt the sunshine warm her face. It was a change from the cold.

She said, 'Us! Well we represent those in the organisation who believe we can grind the Brits down further. If we can rub their faces in the dirt, then the Brits will give us all we want. You know that, don't you?'

'I know the argument,' revealed Liam. 'I just hope that's the only reason why Eugene came after us.'

'You'll see, for sure, Liam,' said Bridget. 'Once we've carried through the attack the Brits will be on the run and the peacemakers will realise we were right and they were wrong. The Brits will capitulate, that's for sure, and we'll get all we bargain for.'

'You may well be right,' suggested Liam, thoughtfully.

'I know I am,' responded Bridget. 'We'll return home in triumph, Liam. Heroes! One and all! Home! Sure, it'll be a place fit for heroes.'

'And we'll all be welcome, will we?' enquired Liam.

'Sure, and you too, Liam,' agreed Bridget.

'I hope you're right, Bridget. I wonder what Damien Devenney thinks about it all?'

'He sanctioned the hit through the leadership, so he did.'

'Who told you that, Bridget?' asked Liam.

'Sean!' offered Bridget, surprise in her voice.

'Does the leopard change its spots, Bridget? Has Damien forgotten and forgiven? Remember, it was me who took his brother's life.'

Bridget replied, 'That was a long time ago now. Sure, there is a time to go forward to victory, Liam, and this is it. The movement must go forward, not stand still.'

Looking into the blue skies above, Liam saw the sparrows circling playfully on the breeze.

'Then I hope we're finished soon, Bridget. I'm tired of running. I want to find peace.'

Sean stood on the corner of the patio listening to the two talking. He carried three wine glasses, a bottle and a corkscrew and placed the articles on the table. He clasped Liam and Bridget on the shoulder and said, 'Peace it is then, my friends. Damien will take you back. Liam, have no fear of that. Enough of this talk. It's been along hard winter and we're all ready for a break. Rest up now. At the weekend we cook and when it's ready we collect the furniture van, load it and attack.'

'You lost the key, remember?' cracked Liam.

'So, I did, Liam,' agreed Sean. 'But not to worry. The van and the contents are safe. A big hammer will have to do the job instead of the key. It's a pity and it'll be noisy. It'll increase suspicion but we'll have to use a hammer, simple as that. You're not the only one who nearly lost his bottle on the bridge that day. But I've got it together again. Trust me. Soon we'll be home as heroes, just as Bridget said.'

Positioning the bulbous glasses on the patio table near to himself, Sean buried a corkscrew into a bottle of red wine. The label indicated a local supermarket and a French table wine. Sean held the bottle's neck and pulled strongly on the corkscrew. The cork popped out and he poured the contents into the glasses. He passed the first to Bridget, following with a glass for Liam. Then he poured himself a generous helping and raised his glass to study the blood red wine settling in the bowl at the top of the stem. He motioned his hand in a circular fashion and watched the liquid wallowing in the glass.

'Peace it is then.' said Sean, raising his glass to his partners, 'But only after the battle.'

They all laughed together, each with their own personal private thoughts as they drank a toast and resigned themselves to a lazy relaxing day in the spring sunshine.

In the far corner of the two-acre garden and overshadowed by a small copse of trees and an overgrown, uncared-for shrubbery stood a small and virtually deserted outhouse. The building was built of breeze block, powered by mains electricity, equipped with water and covered by a good solid timber roof. The rabbits played nearby and the hedgehogs used it to hibernate in during winter.

The building housed an agricultural grinding machine brought to the premises that morning by Sean Brady. Near the grinder, on the concrete floors, was a parcel of Semtex explosives that had been manufactured in Czechoslovakia some years previously. The parcel had been smuggled into the country at Christmas, having been acquired from an Irish Republican contact in Amsterdam. A quantity of detonator cord was neatly coiled and covered by an old tarpaulin on the floor.

Neat to the Semtex lay bags of ordinary farm fertiliser and a quantity of innocent looking household chemicals. A pair of thin marigold gloves completed the requirements. These, together with one or two other minor ingredients, would be compressed tightly through the grinder having been mixed correctly and in the right proportions. They would then produce one of the most feared weapons in the terrorist arsenal: Home-made explosives.

Those who manufacture explosives occasionally talk about 'cooking' when they are involved in preparing the deadly substance. Dermot Dougan taught his eager charge well. Sean had learnt to cook.

Damien Devenney stalked his living room in Derry, backwards and forwards, the perspiration rolling down his forehead and dampening his cheeks. He had just spoken at length with Seamus Kelty from Dundalk. Kelty had brought a message from the peacemakers, the leadership. The leadership were concerned and most unhappy as to the events in London. Damien was a worried and frightened man with no answers and no proposals to make. He would leave the matter in the hands of Eugene Kelly having persuaded Seamus Kelty to have faith. So far, Dermot Dougan and Eamonn Murphy had been accounted for. Sean Brady's misconceived venture was faltering on the rails. Sean would be regrouping. There was still time for Eugene and his Irish contacts in London to locate and destroy the remainder of the ASU.

Damien's argument was good but it was not wholly acceptable to Seamus Kelty. Seamus was a man who could arrange your death from the safety of another country who eventually reluctantly agreed to Damien's protestations. But then he made some more telephone calls and activated friends in Belfast, Liverpool and Birmingham. The leadership could not afford to lose this one. He would make sure of that. Seamus was a winner, not a loser and he had dutifully promised the leadership that the problem would be solved. He took action. Help was on its way to Eugene Kelly.

Time was running out for the peacemakers.

Seamus Kelty unleashed his dogs of war in central London.

Their objective was simple. Help Eugene Kelly destroy the remains of the ASU, by any means possible.

Damien could find no peace with himself. He knew if Eugene failed then he was done for and would be held responsible. Seamus Kelty would sign Damien's death warrant.

Pulling on his long black coat, Damien raised the high collar. He dusted down the sleeves and brushed the front of the overcoat then made his way into Derry town centre. He couldn't hang around the house waiting for news from London since he was agitated and impatient and had plans to make: escape plans in the event of Eugene failing.

Before leaving the house, Damien opened the door between the kitchen and the lounge and inspected the door saddle covering the floor carpet. He removed the thin saddle by unscrewing either end of the slender metal strip. Then he withdrew the saddle to reveal a secret compartment. Reaching into the hole, he pulled out a cash box, checked the contents, and counted the money. Satisfied, he replaced his private fortune and screwed the lid down tight.

Damien's nightmare was simple. He repeatedly saw himself lying in a ditch by the side of the road in South Armagh, blamed for an inability to command his own men, with two bullets in the back of the head from close range. An inability to command and control that derailed the peace process and rejuvenated the long and cruel war.

Meanwhile, on the English mainland. the telephones were ringing again. Those who took the call from Seamus Kelty knew he meant business. All roads led to London. The chase was on. As some planned for peace, others planned for war.

Boyd tidied up the Cheshire office and left a trusted skeleton staff to continue the enquiry into the Montague deaths.

Taking the majority of his team to London, he set up an incident room in New Scotland Yard. He was quite sure in his own mind he would find them near the River Thames and would walk the entire river bank if he had to.

There was a knock on the door and Anthea walked briskly in. The trouser suit had changed colour, now light blue and set off with a lemon-coloured scarf.

'The RUC have arrived,' she announced.

'Show them in and come and join us, Anthea,' replied Boyd.

The two Ulster detectives were both from the Intelligence office at Strand Road police station in Londonderry. The Inspector introduced himself as Roger and the Sergeant as David. After the pleasantries they took a seat and helped themselves to the eternal coffee pot which governed Boyd's office life.

Roger began, 'We understand you have Liam Connelly on your patch. Is that right?'

'Straight to the point, Inspector,' smiled Boyd, 'No time for tittle-tattle I see. Well! Yes, we do think we have Liam Connelly living on us. The point is we don't quite know where he is. Care for a biscuit?'

Boyd offered round a plate of chocolate digestives. There were no takers.

'We want him for a double murder and an arson in Derry in 1986,' pointed out Roger.

'Yes, I know about that,' acknowledged Boyd. 'Anthea told me all about it following her last visit to you. The Shantallow incident, isn't it? Hugh Devenney and Seamus Rafferty were killed, I understand?'

'Correct,' admitted Roger.

'It is nine years ago, Inspector?' reminded Anthea. 'Are the relevant witnesses still alive?'

Roger nodded as the sergeant, David, spoke. 'We can account for the witnesses, Anthea. We're here to take back Liam Connelly once you have him.'

Shuffling uneasily in his seat, Boyd held the cup from his lips as he spoke, 'Interesting! You see, as I see it, one of your main witnesses is Eugene Kelly, is it not?'

'So?' cracked Roger, a challenge in the air.

'Kelly is wanted here for murder,' revealed Boyd. 'I might be wrong, but I believe the other witnesses are Damien Devenney, a commander with the Provos in Derry, and a Bridget Duffy, a blonde woman, also from Derry?'

'You seem to know a lot about our inquiry, Inspector Boyd,' suggested Roger. 'Have you been doing your homework or are you just well informed?'

Refusing to be drawn into an argument, Boyd politely replied, 'I make it my business to know such things, Roger, particularly when such people may be on my patch. You see, Bridget Duffy, Liam Connelly and Sean Brady are all from Derry but they are all wanted here in England for interview in relation to bombings in Oxford Street and Bond Street, as well as a murder or two in Cheshire. It looks like we're going to have to sort something out about all these people when we catch up with them.'

Roger acknowledged, 'It's a bit messy then.'

'That's putting it mildly,' replied Boyd.

'Any suggestions?' asked Roger.

'I'm quite sure you've been following the Intelligence reports,' suggested Boyd. 'I think the first priority remains the same. Find them, then we'll worry about which police force takes them. In the meantime I suggest we all join forces. I have no doubt we can all work together on this. Unless, of course, you have any reservations about that?'

'None whatsoever, inspector,' advised Roger. 'We're well used to working with the mainland forces.'

'I know,' revealed Boyd.

Anthea felt the tension in the air and questioned the RUC men, 'Will your case stick in court?'

David, the sergeant, said convincingly, 'If the witnesses hold to their original statements, yes. If they decide to change their minds, then who knows?'

Changing the mood of the gathering, Boyd suggested, 'I have the bomb disposal guys waiting in the canteen. Perhaps we should go and join them. I need to switch them on to this bomb attack that we reckon is not far away. We can discuss the matter over a drink. Care to join us? You are, after all, our guests. Perhaps, we can share a meal tonight?'

'Sounds like a good idea,' offered Roger. 'We'll listen to what you have to say to the bomb disposal guys and take you up on a night out. I've heard there's a good Chinese restaurant near Leicester Square. One with about six floors, apparently! Do you know it?'

'Indeed I do,' responded Boyd. 'I know exactly where you mean It's something of a legend in the West End. Service is questionable but the food is excellent. No matter, come, the bomb disposal guys are waiting for us. You've probably heard it all before.'

Four detectives rose from their seats and Anthea led the way to the canteen. David opened the door for her as Anthea directed her question to the RUC men, 'Staying long?'

'Long enough to find Connelly and take him back,' said Roger, as he smiled wryly. The door swung closed behind them, the hinges in dispute with the spring-loaded locking mechanism.

The four officers joined the two bomb disposal officers from Explosives Ordnance in the deserted canteen and listened to Boyd's comprehensive briefing. It wasn't so much a briefing as a request from the police to the bomb disposal experts for help when the time came. Boyd put the Explosives Ordnance Disposal Regiment on full-time alert. Another unit involved in the counter-terrorist war repositioned itself for an attack.

At the end of the day it could all boil down to one man trying to defuse a bomb. Bomb maker versus bomb disposal. The police treated the bomb disposal men with respect. They deserved it.

That night the men from Strand Road police station tasted Oriental food in a Leicester Square restaurant. The idea that here was some kind of race on to arrest Liam Connelly was temporarily suspended.

Bold Eric was back at work.

The pounding headaches had gone and the shock of terrible events on Vauxhall Bridge had faded from his mind. The black London taxi had been traded in for an old plumber's van. It was coloured dark blue with a sliding door on the nearside. Eric had especially asked for a sliding door. It would be much easier to escape from next time, he had joked.

Eric was still in charge of the surveillance squad. He gripped the radio handset and moved his team further along the banks of the Thames. It was well after the Easter bank holiday weekend. There was no sign of his quarry. They had gone to ground in the concrete jungle. The watchers were back to square one.

Toni had devised the plan to catch them when they returned. Meanwhile, Eric's team watched and waited and moved slowly and steadily through the traffic hugging the river bank. They checked out the faces in the car parks, the shops and the cafes. The people watchers were back on the streets in force.

Eric and his friends swept through their sector on the first run. They talked and swapped notes of people they had seen and places they had visited. They talked of 'revisits' and 'probables' but were no further forward.

And somewhere out there, a gang of Irish volunteers were looking for the same people. It was a secret war.

When they had finished they would start all over again. They were back to looking for a needle in a haystack.

Liam Connelly stood impatiently by the door to the warehouse, watching Sean and listening to the rasping noise coming from the padlock on the front door. They were at Clive Montague's warehouse down by the river. Bridget was about one hundred yards from the building watching out for anyone who was not a welcome sight.

A black Uzi submachine gun lay with a full magazine in her shoulder bag. It would take her only a moment or two to remove it and level it at the slightest sign of provocation. She would not hesitate.

Sean again eased the chisel between the padlock and the strong wooden door, trying to find a weak point. He took the hammer from his belt and pounded the end of the chisel between the hasp and the wood. He took a step back as Liam held the chisel, which was now partially embedded in the wood. It would have been so much easier and quieter with a key: Clive Montague's key.

Striking the end of the chisel again, Sean saw the wood splinter slightly. He had spent the last five minutes trying desperately to dislodge the padlock from the well built solid door. It seemed like the whole of London would hear them breaking into the warehouse. They were making such a loud noise that their personal security and the integrity of the operation were in jeopardy.

'Try it again. You're nearly through,' suggested Liam.

'Hold it still, to be sure, Liam,' advised Sean.

'Quietly,' snapped Bridget. 'I can hear you from here. For God's sake, be quiet there.'

Sean struck the end of the chisel for all it was worth.

The lock collapsed and fell to the floor, clattering onto the tarmac.

They were in at last. Sean eased the door open and walked into the warehouse.

The building was abandoned, except for the furniture van that stood in the centre. It was the same furniture van that had been brought down from Montagues place in Cheshire but now it bore new registration plates and had been painted dark green.

Liam followed as Bridget moved closer to the warehouse but still remained on guard outside.

'Why didn't you get a spare cut?' asked Liam. 'We could have done without all that noise.'

'Didn't have time, Liam. I'll remember next time, though,' revealed Sean cheekily. 'Come on, let's get it away and get loaded up.'

Sean passed the ignition key to Liam who stepped onto the driver's running board, unlocked the cabin, and climbed in. Reaching over, he unlocked the passenger door just as Sean finished opening the doors to the warehouse. The engine fired and Liam eased the furniture van out of the building into the open air. Stopping outside the warehouse, Sean opened his door and pulled Bridget into the cab beside him.

'Do we close it, Sean?' asked Bridget.

'No, leave it,' answered Sean. 'If someone finds it closed, but with the lock broken, they'll call the police. If we leave it open then it might not cause any suspicion at all. They'll just think it's a deserted warehouse. It's served its purpose and that's an end to it. Come on, Liam, Northfleet, quick as you can. It'll be all over soon.'

'If you hadn't lost the key we could have come early in the morning and taken the damn thing without a sound. Now we're running loose in London, back and forward, in broad daylight,' said Bridget. 'I don't like it one little bit.'

Sean replied, 'Then just keep little Uzi safe, Bridget. Don't concern yourself, woman. We'll be finished soon. We've broken the lock back there and we'll break the next one. Not having the key to the two locks is a problem, but we'll get by. It'll just take us a lot more time than I planned for. That's all, woman. Relax! Let me do the worrying.'

Turning the furniture van south, Liam headed back towards Northfleet. The wind was blowing and the sky was cloudy; rain was in the air. It had the makings of a long and dreary day. Within the hour they had hidden the furniture van at the rear of the house in Northfleet.

Liam reversed the furniture van towards the outhouse, pulled up, and switched the engine off. Bridget was first out of the van and went immediately to the outhouse. Opening the doors wide, she stepped inside. Sean ran to the rear of the van and unbolted the big metal doors that hid the secret of their attack.

Climbing up into the storage compartment, Sean checked the contents. He walked the full length and checked the object hidden inside the van. Then he examined the underside and the walls. All was well. Quickly, he jumped back down and went into the outhouse.

The sheets of homemade explosives had been well prepared and were thinned and sized to the correct length. Sean, Liam and Bridget manhandled the first few sheets from the outhouse into the back of the furniture van. Sean checked the length and breadth confirming measurements were spot on. The calculations were correct.

They worked on, emptying the contents of the outhouse into the furniture van. An old grey tarpaulin covered three high-powered motor cycles that had been bought the day previously by the resourceful Brady. The tarpaulin was drawn back to reveal the scramble bikes, with their pronounced tyre treads poking out underneath the fibre glass mudguards. Each scrambler was equipped with a pillion seat and a large single bore exhaust pipe pointing upwards at the rear of the offside.

A wooden ramp was fixed to the rear of the van and the motor cycles were hurriedly pushed into the van. Sean supervised the loading, taking care that the scramblers were placed along the sides of the van. It didn't take long to load them.

When all was nearly done, Liam climbed back into the driver's seat and fired the engine.

Sean removed the last item from the outhouse and tenderly carried it to the rear compartment. He took a length of detonation cord and threaded it carefully into the explosive sheeting, noting that Dermot's design had indeed been absolutely brilliant. When he finished, Sean connected the detonator cord to the electrical unit and checked that the power was in the 'off' position.

The only thing left was to take the bomb to the target, set the timer and make their escape. The van set off for the heart of London.

Bridget checked the Uzi in her bag.

Sean felt the handgun in his waistband.

Liam pondered the situation, depressed the clutch and selected a higher gear as the van entered the A2 slip road and gathered speed.

The cabin was filled with cigarette smoke as Sean's nerves started to fray and he tipped the end of the cigarette into the ash tray when he sat between Liam and Bridget. He inhaled deeply on the cigarette and ran through the timer mechanism once more in his mind.

The killing time had arrived.

Eric's team found the warehouse as they continued their endless search of the Thames Embankment. Two of the surveillance team entered whilst the rest stayed at a safe distance.

A plumber's van sat on the bridge overlooking the area.

Toni took the radio message and telephoned Boyd. Agreement followed. They both set off independently for the warehouse. The premises loosely fitted the description that Clive Montague's father had supplied. The race was on, courtesy of the starter, Eric, who had found the chequered flag.

Removing a brown manila envelope from his desk drawer, Boyd placed it inside his jacket pocket and switched on the bleeper which he carried in his waistband. His last action was to draw a handgun and several rounds of ammunition from the armoury.

Toni went to her wall safe, carefully dialled the combination and took her handgun from a metal security box. She adorned herself with the shoulder holster, checked the Smith and Wesson, loaded it, and found the envelope in the metal box. She checked the contents of the envelope and placed it in her shoulder bag. Closing the office door behind her, she took the lift to the garage.

Within minutes Toni had eased herself into the city traffic and listened to Eric on the radio net, giving directions to the location of the warehouse. Two members of the bomb disposal team travelled with Boyd. The warehouse had to be pronounced safe.

In a detached house in Kent, a sombre outhouse lying in two acres of garden sat silent and abandoned. In the outhouse a grinding machine slept soundly, its job done. A couple of old and frayed ropes lay on the concrete floor next to empty and discarded plastic bags which had once held fertiliser. Here and there could be seen the cut ends of detonation cord which had been abandoned in the sizing procedure. The brown wax packaging that had held semtex had been thrown into a corner and now nuzzled against an old Pepsi-Cola tin and an empty cigarette packet.

Near an old grey tarpaulin sheet, traces of engine oil seeped into the concrete floor, testament to the assault underway. The detached house was locked, the outhouse and the gardens deserted. Early traffic on the nearby dual carriageway whispered back and forward between Dover and the capital. Daffodils poked through the soil and reached for the heavens. A Kent wind blew the stems northwards, towards London.

And Liam drove the furniture van towards the target.

'Trust, that's what it's all about,' declared Liam suddenly.

'What do you mean, Liam?' asked Sean.

'All these years we've been together. It's all about trust. Trusting one another, that's what got us through,' said Liam.

He signalled as he moved out to overtake a slower moving vehicle.

Sean agreed, 'Sure, you're right there, Liam.'

'Shall we give them a coded warning like in the old days, Sean? When we were young and ferocious,' asked Liam.

'I hadn't planned to. What do you think, Bridget?' asked Sean.

'Seems sensible if you want them to know it was us. Just give them the wrong target though. Once it's gone off we can 'phone in the right target and tell the Brits it's too late,' she chuckled.

'Okay, that's what we'll do. Liam, you make the call. Just like in the old days. Get them running round in the wrong direction. Point them at King's Cross station for starters,' decided Sean.

'In fact, you can make that call, Liam, when we get nearer to the real target, that is. We wouldn't want anyone else claiming the attack. Ring one of the national papers first, then the police, just so they know who it is, no mistake.'

'Leave it to me, Sean. I'll enjoy the call,' said Liam slowing the furniture van as they met the congested city streets. The road narrowed from dual carriageway to single lane and they made for the Thames, still some miles away from their location.

But others were already down by the Thames. Eric's team were buzzing on the radio.

'It's Eugene!' reported one of the surveillance team.

'Where?' enquired Eric.

'Coming towards the warehouse. He's on foot and alone and he's on the footpath, maybe three or four minutes off yet!' came the reply.

Eric dropped the plumber's van down onto the parking area outside the abandoned warehouse. He looked across at Toni and Boyd and asked, 'Do you want him now? It's definitely him. They tell me they can see his shaven head bobbing along.'

'No,' decided Boyd. 'Let's get inside the warehouse and see if he comes to us. Keep your eyes on him and just sit tight in the van. Do me one favour, though?' said Boyd.

'What's that, Inspector?' asked Eric.

'Patch the radio through to Anthea and tell her what's going on. I want her with the river police patrolling the Thames. Tell her I want four armed men on the Thames river police boat available to respond to either the north bank or the south. Once she's on board, she can bring them to the Lambeth area? Okay?'

'Sure thing,' replied Eric.

'Just one more thing,' added Boyd, 'Tell her I want my men with the river police, no uniforms at this stage. Nice and easy, understand?'

'Understood, leave it with me,' replied Eric.

'What do you think?' asked Boyd of the bomb disposal team.

'It's safe. Nothing here to worry about, Inspector. If it's an attack from the river bank, then it isn't here, I would say.'

'Where's the RUC men?' asked Toni.

'They're with Anthea,' replied Boyd.

'Good! Here comes their best witness,' declared Toni.

'And yours, too!' confirmed Boyd.

Eugene Kelly was getting nearer. It was possible to make him out in the distance as he walked along the footpath towards them. His gait was unmistakable.

'Quick! Inside!' ordered Boyd. 'Let's see what he does. Behind the doors. I'll keep an eye on him through the gap between the door and the wall.'

Motionless in the plumber's van, Eric nonchalantly read the newspaper whilst keeping an ear out for the radio. For the first time since the day on Vauxhall Bridge, Eric wondered if Eugene would recognise him as the driver of the taxi. Had Eugene seen him that day or had he been too occupied with chasing Brady and his gang?

The two men from the bomb disposal team, together with Boyd and Toni, moved into Montague's warehouse and pressed their backs against the wall, hiding behind the doors.

Huffing and puffing along the footpath towards them on his search for the remnants of the ASU, Eugene's gun rested beneath his armpit.

Toni felt for the weapon in her shoulder holster and slid the safety catch off. She found the envelope inside her bag and covered it with a silk scarf.

Meanwhile, Boyd crouched low and moved his body slowly so that his eyes followed Eugene's every move through the slender gap between the door and the wall.

Motionless, Eugene looked out across the river towards Pimlico. Battersea power station stood behind him and the New Covent Garden Market ahead. He wasn't far from the roadway and Nine Elms Lane. They were on the south side of the river.

Seconds ticked by as the surveillance team scurried for cover and tried to act as normally as possible.

Eugene used his handkerchief to mop his head and walked on.

'What's he playing at?' asked Boyd.

'Cowboys and Indians!' offered Toni.

'It's about right that, Toni,' said Boyd, 'But the sheriff is in town, so he'd better watch out.'

'Stick the small talk, Boyd. It's not funny anymore. What's he doing now?' enquired Toni.

'Coming this way,' replied Boyd. 'Get ready to whistle up the cavalry if he comes in here, otherwise we'll just follow him along. Perhaps he knows more than we do.'

'Shouldn't be too difficult,' said Toni.

'Now who's making the wisecracks?' whispered Boyd.

Eugene saw the warehouse and the wide-open doors. He looked casually across and realised that it was a deserted shell. He thought nothing of the plumber's van parked outside the warehouse with the driver sat reading a daily paper. Why should such things bother Eugene? He knew who he was looking for. The warehouse meant nothing to him. He stood for a moment.

The Covent Garden Market area was always full of delivery vans and the like. One more fairly nondescript van was not out of place.

Eugene walked on past the hidden eyes, the whispered radio calls and the anticipating guns.

Eric breathed a sigh of relief.

'Does that mean we've got the wrong warehouse?' asked Toni.

'I don't know. It could be that Eugene doesn't know about the warehouse. Who can tell? Let's just keep cool and follow him for a while. We've nothing to lose yet. Eugene isn't stupid. He could still lead us to our goal,' suggested Boyd.

Toni nodded in agreement.

'Apart from that, I've got no intention of taking Eugene alone. We need some good back-up. Swim across to Chelsea barracks, Toni, and see if the boys there can spare a hand,' joked Boyd, using humour to veil his nervousness.

Toni radioed the message to Eric, who circulated the instruction to his team on the radio network. The silent watch continued and the team set off in pursuit.

In the skies above, a helicopter darted in and out of the clouds. The observer patched through the radio to make contact with Eric.

Returning the weapon to her shoulder holster, Toni let out a long sigh of relief and said, 'I wouldn't like to take him on after reading the reports about Vauxhall Bridge, Boyd. What do you think?'

'I think you could have talked him into giving himself up. After all, he's your tout,' replied Boyd.

'Don't I know it?' sighed Toni, elbowing Boyd in the ribs.

'I don't think anyone is safe with that lunatic around, Toni,' said Boyd. 'He's just a loose cannon now. When we take him, we'll make sure he doesn't get away, have no fear of that.'

Eugene made Nine Elms Lane and turned right to walk up Battersea Park Road. Clouds broke and sunshine came through briefly. Battersea Power Station filled the sky line, with the Chelsea road and rail bridges spanning the Thames behind.

Anthea passed under Lambeth Bridge to Eugene's north and headed towards Vauxhall Bridge. The police cruiser sped along at a good rate of knots with Boyd's men holding onto the railings at the side. They passed the Tate Gallery and announced their arrival on the radio net. They made the party just in time - but they'd taken guns instead of balloons.

Less than three miles away, a dark green furniture van with three Irish gatecrashers on board was going to the same party but, like Anthea and her fellow party revellers, they didn't carry balloons and paper hats.

'Once Anthea and the team on the cruiser arrive, we'll call it in and secure the area with patrol cars,' revealed Boyd. 'Then we can take out Eugene whenever we decide.'

Toni said, 'Let's hope you're right, Boyd. Commander Herbert will be at full pace in the control room now.'

In New Scotland Yard the nerve centre was alive.

Commander Herbert plotted the surveillance teams on his map and listened out for reports from the helicopter crew and the officers on the cruiser. He was happy to leave things on the ground to Boyd. Commander Herbert checked the disposition of the uniformed firearm squad and made his plan to seal off the Battersea area with his mobiles.

The Commissioner entered the room, examined the situation and gestured approval at the Commander. The time was approaching.

They would take out Eugene Kelly for starters. Nothing would prevent that.

Once again, Liam crunched the gears as he negotiated the green furniture van round the bend in the road and down a steep hill towards Lambeth and the waiting River Thames. They would be there in about a quarter of an hour provided the traffic remained hospitable. The furniture van was slow moving and a little cumbersome at times, but that didn't present too much of a problem to its occupants.

'Next telephone box, Liam!' suggested Sean.

'I'll pull in as soon as I see a free box, so I will,' nodded Liam.

Bridget checked the nearside mirror and saw a police patrol car behind them moving through the traffic. Gradually, the patrol car moved into a position immediately to the rear of the furniture van and continued to follow them at what seemed to be a discreet distance.

'We've got company,' she said. Bridget strained her neck looking through the side mirror at the police car.

'Keep cool,' instructed Sean. 'We've done nothing wrong. We're not speeding, so just carry on as normal.'

Bridget kept her eyes on the mirror. Liam tried to remain steady at the steering wheel whilst Sean peeked into the rear compartment. The construction inside was still intact and the scramble bikes hadn't moved since the team had left Northfleet. They were still in the same position, pressed to the sides of the van by the weight of the construction.

'Funny, that!' cracked Sean, looking at the blonde.

'What is?' asked Bridget turning to angle her face towards Sean.

'The construction back there. Dermot called it a contraption. He wondered if it would ever work because it was such a hare-brained idea. Now he'll never know. Poor Dermot!'

'We proved it worked on the river at Northfleet. It'll work on the Thames,' said Bridget. 'It's just a pity we had to cart the damn thing back and forward between Northfleet and Lambeth. If we'd had the key it would have been so much more professional, so much easier, so it would.'

'Sure, it couldn't be helped, Bridget,' said Sean. 'It was too near the target area to leave in the warehouse. We could risk losing the furniture van, soon get another, but not the contraption in the back. We needed to keep them separate at all times, only bring them together when we attack. Understand now?'

'I suppose so, Sean,' admitted Bridget.

Liam said, 'There's one!'

Pressing the brake pedal, he slowed the vehicle down in a leisurely but workmanlike manner, looking for a place to park.

The police patrol car following them turned left at a junction and veered away from Bridget's view.

She felt relieved when her eyes left the nearside mirror and she glanced at Sean beside her.

'The cop car's gone,' she said, satisfied.

'I told you not to worry,' replied Sean.

Liam signalled with the nearside indicator and brought the vehicle to a standstill near a row of telephone kiosks outside a small shopping arcade. He applied the handbrake sharply and looked at the offside mirror. There was no following traffic that he could see.

'Coming with me, Sean?' enquired Liam.

'I'll leave it to you, so I will, Liam,' replied Sean.

Opening the driver's door, Liam climbed down from the cab onto the roadway, checked again for traffic, rounded the front of the furniture van, and stepped onto the pavement. Removing some coins from his trouser pocket, he found an empty kiosk. Closing the door behind him, he lifted the 'phone, dialled the number of a daily newspaper, and waited.

It seemed to be a long time before the call was answered.

The tone rang in his ears. Eventually, a polite female voice spoke and Liam asked to be put through to the news desk.

The male reporter was having a bad day. No disasters to report, no bribery and no corruption in the sports world either. This, together with no scandal in the Houses of Parliament, all added up to a quiet day. He needed a story before the deadline was announced.

The reporter lifted the 'phone when it rang and pulled the pencil and pad closer to him. The accent on the other end of the 'phone at first confused the young reporter, then he realised it was an Irishman speaking. The reporter answered the telephone and identified himself.

Liam said, 'Listen to me carefully now! This is the Provisional Irish Republican Army. A bomb will go off in Downing Street soon. You have half an hour.'

'What? Say that again!' said the reporter, scribbling the text of the message.

Liam started again and spoke the agreed codeword very slowly and very clearly.

'Jesus Christ!' said the reporter as he covered the telephone mouthpiece. 'I got a bomb call! Quiet everyone!'

He motioned with his hand in the air for the newsroom to come to a silence.

Liam repeated his claim. 'This is the Provisional Irish Republican Army. A bomb will go off in Downing Street soon. You have half an hour.'

Pressing the button, Liam waited for the dialling tone then made a further call.

The news reporter had a scoop. He arranged a photographic and sound crew, together with a car, and made plans to get to Downing Street as soon as possible. The media had waited for the peace process to fall down. This could be the signal they had been waiting for. The editor collared the reporter as he made for the streets, cooled his enthusiasm, and ordered him to telephone New Scotland Yard.

The control room in New Scotland Yard was following the anticipated arrest of Eugene Kelly. All eyes were focused on Lambeth and the Thames.

A telephone operator flicked the switch in response to the flashing warning light and answered the call. The voice was Irish. She recognised the accent immediately.

'I want to speak to Detective Inspector Billy Boyd,'

'Inspector Boyd doesn't appear to be available just now,' came the reply, terse and to the point.

'Then I'll leave a message for him. Make sure he gets it as soon as possible. It's very, very important,' revealed Liam.

'I'll put you through to the control, hold on,' said the operator. She dialled into the internal system, placing the call into the control room.

'Control room. New Scotland Yard,' said a policeman.

'Give the following message to Detective Inspector Billy Boyd as soon as possible,' instructed Liam. 'It's very, very important.'

He was becoming irritated with the telephone system.

'What's the message?' asked the policeman.

'Tell him the IRA has just 'phoned in to say that a bomb is to go off at Downing Street in half an hour. Tell him he must ignore that call. Tell him the target is the Houses of Parliament. He must look for the green furniture van down at Nine Elms Lane. Check the river. Tell him Pat's friend 'phoned. He'll know who it is. Got that?'

'Yes, I think so. Can I just go through that again?'

Too late, the line was dead. The Irish voice had gone.

Liam left the kiosk and crossed the pavement to rejoin the van. He climbed up into it, turned the ignition key and set off.

The policeman looked towards the duty officer and asked if any calls had been logged in purporting to come from the IRA. It wasn't an unusual request. The control room in New Scotland Yard was well used to regularly dealing with the fools who placed such hoax calls. The supervisor worked his VDU and selected the menu. No such calls had been recorded. the disposition of personnel. Boyd was shown at Lambeth on the Kelly job. More importantly, the red light flashed on the console, signalling an emergency call. The policeman depressed the corresponding switch, adjusted his headset and answered the call. It was a news reporter from a daily newspaper.

The message was passed. There was a bomb due to explode in Downing Street in half an hour. Indeed, by now, in only twenty-five minutes time. Five precious minutes had elapsed since the journalist had received the original call from the Irishman. The reporter divulged that the Irish caller had used a code-word. The policeman knew it was authentic.

Within minutes the Metropolitan police had swung into action. The radio crackled and the sirens blared. Blue flashing lights zoomed in on Downing Street as all available mobiles in the area made for Whitehall.

As the roads were closed and the traffic diverted, Boyd's mobile telephone rang. He raised the short cellular aerial, depressed the green 'talk' button and took the call. It was the control room at New Scotland Yard.

'Downing Street! What? Ignore it because the target is the Houses of Parliament? Is that what he said?' snapped Boyd, as he held the 'phone to one ear whilst covering the other ear with his free hand.

The policeman in the control room relayed, 'The message is Tell Billy Boyd that the IRA have just called in a bomb warning to the effect that a bomb will explode in Downing Street within half an hour. Got that Inspector? He said he was Pat's friend and you should ignore it because the real target was the Houses of Parliament. He said to look for a green furniture van by the river at Nine Elms Lane.'

'A furniture van!' Boyd realised they were on to something.

'How did we respond to that?' probed Boyd.

The policeman revealed, 'Within a few seconds of that call a reporter rang in and said he had taken a call from the IRA. An authentic codeword was used and the message was that a bomb was to go off in the Downing Street area. We've sent everything in the area towards Whitehall. We're cordoning off, diverting traffic and doing the usual with Number Ten's occupants. I think I'm in the best place here!'

'Did your man definitely say he was Pat's friend?' asked Boyd.

'Yes,' replied the policeman.

'That's it then,' declared Boyd. 'Forget Downing Street. It's on the river. It's the Houses of Parliament.'

'Control here is pulling your cars out of Lambeth, Inspector. He wants bomb disposal moved from your patch to Whitehall like it was yesterday,' said the policeman.

'The fool! He's wrong,' declared Boyd. 'I haven't time to explain, but he's wrong. The first caller is right. The attack is here. Tell him he's wrong. Who is it? Put him on the line quick.'

'No can do,' came the reply. 'He's talking to the Commissioner. We're pulling your cars out of Lambeth, Inspector. Sorry.'

'Tell Commander Herbert,' said Boyd.

The line went dead. Boyd's mind raced through the argument. He was so angry.

The green furniture van turned slowly into Nine Elms Lane and eventually found the turning which led between Kirtling Street and Battersea Power Station. Liam slowed the vehicle down to a crawl in the narrow streets. The Thames flowed in the distance.

Locating the jetty on the south side of the Thames, Liam turned the vehicle into the parking area adjacent to the Nine Elms Pier in Kirtling Street. Liam checked the mirror and engaged reverse gear. Crunching through the box again, he carefully drove backwards towards the Thames and came to a standstill.

The sound of police sirens in the distance greeted his ears. The noise was, however, drifting away from him, not towards him.

North of the river, two bomb disposal officers raced towards Downing Street under a fast-moving police escort.

Boyd cursed when the order was passed over the air but he had sent two of the four EOD men requested. Even Boyd wondered if he had been duped. New Scotland Yard were taking no chances. They were deploying their resources as best they could.

The lights flashed as the police escort threaded his charge through the London traffic, slowing slightly on the approach to traffic lights before accelerating to the next junction. Pedestrians scattered as a Metropolitan police traffic mobile pulled up sharply near the Ministry of Defence building in Whitehall, its siren blaring and blue lights flashing across its roof.

Across the road stood Downing Street with its black iron gates locked fast to the passer-by. Number Ten, the heart of government, was inside the blast area that would result from a large vehicle bomb. In any case, a mortar attack could come from anywhere.

By the pavement, an old and battered orange Transit van had been abandoned. It was locked. A note on the windscreen told the first traffic policeman at the scene that the vehicle had broken down. The driver would be back in a few minutes. The policeman checked the rear of the van. The windows were blacked out and he was unable to inspect the rear compartment. He reached for his radio. The uniformed officer moved to the front of the van again. In the front passenger well the wires from an old, broken transistor radio were visible. The wires disappeared under the driver's seat, out of view. This was it.

An officer from the Ministry of Defence Police arrived and agreed with the traffic officer. They thought they'd found the suspect bomb. The Transit bore all the hallmarks.

The area was being evacuated.

Blind panic struck the streets of London as the word spread like wildfire.

A police Land Rover slewed across the road between Downing Street and King Charles Street, near the Cenotaph. The occupants leapt onto the highway and donned fluorescent jackets. Further along, at the end of Parliament Street, two larger patrol cars blocked the street, preventing traffic from entering. Taxi drivers sought alternative routes whilst motorcycle couriers became impatient.

At the top end of Whitehall, near Charing Cross station, police cordoned off Whitehall and prevented vehicles from travelling down the road. The heavy traffic became even more congested as yet another route was denied to the frustrated motorist.

Nelson looked down from his column in Trafalgar Square and saw the tourists in Whitehall being guided backwards by the uniformed men and women of London's police force. Admiral Lord Horatio Nelson had seen it all before. It was often demonstrations or New Year celebrations. Today it was people running away from a bomb threat.

The police tried to prevent panic by quietly moving the pedestrians away from the orange van. It was difficult. As the young men and women in blue uniforms covered by fluorescent jackets spread out their arms in an appeal to stop or go backwards, the reality of the situation slowly hit the minds of the hundreds of tourists in the area.

Suddenly, Horse Guards Parade and the splendour of the Household Cavalry didn't seem quite so attractive to London's visitors. Something was wrong! Why were the police concerned about the orange van? Why were there so many of them in the area?

Someone said, 'Bomb! Bomb!'

The slow walk became a trot followed by a full-blooded run. Soon it would be a frenzied gallop.

Mothers grabbed their children as concerned fathers shielded their families from the maddening crowd.

'Bomb!' Someone said, 'Bomb!'

Pavements filled with secretaries and clerks, mingling with Japanese and American tourists with their cameras around their necks and their plastic police helmets perched comically on their heads. 'Kiss me quick' hats fell to the ground as the throng realised what was happening.

The slow walk became a terrified run as the crowd swelled and headed for Trafalgar Square.

An American tourist fell at the front of the crowd and was trampled underfoot by the screaming mass.

A London taxi driver saw the crowd approaching him and mounted the pavement in order to miss the people. The front of his taxi collided with a litter bin and the rear end of the cab bounced round onto the roadway, causing further mayhem and a temporary distraction.

It was the loudspeaker that brought the crowd under control, and not a moment too soon. It shrilled and pierced the airwaves as the officer pressed the button. One of the police officers got out of his patrol car and used the loudspeaker on his radio to address the stampeding crowd.

'This is a police message. There is no danger! Walk! Don't run! Slow down and walk quietly into the square in front of you. There is no need to panic.'

The radio whistled before the policeman continued.

'Slow down! There is no danger.'

His colleague strode into the roadway and dominated the scene in his bright fluorescent jacket. He raised his hands and the London traffic dutifully ceased its constant navigation of the famous square. Gradually, as the traffic built up behind the vehicles on the approaches to Trafalgar Square, the scene came to a standstill. The policeman calmly repeated the loudspeaker message again and again, as gradually the crowd reduced its clamouring and regained its brain cells.

The jostling and the pushing stopped and families found themselves reunited. Eventually, normality returned to the street.

Boyd was still south of the Thames in Lambeth. He had not moved his position. He was steadfast, resolved, convinced the action would be in the Lambeth area. Toni stood by his side. His men patrolled the river, with Anthea standing at the helm next to the River Police sergeant.

The furniture van reversed towards the jetty, the hidden load ready to be unleashed. Overhead the police helicopter ignored the green furniture van, flew across the river near the Houses of Parliament and made for the Downing Street area. As the helicopter neared its target the observer switched on the external recording cameras and focused on the orange Transit van that was causing so much consternation.

Commander James Herbert sat in the special operations control room and wondered what Boyd had decided upon. The radio airwaves were full of calls about evacuation and parked vehicles all over the Whitehall area. Each one was a potential bomb. Each one was a real threat. Each one a daily headache for the boys and girls in blue. The radio network was crammed with call after call about suspect parcels and suspect bombs.

The Commissioner made it clear. Downing Street was the target, just as he had forecast months ago. It was to Downing Street that resources would be deployed. There was no time for argument, no time for rationale. The IRA had done the usual thing and given only a scant warning. Commander James Herbert, beloved and respected by all around him, studied the disposition display on the VDU in front of him.

He could clearly see that Boyd's team was diminishing fast. The importance of Eugene Kelly and the unfolding drama in Nine Elms Lane paled into insignificance following the receipt of one coded telephone call. Very soon Boyd and his dedicated team would be on their own.

'Commissioner!' advised Commander Herbert. 'We're forgetting the Lambeth incident.'

'I'm not forgetting Lambeth at all, Commander. I'm making damn sure Downing Street is protected and if I have to use every damn copper in London to do it then I will,' replied the Commissioner emphatically.

'Yes, but there may be an attack from the Nine Elms area,' argued Commander Herbert.

'Just tell me where then, Commander, if you're so sure of yourself?' replied the Commissioner.

Commander Herbert suggested, 'Downing Street could be a diversionary call to get us to move our resources from the main target. Look!'

The Commander pointed to the map of central London and advised, 'Down there in Nine Elms there's the old Battersea Power Station, Covent Garden Market, Chelsea Barracks and even the Chelsea Royal Hospital. God! Millbank Tower is a mountain of glass. There's also these other sites!'

Commander Herbert fingered further potential targets in the vicinity of Nine Elms. The Commissioner thought for a moment and then nodded to the detective.

'Alright, I suggest I look after the Downing Street incident whilst you look after Battersea Dogs Home,' said the Commissioner, scathingly. More seriously, the police chief continued, 'I don't think your analysis is correct. There is no major worthwhile target in that area, not major, you understand. However, get yourself down there and you may feel happier about it. You can't beat being on the ground to get the feel of things. It's Downing Street, I say, but I have no objection to you using what's left down by the river. Okay?'

'Fine,' replied Commander Herbert. 'The duty Inspector can monitor the radio channels and keep me updated on both incidents. I'll get south of the river as soon as possible.'

The Commissioner dismissed the elderly detective with a wave of his hand and resumed his deliberations on the Downing Street scenario.

He keyed into the computer screen and listened to the radio giving advice and issuing orders to his nearest confidants.

Commander Herbert watched. It was too much for him. He'd had enough. He'd driven a desk for too long and played politician too long with the budget. He knew where real policing took place and he knew that policing was about people, not politics and money. The Commander slowly rose from his seat and quietly left the room. He took the lift to the garage in the basement.

Finding his car, he drove up the ramp into the city streets. The Commander acknowledged the car park attendant with a wave of the hand, shook his head at the edifice of New Scotland Yard, and plotted his course for the borough of Lambeth and the action that he was sure was to follow. It would not take him long to drive from his central location near St James tube station to Lambeth. He would go where he was wanted and join Boyd, Toni and Anthea.

Commander Herbert made for the bridge across the river. He wound the driver's window down and fixed the portable blue light to the car roof. He found his youth from a bygone age, changed down a gear, pulled out to overtake a line of traffic and put his foot to the floor. The killing time was nigh, but whereabouts?

The Thames was broad, deep, and murky with a lazy attitude at this crucial point on its journey towards the sea. The current was, however, mysteriously deceptive and fairly moderate in its speed, having mastered the Chelsea Reach and turned gradually to the north in the direction of Westminster. It was the slow northward bend at Nine Elms that initially reduced but then increased the flow of the river.

Indeed, here was the secret of Dermot Dougan's exhilarating and inspirational plan. He noticed that a floating object, such as a block of wood, when thrown casually into the river from the centre of Chelsea Bridge would first float across to the southern side of the river near Nine Elms. But from thereon, the object would move into the centre of the river near Vauxhall Bridge. By the time it reached Lambeth Bridge it was floating nearer to the northern bank than at any other time in its journey. Just east of Lambeth Bridge and close to the heart of the city lay the dominant structure the British people know as the Houses of Parliament.

Dermot Dougan had been mentally astute for he had noted the occurrence with the floating object on the river twelve months previously. It had puzzled him ever since but he cleverly worked out the flow, the river speed, the movements, the wind speed and the activity on the Thames. Slowly and patiently, he put the puzzle together, piece by piece, before producing his violent and awesome blueprint.

It had been Dermot's idea to build the floating wooden barge. The 'contraption', they called it. It was no more than a well built wooden structure that resembled a barge which had been tested on the Thames near Northfleet and found to be feasible. The wooden contraption floated well and the complicated mathematical formula the resourceful Dermot used had proved correct.

Now the contraption would be used in anger. When the contraption drew parallel to the Houses of Parliament, the timer would complete its course and the bomb would explode. A massive amount of home-made explosives, together with a proportionate amount of semtex, would decimate the Houses of Parliament and terrify the British people.

The terrorists reckoned the enormous blast wave from the device would alone bring down massive splinters of glass onto the physical targets below. The blast wave, having shattered the impressive glass frontage of the Parliamentary Gallery which overlooks the Thames, would catapult the interior furniture into an uncontrollable fit of death, destruction and mayhem

The likelihood existed that the flying furniture would take out further bodily targets and provide the active service unit with a bloody and spectacular onslaught.

The tables, chairs, cutlery, paintings and regalia which adorned the majestic walls would perish as the explosion destroyed all in its path. Indeed, the very foundations of the political establishment would quake in terror at the ferocity of the attack.

Thereafter, the bomb blast and its tremendous trail of destruction would rebound against the ancient walls and roof of the Parliament building. The weakened structure would crumble in some critical places and fall onto the unsuspecting honourable Members of Parliament below. Death could rain from above, on the unwary, the unprepared.

The result would be terrifying.

A pall of smoke and debris would climb into the heavens, equalling the enormous Bishopsgate bomb that had recently exploded in the heart of the City. Dermot prophesied that the familiar mushroom effect would be smaller, since there were fewer high buildings in the immediate area to contribute to the bomb affect. Nevertheless, the clever bomb maker foresaw political upheaval for the Brits and a major victory for those elements of the Republican movement who wished to continue the struggle. Dermot, although deceased, had ensured their success.

St Thomas hospital and its famous medical school across the river from the Houses of Parliament would feel the full force of the blast. Glass would fracture; the ground would shake and objects would take on a life of their own, flying through the air. Hundreds of patients would be injured in the atrocity, along with the attendant medical and nursing staff unlucky enough to be caught in the blast area at the time.

It was whilst talking about flying furniture, caused by bomb blasts, that Sean suggested transporting the contraption in a furniture van.

Somewhere in Sean's mind lurked a sick and evil note of black comedy. Dermot had systematically checked his calculations regarding size and shape before he agreed. The furniture van had been acquired from a shady dealer in the Midlands. The plan had been made. Dermot built the strange contraption to hide in the furniture van. The rest would prove to be history.

But throughout the planning, Dermot made it clear that he could never be truly sure of whether the bomb would totally destroy the Houses of Parliament. To Sean, it was an irrelevance. The gesture was much more important. Furthermore, martyrdom was as attractive as outright victory to the dedicated terrorist. The attack from the river on the heart of Government would be spectacular enough to undoubtedly capture the close attention of the world's media. The assault, whether totally or partially successful, was guaranteed to dominate every television screen and the front page of every newspaper in the democratic world. The vital search for peace would be mutilated and lie forever in the bombed ruins of the mighty Houses of Parliament.

The British Parliament would need to seek revenge to placate the masses and, with revenge, the hate and violence of centuries past would be resurrected.

The fragile peace, that had been so hard won, would be broken.

Where Guy Fawkes and his conspirators had once attacked the Houses of Parliament from the underground cellars, Sean Brady and his terrorist guerrillas would attack Parliament from the river. They were guaranteed success and a place in the long, bloody, violent history of the Republican movement.

Liam Connelly sat quietly in the driver's seat, looking all around him for some sign of Boyd's men. The jetty area was deserted. There were no more than a handful of meaningless craft chugging up and down the Thames, going about their daily business.

'Now,' said Sean Brady. 'It's time.'

Liam, Sean and Bridget alighted from the front of the furniture van and moved casually to the rear.

Sean climbed onto the step board and withdrew the iron bolts from the rear door.

Liam climbed onto the tailgate and the two men slowly opened the rear door and carefully lowered the wooden ramp which lay inside the van. A low creaking noise could be heard as the hinges on the door were

246

worked. The mysterious contraption was painted in a grey- black shade, in order to match the colour of the water when seen from afar.

The blonde woman, Bridget Duffy, supervised the lowering of the ramp and checked both upstream and downstream to ensure no one interrupted their final onslaught. The venomous Uzi submachine gun hung from its sling underneath her armpit, only partially hidden by her tight leather blouson jacket. Her hair blew backwards as it reacted to the breeze from the river. She drew her jacket closer to her body in an effort to defeat the elements.

Inside the interior of the furniture van, Sean manhandled the three scramble bikes down the wooden ramp and laid them at the side of the furniture van. Checking the engine mountings, he made sure that the petrol taps were turned to the 'on' position. Next, he unscrewed the filler cap on each petrol tank and confirmed that the bikes were fully fuelled and ready for immediate use.

The plan catered for a quick escape from the area. Once the contraption had been launched on the river, the team would evacuate the jetty, leave the furniture van abandoned in the road, and make speed for their hiding place in the west country.

The three terrorists worked together inside the van. Sean climbed into the contraption and found the timing mechanism. His thin nimble fingers finally located the black plastic cover that secreted the heart of the bomb. The mechanism was simple but effective. Sean checked that the slender wooden dowel pin was in place. He knew that once he removed the dowel pin the timer would start and within minutes its course would be run. The detonation wiring was in place. The explosion would be heard for miles around. The bomb was still safe, but for the moment only.

The contraption was heavy. They pulled it down the ramp and, for the first time, wondered if it would really work.

Liam looked again for Boyd. The jetty remained deserted.

'What you looking for?' remarked Bridget.

'Just checking we're still alone, so I am,' replied Liam.

Liam had parked the furniture van about twenty yards from the pier head. It was the nearest point for vehicle access. The perspiration ran. The respiration increased. And the adrenalin flowed as three terrorists bounced the deadly contraption towards the water's edge.

The entrance to Nine Elms Pier was controlled by a metal security gate that was locked tight with a padlock. The key that had belonged to Clive Montague and which had been lost by Sean on Vauxhall Bridge fitted the security gate padlock as well as the Montague warehouse. With the key, the trio could have merely unlocked the gate, dragged the contraption over a short walkway above the Thames and dropped it into the deep water side of the quay. Now, there was no key. The trio could not access the water directly.

Instead, they had to manhandle the device over the low security fencing and onto the mud bank that lay beneath the pier. The device was heavy and difficult to handle. It took time to position, and time was vital to them. They had no desire to stay in the area any longer than was necessary. They worked quickly. Gently, the contraption was lowered towards the water.

Sean said, 'Jaysus! How I wish I had that key, to be sure. This bloody contraption is going to break my back, so it is.'

'Too late now, Sean,' replied Bridget. 'Just get on with it. So, it'll take ten minutes to launch instead of two, but launch it we will.'

The trio introduced the contraption to the water when the Thames lapped against the wooden structure at the waterside.

Boyd swung the car into Kirtling Street and bounced over the rough track towards the jetty area. He cursed the withdrawal of the police helicopter. Now his reduced team had to check out every nook and cranny in the Nine Elms area themselves. It took up time, and time was the very thing that the impatient Boyd was running out of.

The furniture van couldn't be missed, big and painted green. The rear doors were open and its ramp down. The scramble bikes were clearly visible, parked against the side of the big green van.

As soon as Boyd saw the vehicle, he spotted the attack site. There were two men and a woman standing near the rear of the furniture van. One of the men jumped from the jetty onto a wooden barge-like structure that Boyd was at a loss to describe in the heat of the moment. The man Boyd was particularly watching was now inside the contraption, fiddling with a package of some kind at the rear of the wooden structure.

Boyd reached for the radio.

The word 'boat' came to mind as he tried to illustrate the scene in his mind before speaking to control. Boyd made the call, looked at Toni sitting beside him, and felt for the gun in his holster. They had just run out of time. Boyd continued to drive towards the jetty with the two bomb disposal officers in the rear of the car sitting uneasily.

Concentrating on the timing device, Sean pulled the slender dowel pin from the bomb and jumped from the contraption to the bank. There was no more than a foot gap between the contraption and the river bank when he breached the Thames and took a foothold on the rough tarmac. The contraption made the deep water at last, following a great deal of physical exertion by the determined Sean.

Once he was on dry land Sean gave the contraption a gentle push with his outstretched foot and it began to move into the river flow. The current gradually embraced the structure as it moved away from the side of the jetty. The timer was ticking. The bomb was live and targeted towards the bulls eye. The archer had released his bow and his arrow flew towards the heart of the British Establishment.

The current caught the contraption and it headed for the middle of the river. The gently churning Thames welcomed the float and bobbed it up and down as it finally met the main current which was to propel it northwards towards its destination.

'Thanks for your help!' cracked Bridget to Liam sarcastically. 'You could have given us a push to get it started.'

Liam ignored the remark. The dice were rolling. Liam looked inland and, to his trepidation, saw Eugene Kelly approaching them.

Eugene, too, had searched the area all day. He had passed the open warehouse that had once belonged to Clive Montague and dismissed it from his mind. Eugene's hand went to his gun as he closed with the remnants of the active service unit and his heart beat faster; pounding, thundering inside his muscular chest. His killing time had arrived once more.

Toni shouted, 'Eugene! Look, it's Eugene! He's back. Watch him, Boyd!'

'Where?'

'To your right, look over there,' responded Toni.

Boyd saw the familiar shaven head of the demon from Derry and slowed the vehicle, weighing up in his mind what to do next. He knew it was decision time.

Boyd scanned the Thames for Anthea and her navy, but there was no sign of the armada. The contraption gathered speed and circled in the current which still continued to push it mercilessly towards Vauxhall Bridge.

Seconds ticked by, the clock still running, the killing time approached.

Making a radio call again, Boyd decided to press the accelerator to the floor. The tyres screeched on the loose gravel as the rubber sought purchase on the road surface when Boyd increased speed.

Commander Herbert heard the radio call. It was Boyd's voice shouting for assistance. The Commander responded by lifting his own radio handset and issuing instructions to control.

Changing into a lower gear, the Commander increased his speed towards the danger zone, swinging the car towards Nine Elms.

Anthea also heard the call on the river police radio net. The boat turned and headed towards Vauxhall Bridge, with the bow cutting through the Thames and displacing the water as it rushed towards the fray.

'It's Eugene!' warned Liam.

Bridget opened her blouson jacket, unearthed her Uzi, and turned to face the approaching man from Derry. Eugene Kelly was about fifty yards or so from the trio.

'Easy!' cracked Sean. 'The bikes, take to the bikes. Let's go. We're finished here.'

'I can take him now,' said Bridget levelling the weapon in anticipation. The safety catch moved to the 'off' position. The trigger warmed to the female touch as her fingers embraced the trigger guard.

'No need!' said Sean. 'The bomb is in the water, nothing's going to stop it now. Take to the bikes and go. Come on, get out of it!'

The sound of a car engine revving loudly filled their ears as Boyd and his crew came into full view. The terrorists were aghast, not quite understanding what was happening. Eugene they understood, but who was in the car?

Boyd pulled the handbrake at the last moment and swung the car broadside to come to a stop some fifty yards from the furniture van.

'Out!' shouted Boyd to the bomb disposal officers and Toni. 'Out! Take cover quickly!'

Leaping from the nearside of the car, Toni withdrew her weapon and pointed it towards the ASU, using the car for cover and the car roof for weapon stability.

Boyd opened the driver's door and rolled onto the dirt. He, too, removed his gun and used the driver's door for cover.

The two bomb disposal officers crept to the rear of Boyd's vehicle and peered through the windows to observe the action whilst using the car body as a shield.

'Armed Police! Stand still!' ordered Boyd.

Sean's hand went to his trouser belt, found the handgun, and withdrew the weapon.

Liam thought it was too late and began to run to the far side of the furniture van, out of the line of fire from Boyd and the red-headed woman whom he did not know.

The sound of shots echoed across the skyline as Eugene Kelly opened up on Sean Brady.

Eugene stood tall and fired towards Sean without hitting him.

Bridget returned the fire on behalf of Sean, her Uzi eating up the earth directly in front of the demonic Kelly.

Straddling the scrambler, Sean kick-started the motorbike into life and ignored the bullets whistling through the air above his head.

Boyd knelt by his car and yelled, 'You are surrounded. Throw down your weapons! Give yourselves up! We are armed police officers.'

There was a tremendous crash when bullets from Bridget's Uzi blasted the windscreen of Boyd's car and raked towards the car door that he hid behind. The windows shattered as the bomb disposal officers at the rear of the car dropped flat to the ground to protect themselves from the deadly assault.

Leaping away from the vehicle, Boyd rolled over and over towards a collection of old oil drums that were gathering rust near the jetty. Seeing the beams of timber stacked nearby, Boyd jumped towards them, looking for cover as the bullets followed him, intent on bringing the detective to the ground and certain death.

Boyd slid behind a pile of oak beams as the cargo of death from Bridget's Uzi ripped through the forsaken oil drums and wooden beams. The bullets sliced a path towards Boyd's legs as he scurried for cover and protection from the onslaught. There was a tumultuous explosion in Boyd's eardrums as the long-forgotten contents of two oil drums erupted into the atmosphere, sending a plume of fire and black acrid smoke into the sky. The contents of the old barrels appeared to have been some form of chemical residue since the ball of fire sucked the oxygen inwards and deposited a noxious and horrible odour in its place.

Boyd's nostrils tingled as the back of his throat experienced the sensation of an unknown chemical reaction. His eyes watered and he fought to hold together consciousness as the violent fire raged around him. Toni engaged Bridget from the other side of the car. She switched her gun towards the Irishwoman and returned fire as best she could.

Toni emptied her chamber before dropping behind the car to take cover and reload with a speed-six capsule. Again, lifting her head above the parapet, Toni saw her target and pulled the trigger. Her bullets penetrated thin air as she missed Bridget by inches and then slammed into the side of the furniture van, ripping the metal to pieces, leaving a jagged signature.

Sean pulled in the clutch and kicked a gear down with his right foot. Setting off with full throttle, the front of the scrambler did a wheelie causing Sean to crash into the furniture van. He was thrown to the side where he caught a glimpse of petrol discharging from the scrambler's tank when he rolled away from the motor cycle.

Unarmed, Liam threw himself underneath the furniture van in order to try and escape the developing fire fight. He crawled beneath the vehicle and sought refuge from those above.

Bridget was in a dilemma. The man and woman who must be police were firing at her as well as at Eugene. But she took it all in her stride and slowly walked towards the second scramble bike, firing first at the redheaded woman, and then at Eugene. She alternated her fire as the Uzi spat out its deadly cargo. She fired again and again, engulfing the area with rapid fire. A deluge of hate spat from the Uzi.

When she had emptied the magazine, Bridget calmly dropped to one knee, took a replacement magazine from her shoulder bag and commenced firing once again.

Petrol from Sean's discarded scramble bike leaked onto the tarmac surface and slowly flowed towards the waterside.

Bridget made the second scrambled and kicked it into action. The shooting continued as Toni carefully took aim and held the terrorists at bay. Eugene dropped behind a massive coil of rope and reloaded his gun with his back to the action.

Rolling further from the smoke and fire, Boyd saw a clear pathway and fired towards Bridget. The bullets tailed off into oblivion.

Meanwhile, the contraption bobbed up and down on the Thames moving closer to its target. In the distance, the London traffic appeared to have ceased. Blue lights crossed Vauxhall Bridge, rushing towards Nine Elms and the shoot-out on the river bank.

A cacophony of sound filled the air as the wailing sirens grew in an orchestra of emergency vehicles.

Finally righting his scrambler, Sean mounted it for the second time, found the correct gear, and got the bike under control. He set off towards the Kirtling Street entrance.

Commander Herbert turned off Nine Elms Lane into Kirtling Street. He could hear the fire-fight taking place and saw smoke from burning oil drums rising above the jetty in a sickening pointer to the violent encounter.

Eugene anticipated Sean's escape route. Rolling from his position behind the coiled ropes and, whilst lying on the ground, he aimed directly at the escaping Sean. His bullets missed their destination but ripped the front tyre to shreds causing the scrambler bike to crash into the front of Boyd's abandoned police car.

Winded, Sean lay motionless for a moment or two as the hot lead flew across the open space that had been declared the killing zone. Then he climbed into Boyd's forlorn wreck and turned the ignition key. The car surprisingly burst into life.

Blood from a head wound spilled onto Brady's hands as he pressed the clutch and selected reverse gear. Petrol which had been leaking from the first scrambler finally married sparks from an ignited oil drum. A ribbon of fire followed the leaking fuel and engulfed the scrambler in flames. There was an explosion when the petrol tank on the motor bike became another casualty of the troubled jetty.

Bridget targeted Boyd and closed with him when Toni took cover and reloaded.

Boyd was at her mercy, constantly rolling from one side to another, using the wooden beams for cover. Cat and mouse on the quayside.

Bridget could not miss. Her fingers coiled round the trigger. Her sights were on Boyd's head. His time had come. It was Bridget's time to kill for the cause of freedom. She exhaled slowly, concentrating on the path of her dedicated bullet.

The bugle did not sound when the cavalry arrived. Indeed, there was no cavalry, only a red-headed Detective Sergeant called Anthea who stood out on the bow of the police boat, raised her small handgun and took long and careful aim. She saw Bridget move in for the kill.

One microsecond before Bridget pulled the trigger, Anthea fired.

The bullet entered the back of Bridget Duffys head and exited through her left cheek. The bullet from Anthea's gun continued its flight and buried itself in the side of the furniture van. The Irish terrorist fell forward and was dead before she hit the London tarmac. The Uzi clattered onto the ground and fell underneath the furniture van.

Liam saw the fallen Uzi from his hidden lair beneath the big green van. He stretched out his arm to gather it in, but then thought better of it and retreated out of sight once more.

Anthea only fired one shot before the patrol boat cruised on, passing the jetty at speed. It was enough. Boyd lived. Bridget Duffy died.

Standing up, Boyd waved at Anthea who looked back towards him with a face sombre and devoid of sparkle.

The patrol boat circled in the middle of the river and made as if to set off in pursuit of the contraption. The vessel bobbed like a cork as the pilot wrestled with the current.

Reading the situation expertly, the bomb disposal officers moved swiftly from their cover and waved their arms in the air. They ran swiftly towards the river bank, calling to be picked up by the police boat.

Boyd's team on the police launch recognised the men and signalled the vessel's pilot to quickly pull about and collect the two men.

Meanwhile, the fire on the quay raged on.

Anthea had never fired a weapon in anger before, never mind kill someone. She stood motionless at the front of the vessel, perched on the bow like a statue. A snapshot in time captured her moment A memory to be printed forever on Boyd's brain.

Creping towards the furniture van, Eugene was intent on seeking out Liam Connelly.

Toni was still in the game and smoothly closed the chamber on her Smith and Wesson. She made stealthily towards the furniture van.

Boyd regained his composure and saw his car reversing from the fireball caused by a burning scrambler.

Pulling away from the inferno, Sean rammed the car into first gear, pressed his foot to the floor, and took off with the car shuddering under the pressure of acceleration. He moved his feet on the clutch pedal and the throttle and ran the gear stick through into third gear with the tyres squealing in anguish.

The Commander arrived with his car bouncing along the road towards the jetty and a blue light rotating on the roof. It was to no avail. Commander James Herbert had no time to take evasive action. When the panic-stricken Sean headed directly for Nine Elms Lane in Boyd's car, he failed to recognise the danger. Cornering Kirtling Street into Nine Elms, Sean lost control and careered into Commander Herbert's car full on.

The policeman was wearing his seatbelt and saw the missile coming towards him. Brady did not. The front of Boyd's car crumpled on impact, metal merging with metal in a horrible debacle of destruction as two vehicles locked themselves in mortal combat. Both cars died, neither won.

Sean was thrown from the driver's seat through the windscreen screaming when his head penetrated the glass windscreen and tore the skin from his cheekbones. His body twisted against the window frame seizing him upwards in a painful arc.

Brady's eyes were wide open and caught a fleeting glance of an older man at the wheel of the other car. The Commander braced himself and braked hard, but felt the sickening thud as Sean Brady landed crazily on the bonnet of his car.

Sean broke his neck when his body bounced upwards from the bonnet and struck the roof of the rival car driven by the Commander. Sean's eyes again glanced at the Commander in his final flight of death.

As the two police cars married together in an astonishing embrace of death and destruction, Sean's dying body spun horribly through the Nine Elms air and bounced finally onto the road surface behind the two cars. Steam from two spent radiators rose upwards towards the sky and hissed quietly. It was the only sound left from the terrible crash once the metallic parts of both vehicles had reconstituted their jagged form.

Commander Herbert lay unconscious in his vehicle bleeding slightly from a small wound on his forehead. He was not seriously hurt and would recover fully in a matter of days. Irreverently, the blue light on the Commander's roof had been undamaged. The light flashed on, a beacon of despair, a signal of attrition.

Sean moved. His fingers sought life, the nerve ends alive, then there was a final movement when his chest deflated and his legs straightened. The body of Sean Brady twitched in its final death throes before his soul inexorably left his body and began its journey to the heaven or the hell that God earmarked for the leader of the terrorist unit.

In Kirtling Street, a child aged about twelve years had witnessed the unholy coupling of the two police cars. A tear formed in the child's eye. A door opened in the quiet terraced street and a worried mother, who wanted no part in the proceedings, gathered her child into her arms and took him fittingly inside. The door closed on the carnage outside.

An eerie silence in Kirtling Street was not matched by the raging fire on the jetty nearby. The fire hungered and oil drums burned on licking nearby wooden beams and sucking the oxygen from the air. Petrol from the scrambler bikes added to the fire as one of the vehicles burnt itself slowly out.

An acrid smell of burning rubber from motor cycle tyres, together with the residue of petrol fumes, fouled the human nostrils and struck deep into the heart of the human stomach. Ugly black smoke spiralled upwards into the air and drifted downstream on the wind.

Liam succumbed to fear and self-protection and finally recovered the Uzi. Carefully, he climbed into the rear of the furniture van and crouched low in one corner with Bridget's Uzi in his hands. He contemplated resting there a while and wondered if he could smash the cab window with the stock of the Uzi and climb from the rear of the van into the small cabin area and the driver's seat. It was a means of escape within his grasp.

Hearing movement inside the rear of the green furniture van, Eugene made towards the ramp at the back of the vehicle. He crept low, hugging one side of the van and listening for any movement inside.

Toni saw the Irishman. Once she had controlled Eugene Kelly and he had obeyed her every command. Now she feared him. She prepared her mind for combat again and looked for Boyd as she felt for her weapon and examined its chamber. It was fully loaded.

Reassured, she levelled the six-shooter revolver before her. Boyd had similar thoughts on his mind. He checked that his weapon was fully loaded and signalled across to Toni that he would take the nearside of the vehicle if she approached from the offside. The fingers pointed in the air at the decided directions.

They nodded to each other in agreement and made their way forward into position. They would enter the rear of the van simultaneously from either side and attempt to block any escape route. Although in the past they had to some extent been adversaries, virtually rivals, certainly competitors, they were together when the chips were down. They were still a team when it really mattered.

Thinking he was alone, safe, forgotten, Liam felt a pane of glass with his fingers and looked through the window into the front cab. He could see through the windscreen and took in the fire raging before him. Liam looked out and knew there were people out there. Which one would be Boyd, he wondered? His eyes scanned the jetty looking for a tell-tale sign that would assist him to identify the detective.

There was a creak on the wooden ramp behind him. Liam turned his head. Eugene's shaven skull came into view. Liam's heart missed a beat when terror struck into his brain.

Eugene stepped heavily onto the ramp, his weight betraying his presence. He peered inside the dark furniture van and located Liam's shadowy form in the depths of the van. Raising the handgun higher, his arms outstretched, Eugene sought a bead on Liam's forehead.

Flames from burning petrol started to lick the underside of the green furniture van. Fire slowly began to consume the vehicle. Black smoke began to seep into the rear compartment of the van, finding its way through the cracks in rotting wooden floorboards.

Two bomb disposal men climbed on board Anthea's patrol boat and headed for the contraption at full speed, its bow breaking over the churning Thames making light of the dark grey choppy waters. The solid wooden contraption Dermot Dougan had lovingly constructed was also at full speed with the current flow driving it downstream.

The barge passed the Millbank Tower and closed with Lambeth Bridge. It would soon be close to Victoria Tower Gardens and the mighty Houses of Parliament. Big Ben struck the hour, scattering the pigeons from the lawn in Parliament Square. A uniformed policeman stepped off the pavement and stopped traffic as a chauffeur-driven Rover delivered yet another honourable member to his eloquent place of work.

The timer in the rear of the barge moved slowly on towards its point of detonation. Time was running out. The floating bomb was well ahead of the police patrol boat.

The duty Inspector had picked up Anthea's frantic radio calls in the control room at New Scotland Yard and called in the spy in the sky. The sound of the helicopter engine could be heard faintly overhead returning to the scene.

The police helicopter pilot soon located the floating barge between Vauxhall Bridge and Lambeth Bridge.

The grey paint which covered the wooden contraption had indeed made identification difficult but not impossible. Anthea, on the police patrol boat, had seen to that.

The resourceful sergeant had reported the location of the barge to the pilot on the radio net and talked the pilot in until he was above the object. The contraption passed underneath Lambeth Bridge and moved towards the north bank and closer to its target: the Houses of Parliament.

Nearby, Fire Service personnel on duty at Lambeth High Street headquarters responded to an alarm bell and ran quickly to the fire rescue vessel moored off the Embankment. London's Fire Service set course for Westminster as their crew made ready with the water cannon. Desperate measures were called for.

The helicopter pilot ignored every rule in the book and audaciously pushed the control stick defiantly downwards. The police helicopter drew closer to the river and hovered dominantly above Old Father Thames.

The Fire Service vessel steamed beneath Lambeth Bridge and into the fray.

The police helicopter dropped still further towards the river.

Water churned indignantly at the unwelcome attention from above. The tactic helped. Downdraught from rotor blades on the helicopter seemed to stem the movement of the dangerous wooden contraption as it bobbed up and down in the water. It was apparently held for a slender moment by the pressure exerted by the rotor blades. For an instant the potentially lethal contraption faltered and changed course as the helicopter pilot manoeuvred to the north of the barge and dipped his nose. The downdraught tangled towards the side of the floating bomb and pushed it away from the north bank, back into the middle of the Thames.

It was a personal battle.

The pilot was alone in his thoughts, fighting his own war in the greying peaceful skies above London. Decades previously the 'Few' had also fought the enemy above the London skies. This day in 1995 saw a different enemy and a different type of skirmish, but London is used to being regarded as a battleground for the malcontent. It is also used to its heroes. They are all around, but seldom seen.

But still the contraption floated on.

Anthea held on for grim death as a river police sergeant took command of the operation. The floating bomb bobbed up and down like an abandoned autumn leaf as the murky Thames gurgled and churned ceaselessly in its frightening unholy alliance with the helicopter above.

Eventually, the police boat closed alongside the floating bomb and they careered together in a sickening act of marriage down the Thames towards the Houses of Parliament. The awesome helicopter hovered overhead with the hard working pilot constantly changing position to push back the contraption with the rotor blade down draught. Frightened pedestrians on a nearby walkway hurriedly ran for cover as the helicopter's noise drowned out the sound of normal speech and brought an alarming temporary chaos to the normally enchanted area. They fled wisely for the safety of cover, not realising the drama that was being acted out above them and in the river beside them.

The boughs of the trees bent slightly and litter lying in the gutters blew high into the sky and scattered to the four winds like coloured pieces of confetti at a wedding. The noise of the helicopter was deafening as the pilot brought his aircraft further and further downwards in his lonely and determined battle with the barge. It was just as well people ran for cover. If the bomb exploded they would all need to seek cover. At the same time the police launch positioned itself near the northern riverbank and physically pushed the floating bomb away from the target into the middle of the river. But the middle of the river elected the strongest part of the current. The dilemma continued.

The Fire Service arrived, uniquely in a launch, and joined forces with the police. Reading the situation admirably, the Fire Service vessel added its weight to the job in hand and pushed the contraption away from the north bank of the Thames. Together the emergency services fought to solve the problem of the current and the flow.

His job was done. He could do no more. The helicopter pilot withdrew and climbed into the sky. The pilot knew that the downdraught from the machine would prevent the bomb disposal men from boarding the contraption. It was time for the helicopter to depart. The craft simply climbed high into the sky, circled, and headed south over the river. The fuel load was low, just enough to make the air base, but no more.

As the helicopter withdrew, an eerie calm settled over the river. The police boat drew alongside the contraption. Grappling irons were thrown by the crew and the two vessels were hastily fixed together. The bomb disposal officers made themselves ready and prepared to board the contraption.

There was a young, fairly inexperienced corporal and an older, time-served Major, who had relished the challenge for more years than he cared to remember. Grey tinged the older man's temples. Some in the armed services said the Major was past his sell-by date at forty years of age. He knew better. The two men from two different generations had chosen their path in life and responded as unsung heroes do.

Liam was scared, his time had come.
Eugene stood above him with the gun pointed into Liam's temple.
Liam was on all fours, the Uzi lying beneath him on the floorboards.
Eugene's finger gripped the trigger.
'Freeze!' screamed Toni, the Smith and Wesson outstretched in front of her shaking slightly. Perhaps it was the voice. A voice from the past returning to haunt him. Whatever it was, it worked. Eugene recognised the female's command and froze as a statue. The gun remained pointed at Liam's head, millimetres from his temple.
'Sure, I've got the wee bastard, so I have,' cracked Eugene without turning his head. 'I can finish it now, so I can.'
Toni climbed into the furniture van, carefully holding the gun out before her. Nervous, she fought to control her wavering gun.

'Move, Eugene, and I'll blow your bloody head off,' warned Toni emphatically. She straightened up once inside the vehicle, confidence growing by the second.

'Sure, I'll save you all the trouble now,' suggested Eugene. 'I'll do him for you. No one will know any different.'

The gun remained at Liam's head, but closer.

'Except me,' offered Boyd, climbing into the furniture van seconds after Toni.

Eugene moved his head ever so slightly and took in Boyd at the entrance to the furniture van. The red-head he had known so long stood at the other side of the van. They both pointed their guns towards him. Two against one, but Eugene was still playing the odds and had an ace up his sleeve. It was time to play it.

'Police, is it now?' asked Eugene. 'Or are you with her mob?'

'The police,' replied Boyd. 'You're nicked. It's your choice. Put the gun down or I'll kill you where you stand. It makes no difference to me.'

Boyd moved slowly closer, inching along the side of the van. Toni saw him move and started the same action along her side of the van, slowly, calmly.

The offside of the vehicle was warming up.

She was aware of the heat.

Flames outside melted the rubber tyres and engulfed the underside of the engine block. Decaying wooden panels that formed the underside of the vehicle began to surrender to the gathering inferno.

A blue Vauxhall Cavalier sped over Lambeth Bridge towards the jetty with its blue light flashing incessantly across its rooftop and the siren screaming an impish cry. The control unit had alerted the two RUC officers in London to arrest Liam Connelly.

The Irish policemen drove at high speed, carving a path through the traffic, determined. They wanted Liam Connelly badly.

Back at Nine Elms the drama continued.

'That wasn't the deal as I remember it,' suggested Eugene.

'I made no deal with you,' said Boyd. 'Drop the gun. I'm an impatient northerner with a bad temper and better things to do. Slowly now, drop the gun on the floor and place your hands on your head. One false move and so help me I'll take your head off your shoulders.'

Eugene pressed the gun into the back of Liam's head and looked at Boyd, smiling, challenging the detective.

'I made a deal,' reminded Eugene.

'With me you did,' admitted Toni. 'But it didn't include shooting up half of London and committing murder. You've never been above the law, Kelly.'

'Sure, what about all the years I worked for you?' asked Eugene.

Liam turned his neck, startled at the admission by the PIRA enforcer from Derry.

'Don't even twitch,' threatened Eugene, pressing the gun further into Liam's head, 'Or I'll blow you in half and send you back to Derry in a box.'

Afraid, Liam was in fear, remaining motionless in his anguish.

'Kill him,' challenged Boyd, testing, probing weaknesses in his adversary. 'He's a nobody.'

Liam Connelly saw Boyd out of the corner of his eye and wondered if Padraigh O'Toole had made the wrong decision about his policeman friend. In an instant, Liam looked death in the eye. He had to make his move soon, his bid for freedom and escape.

'No, my friend. I know the police better than that. You won't kill me while I have this one,' suggested Eugene.

'What makes you think that?' queried Toni, joining in the verbal battle, stretching out time.

'You, woman! Where's my money? We had a deal,' snapped Eugene.

Before Toni could answer, Liam seized the moment. He dropped downwards further onto the ground, arched his back, and pushed his backside into Eugene's bloated stomach. The shaven head bobbed backwards when Eugene lost his balance and dropped the handgun.

Liam seized the Uzi beneath him.

Eugene realised his folly, regained his posture and threw himself at Connelly.

The two Irishmen grappled together trying to assert their authority over each other. They wrestled on the floor of the vehicle, lightweight and heavyweight. Liam tried to draw a bead on Eugene with the Uzi as the man with the shaven head reached desperately for the handgun he had so carelessly dropped.

Smoke thickened and jutted upwards through the floor cracks.

Eugene coughed and Toni gagged as the four occupants of the van became more and more conscious of their predicament inside the burning van. Toni reacted first and rushed towards the struggling Irishmen.

Boyd backed her up, more conscious.

The four bodies closed with each other.

Suddenly, it was finished. Eugene found his gun and pointed it directly at Toni who aimed her weapon back at Eugene.

Liam fingered the Uzi and trained it at Boyd.

Boyd found himself kneeling on the floor with his handgun pointed at Liam. The atmosphere was of uncertainty, hate, fear, people on edge, expecting the worst.

There was a silence as the combatants weighed each other up and thought out their next move. Fire raged beneath. Flames licked the sides of the furniture van and reached for the rooftop.

Back on the road, the RUC officers gunned their vehicle down Nine Elms Lane looking desperately for the turnoff into Kirtling Street.

On the river, the bomb disposal officers were in command of the contraption. They worked feverishly at the improvised device trying to figure out Dermot's blueprint.

'Let's leave it,' suggested the EOD corporal. 'We'll go up with it ourselves if we're not careful.'

'No!' snapped the bomb disposal Major. 'We've probably got a minute or two left, if that. I think I've got it. It's simple. A big bomb, but simple. Pass me the tool bag. I'm going to go for it.'

The corporal did as he was told, obedient.

'One more thing,' said the Major, 'Ring control and book a squash court for tonight. I fancy we can make it back in time if our luck holds.'

The corporal shook his head at the typical black humour from his superior. The two men worked on; peace in their hands.

In the burning furniture van the tension steadied. A mystery deepened, developed, twisted and turned.

'Put it down, Eugene,' said Toni. 'I have something for you.'

'What would that be now?' asked the Irishman.

'Pay day, just like I promised,' revealed Toni.

'You promised many things, woman, but it was always promises. Tomorrow, you said, always tomorrow, and never today,' replied Eugene, still training the gun towards her.

'Today has arrived. Now, lay down the gun.'

'And let you shoot me? No way, woman,' commented Eugene.

'Do you want this?' asked Toni producing a brown manila envelope which she held up for his inspection.

Intrigued, Eugene peered at the bulky envelope and enquired, 'How much?'

'Enough!' she replied.

'How much, woman?' asked Eugene again, demanding, evil.

Toni shrugged a reply with her shoulders, buying time.

'Pass it here, then,' ordered Eugene.

The flames around them began to penetrate the sides of the vehicle as it continued to fill with smoke.

Liam coughed. Underneath the furniture van, fire poked and teased the fuel tank. A dark blue flame caressed hot metal.

Toni decided to change the roles and threw the envelope to her right and into the corner of the vehicle.

'Go for it, Eugene. You always wanted it,' she said.

The envelope landed on the wooden floor. A seal burst and a bundle of twenty pound notes sprayed out onto the floorboards.

'There's fifty thousand there for you,' said Toni. 'Take it and go. Leave the gun behind. Our business is concluded. We will not meet again.'

Eugene had played the odds and picked the winner. Fifty thousand pounds! Enough to start a new life in a new country, what with that money and what he had managed to save over the years. Eugene slowly crawled to the corner of the van to collect his winnings. He felt elated and moved towards his money, still training the gun at Toni.

'But he's wanted!' queried Boyd.

'So is Liam,' returned Toni.

'But not in the same way,' replied Boyd.

Toni offered, 'No matter! Eugene must walk. He's too much of an embarrassment to us all. The system would fall down if it came out that an agent of ours had shot up half of London. The public mustn't know.'

'You worked that one out, did you, woman?' said Eugene, his ace played, no trump.

Liam looked directly into Boyd's eyes and said, 'I trusted you.'

'No,' corrected Boyd. 'You trusted Uncle Pat.'

'Who's uncle Pat?' queried Toni, seeking Boyd's eyes.

In Nine Elms the RUC came to a standstill in the middle of Kirtling Street, the road blocked by the accident caused by Sean Brady and Commander Herbert.

'Where?' shouted the RUC men as they alighted from their vehicle.

'That way,' replied the dazed Commander Herbert, pointing towards the jetty area. Blue lights flashing, static beacons watching fire and smoke.

The RUC men set off on foot, breaking into a jog at the end of the street.

Eugene reached the money and started to count it in the corner.

The floorboards on which he was kneeling were warming up.

Toni's question remained unanswered.

'I trusted Pat. He said I should trust you, even though we've never met,' said Liam. 'Pat told me that you would understand, that you would see it right.'

'He was right to tell you that,' said Boyd.

'Why should I think that now? It seems like the whole world wants me. Yous boys! The RUC! Him!' offered Liam, pointing to Eugene. 'A

262

feather in your cap if you took me out, hey? You used Pat and you used me. We should never have trusted you.'

Reaching inside his jacket pocket, Boyd withdrew the brown manila envelope he had brought in the briefcase from the north. He tossed it towards Liam, but slightly askew, and it landed in the nearside corner of the van.

Liam watched the envelope fly through the air.

Eugene ignored it. He had one eye on Toni and one eye on his pot of gold.

Toni was mystified. What was in the envelope, she wondered.

Boyd slowly stood up, changing the atmosphere and deciding that the time was approaching to vacate the vehicle lest they all go up in flames.

'Trust me you can, Liam Connelly,' said Boyd. 'Pat gave me this for you. I promised to deliver it and I did. It's for you, see. Come on, it's time to go.'

Eugene heard the remark and turned the gun on Boyd.

'Stand still or I'll drop you. No one leaves until I check my money.'

Toni felt the heat around her and the perspiration soaking her blouse. She eased herself backwards towards the opening and freedom.

Opening his envelope, Liam examined the contents. He counted out money and inspected a passport Padraigh O'Toole had doctored for his nephew. The passport photograph was an old one but it was still a good likeness of Liam Connelly. Inside the pages of the small maroon passport, lay Liam's air tickets for Tenerife and a piece of paper in Padraigh O'Toole's handwriting.

The written note bore the address of an apartment in La Caleta, north of Playa de Las Americas, where the Atlantic pounds the rocky coast and no more than a dozen beach chalets look out on the mighty ocean as it basks in the tropical sunshine.

Padraigh O'Toole, as well as providing the flight to freedom, had delivered his own safe house to his nephew, courtesy of Detective Inspector Billyboy Boyd.

'How?' asked Liam, puzzled. 'Why?'

'He loves you like a son, Liam,' said Boyd. 'All you have to do is put down the Uzi and take off. Only I know the destination. Perhaps one day we'll meet again?'

Placing the Uzi on the floor, Liam pocketed the few hundred pounds and the papers that would give him a chance to start a new life in a new country. He slowly slid along the side of the furniture van, conscious of Eugene who was as puzzled as Toni with the proceedings developing before them. But Eugene's greed was evident as the demon from Derry licked the end of his index finger and continued to count the wad of notes that Toni had provided.

'I believe there's one bike outside that hasn't been touched,' suggested Boyd.

Nodding in agreement, Liam declared, 'God made the land and God made the sea!'

Boyd finished it, saying. 'He shone down on you .Goodbye!'

Then suddenly, 'You bitch!' screamed Eugene. 'There's not fifty thousand here!'

The atmosphere erupted into a cauldron of hatred.

Eugene hurled the banknotes into the air and took a firm two-handed grip on his handgun.

Liam jumped for safety as Eugene eventually realised that his envelope contained nowhere near fifty thousand pounds.

Liam was out of it. Gone! Lucky!

Eugene levelled his weapon at Toni and pulled his finger inwards around the trigger. The pressure squeezed the trigger. The killing time!

Responding, Boyd turned, raised his gun, aimed and pulled the trigger through in a split second. He shot Eugene Kelly through the chest.

Eugene slowly fell forwards, clutching his breast where the bullet had entered his body. The blood gurgled and pulsed outwards onto the van floor. In that same instant, Eugene loosed off a final death-defying round of shots into the side of the van. He lost all control over his bodily functions. His death throes were accelerated when the fuel tank underneath him exploded in final surrender to the raging fire.

Toni turned and jumped from the ramp onto the ground outside, holding Boyd's hand as they leapt through the air and strove for safety.

Floorboards erupted and snared the dying body of Eugene Kelly in an enormous ball of fire.

The inferno raged on, uncontrollable, independent, as at last the fire found its mark and consumed the contents of the furniture van.

The remnants of Eugene Kelly's life were spent in horrific and terrifying pain. The tremendous heat from the fire firstly ripped the hairs from his body before frying his skin.

The screams of Eugene's death were heard in Kirtling Street when the demon from Derry went to hell.

After a few moments the screams were replaced by a strange but welcome silence.

Toni held Boyd's hand as they lay on the tarmac where they had landed. She recovered first and tended to Boyd who was dazed. They coughed and spluttered their way back into the fresh air and the daylight.

A motor cycle engine burst into life nearby.

Boyd propped himself up onto his elbow and saw the burning inferno that once was a green furniture van.

Near to the burning vehicle he saw Liam Connelly astride the remaining scrambler bike, preparing to depart. Liam turned his head and looked over his shoulder. He fastened the safety helmet round his chin and engaged Boyd's eyes, saying, 'If you're ever in ...'

Boyd nodded, smiled and replied, 'I know.'

'Tell Pat,' said Liam, 'Just tell Pat,' the Irishman was lost for words. 'Tell him, thanks.'

'I will,' answered Boyd. 'You can count on me, Liam Connelly. Trust me.'

Liam twisted the throttle grip, pulled in the clutch and tapped in a gear with his foot. He smiled and nodded at Boyd before roaring off at speed, the rear wheel scorching the tarmac as Liam headed for freedom.

On the contraption, the Major celebrated silent victory. He cut the cable and rendered the bomb safe. There would be no explosion on the river and no detonation at the Houses of Parliament.

'Blast!' cracked the Major.

'What's wrong, sir?' asked the corporal.

'Well, I can't play squash, young man. Still, you can teach me. Now, where's that police boat with the red-head on? I wonder if she can play?' remarked the Major.

The two bomb disposal men sat waiting to be picked up, stowing their equipment in the regulation holdall provided. A good job done.

London breathed a sigh of relief again.

The two RUC men arrived at the scene, too late and out of breath. They surveyed the quayside that had been turned into a killing zone. They passed the body of Sean Brady on the road near Commander Herbert. Now they inspected the lifeless corpse of Bridget Duffy and peered towards the burning furniture van, the charred oil drums, and the wrecked motor cycles littering the quay.

'Where is he?' asked the RUC Inspector to Boyd.

'Who?' asked Boyd.

'Liam Connelly, for God's sake!' snapped the irritated RUC man.

Toni replied immediately, startling Boyd with her incisive manner. 'In there!'

Antonia Harston-Browne pointed to the burning furniture van and said, 'Liam Connelly is dead. He's in there, what's left of him.'

The RUC man smiled and looked towards his sergeant. 'Good! It's the best place for him. It'll save a trial or two.'

The RUC sergeant nodded in agreement with his boss but added, 'Kelly! What of Kelly?'

Both men turned to face the red-headed woman. Toni replied, 'Eugene Kelly made the call that led us here. If it hadn't been for Eugene, we wouldn't have caught them in time and the bomb would have gone off.' Toni continued, 'Sorry, I couldn't call you to join in the fun at the end but it all happened so quickly. When Eugene phoned in we moved fast.'

The RUC men nodded, wisely understanding the lady's predicament, experienced.

The RUC Inspector said, more softly, 'Where is Eugene Kelly now then, Miss?'

Toni lied again. 'Gone! With the thanks of Her Majesty's Government. I'm sure you understand?'

The RUC men nodded again. She was a charlatan in their eyes, but had successfully convinced Eugene Kelly to work for her all these years. They understood.

'Pity, but understandable,' remarked the RUC Inspector. 'Eugene was a good tout. Probably one of the best. Still, time he got out of it, I suppose.'

Boyd remained silent. He pursed his lips and held his own counsel as in the distance the sound of a motor cycle scramble bike found the roadway north and headed out towards Heathrow Airport. Boyd knew the open ticket would see his adversary in safe territory within twenty-four hours. Boyd held inside himself in quiet pride. He had honoured his contract with Padraigh O'Toole. His mind strayed north.

The RUC man walked away from the burning van, content to examine the remains of Liam Connelly's body later in the mortuary. He bent beside the dead body of Bridget Duffy. Her blonde hair fanned out across the tarmac in a profusion of crimson.

Toni and Boyd found themselves alone again, out of earshot from the RUC men, conspiratorial.

'Nice one, Toni,' mentioned Boyd.

'What do you mean?' asked Toni.

'The money! How much was there?' asked Boyd.

'Just under two thousand pounds,' she replied.

'So Eugene fell for it!' said Boyd.

'Looks that way!' she replied.

'Where did you get it?' asked Boyd.

Toni laughed. 'It was your hotel expenses for the last three months.'

Boyd couldn't work out whether she was serious or not. The fire burned on. The patrol boat came into view again and the helicopter returned from its refuelling.

Boyd helped the lady to her feet and held her hand.

'Thanks,' he said.

She looked at him and remarked, 'No! Thank you. We've had our differences but we got there in the end.'

Nothing else to say, she engaged his eyes, reflecting on the past. He was handsome, had she missed her chance?

'We did it together,' said Boyd, friendly, respectful.

He kissed her lightly on the forehead and placed his hand round her shoulder. They turned and walked towards Kirtling Street as the cavalry arrived in force. A light breeze whisked across the scene and freshened the atmosphere. The breeze carried the smell away from the quayside and dissipated it into the atmosphere.

Blue uniforms, wailing sirens and blue flashing lights filled the jetty area within minutes. The two comrades walked casually away from the river and saw Commander Herbert walking unsteadily towards them. He escorted them both through the growing crowds and into a conveniently parked police car.

He found them the moment of peace they so richly deserved. The day moved into twilight, then the night darkened fully and Nine Elms slept peacefully.

Shortly after midnight that night Liam Connelly passed through Heathrow Airport security controls using a false passport and a cheeky Irish smile. He boarded an aeroplane and by lunchtime the next day was basking in the tropical sunshine at La Caleta on the island of Tenerife.

To the RUC in Londonderry, to PIRA in Northern Ireland, and to the British police forces on the mainland, Liam Connelly was a dead man. A terrorist who had died in the inferno of a green furniture van on a jetty near the River Thames at Nine Elms Pier. A body burned beyond recognition. No fingerprints, no dental evidence. A wanted man no longer sought A case file closed forever.

Liam Connelly, the reformed terrorist from Shantallow, Northern Ireland, had found his peace. The sun burned down upon him and tanned his Irish skin. The Atlantic roared and smashed once more against the rocky coast guarding the hamlet of La Caleta. The two-roomed apartment that formed Liam's new home stood out proud with its balcony jutting out slightly over the pebbles on the beach beneath. Towards the distant horizon the ferries hurried their tourist cargo from island to island, fuelling the pockets of the Canarian businessman.

In the small bay dominating La Caleta, scuba divers plunged once again to the bottom of their ceaseless search for adventure and mystery. On the surface, wind surfers soaked up the sun and leaned backwards to catch a sea breeze, their hands trailing in the wake of the ocean.

Liam took it all in and brought the ice cold beer to his lips once more. It wasn't a Murphy's beer, but then he wasn't a bitter man. The smooth, cold, Canarian beer slid down his Irish throat as he leaned backwards into the canvas beach chair that once young Padraigh O'Toole had occupied, when he had been on the run from the police over two decades ago.

Liam Connelly looked down at the woman sleeping soundly at his feet and fingered her hair softly with his hands. She was so beautiful. Liam wondered to himself if he would ever see Boyd again as his thoughts privately strayed to the hospital in England where his dear Uncle Pat lay.

A man drove alone with only a radio, a suitcase and some private thoughts for company. He drummed the steering wheel with his fingers in time to the soft music. He left the capital far behind him. Time to leave, time to move on, time to start again.

The journey from the south was long and arduous but the climb towards the north and the Scottish border was well worth it. Hectic urban carriageways gradually conceded to a quieter rural highway where concrete jungles bordering the motorway gave way to rolling hills and the green fields of England.

Boyd pulled out swiftly into the fast lane, overtook the line of heavy goods vehicles and pushed his black sports car harder up the motorway into the hills. He selected top gear and travelled underneath the narrow motorway bridges at high speed. The Friesian cattle on the bridge above him made their lethargic way back to the farm for the night. Boyd saw the bold Cumbrian fells in the distance and knew his home in the north was drawing near. Checking his rear view mirror, he carefully moved the nifty little vehicle to the nearside lane as traffic flow became lighter the further north he progressed.

Soon, the amber neon lights of the city ahead filled his tired eyes and welcomed him home. He removed his right foot from the throttle and slowly decelerated up the steep exit road, leaving the motorway to find its own way north into the lowlands of Scotland. It was a beautiful evening. Slowing the sports car down, he negotiated the roundabout using the slick gearbox to good advantage.

The broad expansive road into the city was still there, with the well kept detached houses set conveniently back from the busy roadway. It had not changed at all and he smiled at the coat of arms and welcome sign announcing the city boundary. He casually examined the flowering gardens en route into the serene historic city. It was approaching twilight, only a few days after the events on Nine Elms Pier. The city was in early summer bloom. Boyd braked to coincide with the speed limit and dropped into the line of congested city traffic.

The weary Cumbrian eventually found the car park in the hospital, parked the vehicle and made his now familiar way to the quiet terminal ward where Pat lay.

Sister Meg greeted him in the outer office. Boyd took her closely in his arms and ignored the knowing looks from the nursing staff working on the ward. He held her close to him and knew that he would never let her go. He sought her lips and smothered them. She did not resist and melted into his life from that point on.

'Pat?' asked Boyd, as he lifted his face from hers.

'Not long,' she replied sadly.

'Where?' he asked.

'Side ward,' she said, pointing down the corridor. 'Same place as you found him last time.'

Boyd loosed his arms from the dark blue uniform and made his way to the room where his friend's life was slowly ebbing away. He pushed the door gently and walked in. The room was bedecked with flowers and get well cards. Boyd greeted Pat's wife and Michael, her son. The trio sat by the bedside near to Pat who glanced towards the tall Englishman as he filled the room. Pat smiled through the thin gaunt mask that tried without success to hide the pain the Irishman was enduring.

He raised a hand and twitched his fingers, commanding Boyd to come nearer. Pat spoke softly, quietly, every word wrapped in the pain of his terminal illness. 'Liam, Billyboy?' said Pat.

'Safe and on the island, Pat,' said Boyd. 'He's out of it for good. Everything worked out okay, just like you said it would. He came up trumps. He must have remembered what you said to him. He's probably taking it easy in the sunshine.'

Padraigh O'Toole smiled and tightened the grip on his wife's hand. He found Michael with the other and held them both close for what seemed like an eternity.

'Look after them for me, Billyboy, all three,' said the Irishman faintly.

'I will. You can always count on me, Pat,' said Boyd.

'I know,' said Pat.

The staff nurse, Vikki, walked into the ward and handed Pat a postcard. She was examining the colour photograph on the front of the card.

'Mail, Pat!' said Vikki. 'Very nice, too. Lots of sunshine there, so there is.'

Pat took the post card and read it. He smiled and handed it to Boyd. The policeman read the writing on the postcard out loud for the benefit of the family, who looked on with interest.

Boyd said, 'Dear Uncle Pat, Thanks. All is well. Liam and Shelagh.'

Boyd shook his head and passed the card to Linda. Boyd said, 'Shelagh! How did that happen?'

Pat revealed, 'There were two envelopes with passports in them. You gave one to Liam. Michael posted the other to Shelagh for me.'

Michael winked at Boyd and was happy to be seen as a conspirator in his father's plan.

'You're a cunning old fox, Pat!'

Pat ignored the remark and winked at Michael.

'The Blues, Billyboy? What of them? Did we win?' asked Pat.

'Lost by the odd goal. The southerners beat us in extra time but we played with pride and enjoyed the Wembley carnival,' said Boyd. 'They played in blue. We played in the away colours, green, white and red. It reminded me a bit of the colours of the Tricolour. Perhaps it was in honour of you.'

Boyd smiled at his Irish friend.

'I doubt it, Billyboy. The deck chair strip was it, then? Good colours, pity about the result. Next year, then?' queried Pat.

'Perhaps, it's only a game, Pat,' said Boyd.

'Shankley didn't think so!' said Pat.

'Life's just a game, Pat,' suggested Boyd.

Pat let go his hands and settled back onto the pillow. His wife fussed the sheets and Michael poured the ailing man a small drink of water.

'A game to be won or a game to be lost, is it then?' said Pat quietly as he sipped the cool water.

'Maybe just playing is important, I don't know,' said Boyd.

'But Liam has his peace, Billyboy?' stated Pat.

'He does that, and good luck to him, I say,' said Boyd.

'Do you think the peace will hold, Billyboy?' asked Pat.

'That depends on the Irish, my friend,' replied Boyd. 'If they want it, they'll find it somehow.'

'It's time for peace, Billyboy, time for peace,' said Pat.

Padraigh O'Toole fell backwards into a long and deep sleep, conscious of his loved ones around him. The daffodils in the glass vase remained staunch and upright as the Irishman bent towards the final whistle. There would be no extra time. The gathering talked quietly together as Pat slept his peaceful sleep. The ward closed down for the night and Sister Meg slid quietly to her home. Boyd eventually retired from the hospital bedside to leave his old friend with the family that the Irishman loved so much.

When Boyd closed the door on the ward there was a tear in the corner of his eye. He knew he would not see Pat alive again. They would not pot the black together that night or any other night.

And so it was that during the night Padraigh O'Toole passed on. The Irishman found his lasting peace.

Boyd retraced his steps to the hospital car park, intent on visiting Meg before the end of day. Thereafter, he would travel to the Eden valley and plan the rest of his life. Meg would be part of it, of that he had no doubt.

Boyd strode towards the car. He thought sadly to himself of his friend.

'Don't look back as you walk away, with tomorrow there comes another day. Pat would want it like that.'

Billy Boyd fired the car engine, pulled into the night time traffic and headed through the city. He switched on the car radio and pressed the tape cassette button. The music filled the hooded sports car and he fast-forwarded the tape to find the selection of his choice. He loved jazz at this time of night and sought solace in his music.

In the south, the twin towers of Wembley stood tall and proud, watching over the capital that relaxed in harmony with the world. The hallowed green turf that had once originated from the distant Solway Coast lay brilliantly smooth and ever so silent.

The crowds had gone. The litter had been cleared. The stadium was hushed, waiting patiently for the next exciting drama to unfold.

The grey Cumbrian mountains grew tired and closed their weary, enchanting eyes for the night. For the walkers, for the photographers and for those who just liked to sit and watch the beauty of it all, the Fells slept on, silent guardians to the serenity of the lakes.

Far across the Irish Sea, in another land and in another place, the people of Ireland drew their families around them and talked of the future. To the people of Ireland, little had changed. In the South the ocean still dashed against the rocks in Tramore Bay, whilst the crystal in Waterford continued to twinkle an Irish smile. But in the occupied counties of the north, once divided, frightened factions cautiously watered the seeds of peace. Where the Provos once carried guns, they now carried sticks. Where the Loyalists once reacted to violence, they now courted the fragile chalice on offer and looked to the Crown to preserve their future.

To the men of violence, the reality dawned that war could be won with peace as well as bullets and bombs. The British Army moved cautiously indoors and made tentative plans for a long strategic withdrawal to the mainland. The RUC braced itself for a return to the normality that anchors democracy and recognised a need to win again the hearts and minds of its future charge.

Perhaps a glimmer of hope could be seen shining on the Emerald Isle. There were no winners in the' Troubles.' No one wins a war.

It wasn't a perfect world for the Irish but a start had been made where once the finish had not been in sight.

To people like Boyd and Anthea, the conflict went on, and in any case, another conflict in another place was always waiting just around the corner. There was always a secret war to fight, a peace to win, a peace to keep.

As the night's curtain drew across the skyline, the dark clouds pushed the remnants of daylight to the sidelines and Padraigh O'Toole's soul moved proudly and reverently to its final resting place.

Boyd listened to the music and held back the gathering tears at the sound of Johnny Hooper's saxophone softly playing 'Silhouette' in the background. It was one of Johnny's lazy, but beautiful, compositions that closed the chapter on this part of so many lives.

The tune was haunting but melodic, and reminded Billy Boyd of the shadowy world in which so much of his later years had been spent. He thought of the former terrorist, Padraigh O'Toole, and how he had come to cherish the old man that so many others could so easily have hated, had they known of his earlier bomb making days.

He thought of Toni and of Anthea and of the others who had been so much a part of the quiet unseen conflict that carried on from day to day. Boyd had no more words for the past, only thoughts for the future and tired eyes that needed to rest.

William Miller Boyd, better known as 'Billyboy' in some quarters, dropped a gear, took the turning for Meg's home, found the open road and gunned the sports car quickly into the rest of his life. He had no regrets, just memories.

This was my story.

The story has been told.

A story of hate, a story of passion and a story of love.

For some, peace had been found.

For others, peace was there for the taking.

*

The Fragile Peace
***

A fragile peace,
A fragile land,
A fragile people,
Do we understand?
A time for me,
A time for you,
A time for us,
A peace is due.

A time to kill?
A time to mourn?
A time to hate?
No! A peace is born!
A time to remember,
A time to weep,
A time for tomorrow,
A peace, to keep.
A time to dream,
A time to cry,
A time for love,
Before I die.
A fragile peace,
A fragile land,
A fragile people,
A peace! Seize it in your hand!

PAUL ANTHONY

THE WAR

1969, August...... 15th August: The army is sent into Northern Ireland following civic unrest and in support of the RUC. The hostilities commence. Twenty five years of bombings, shootings, death, destruction, violence and terrorism follow.

1969, August...... 26th August: The Times newspaper carries a report showing that Bernadette Devlin, (later to be a Member of Parliament) had visited the USA on behalf of the Northern Ireland Civil Rights Association and claimed to have received pledges of 650,000 dollars for the homeless of the six counties.

1969, December...... The Provisional Army Council splits from the Irish Republican Army, and calls on Irish people at home, and 'in exile' for increased support towards their people in the north, and the eventual acknowledgement of the full political, social, economic, and cultural freedom of Ireland. The call is primarily aimed at the USA and leads to the subsequent formation of NORAID and the formation of the Provisional Irish Republican Army, henceforth referred to as PIRA.

1970, April...... NORAID is founded in New York City, USA, by Mick Flannery, Jack McCarthy and John McGowan. NORAID is consistent in its boasts for a) remitting large amounts of cash to Joe Cahill, who in 1973 was convicted of gun running using the vessel Claudia; (b) the purchase of arms; (c) support of the provisional campaign; and (d) allowing those on 'the other side' to use the funds as they saw fit. NORAID is therefore an Irish-American organisation founded to support the Provisionals by financial means.

1970, April...... B Specials disbanded. The Ulster Defence Regiment is formed (Later renamed The Royal Irish Regiment in 1992)

1971, August...... Internment is introduced

1971, November...... 16th November: Of seven individuals who break out of Crumlin Road Gaol, five are recaptured in the north.

1971, December...... 2nd December: Three more prisoners escape from Crumlin Road Gaol

1971, December...... 15 people are killed in an Ulster Volunteer Force bomb attack on McGurk's Bar, Belfast

1971, December...... 22nd December: Three PIRA members re arrested in County Donegal, occasioning serious riots in the area.

1972, January...... 30th January: Bloody Sunday. 1st Battalion Parachute Regiment kills 13 people during a civil rights march in Londonderry.

1972, February...... Aldershot bombing. Seven killed and 15 hurt in Parachute Regiment HQ bomb attack. This signals the start of the mainland PIRA campaign.

1972, March...... Stormont Government is suspended and direct rule is instituted.

1972, July...... Bloody Friday, 21st: 11 killed and 130 injured following the detonation of 26 PIRA bombs in Belfast.

1972, July...... Secret talks take place between PIRA and William Whitelaw, Secretary of State for Northern Ireland

1972, July...... During Operation Motorman the military break down no-go areas in Londonderry and Belfast.

1972...... Approximately 30,000 troops are stationed in Northern Ireland, the highest number throughout the entire campaign.

1973...... House of Commons Official Reports show that between 15th February, 1971 and 20th February, 1973, 282 different types of weapons from 15 different countries had been seized by security forces in Northern Ireland.

1973, March...... 28th March: The 298 ton coaster Claudia is intercepted by the Irish Navy off Helvick Head, County Waterford. Five tons of arms bound for the IRA are seized. Amongst those arrested is Joe Cahill. The arms consist of 250 AK 47 self loading rifles, 247 Webley revolvers, 20,000 rounds of ammunition, 100 anti-tank mines, 100 anti-personnel mines, 600 lb of TNT, 500 lb of gelignite and 300 hand grenades. The evidence points to Libyan involvement, despite the vessel being registered in Cyprus by a German shipping company which is partially owned by a man convicted in 1967 of attempting to smuggle arms from Czechoslovakia to Kurdish rebels. This case showed how Irish Republican terrorism had exceeded the boundaries of the Province.

1973...... Charles Malone, NORAID member of San Francisco, and James O'Gara, NORAID member of New York, are convicted of arms charges in the USA.

1974...... The Royal Canadian Mounted Police and the Irish Police between 1973 and 1974 in parts of Canada, Toronto and Dublin, in joint operations and collaborations, recover 32 rifles, 5 sten guns, 12 handguns, 47,000 rounds of ammunition, 10 hand grenades and 60 lb of gunpowder.

1974, April...... 14th April: Captain Anthony Pollen, 14 Intelligence Company, is killed on active service.

1974...... Between May, 1972 and February, 1974, the Irish Courts in Eire convicted 338 persons for 'IRA' offences relative, in the main, to the possession of arms and explosives.

1974...... Between 1969 and 1974, Lieutenant Colonel George Styles was Officer Commanding the British Army Bomb Disposal Teams

1974...... Unnamed Protestant extremists are generally held responsible for a series of car bombings in Dublin and Monaghan. During a three hour period 28 lives are lost.

1974...... The Ulster Workers Council Strike.

1974...... Two Irish men and two Irish-Americans are convicted in Baltimore, Maryland, USA, of conspiring to smuggle 158 semi-automatic rifles and armour piercing shells from New York to Ireland.

1974, February...... 12 soldiers killed following bomb attack on the M62 motorway, near Leeds. A bomb, laid down by PIRA, explodes in the luggage compartment of a coach.

1974, November...... Birmingham pub bombings. 21 killed in two pubs.

1975...... London. The Balcombe Street Siege.

1975...... The Republican Movement splits. The INLA breaks away from the PIRA and forms its own organisation.

276

1975, March...... 7th March: Mortar attack on Aldergrove airport, near Belfast.

1975, May...... Internment is ended.

1975, August...... Three members of the Miami Showband are killed by the UVF

1975, November...... 29th November: Bomb explosion at Dublin airport is claimed by the UDA. One person killed, several others injured.

1976, January...... First SAS troop of 12 men deployed to Ulster.

1976, March...... Frank Grady is convicted in New York of illegally exporting arms and falsifying documents.

1976, March...... Betty Williams and Mairead Corrigan are generally associated with the 'Peace People', based on the Christian faith and tolerance. They receive the Novel Peace Prize in 1977. Up to 31st March, 1978, the sum of only £900 has been donated from the USA towards the peace.

1976, March...... IRA member Sean McKenna is arrested after alleged illegal abduction by the SAS from the Republic of Eire.

1976...... A ceasefire lasts approximately nine months.

1977, February...... Brendan Swords, arrested in Eire, is linked to a PIRA arsenal recovered in London in 1976. Dublin High Court ruled that allegations were 'political' and, as a result, he was immune from extradition.

1977, July...... Seamus Harvey, IRA member, is shot dead by the SAS in Culderry.

1977, August...... 15th August: On the eight anniversary of 'The Troubles'. The Times reveals that since 1969, 902,554 rounds of ammunition, 257,489lb of explosives, 297 machine guns, 2,667 rifles, 2,962 pistols, 881 shotguns, 18 rocket launchers, 57 rockets, 427 mortar tubes and 441 mortar shells were recovered by security forces. 2,828 bombs were defused.

1977, September...... Dominic McGlinchey is arrested in Eire and subsequently convicted of his part in a mail van robbery. He receives four years imprisonment. He had previously been involved with PIRA in the seventies and had served time for illegal possession of arms. An extradition warrant had been issued by the RUC for the murder of an elderly woman on 28th March 1977. Extradition law becomes the focus of media and legal attention, particularly when extradition is refused on the grounds of a 'political offence.'

1977, December...... Colm McNutt, INLA member, is killed by a soldier from the 14 Intelligence Company in Londonderry

1978...... British Army Garrison in Northern Ireland stands at 13,000 troops.

1978, February...... 22nd February: PIRA claims responsibility for bomb attack on army officer's mess in Aldershot. Six civilians are killed and one Roman Catholic Chaplain.

1978, February...... The La Mon House massacre. 12 Protestants are killed at a restaurant in Comber, County Down.

1978, February...... Paul Duffy, IRA member, is killed during an SAS ambush at Ardhoe.

1978, April...... 'Dirty' blanket protest begins at the Maze Prison.

1978, June...... 20th June: Three IRA men and one Protestant bystander are killed by the SAS and the RUC in the Ballysillan Postal Incident.

1978, June...... 19th June: The Irish Times indicates that their correspondent, Conor O'Cleary, has interviewed a colonel in the Palestine Liberation Organisation who admits advising a small number of IRA members who received instructions in explosives and guerrilla warfare in the Lebanon.

1978, November...... 24th November: IRA man Patrick Duffy is shot dead by the SAS at an arms cache in Culderry

1978, December...... 15th December: Five men are convicted of offences relating to kidnap, murder, manslaughter, and associated forearms charges, following the kidnap of army intelligence officer,

Captain Nairac. Nairac was kidnapped in Ulster and taken across the border into Eire. This trail followed the conviction on 8th November, 1977, of a sixth person, Liam Townson, for the murder,

1979, March...... Airey Neave, MP, killed by an INLA bomb in his car when leaving the Houses of Parliament in London.

1979, March...... Sir Richard Sykes, British Ambassador to The Netherlands, is murdered by the IRA.

1979, August...... 18 soldiers killed in a double bombing attack at Warren Point. Hours earlier Lord Mountbatten is killed by an IRA bomb when his boat is blown up in County Sligo, Eire.

1980...... Thomas McMahon is convicted of the murder of Lord Mountbatten.

1980, September...... The SAS apprehend two IRA men from Dungannon at an arms cache in Tyrone.

1981, May...... 5th May: Bobby Sands dies during a hunger strike, the first of 10 PIRA and INLA individuals who take their own lives in this manner.

1981, January...... Sir Norman Stronge is murdered by the IRA at Tynan Abbey.

1981, March...... Four IRA men are captured by the SAS at Rosslea

1981, November...... 21st November: Christopher Black of the Ardoyne, Belfast, is arrested at an IRA roadblock and on 24th November is granted immunity from prosecution. Black signals the start of the 'Supergrass' system and during a nine month trial that ended in August, 1983, Black gives evidence against 38 accused. 35 are convicted as a result of his testimony.

1982...... Between November, 1981 and November 1983, seven Loyalist and 18 Republican supergrasses were responsible for the arrest of 519 persons in relation to paramilitary activity.

1982, March...... 2nd March: A failed assassination attempt on Lord Lowry, Lord Chief Justice of Northern Ireland, takes place at Queen's University, Belfast.

1982, March...... 11th March: Ex UDR man is shot dead in Newry six years after leaving the regiment.

1982, March...... 15th March: A PIRA bomb explodes in Banbridge town centre, County Down. 15 persons are injured and one 11 year old boy, Alan McCrum, is killed.

1982, July...... Gerard Tuite is convicted in Dublin of possessing explosives in England between 1978 and 1979

1982, July...... 11 soldiers are killed and 50 injured in a bomb attack on the Household Cavalry in London. One horse, Sefton, is injured, and many horses killed.

1982, August...... IRA man, Raymond Gilmour, turns supergrass and compromises IRA operations in Londonderry.

1982, October...... 27th October: Three IRA members are killed by the RUC near Lurgan. This is the first of three incidents that led to the Stalker enquiry.

1982, November...... 24th November: One IRA man is killed by the RUC at Lurgan.

1982, December....... Ballykelly bombing. The INLA bombs the Droppin' Well Bar, killing 17 people, 11 of them soldiers.

1983...... Between 1969 and 1983, 2,200 lives are lost in Northern Ireland as a result of terrorist related violence. 165 lives were lost in countries outside Ulster.

1983, December...... 4th December: The SAS kill two IRA members near Coalisland.

1983, December...... The Harrods bomb, London. Six people are killed, three of them police officers, and 90 people are injured.

1984, March...... 14th March: UFF gunmen seriously injure Gerry Adams.

1984, May...... 24th May: John Stalker, Deputy Chief Constable of Greater Manchester Police, is appointed to the 'shoot to kill' enquiry.

1984, October...... The Grand Hotel, Brighton. Five killed, 30 injured, during the Conservative Party Conference. Margaret Thatcher escapes harm.

1985, February...... Newry. RUC Station is attacked by a mortar and nine police officers killed.

1986, May....... John Stalker is removed from the 'shoot to kill' enquiry.

1986, July...... 2nd July: Three RUC men are shot dead by PIRA in Newry.

1987, May...... Loughall shooting. An eight man IRA unit is killed by SAS during an ambush on the town's police station.

1987, November...... Poppy Day. 11 killed during the Remembrance Day Service Day at Enniskillen. The Wilson family receive national prominence in their plea for peace and sanity.

1988, February...... Pat Finucane, a solicitor representing Republican defendants, is murdered by the Loyalists.

1988, March...... Gibraltar. SAS kills three IRA members, allegedly on active service.

1988, March...... Belfast. Michael Stone kills three mourners at the subsequent funeral in Belfast. Two army corporals inadvertently drive into one of the funerals and are killed.

1988, June...... Fun Run bombing at Lisburn, County Antrim. Six soldiers killed.

1988, August...... Ballygawley. Eight soldiers killed and 27 injured in a bus.

1989, July...... Ian Gow, MP, killed in a car bomb attack at his home in West Sussex.

1989, September...... Deal Barracks. 11 Marine bandsmen killed in a bomb attack at the Royal School of Music.

1989, October...... Buncrana Border Crossing near Londonderry. Man strapped in his car as a 'proxy' bomb is killed along with five others.

1992, January...... Eight Protestants killed leaving an army base in Tyrone

1992, February...... Five Catholics killed in Ulster Freedom Fighters attack on Ormeau Road bookmakers in Belfast

1992, April...... Derby. Members of INLA shoot army recruiting sergeant Michael Newman.

1992, April...... North Shields. Bombs explode at oil refinery

1992, April...... Baltic Exchange bomb, London. Three killed.

1992, August...... Large consignment of explosives recovered from a motor lorry in London

1992, August...... Firebomb attacks, Shrewsbury.

1992, October...... London 'Dungeon; public house bombs

1992, October...... Quantity of semtex found in a tea chest in a shop in London. Vincent Woods is arrested. Plans of John Major's house recovered.

1992, October...... Downing Street, London. 'Proxy' bomb attempt fails after taxi driver is forced by passengers to drive a bomb-laden taxi at gunpoint into Whitehall.

1993, February...... 6th February: Members of INLA attempt to steal explosives from Westbury-sub-Mendip quarry in Somerset. Arrests are made by Avon and Somerset Constabulary. Convictions follow.

1993, February...... Bomb explode at Warrington Gas Works

1993, March...... Warrington bombing. Two bombs kill Jonathan Ball, aged 12, and Timothy Parry, aged 3. Both are killed in Warrington town centre.

1993, April...... Bishopsgate bomb, London. Major devastation caused in City of London by a bomb hidden in a heavy goods vehicle.

This incident represents one of the largest and most costly bombs (in economic terms) in the entire history of 'The Troubles'.

1993, August...... PIRA bomb attacks take place in Bournemouth and along the south coast of England.

1993, October......Ten killed by PIRA bomb attack in Shankhill Road, Belfast. It is said that the man who planted the bomb in the Protestant enclave was killed by his own device when it explodes prematurely.

1993, October...... Seven Catholics killed by UFF gunmen at Rising Sun Bar, Greysteel, Londonderry. The offenders enter a public house and spray the occupants with bullets.

1993, October...... The Downing Street Declaration.

1994, June...... Loughinisland Massacre. Six Catholics killed in O'Toole's Bar whilst watching the World Cup on TV

1994, June...... Helicopter crash. West Scotland. Members of the RUC Special Branch, Army Intelligence Corps and the Security Service are killed on their way to a conference on terrorism.

1994, July...... Heysham, Lancashire. A massive bomb is found in a flatback wagon at Heysham port, having been shipped from Northern Ireland.

There is both a human cost and an economic cost which can be attributed to the violent acts of terrorism. During 'The Troubles', well over 3,000 people lost their lives as a result of terrorist activity. Thousands more were injured. The economic cost from bombings runs into millions of pounds.

THE PEACE

1994, August...... 31st August, midnight. PIRA declare a total cessation of military operations.

1994, September...... A son is born to Mairead Doherty, the first child born in Belfast after the ceasefire.

1994, October...... 14th October: The Loyalist paramilitaries announce a ceasefire and express regret at loss of life during 'The Troubles'. A fragile peace ensues.

1995, February...... 2nd February: A framework document revealing new political and constitutional arrangements for Northern Ireland is leaked to the media.

1995, February...... 22nd February: Joint framework document published by the Prime Ministers of Britain and Eire in Belfast outlining new political and constitutional arrangement for Northern Ireland.

1995, February...... Provisional Sinn Fein chairman offers olive branch to Unionists while speaking in Dublin, contending there is a place for those in Northern Ireland who wish to remain British.

1995, March...... The month marks the 150th anniversary of the Great Irish Famine. The event is recalled on British television. Some commentators argue that the Famine lasted unnecessarily long, due to the uninterested attitude to Ireland and an inadequate response to the famine from the British Government. Channel 4 runs a documentary on Irish Affairs every evening for one week.

1995, March....... 14th March: Prime Minister John Major whilst on a tour of the Middle East meets Yasser Arafat, leader of the Palestine Liberation Organisation and former international terrorist. The meeting takes place at the Gaza Strip.

14th March: Gerry Adams, leader of Provisional Sinn Fein, travels to the United States of America for talks with President Clinton. John Major advises President Clinton against the meeting.

14th March: The British Government announces that 400 soldiers from the Artillery Regiment are to be withdrawn from Northern Ireland and returned to their base in Yorkshire. This represents the biggest withdrawal of personnel in many years and follows the abandonment of daytime military patrols. Neither Loyalist nor Republican terrorist groupings has surrendered any arms, ammunition or explosives.

14th March: Loyalist prisoners at the Maze Prison in Northern Ireland riot and go on the rampage, brandishing firearms from the roof of the burning prison. 50 prison officers are inured, some seriously, before the authorities regain control.

17th March: A bomb is planted in a Texas shopping store in the town of Newry, A warning is given and the device is defused.

24th March: Commentators report on the position of the British Government, revealing that Government ministers will not meet Sinn Fein representatives unless weapons are decommissioned as opposed to demilitarised., An argument over 'words' ensues.

26th March: Army patrols are taken off the streets of Belfast. Democratic Unionist, Peter Robinson, says that the British Government has demilitarised before PIRA.

1995, April...... 1st April: Relationship between Britain and the USA reaches a low point when John Major criticises President Clinton for his dealings with Gerry Adams and in particular his decision to grant an unrestricted United States visa to Adams in March.

3rd April: Gerry Adams, Sinn Fein, announces he has lost confidence in John Major. The Prime Minister replies, pointing out that PIRA decline to discuss decommissioning of weapons and therefore cannot reasonably expect to enter negotiations with other parties in the democratic process.

4th April: President Clinton calls upon paramilitaries to lay down their arms and enter the democratic process. The rift between the USA and the UK is healed somewhat when Clinton praises Major for his part in the Ulster peace process.

5th April: Four suspected members of the INLA are arrested at Balbriggan, north Dublin, by the Garda Siochana, in possession of 26 guns and 2000 rounds of ammunition which are recovered from a van and a car. The suspects are held under the Offences Against the State Act of 1939. INLA remains an outlawed Republican terrorist group which broke away from the IRA in the mid 1970's and to date has not declared a ceasefire.

11th April: British Government announces the withdrawal from the province of 400 troops from the 40th Regiment, Royal Artillery.

12th April: Sir Patrick Mayhew, Secretary of State for Northern Ireland, announces multilateral talks involving all parties in Northern Ireland. Speculation mounts that Sinn Fein and British Government ministers will soon meet.

12th April: The Irish Government in Dublin announce that seven more IRA terrorists are to be released early, bringing the total to 20. The inmates are to be freed on Thursday, 13th April, 1995, approximately one year earlier than their anticipated release date.

13th April: The RUC seal off a four storey building and outhouses in Hollywood, County Down, and seize approximately 40 guns and boxes of ammunition. Police believe the cache is destined for the UVF. Four men and one woman are arrested. Speculation exists that the RUC are searching for a UVF arms factory where home-made weapons are manufactured.

14th April: In Ouston, County Durham, on the mainland, Des Lindop, employed by the Royal Ordnance Factory at Birtley, Tyne and Wear, is arrested by English police assisting the RUC in the Hollywood UVF arms cache enquiry. He and other family members eventually appear in court on firearms charges. On 17th April, Durham police announce the recovery of sub-machine guns and weapons from the Ouston house.

16th April, Easter Sunday: Bank Holiday newspapers report that Gerry Adams, President of Sinn Fein, expects that it is unlikely that the Provisionals will hand in their arms. Commentators speculate on the proposition that both the Republicans and the Loyalists are still engaged in acquiring arms and ammunition despite the ongoing peace initiative.

16th April, Dublin: Gerry Adams, whilst speaking at a ceremony to make the 79th anniversary of the rise against British rule, accuses the British Government of attempting to suborn the peace process by seeking a victory within the peace that could never be achieved against the IRA during the war. Masked IRA men, throughout Northern Ireland, speak at Easter Commemoration services.

25th April: An announcement is made that Ulster Minister, Michael Ancram, is to meet Martin McGuiness, Sinn Fein. It is reported that the decommissioning of IRA arms and the withdrawal of troops from Northern Ireland are to be discussed. Democratic Unionist, Ian Paisley, retaliates by accusing the British Government of 'surrender'.

30th April: Watch company, MDM, present Gerry Adams, Sinn Fein, with a watch valued at £1,000. The gift comprises the Thorr 'Peace' Award which is made annually to a person who has made a significant contribution to peace and democracy. Many British Ministers are reported to be outraged at the award.

3rd May: The Prime Minister, John Major, visits Londonderry. He intends to visit the Tower Museum where an exhibition commemorates the role of Londonderry people in the World War Two 'Battle of the Atlantic'. A Sinn Fein and Republican demonstration is held at Union Hall Place near the entrance to the museum. Demonstrators call for 'peace through British withdrawal and the disbandment of the RUC'. The demonstration becomes violent when the RUC need to clear the mass of people. Fighting breaks out and for an hour 150 demonstrators clash with police. Missiles are thrown. 12 RUC officers and one Sinn Fein councillor are injured in the fighting. Major seeks a denunciation of the violence but Mitchel McLaughlin, National Chairman of Sinn Fein, declines to condemn the demonstrators, stating the situation was mishandled on both sides. Major threatens to postpone the Ancram-McGuinness peace talks.

4th May: During an Orange Order march through Belfast, violence erupts when the marchers pass a Catholic area. In the subsequent violence, over 20 RUC officers are injured and at least ten persons arrested for offences of serious public disorder and criminality. Fires are started, missiles thrown and shops looted. One off-licence is targeted by the mob and about £30,000 worth of tobacco, beer and spirits is stolen. The violence evident on this night appears to be far in excess of the previous night's events in Londonderry, yet receives little attention from the British national newspapers due to the local elections which take place on this date. Some commentators, however, foresee problems for the summer marching season in Northern Ireland. The Orange Order is a Protestant organisation with no unduly adverse history of involvement with Loyalist paramilitary organisations.

1995, May   7th May: The Fourteenth Anniversary of the death of hunger striker Bobby Sands is marked by Republicans in Belfast with a commemorative march through the city.

8th May: The British nation celebrates VE Day and recalls the victory in Europe 50 years earlier.

10th May: Michael Ancram, Northern Ireland Minister, meets Martin McGuinness, Sinn Fein, at Stormont Castle, Belfast.

16th May: The leader of the SDLP, John Hulme, and his wife, Pat, are awarded the title 'Europeans of the Year' by the French magazine La Vie. The magazine awards the title annually to the person who has made a major contribution to world peace.

17th May: The Independent carries a small newspiece revealing that a 25 year old man is recovering in hospital after being beaten by a Republican punishment squad armed with iron bars and baseball bats in West Belfast.

17th May: Junior Northern Ireland Minister, Malcolm Moss, meets Mitchel McLaughlin, Sinn Fein Chairman, during a visit to Londonderry.

17th May: Republicans are blamed for an attack on the Creggan estate, Londonderry, in which two persons are badly injured by several masked men carrying iron bars, and wooden cudgels with nails.

18th May: David John Adams, Robert Crawford and Paul Stitt are convicted at Belfast Crown Court of conspiracy to murder, conspiracy to cause an explosion and possession of guns and explosives with intent to endanger life. Sentence – 25 years. Adams is the cousin of Sinn Fein President, Gerry Adams.

18th May: Sir Patrick Mayhew invites Gerry Adams to meet him at a White House Conference on 'trade and investment in Ireland' whilst the two are in Washington during May. Adams has in the past been interned without trial, gaoled and excluded from Britain on security grounds under the Prevention of Terrorism Act. Adams agrees to the meeting, which is seen as an incremental step in the peace process.

19th May: South African police name the IRA as part of a £40 million criminal plot to take over three diamond firms. Three arrests are made and 13 people, British, Irish and South African, are suspected of involvement in one of the country's biggest ever fraud cases.

19th May: James Molyneux, Ulster Unionist, and Ian Paisley, Democratic Unionist, pull out of key talks in anger over Sir Patrick Mayhew's plans to meet Gerry Adams in America.

21st May: President Clinton tells the Northern Irish magazine Omnibus that decommissioning of weapon is essential to peace.

21st May: The Protestant Action Force admits that five traffickers in Larne face execution if they continue to ignore warnings to stop drug dealing.

30th May: Prince Charles visits Eire and is the first British Royal to visit the Republic since 1917. A home-made bomb is found at Classiebawn Castle, Mullaghmore, County Sligo, the holiday home of the late Lord Mountbatten, the Prince's uncle, who was killed by the IRA in 1979. Two incendiary devices explode in a Dublin book store. The INLA are suspected of involvement partly because, unlike the IRA, they have not announced a ceasefire.

30th May: Several thousand people stage a protest march to Dublin Castle, where Prince Charles is guest of honour at a banquet hosted by the Taoiseach, John Bruton. Anti-British chants and placards denoting Oliver Cromwell and the Great Irish Famine are prominent.

31st May: Three men are treated in hospital after separate punishment beatings in North Belfast.

1995, June   4th June: Edinburgh. 400 persons participate in a march to commemorate James Connolly (born in Edinburgh), one of the leaders of the 1916 Ester Rebellion. Police detain 47 Loyalists in South Clerk Street, Edinburgh, to prevent a disturbance. In a subsequent clash between the factions, 16 arrests are made.

4th June: Athlone, Reports emerge that PIRA have begun to hand in weapons to the Irish army. These include guns, ammunition and two heavy-calibre machine guns, capable of bringing down helicopters. The weapons are handed in at Athlone Barracks in the Republic of Eire.

13th June: Sir Patrick Mayhew announces an independent review of anti-terrorism legislation and an extension of compassionate leave for terrorist prisoners.

13th June: The Royal Engineers begin to dismantle a checkpoint in Clady, County Tyrone, the first such action since the ceasefire.

1995, June   The peace process appears to flounder when John Major calls an election to determine leadership of the Conservative Party. Foreign Minister Dick Spring, in Dublin, maintains impetus and calls for the decommissioning of arms.

1995, July.   3rd July: Private Lee Clegg, Paratrooper, is released from prison having served 4½ years for the murder of Karen Reilly: a passenger in a stolen car which failed to stop at a road check in Belfast in 1990. On the night of his release, over 100 vehicles are hijacked and set on fire in Belfast, Londonderry and Lurgan. The RUC recover 100 petrol bombs in the Ardoyne. Civic unrest returns to Northern Ireland. John Hume calls the decision to release Clegg 'insensitive' at the start of the marching season. Army bomb disposal officers carry out a number of controlled explosions on suspect devices during this period. Martin McGuinness calls the Clegg decision 'disgraceful and despicable. The British Government haven't taken the peace process seriously and have thrown it back in our face.' Dick Spring 'conveys concern'. Seamus Mallon, SDLP, Newry and Armagh, says there are 'serious implications for the peace process.' Gary McMichael, UDP says, 'All political prisoners should now be freed.'

9th July: Garvachy Road, Portadown, is the scene of a proposed Loyalist march, when over 500 Orangemen try to walk through Nationalist-Republican area for the 189th successive year, to commemorate the victory of the Battle of the Boyne. The RUC deny access to the road and block the route with Land Rovers. A standoff follows. David Trimble, Ulster Unionist MP, and Ian Paisley, DUP leader, negotiate with police. Cathal Daly worries over the peace process. Local Orange Leader, Harold Gracey, says, 'We will not be moving until we walk our traditional route home.' Violence flares across Ulster in support of the Orangemen. A compromise is reached; the march takes place.
July, 1995   12th July: The Reverend Martin Smyth, Grand Master of the Orange Order, says, 'Loyalists will never accept a United Ireland based on the framework document.'

The marching season passes off without further incident.

16th July: The RUC confirms that in the ten day period following Clegg's release, there were 150 attacks on police officers. In addition, 227 vehicles were hijacked and burnt out; 150 petrol bomb attacks were recorded; 130 people were injured; 117 arrests were made.

16th July: Two arson attacks occur at a Belfast Orange Lodge and Drumcree Church Hall, Portadown.

21st July: During a demonstration in the centre of Belfast, a number of Republican marchers are arrested in violent clashes with the RUC

22nd July: Americans visit Northern Ireland to examine what assistance can be given to the stagnated peace process.

31st August, 1995... The 'ceasefire' is one year old.

*

Paul Anthony's Book Shop
~
Welcome to Paul Anthony's book shop.

Paul Anthony is a retired British detective who has served extensively throughout the U.K and elsewhere. This is his current collection. You will find all these books in print and kindle, and all the other formats, from either Amazon, Smashwords, Lulu or Venture Galleries.. I recommend Lulu for the cheapest print versions and either Amazon or Venture Galleries for the ebook versions. Thank you.

*

Paul Anthony
'One of the best thriller and mystery writers in the United Kingdom today'. Caleb Pirtle 111, International Best Selling Author of 'Place of Skulls', screenplay writer, and Founder and Editorial Director at Venture Galleries, Owner and Director of CP3 Productions

Paul Anthony is one of the best Thriller Mystery Writers of our times!
Dennis Sheehan, International Best Selling Author of 'Purchased Power'.

*

THE CONCHENTA CONUNDRUM
Murder Mystery/Crime/Detective
Book Description
Two beautiful and mysterious women are murdered in the same week. The local police chief believes both killings are the work of one man and instructs his officers to bring about a swift conclusion to the investigation. Davies King, the hardnosed, chess playing detective, reckons the game is much more complex and refuses to accept an apparent checkmate. With the odds stacking up against him, Davies tries to shuffle all the pieces and capture the guilty party before an innocent man is wrongly arrested. But the clock is counting down, there''s a bomb explosion imminent, and he's running out of time.... With enigmatic characters that are credible and authentic it doesn't take long to become engrossed in a well crafted and gripping plot. Paul Anthony's mesmerizing conspiracy carries the reader all the way and skilfully builds to an exhilarating and explosive finale.

My favourite detective novel so far from a most remarkable novelist, gripping to the last...'
Nick Gordon, International award winning screenwriter

One of the best books I have ever read. The story is well written and holds you from start to finish. I really like the character Davies king and would love to read more books with this character in it.

Susan Murray, Reader

The Conchenta Conundrum sets the standard for murder mysteries. You can get the sense that the author is a real life detective, civilians wouldn't have the insight nor the technical know how to write like this. Once you start reading you won't be able to put it down. I highly recommend this book....

Dennis Sheehan, Best Selling Author of 'Purchased Power'

*

THE LEGACY OF THE NINTH
Espionage Thriller/Crime/Historic Fiction
Book description

Packed with action, stacked with intrigue, and sprinkled with ingenious conspiracy, The Legacy of the Ninth is a whirlwind thriller of bitter conflict and religious mystique, echoing through the centuries of time from the desert wastes of the Roman Empire to the luscious green valley of the River Eden and the land of the Lakes. Behold, the noble Domitian: a valiant Roman Centurion who witnesses an appalling act of mass suicide in the Negev desert, and Hussein who plunders a Jewish artefact from its rightful owner. Centuries later, Boyd, the detective, tries to find out why events in Masada are now so closely linked with nearby Hadrian's Wall. Indeed, against all the odds, Boyd realises that the links are so strong that prospects of peace in the Middle East are in danger of collapsing...Things can't get any worse, can they?

'Full of intrigue, espionage and cold-blooded murder; the action is on-going, the descriptions vivid....'

The Keswick Reminder

'A thriller mixing fact and fiction, stacked with intrigue.'...

The Cumberland News

The Legacy of the Ninth takes the reader on a breathtaking journey, following the traces of a certain ancient artefact all the way from the desolate deserts of the devastated by Romans Judea to the modern day Britain and the Middle East.

Victorious Roman legions, fierce ancient Scots, British and Israeli Intelligence, terrorists camps in Lebanon, undercover police officers, drug dealers, fishermen - you get to meet them all, while the action never slacks, never let you relax and pause for breath. You finish this story breathless, unable to let the book go before you know how it ends.

This novel is very well written and deeply satisfying. It analyzes all aspects of human nature, never turning to the easy solution of the good and the bad. The multiple points of view are astounding. Every angle of the unfolding story fascinates you with its different points of view, which exploring the inner worlds of various people of various cultures. The depth of the historical research is amazing and reminds us that life was brutal and cheap through all times, the modern days included.

A very rewarding, enjoyable read that I would recommend to anyone.

Zoe Saadia, Eminent Respected Author of The Cahokian.

I began reading The Legacy of the Ninth thinking that it was a story of the Roman Empire, but was not disappointed when it morphed into present day England where an artifact carried there from the Middle East by the Ninth Legion is uncovered. Its discovery becomes the catalyst for a new battle in the continuing conflict between Arabs and Jews.

Paul Anthony populated this story with a host of three-dimensional characters engaged in the conflict from different venues, England, Istanbul, Lebanon, and Israel. One in particular, a British policeman reassigned from undercover work in London to leading Bobbies in Cumbria, faces the daunting task of reigniting pride in a group that has been allowed to languish in mediocrity. This challenge alone would be sufficient foundation for a good story. In The Legacy of the Ninth, it is but one facet of a complex tale with plots within plots. Paul Anthony varies his pace, lingering on details to establish the milieu, and racing ahead with action to make it exciting.

Jack Durish, famous author of Rebels on the Mountain

*

BUSHFIRE
Espionage Thriller/Historic Fiction/Crime
Book Description
A terrifying thriller of greed and deceit.

The action spans the oceans; from Northern Ireland, to Portugal, from Colombia to the British Isles, and is set against the inferno of a raging drugs culture. Cumbrian undercover detective, Boyd, working with two Portuguese investigators, a determined female British Intelligence officer, an American drug-busting legend, and the covert power of the State, battle against globally organised crime syndicates unaware that some amongst them have different plans...

Private and personal revenge...

'A gripping story.... Take a bow...' The Cumberland News

'A fast paced, expertly written, brilliant tale of crime and suspense. The plot is clever, multi layers, detailed and precise. The writing has great depth which makes the reader feel as though they are right there, in the middle of this dangerous world of crime. This book is captivating and filled with adventure, excitement and drama. In a

294

nutshell, this story has all the hallmarks of a Martina Cole book, but the big difference between the two is that what Paul Anthony has created in 'Bushfire' feels real, raw and grown-up.

It opened my eyes to the world of organised crime and those who bravely fight it. It tackles deep social issues and forces your mind beyond the normal bounds of society into the terrifying underworld of drugs and terrorism.

I found myself connecting with the main crime fighting characters, routing for them, supporting them and wishing I could get into the book and warn them of dangers only the reader could see.

The criminals terrified me as I glimpsed the inner workings of a world I didn't know existed. The very darkest side of human nature – greed, illicit drug trafficking, organised crime and terrorism. It is a story of a world only few can really understand.

This is a book that will keep you on the edge of your seat from the first page to the last. I have only ever read one crime thriller which felt absolutely real – 'Bushfire' by Paul Anthony

Elizabeth Marshall, Book Reviewer, Travel Critic and International Author of 'When Fate Dictates'...

"Bushfire" by Paul Anthony is about the illegal drug industry in 1990's spanning Ireland, Portugal, and across the ocean to South American connections. This complex, well-written crime story follows layers of characters, from the criminals, the law enforcement, and the go-betweens as they make plans and interact with each other, making a non-stop story that is almost impossible to put down. I highly recommend this novel to readers that enjoy being pulled into the dangerous, intense world of international crime fighting. Five stars!

C.C. Cole, Award Winning Author of the 'Gastar' Dark Fantasy series.

I could not put the book down. It was fast and moving. Even in the midst of the mayhem that this story produced, Paul Anthony managed to use pleasing language to describe the surroundings. It seemed that when he described a beautiful spot, it got marred by the incidents surrounding it. I found that appealing in that it gave me a contrast between "normal" life and the lives of criminals and the havoc they reek on society.

Sonia Rumzi, International Best Selling Author of 'Simple Conversation', 'Caring for Eleanor' and many others works of 'Woman's literature'.

What an excellent book. I thoroughly enjoyed it.

This story has held me more and interested me more than the last two Clive Cussler books I have read and that is saying something as Clive Cussler is one of my favourite authors. I do believe I have found a new favourite author. The plot is brilliantly gripping and the characters are vividly real. It has an excellent pace and is crammed full of adventure, suspense and twists.

Andrew Brown, Book Critic and Reader.

Paul Anthony has written a winner with Bushfire. He takes the reader into the dark and dangerous world of narcotics trafficking and terrorism. The realism is in every page because the author moved in this world as a British detective investigating these crimes. The story centres on a group of British detectives attending a Europol conference in Portugal. They are led by Detective Inspector William Boyd, a dedicated and seasoned police officer. During the conference, Boyd goes for a run and spots an IRA terrorist. This leads to a joint investigation with the British detectives, Portugal authorities and DEA.

The investigation leads to a drug kingpin named Klaus from whom IRA terrorists want a load of drugs. However, terrorists decide they want everything Klaus has and kill his guards and hold Klaus and his wife prisoner. The detectives are hot on their trail and in a series of violent confrontations, take down Klaus' operation, but the IRA men escape on Klaus' boat. But not for long. Shadowed by a British submarine, Boyd and his detectives know the IRA is headed for Britain and approximately where. With the help of British Customs and British Intelligence, the terrorists and drug dealers are cornered in a climatic confrontation.

Bushfire is action filled and gripping. A must read if you like action/adventure novels.

Mike McNeff, Arizona Highway Patrol Academy; the DEA Narcotics Commanders' School, the Arizona Law Enforcement Academy, the Chandler/Gilbert Law Enforcement Academy, former Deputy County Attorney and Prosecuting Attorney...

... and successful author of the GOTU series.

*

THE FRAGILE PEACE
Historic Fiction/Thriller /
Love Story/Crime/Espionage/Terrorism
Book Description:

The Fragile Peace is a thriller of violent prejudices and divided loyalties. This Ulster novel reaches to the very roots of sectarian life and death. Written by a member of the security forces, it reveals a human landscape that is unknown, yet startingly believable. It is a world where sworn enemies may exchange confidences over a game of snooker; where a kneecapping operation turns into a deadly vendetta fuelled by sexual jealousy and where the fate of the United Kingdom could rest in the hands of one punch-drunk bruiser with a dangerous addiction. Everything is here, from the glamour of hi-tech intelligence work to the despairing pub-talk of men locked in the past. Trace the origins of these relentless tit-for-tat killings, often starting in childhood and see how the lives of

296

vastly different people may be mysteriously linked forever against the fatally beautiful backdrop of Northern Ireland.

'A powerful novel... A hard hitting tale of intrigue and suspicion, treachery and tension...'

The Keswick Reminder

A remarkably balanced piece of fiction... Gripping...'
The News and Star

'Selected in 2011 as the first audio book in the Dyslexia Foundation UK audio Library...'
Steve O'Brien, The Dyslexia Foundation UK

'A book that has accompanied me around the world. A great read, time & time again...'
Eddie Lightfoot, Book Critic and Reader

*

SUNSET
POETRY COLLECTION
Book description
Sunset is a collection of poetry tracing the life of a relaxed carefree teenager in the Sixties to a man at the dawn of the Twenty First Century. The journey captures an age of experiences; peaceful and pleasant, violent and murderous. The voyage from one century to another smoothly results in a unique portrayal of the era in which we live. From love and romance, war and peace, sorrow and surrender, to private fears and unknown tears, Paul Anthony_delivers a roller-coaster of poetic emotion in his third book, Sunset.

'From boy to man in seventy seven poems...'
The Cumberland News

'A very touching and wonderful collection of poetry from an author who has experience and has worked with teenagers and adults alike. Paul Anthony does a wonderful job of portraying the era in which we live with its known and unknown fears. The author uses his expertise as a crime-fighter to depict the diversity of emotions both good and bad that we all share in common with one another. I encourage all to read it when you get a chance...
Jeannie Walker, author of the True Crime Story 'Fighting the Devil', 2011 National Indie Excellence Awards (True Crime Finalist) and 2010 winner of the Silver Medal for Book of the Year True Crime Awards.

This was a wonderful read. I really enjoyed it.'
Arlena Dean, Reader...

http://paulanthonys.blogspot.com/

Printed in Great Britain
by Amazon